*An Ethnic History of Europe
Since 1945*

Pearson Education

We work with leading authors to develop the strongest educational materials in History, bringing cutting edge thinking and best learning parctice to a global market.

Under a range of well-known imprints, including Longman, we craft high quality print and electronic publications which help readers to understand and apply their content, whether studying or at work.

To find out about the complete range of our publishing please visit us on the World Wide Web at:

www.pearsoned.ema.com

An Ethnic History
of Europe
Since 1945
NATIONS, STATES AND
MINORITIES

Panikos Panayi

LONGMAN

An imprint of **PEARSON EDUCATION**

Harlow, England · London · New York · Reading, Massachusetts · San Francisco · Toronto · Don Mills, Ontario · Sydney
Tokyo · Singapore · Hong Kong · Seoul · Taipei · Cape Town · Madrid · Mexico City · Amsterdam · Munich · Paris · Milan

Pearson Education Ltd
Edinburgh Gate
Harlow
Essex CM20 2JE
England
and Associated Companies throughout the World.

Visit us on the World Wide Web at:
www.pearsoned-ema.com

First published 2000

ISBN 0-582-38135-5 CSD
ISBN 0-582-38134-7 PPR

British Library Cataloguing in Publication Data

A catalogue record for this book is available from the British Library

Library of Congress Cataloging-in-Publication Data

Available from the publisher

10 9 8 7 6 5 4 3 2 1
05 04 03 02 01 00

Typeset in 10/12pt Bembo by 35
Produced by Addison Wesley Longman (Pte) Ltd,
Printed in Singapore

Contents

Lists of Maps and Tables

Acknowledgements

The idea for the following volume first appeared on paper in January 1994, when I decided to write a definitive history of minorities in post-War Europe. In fact, this current book actually represents the second volume of my original plan: the first, tracing the reasons for the existence of ethnic groupings in Europe, appears as *Outsiders: A History of European Minorities* (London, 1999). The present volume focuses upon the situation of European minorities after 1945.

During the five years of working upon *An Ethnic History of Europe*, I have received support from numerous institutions and individuals, the most important of whom I would like to acknowledge. To begin with, I obtained financial assistance from the British Academy, the Nuffield Foundation, the Alexander von Humboldt Foundation and De Montfort University, which, collectively, allowed the employment of three research assistants and visits to libraries in London and Germany. I am very grateful to the three researchers who gathered information for the project: Joanne Reilly, Paula Kitching and Matthew Britnell.

My own research for the book took place in five cities, involving a large number of libraries, and I am grateful to the staffs of all of these: in Leicester, De Montfort University, Leicester University and Leicester County Council; in London, the British Library of Political and Economic Science, the British Library, and the libraries of the School of Slavonic and East European Studies, the School of Oriental and African Studies, the German Historical Institute, Amnesty International and the British Refugee Council, as well as Hornsey and Wood Green public libraries; in Osnabrück, the University library and the library of the Institut für Migrationsforschung und Interkulturelle Studien; in Berlin, the Staatsbibliothek; and in Stuttgart the libraries of the Institut für Auslandsbeziehungen and the Institut für Zeitgeschichte, as well as the Württembergische Landesbibliothek.

Furthermore, I would also like to acknowledge the assistance of numerous individuals who helped me in numerous ways. I am especially grateful to Andrew MacLennan of Longman for accepting this book and diagnosing the faults in the original manuscript. I would also like to mention the administrative staff at De Montfort, including Viv Andrews, Val Bell, Steve Gamble, John Mackintosh and Barrat Patel. My academic colleagues, who helped in various ways, by either reading parts of the manuscript or offering advice with sources, include Lorna Chessum, Pierre Lanfranchi, Mark Sandle and Gurharpal Singh. Outside De Montfort, I am especially grateful to Klaus J. Bade, who allowed me to work at his Institut für Migrationsforschung und Interkulturelle Studien, as well as Tony Kushner, Johannes Dieter Steinert and John Stevenson. I would also like to thank Mark Thompson for allowing me to use his map of 'National and Ethnic Distribution in Yugoslavia'.

As ever, I am grateful to my parents, at whose home in Hornsey I stayed when I carried out the London research and where I also wrote some of the manuscript. Many students also helped to keep the work in perspective, including Stuart Blackmore, John Davies, Mundeep Deogan, Adam Gillogley-Mari, Lyndon MaCerlaine, Alex Peach, Helen Ward and Scott Zlotak. The book is dedicated to Rebecca Axten, Lindsay Garratt and Lucie Parkes.

Glossary and Abbreviations

AAE	Amicale de Algériens en Europe (Association of Algerians in Europe)
ASSR	Autonomous Soviet Socialist Republic
BBC	British Broadcasting Corporation
Beur	Second-generation North African immigrant in France
Bidonville	Immigrant shanty town in France
CARD	Campaign Against Racial Discrimination [in Britain]
CPY	Communist Party of Yugoslavia
CRE	Commission for Racial Equality [in Britain]
DEMOS	Democratic Opposition Coalition of Slovenia
DP	Displaced person
DVU	Deutsche Volksunion (German People's Party)
Enosis	Greek Cypriot ideology of union with Greece
EOKA	Ethniki Organosis Kyprion Agoniston (National Organisation of Cypriot Fighters)
ETA	Euskadi ta Askatasuna (Basque Land and Freedom)
EU	European Union
FN	Front National [of France]
FNC	Front Nacional de Catalunya (National Front of Catalonia)
FOC	Front Obrer de Catalunya (Workers' Front of Catalonia)
FPÖ	Freiheitliche Partei Österreichs (Liberal Party of Austria)
GDP	Gross domestic product
GDR	German Democratic Republic
GNP	Gross national product
Gorgio	Gypsy word for non-Gypsy
HEP	Halkin Emek Partisi (People's Labour Party [of Kurdistan])
HTV	Harlech Television
ICERD	International Convention for the Elimination of All Forms of Racial Discrimination
IRA	Irish Republican Army
IWA	Indian Workers' Association [of Britain]

Jus sanguinis	Nationality law principle based upon origin
Jus solis	Nationality law principle based upon place of birth
LYC	League of Yugoslav Communists
MDS	Movement for a Democratic Slovakia
MSC	Moviment Socialista de Catalunya (Socialist Movement of Catalonia)
MSI	Movimento Sociale Italiano (Italian Social Movement)
NATO	North Atlantic Treaty Organisation
NF	National Front [of Britain]
NPD	Nationaldemokratische Partei Deutschlands (National Democratic Party of Germany)
NVU	Nederlandse Volksunie (Dutch People's Union)
PDA	Party of Democratic Action [of Bosnian Muslims]
Pied-noir	Ethnic French person born in Algeria
PKK	Partiya Karkaren Kurdistan (Kurdistan Communist Party)
PNV	Partita Nacionalista Vasco (Basque Nationalist Party)
RSFSR	Russian Soviet Federal Socialist Republic
RUC	Royal Ulster Constabulary
SDLP	Social Democratic Labour Party [of Northern Ireland]
SGB	Schweizerischer Gewerkschaftsbund (Swiss Federation of Trade Unions)
SNP	Scottish National Party
Stasi	State Security Police of the GDR
SVP	Südtiroler Volkspartei (South Tyrolean People's Party)
Taksim	Turkish Cypriot ideology of partition of Cyprus
TMT	Türk Müdafaa Teskilati (Turkish Defence Organisation [of Cyprus])
TRT	Türkische Radio-TV-Cooperation
UFF	Union et Fraternité Française (French Union and Fraternity)
UN	United Nations
USSR	Union of Soviet Socialist Republics
VB	Vlaams Blok (Flemish Bloc [of Belgium])
WDR	Westdeutscher Rundfunk

TABLE 1
CONTEMPORARY EUROPEAN STATES WITH THEIR SIGNIFICANT MINORITIES SINCE 1945

Nation state	Type of minority		
	Dispersed	Localised	Immigrants and refugees
Albania	Gypsies	Greeks, Vlachs	
Armenia	Muslims (Azerbaijanis)	Armenians	
Azerbaijan			
Austria		Croats, Slovenians	Hungarians, Spaniards, Tunisians, Turks, Yugoslavs
Belgium	Germans, Jews	Flemings, Walloons	Italians, Turks
Belorussia		Russians	
Bosnia-Herzegovina	Gypsies, Muslims	Croats, Serbs	
Bulgaria	Gypsies, Muslims (Turks)	Vlachs	
Croatia	Gypsies, Muslims	Serbs	
Cyprus	Muslims (Turks)		
Czech Republic	Gypsies	Poles, Slovaks	Russians
Denmark	Germans, Jews		Norwegians, Turks
Estonia			Russians
Finland		Lapps, Swedes	
France	Gypsies, Jews	Bretons, Corsicans	Algerians, Italians, Moroccans, Portuguese, Spaniards, Tunisians, West Indians
Georgia	Muslims (Abhzians, Adzhanas, Azerbaijanis)	Armenians, Ossetians	Russians
Germany	Gypsies, Jews	Danes, Sorbs	Bosnians, Croatians, Greeks, Italians, Moroccans, Poles, Portuguese, Russians, Serbs, Spaniards, Turks
Greece	Gypsies, Muslims (Turks)	Vlachs	Albanians, Egyptians, Filipinos, Poles, Moroccans, Turks, West Indians
Netherlands	Jews	West Frisians	

Table 1

Country			
Hungary	Gypsies, Jews		
Italy	Germans (South Tyroleans), Jews	Albanian speakers, Slovenians	Albanians, Filipinos, Moroccans, Tunisians
Latvia			Russians
Lithuania	Jews		Russians
Macedonia	Gypsies, Muslims (Albanians, Turks)	Vlachs	
Moldova	Gypsies	Poles	
Norway		Finns, Lapps	
Poland	Germans, Gypsies, Jews	Belorussians, Czechs, Slovaks, Ukrainians	
Portugal			Angolans, Britons, Mozambicans
Romania	Germans, Gypsies, Jews	Hungarians	
Russia	Germans, Gypsies, Jews, Muslims (including Azerbaijanis and Tatars)	Belorussians, Chechens, Estonians, Latvians, Lithuanians, Moldavians, Ukrainians	
Slovakia	Gypsies	Czechs, Hungarians, Ruthenians	
Spain	Gypsies, Jews	Basques, Catalans, Galicians	
Sweden	Gypsies, Jews	Finns, Lapps	Finns
Switzerland	Jews	French, Germans, Italians, Romantschians	Italians, Spaniards, Turks
Turkey	Gypsies, Jews	Armenians, Greeks, Kurds	
Ukraine	Gypsies, Jews, Muslims (Tatars)	Russians	
United Kingdom	Gypsies, Jews	Irish, Scots, Welsh	Bangladeshis, Chinese, Cypriots, Indians, Irish, Italians, Pakistanis, Poles, West Indians
Yugoslavia	Gypsies, Muslims (Bosnians, Albanians)	Croats, Hungarians, Macedonians, Montenegrins, Slovenians	

SECTION ONE

Introduction

CHAPTER 1

Minorities in European History

THE UNDERLYING CONCEPTS

In 1945 Europe emerged torn apart by a war in which ethnic, national and racial differences had determined allies and enemies. Superficially, the following five decades of European history appear to represent an attempt to heal the wounds of centuries of conflict. In reality, ethnic differences have continued to perform a fundamental role in the development of all nation states and systems of government within Europe, in societies in which origin plays a central role in determining which individuals obtain economic and political rewards. Despite this, and despite the countless studies of countless minorities in numerous countries throughout Europe, no book by a single author has attempted to examine the European ethnic mosaic since the end of the Second World War. The present volume is therefore the first attempt by an individual author to rectify this situation. Its geographical scope ranges from Scandinavia to Turkey, and from Great Britain to the Soviet Union. The approach is thematic, with examples introduced to illustrate the areas covered by the three core sections of the book: it will not examine every minority in every nation state. Instead, it focuses upon those countries with the largest populations, including the Soviet Union, Britain, France and Germany, as well as those with the most obvious ethnic problems, which, in addition to the above, include Romania, Yugoslavia and Cyprus. However, hardly any country is ignored and the book is certainly not a study simply of those seven states. Attention will focus upon all categories of minorities including immigrants and refugees, localised ethnic groupings, and dispersed peoples.

The central theme of the book is the relationship between nation states and minorities which do not form part of the dominant ethnic grouping. All periods of human history have almost certainly witnessed intolerance by one group of people towards another, justified by the concept of superiority even in pre-literate cultures. The age of nationalism, both before and after the Second World War, fits into this historical pattern.

The present study will use throughout a series of terms which need defining at the outset. The most important of these words consist of: ethnicity, nation, nationalism, nation state and minority. Each of these terms has a very precise meaning, which have become confused in recent decades by over-use in the media and social science discourse.

Whether they like it or not, all individuals in Europe have some sort of ethnic identification. So what does 'ethnic' mean? The *correct* meaning is indicated by the origins of the term. It comes from the Greek word, *ethnos*, which simply means 'nation'. The full significance of this fact is that no difference exists between an ethnic group and a nation, in the true sense of the meaning of the latter word, applying to a group of people with shared characteristics. This relates equally to majorities and minorities.

The shared characteristics cover one or more of the following areas: appearance, language and religion. Appearance represents the most controversial signifier of difference, usually referring, at a fundamental level, to physiognomy or skin colour – although this does not mean, for instance, that all black or Asian people constitute the same ethnic group. Appearance of groups also manifests itself in other ways, notably dress, which especially distinguishes particular groups of post-War immigrants. Food, which can be regarded as another aspect of appearance, also differentiates one ethnic group from another. Appearance, encompassing dress and food, represents a basis for difference, but the last two are not built upon to any great extent by ethnic ideologues.

However, this cannot be said to hold true of language, perhaps the most important basis for the development of political ethnicity. Nevertheless, we need to recognise the fact that all modern literary languages are artificial constructs of modernity. Pre-literate societies communicate in dialects which thousands rather than millions of people speak. The act of creating a literary language in a particular area destroys the sum of its parts. Such an action represents a move towards a politically based ethnicity because no group can regard itself as a nation unless it possesses its own language.

While language is central to the claim of most ethnic groups which wish to describe themselves as distinct entities, religion is only slightly less important. Attending a religious service in many parts of Europe today is the most important way for members of some groups to display their difference from the dominant population in the state in which they live. Clearly, religion is just as important for majorities as minorities, with Eastern Orthodoxism, Roman Catholicism and various forms of Protestantism forming a basis of majority ethnicity throughout Europe.

The above differences merely form the basis of ethnicity, which becomes conscious when members of a particular minority face threats from an expanding state and its nationalist ideology. In this situation, leaders of a group of people develop a political consciousness, based upon a combination of the differences outlined above. In essence, ethnicity is a political ideology which revolves around one or more of the factors of appearance, language and religion.[1]

1 A fuller explanation of ethnicity can be found in Chapters 4 and 5.

Ethnicity is essentially a reaction against nationalism, but it also represents its basis. The latter ideology has evolved in Europe during the past two centuries. Before the nineteenth century political ideologies, revolving primarily around Christianity and kingship, acted as the basis for state authority. But, since the middle of the eighteenth century, nationalism has gradually evolved as the only legitimate form of political control. 'Received opinion holds that nationalism in the modern sense does not date back further than the revolutionary political turmoil that troubled the second half of the eighteenth century',[2] meaning, of course, the American and French Revolutions.[3] Nationalism has been like a Pandora's box: once opened, in 1776, the release of its US personification was followed, within the European continent – initially in the west and gradually moving eastward – by further spirits describing themselves as nationalities, so that there exist an endless number of groupings wishing to organise themselves as nation states.

Nationalism did not spring up overnight because it has ethnic origins.[4] A political, social and economic transformation needs to take place in order for ethnicity to evolve into nationalism followed by a nation state. Nations and states differ and there is nothing inevitable in the existence of the nation state. In early modern Europe the main forms of political control included empires, notably the Habsburg and Ottoman, monarchical states, such as Sweden, France and England, and city states, especially in Germany and Italy. But none of these was actually a nation state. In the case of monarchical states, the monarch, rather than the people, represented the embodiment of nation and 'national historiography . . . extolled the nation in terms of its landscapes and resources rather than the character of its inhabitants'.[5] Nationalism has essentially represented a transformation of the state since the eighteenth century to focus, in theory, upon the people who live within it.

At the end of the twentieth century the nation state 'is a construct which we now take for granted as a "natural" or eternal political state of affairs'.[6] Nationalism seized control of Europe fairly rapidly so that by 1914 millions of people were prepared to *die* for their country. The reasons for these developments lie in a complex series of changes in Europe, affecting economy, society, politics and culture. The main social and economic change in European society during the past two centuries has clearly been the transformation of virtually the entire continent from one in which the agrarian means of production dominated to one in which industry has become central.

Nationalism is usually regarded as the ideology of a growing bourgeoisie, used to divide proletarians of one nation from those of another and therefore

---

2 Peter Alter, *Nationalism*, 2nd edn (London, 1994), p. 39.
3 But see Adrian Hastings, *The Construction of Nationhood: Ethnicity, Religion and Nationalism* (Cambridge, 1997), who writes of England as a nation state from the eleventh century at the latest.
4 See Anthony D. Smith, *The Ethnic Origins of Nations* (Oxford, 1986).
5 John Breuilly, *Nationalism and the State* (Manchester, 1982), p. 45.
6 Gérard Chaliand, 'Minority Peoples in the Age of Nation States', in Chaliand (ed.), *Minority Peoples in the Age of Nation States* (London, 1989), p. 1.

allowing bourgeois values to become dominant. This process was integral in the evolution from feudalism to capitalism.[7] 'The chief problem for the young bourgeoisie is the problem of the market. Its aim is to sell goods and to emerge victorious from competition with the bourgeoisie of another nationality. Hence its desire to secure its "own", its "home" market.'[8] The new industrial economies further need a national culture in which all sections of the population can communicate for the purpose of increasing affluence. In pre-industrial economies only a minority bureaucratic class required education, while the bulk of the population got on with subsistence food production.[9] In more purely ideological terms, nationalism originates in the late eighteenth and early nineteenth centuries, with the emergence of the individual and collective desire to achieve self-determination, epitomised by German nationalists before 1848.[10]

Like the goods produced in the age of industry and nationalism, all national ideas are artificial. While some may have agrarian origins, the essence of nationalism lies in the fact that it arrives with the age of industrialisation and therefore creates new ideas in a new age of economic activity.[11] Since the late nineteenth century European nation states have invented traditions about themselves which have involved creating national education systems, public ceremonies and public monuments.[12] Furthermore, 'imagined communities' have developed within nation states 'because the members of even the smallest nation will never know most of their fellow-members, meet them, or even hear of them, yet in the minds of each lives the image of their communion'.[13]

Nationalism is therefore inextricably linked with the process of industrialisation. While nation states may have deep-rooted origins, which represent a basis for subsequent elaboration, they are human creations. Like the modern age and the industry which accompanies it, their essence is standardisation, rationalisation and centralisation. The end product therefore represents an artificial entity in the form of the nation state, as artificial as the goods produced by the industry which dominates the new form of political organisation. These new political creations initially came into existence for the benefit of the classes who would gain most advantage by the creation of an internal market which allowed free movement of their goods, namely industrialists. However, during the course of the nineteenth and twentieth centuries, the working classes have been made to believe in the nation state, while, for the national movements emerging throughout Europe during the last two centuries, proletarians have often been needed as fodder in the political insurrection needed for the overthrow of imperial domination by a 'foreign' power.

---

7 Walker Connor, *The National Question in Marxist–Leninist Theory and Strategy* (Princeton, 1984), pp. 6–9.
8 Joseph Stalin, *Marxism and the National and Colonial Question* (London, 1936), pp. 13, 15.
9 See Ernest Gellner, *Nations and Nationalism* (Oxford, 1983).
10 Elie Kedourie, *Nationalism*, 4th edn (Oxford, 1993).
11 Gellner, *Nations and Nationalism*, pp. 48–52.
12 Eric Hobsbawm, 'Mass-Producing Traditions: Europe, 1870–1914', in Eric Hobsbawm and Terence Ranger (eds), *The Invention of Tradition* (Cambridge, 1983), pp. 263–83.
13 Benedict Anderson, *Imagined Communities* (London, 1991), p. 6.

By the start of the twentieth century, nation states had become accepted as the only legitimate form of political organisation within Europe, which meant that the Ottoman and Austro-Hungarian Empires were doomed. The division of Europe into nation states was by this time inevitable, although there was nothing inevitable about which countries would come into existence. However, the new states in Europe, especially in its eastern half, would also contain minorities within their new borders because of the complexity of historically evolved settlement patterns. The determinants of the boundaries of new nation states included the linguistic and religious characteristics of particular areas, the size of individual ethnic groups, their ability to mobilise themselves into national movements, and the attitudes of the Great Powers. These factors have remained important up to the end of the twentieth century (indicated by the collapse of communism) and they also had a part in the state-building processes at the end of the two World Wars, when the attitudes of the victorious powers played the determining role.

A definition of a 'nation state' creates problems. While not rejecting the idea that some nation states are more 'real' than others, in the sense that they may consist of a more ethnically composite people, the basis of my argument so far rests upon the artificiality of nationalism and its creations. All 'objective definitions have failed, for the obvious reason that, since only some members of the large class of entities which fit such definitions can at any time be described as "nations", exceptions can always be found'.[14] In 1971, 'out of 132 entities generally considered to be states', only 12 or 9.1 per cent 'can justifiably be described as nation states', with a unitary ethnic group,[15] although even this seems an exaggerated figure.

The essence of the nation state is political control: 'Nationalism is primarily a political principle, which holds that the political and the national unit should be congruent.'[16] Taking the above discussion into account, my definition of a nation state would be as follows. It is a method of political organisation which has developed in the age of industrialisation and in which the life-blood consists of an artificial culture which has been introduced by those who dominate political power, who usually control the economy. It aims at standardisation and efficiency, achieved through the establishment of a series of institutions which facilitate the passage of culture through the whole economy. The most important of these is a national education system, which spreads knowledge of the national language and educates children primarily in the geography, history and literature of their own state. In addition, a series of more political organs holds the nation state together including representative institutions (whatever the system of government), an army (in which those who claim citizenship should be prepared to die), and a national taxation system (an

14 Eric Hobsbawm, *Nations and Nationalism Since 1780: Programme, Myth and Reality*, 2nd edn (Cambridge, 1992), pp. 5–6.
15 Walker Connor, 'A Nation is a Nation, is a State, is an Ethnic Group is a . . .', *Ethnic and Racial Studies* 1 (1978), p. 382.
16 Gellner, *Nations and Nationalism*, p. 1.

essential lubricant in keeping the nation state together). There exist further the clothes – or symbols of nationalism – which display the existence of a nation state, including the national flag, the national anthem, and a national football team, without which a country would remain naked, a primitive and not fully developed nation state. Finally, the sacred national boundaries define the extent of the nation state.

Not all states in post-War Europe fit comfortably into the above definition. The Soviet Union, together with other federal states, such as Switzerland and Yugoslavia, allowed varying degrees of autonomy, demonstrated in language use, education and local self-rule. However, above these there still existed, ultimately, the concept of a Soviet people, a Swiss people and a Yugoslav people, with central representative institutions, national citizenship, national flags and national anthems. Even in the Soviet Union, with its confused nationalities policy – especially during its early years – the idea of a Soviet people began to spread after the Second World War, and became legalised in the 1977 constitution. Furthermore, there also existed the lubricant of Russian culture, despite the aspects of local autonomy.[17]

It is not possible for all members of a nation state to fit into the strait-jacket created by nationalism, which inevitably leads to the creation of minorities. In liberal democracies, these can be social minorities, particularly in the early stages of industrialisation when bourgeois culture is first imposed from above, meaning that the working classes develop their own alternative culture,[18] while the peasantry, in the short run, remain outside either of these new cultures, continuing to live their lives as they always have done until the instruments of the nation state eventually manage to reel them into the body politic.

Our concern lies with minorities of another sort, who can all be described by the catch-all term of 'ethnic' minorities, which, however, encompasses a large variety of groupings in modern European history. It would be wrong to suggest that all minorities came into existence simply as a result of the growth of nationalism. The history of medieval European Jewry would warn us against this, both because of their residential segregation and because of the persecution they faced, particularly during the Crusades. During the Middle Ages the essence of Jewish minority status lay in religion together with a distinct economic activity in the form of money-lending.[19] Upon their arrival in medieval and early modern Europe, the Gypsies were automatically recognised as different and faced universal hostility.[20]

The process of state creation from the end of the eighteenth century resulted in new minorities where they did not previously exist as such in the empires

---

17 Alexander J. Motyl, *Will the Non-Russians Rebel? State, Ethnicity, and Stability in the USSR* (London, 1987), pp. 38–9; René Tangac, 'The Soviet Response to the Minority Problem', in Chaliand, *Minority Peoples*, p. 105; Connor, *National Question*, pp. 392–407.
18 See Hobsbawm, 'Mass-Producing Traditions', pp. 283–91.
19 A good account of outgroups in medieval Europe is David Nirenberg, *Communities of Violence: Persecution of Minorities in the Middle Ages* (Princeton, 1996).
20 See, for instance, Ian Hancock, *The Pariah Syndrome: An Account of Gypsy Slavery and Persecution* (London, 1987).

which controlled early modern central and eastern Europe. This is not to deny that these peoples with their own distinctive language and folklore had not already lived in these areas. Thus, while Albanians may have existed as a group for centuries, the creation of new states in the areas where they lived – with more direct control and with the implementation of a state culture claiming to represent all members of the population who lived within the artificial boundaries which had been drawn up – inevitably resulted in a reaction against the new, more direct form of political control by groups of people who spoke a different language, practised a different religion or felt themselves to be different in other ways.[21]

This brings us on to a definition of 'minorities'. Four factors can contribute to the existence of ethnic minorities, revolving around the issues of difference, power, size and geographical concentration. All of the minorities which exist in contemporary Europe possess each of the above characteristics to some degree, and have done throughout their history as minorities. A perfect minority, for the sake of argument, is smaller than the majority grouping, concentrates in particular locations, looks outwardly different and lacks power *vis-à-vis* the dominant population.

Difference revolves around origin and manifests itself, as we have seen, in appearance, language and religion. Minorities often possess more than one of these characteristics or all of them. The minorities 'are subcultures' maintaining some or all of the above 'behavioural characteristics' that 'in some degree, set them off from society's mainstream or modal, culture'. They feel these differences provide them with 'sense of community' which differentiates them from the dominant group within any nation state.[22] Consequently, most minorities are a product of nationalism, because they would have regarded these differences as natural in an age before nation states, and would not have felt the need to demonstrate their differences to a centralising culture with which they had no connection. 'The problem of national minorities arises out of the conflict between the ideal of the homogeneous nation state and the reality of ethnic heterogeneity'[23] in any given geographical area which is turned into a nation state by drawing lines on maps described as national boundaries. Following on from this, the second universal characteristic inherent in all minority groups consists of the fact that 'they are relatively lacking in power and hence are subjected to certain exclusions, discriminations, and other differential treatments'.[24] This does not mean, of course, that all minorities are completely powerless, or that they all suffer the same types and level of prejudice, as this varies from one instance to another. The number of members of a particular minority varies enormously in contemporary Europe. No groups

21 See Miranda Vickers, *The Albanians: A Modern History* (London, 1995).
22 Martin N. Maryer, *Race and Ethnic Relations: American and Global Perspectives*, 2nd edn (Belmont, CA, 1991), pp. 12–13.
23 I. L. Claude, *National Minorities: An International Problem*, 2nd edn (Cambridge, MA, 1969), p. 1.
24 Arnold M. Rose, 'Minorities', in David L. Sill (ed.), *International Encyclopedia of the Social Sciences*, Vol. 10 (New York, 1968), p. 365.

form a majority within any particular nation state, although they can do within a particular area of that nation state, such as, to give one of many examples, the Basques in Spain. In all cases, minorities do concentrate geographically, whether within regions or cities, although this does not mean that all members of a particular group live in one location. In some nation states two groupings of similar numerical size exist (such as Belgium), in which it is difficult to apply the term 'minority', and where 'ethnic groupings' can act as an alternative term.

TYPES OF EUROPEAN MINORITIES

The long history of settlement within Europe has meant that there exists within the continent as a whole an enormous variety of minorities. They consist of those who were indigenous before 1945, some of whom moved into or across Europe tens, hundreds or thousands of years before the twentieth century, and immigrants, migrants and refugees, who settled in a new area after the Second World War. Indigenous minorities include people distinguished from dominant groupings for a wide variety of reasons, whether religion (as in the case of Jews and Balkan Muslims), language (of which there are countless examples), allegiance to another state (such as east European Germans), or way of life (as in the case of Gypsies).

In fact, it is most useful to divide European minorities into three categories, consisting of dispersed peoples, localised minorities and post-War immigrants and refugees. All have the basic characteristic of counting small numbers within a particular state, distinguishing themselves through appearance, language or religion, and having limited political power. They have, collectively, evolved as minorities over the course of periods of time varying from decades to centuries.

The dispersed European minorities divide comfortably into four groups. The first of these, Jews, already lived in Europe during the classical period and gradually moved west and north over subsequent centuries. Gypsies appeared in eastern Europe, originating in India, from about the twelfth century and, again, moved west and north. These two minorities have always been outsiders throughout European history, both before and after the age of the nation state.[25]

Slightly different are two dispersed groupings concentrated in the eastern half of the continent in the form of Germans and Muslims. The former moved eastward from a variety of areas of core German settlement from as early as the tenth century to find themselves, by 1919, living throughout the newly created states which followed the collapse of the Austro-Hungarian and Ottoman Empires, but focused especially upon Czechoslovakia, Hungary, Poland and Romania. Their numbers declined drastically at the end of the Second World War due to ethnic cleansing, but small concentrations remained.[26]

25 Good introductions to the history of both of these groups can be found in Gérard Chaliand and Jean-Pierre Rageau, *The Penguin Atlas of Diasporas* (London, 1995).
26 See contributions to Klaus J. Bade (ed.), *Deutsche im Ausland – Fremde in Deutschland: Migration in Geschichte und Gegenwart* (Munich, 1992).

Muslims moved into eastern Europe and Russia from further east, in their case in connection with the Ottoman and Mongol invasions. Like the Germans, those living in eastern Europe found themselves as minorities in the new states which followed the collapse of the great European empires at the start of the twentieth century. A significant difference between Muslims and Germans is that the former also consist, in some instances, of the descendants of indigenous peoples who converted to Islam following the Ottoman invasions of Bosnia, Bulgaria, Cyprus and Greece.[27]

The other major category of indigenous minorities consists of those which are particular to small areas of Europe or to individual states, all of which, to a greater or lesser degree, have become ethnic groupings because of state creation and extension in areas in which they have not conformed to the dominant economic, social and cultural norms. These minorities can be divided further. In the first place we can identify peripheral peoples who found themselves upon the edge of particular expanding states, which have tended to develop over the course of centuries. The best examples of such minorities include the Celtic fringe in Britain, essentially subjects of an expanding English kingdom,[28] the Sami people, who retained their differences despite the continual northward movement of the Scandinavian states from the Middle Ages,[29] and the peripheral peoples of Russia and the Soviet Union, who remained distinct from an expanding empire.[30]

Another type of localised minority is that which has developed due to a process of state creation through unification. In such a situation a dominant culture emerges, usually that of the group which played the leading role in the birth of the new state. Such developments have occurred throughout the course of European history. Examples have included the unification of Spain in the fifteenth century, which ignored the wishes of Basques and Catalans in particular;[31] the creation of Italy and Germany during the nineteenth century, both of which contained linguistic minorities;[32] and the formation of Yugoslavia and Czechoslovakia at the end of the First World War.[33]

Numerous localised groupings simply represent victims of boundary changes, resulting especially from the peace treaties which have concluded

27 See contributions to M. Bainbridge (ed.), *The Turkic Peoples of the World* (London, 1993).
28 The best exponent of this argument is Michael Hechter, *Internal Colonialism: The Celtic Fringe in British Development, 1546–1966* (London, 1975).
29 See Helge Salvesen, 'Sami Æednan: Four States – One Nation? Nordic Minority Policy and the History of the Sami', in Sven Tägil (ed.), *Ethnicity and Nation Building in the Nordic World* (London, 1995), pp. 106–44.
30 For an outline of Russian expansion see Lionel Kochan and Richard Abraham, *The Making of Modern Russia*, 2nd edn (Harmondsworth, 1983).
31 See, for instance, J. H. Elliot, *Imperial Spain, 1469–1716* (Harmondsworth, 1970).
32 For Italy see Anna Laura Lepschy, Giulio Lepschy and Miriam Voghera, 'Linguistic Variety in Italy', in Carl Levy (ed.), *Italian Regionalism: History, Identity and Politics* (Oxford, 1996), pp. 69–80. For the main linguistic group in Germany see Gerald Stone, *The Smallest Slavonic Nation: The Sorbs of Lusatia* (London, 1972).
33 See the contributions of Ann Lane, on Yugoslavia, and W. V. Wallace, on Czechoslovakia, in Seamus Dunn and T. G. Fraser (eds), *Europe and Ethnicity: World War I and Contemporary Ethnic Conflict* (London, 1996).

twentieth-century conflicts, especially the First and Second World Wars. In such situations the fate of peoples in particular areas was far less important than the concerns of the balance of power being shifted in favour of victors. Such minorities have existed particularly in central Europe and the Balkans in the form of, for instance, Hungarians in Romania[34] and Greeks in Albania.[35]

A few minority groups remain within the heart of particular nation states. Good examples of such peoples include the Vlachs, who reside in various Balkan states,[36] and the Kurds of Turkey.[37] The main characteristic of such peoples consists of the fact that they came second in the development of ethnic consciousness, which has meant that they often find themselves trying to form their own political structures in the historical heart of an existing nation state.

Migrants, immigrants and refugees are post-War arrivals. Since 1945 the entire continent has been affected at some stage either by taking up population or by surrendering people to another part of Europe. All newcomers arriving in already existing states after 1945 have automatically become minorities upon their first arrival. Population movements in post-War Europe fall comfortably, though not perfectly, into three phases.

The first of these covers the years immediately following the end of the War and the population movements during the initial years of peace, which particularly affected the areas which the Nazis had controlled. The tens of millions of people on the move included victims of Nazism, in the form of foreign workers used by the German economy and former inmates of the camp system, German expellees from the victorious and vindictive regimes which followed the defeat of the Nazis, and victims of Stalinism, attempting to escape from that particular system of totalitarianism, but in many cases forced back by the agreements of the Allies at the end of the War. Many of the refugees of this period moved to states with populations which shared their ethnic characteristics, meaning that they disappeared into the surrounding population fairly quickly. But some Poles and Germans, as well as Soviet citizens, moved into western European states, where they stood out as minorities.[38]

The second phase of European migration essentially represents the search for labour supplies to act as fodder for the expansion of the European economies which took place until the early 1970s. For those states with colonies, notably Britain, France and the Netherlands, they had obvious supplies of labour, but they also used workers from Mediterranean states, as did Germany and Switzerland and virtually the rest of north-west Europe. Push factors play a subordinate role in this second phase of migration because the determining factor in causing population movement consisted of the initiative of business and industry in the receiving state. However, in many cases, such as Turkey

---

34 See Elemér Illyés, *National Minorities in Romania: Change in Transylvania* (New York, 1982).
35 Christodoulos Stavrou, *Die griechische Minderheit in Albanien* (Frankfurt, 1993).
36 T. J. Winnifrith, *The Vlachs: The History of a Balkan People* (London, 1987).
37 David McDowall, *A Modern History of the Kurds* (London, 1996).
38 A good account of this period can be found in Michael R. Marrus, *The Unwanted: European Refugees in the Twentieth Century* (Oxford, 1985), pp. 296–346.

and Italy, the government of the sending society pursued a policy of exporting population as part of a solution to domestic overpopulation and underdevelopment. Tens of millions of people migrated to western Europe during this period, which finally ended by the mid-1970s.[39] In the eastern half of the continent a few foreign workers moved to the German Democratic Republic,[40] while millions of people migrated within the Soviet Union, especially Russians who moved to the Baltic Republics and Central Asia in an attempt to develop the economies of those regions.[41]

The third phase of post-War European migration, from the middle of the 1970s, has involved several contradictory developments. First, the slamming shut of doors by the western European industrial democracies to migrants from all over the world. Second, an increase in the number of people who actually wish to move towards the wealthy parts of western Europe, especially following the political changes consequent upon the Cold War. Furthermore, many of the countries on the Mediterranean periphery which previously experienced emigration now find themselves acting as importers of migrants from eastern Europe and North Africa. More recently, following the collapse of communism, much migration has also begun to occur between and towards former Soviet bloc states. At the same time, the fact that the EU allows free movement of labour has meant that many nationals of Italy, Greece, Spain and Portugal can now move into north and western Europe without the need for labour transfer agreements previously necessary.[42]

As a result of hundreds of years of migration, exclusion and state creation in Europe, every country contains ethnic minorities, in most cases forming a significant percentage of the population. At the end of the twentieth century most European states act as home to representatives of each of the three types of European minorities outlined above. Ethnic cleansing and genocide during the twentieth century have certainly changed the population make-up of many states, especially in Central and Eastern Europe, but then so has post-War immigration, particularly in the western half of the continent.

MINORITIES IN EUROPE SINCE 1945

Having provided a conceptual and historical background,[43] we now need to outline the contents of the present book. It examines the relationship between the nation state, majority populations and ethnic minorities in Europe since

39 See Stephen Castles, *Here for Good: Western Europe's New Ethnic Minorities* (London, 1987), pp. 11–95.
40 See, for instance, A. W. Stack and S. Hussain, *Ausländer in der DDR: Ein Ruckblick* (Berlin, 1991).
41 See, for instance, Paul Kolstoe, *Russians in the Former Soviet Republics* (London, 1995).
42 See, for instance, Stephen Castles and Mark J. Miller, *The Age of Migration: International Population Movements in the Modern World* (London, 1993).
43 A more detailed account of the history of the minorities examined in this volume, focusing upon their creation, can be found in Panikos Panayi, *Outsiders: A History of European Minorities* (London, 1999).

1945. It argues that most minorities in most states find themselves worse off than those members of the population holding the correct ethnic credentials within the same state, meaning that ethnic minorities have no choice but to form their own ethnic organisations based upon their ethnic difference.

The remainder of the book divides into three sections, each containing two chapters. Section Two examines 'Minorities Within European Society and Economy', as the social and economic characteristics of a group usually distinguish it from the dominant population and form the basis of its powerless position. Although exceptions exist, minorities tend to have higher fertility rates and reside in poorer areas than the dominant populations of a particular state. Often they live in more rural environments or if they are concentrated in cities, they tend to find themselves residing in the poorest areas. Furthermore, in the case of some minorities, such as the Lapps, they live in peripheral areas of states in which they will always remain marginalised. They have no hope of controlling these political entities unless they fully assimilate themselves into the dominant population. They are essentially victims of internal colonialism. In addition, they tend to reside in poorer housing conditions. Exceptions certainly exist to this situation, notably the long-established Jewish communities.

The geographic and demographic patterns of minorities on the European continent replicate themselves in their economic and social structure. Indeed, all aspects of the social and economic life of peoples throughout the European continent remain closely linked. In the classic pattern, the groupings residing in the worst housing conditions with the highest birth and mortality rates would find themselves employed in the least desirable occupations shunned by the dominant grouping. This is the most common paradigm, but a few European minorities have low birth rates and reside in predominantly urban environments, often of a high quality, and also have a superior occupational and economic position. These include the long-established Jews who have managed to emerge from thousands of years of prejudice to work in professional and commercial occupations. Similarly, some localised groupings would fit into this pattern, such as Armenians, Georgians and Baltic peoples within the Soviet Union, as well as some immigrants who have managed to establish their own small businesses throughout western Europe.

The majority of immigrants, in keeping with the reasons for their importation into western Europe, have found themselves concentrated in working-class occupations, especially in construction and factory work. Elsewhere, the areas in which localised minorities live tend to have a lower level of economic development than the core of any particular state, a situation which can have various causes including a lack of resources and exploitation by the centre. The former point would apply to Kosovo within former Yugoslavia, while the latter describes the Ukraine within the Soviet Union.

Members of some minorities remain outside the dominant social and economic structure. This would apply, for instance, to English Gypsies who have pursued occupations which are distinct from those carried out by all other sections of English society. Many immigrants have endured high rates of unemployment due to both prejudice as well as their concentration in occupations which have suffered decline since the 1970s.

Section Three of the present study tackles the question of ethnicity, arguing that, while it has a basis, it has become a highly politicised concept since 1945. Chapter 4 examines 'The Basis of Difference', focusing upon appearance, language and religion. With regard to physical characteristics, long-standing European populations clearly differ from the newcomers who have moved to the continent from Asia and Africa since the end of the Second World War. Similarly, dress plays a central role in differentiating, for instance, Asian and North African immigrants – in Britain and France respectively – from the autochthonous population. Diet also helps to maintain ethnic differences, again especially in the case of immigrants.

Language plays a key role in distinguishing a minority from the dominant community, although there are instances in which members of ethnic groups do not speak a different language from the dominant population, including Jews, some Gypsies and the people of Yugoslavia, most of whom spoke Serbo-Croat. If a language has developed sufficiently and an ethnic group has established some sort of political power, an existing nation state often gives the language recognition, allowing it to be taught to varying degrees, depending upon the power of the group which speaks it. Welsh is a prime example.

Religion has, historically, played a central role in distinguishing ethnic groups and continues to do so. In some cases, notably the ubiquitous Jews, their faith is the source from which all aspects of their lives spring. Religion is also a characteristic of ethnic life in particular parts of the continent. The most obvious examples are the areas formerly under Ottoman rule in the Balkans. Just as important is the Soviet Union where not only Judaism survived Stalin and his successors, but also Islam in the southern periphery, Protestantism in the Baltic, and the Uniate and Orthodox Churches in the Ukraine. The arrival of immigrants from the Middle East, North Africa and South Asia has also introduced Islam in a big way to much of western Europe, especially Britain, France and Germany, while also reaching countries such as Norway, where refugees from Iran have been instrumental in its introduction.

Ethnicity becomes conscious and politicised following a series of developments. In the first place, a culture develops, springing forth from a literary language, which leads to the evolution of literature, theatre and music. Support from the existing state plays a leading role in this process. Political ethnicity becomes possible with the backing of an ethnic media and the stereotypes which it perpetuates. In many parts of Europe this would encompass the development of newspapers in the language of the grouping in that area, such as Catalonia or Northern Ireland. Such groups can also develop a national myth through their media, even though they do not have their own nation states. In other instances, such as Gypsies, the lack of literacy hinders the development of political ethnicity.

Participation in the political process represents the highest level of ethnic consciousness. Activism can take a variety of forms. Amongst immigrants it can simply consist of bodies campaigning for the rights of a particular group within the country of settlement. Refugees, meanwhile, usually continue their previous activities in their new country. For indigenous minorities, the development of full-blown nationalist organisations represents at least the desire for autonomy and, usually, independence. Numerous examples of such bodies have existed throughout Europe since 1945, including the SNP and the Vlaams Bloc (amongst non-violent groupings), and ETA and the IRA (of those prepared to use any means to fulfil their objectives).

Section Four examines the relationship between 'Nation States, Majorities and Minorities'. It essentially argues that the status of minorities is perpetuated by an exclusionary government and public opinion. The experience of minorities varies from one state to another and depends upon a series of factors which have included historical traditions of a particular nation state, the system of government and immediate circumstances.

National governments try to accommodate and yet discriminate against non-dominant groupings. In societies with large pre-modern minorities, numerous attempts have been made at some form of power sharing on a national level, some of them successful, most notably Switzerland and Britain, which have evolved historically. Newer states such as Romania, Yugoslavia and the Soviet Union pursued fairly successful forms of power sharing for a period but, in the case of the last two, collapsed with the fall of communism. Many western states with immigrant populations have passed legislation to create 'multiracial' societies. While immigrant minorities may obtain the chance to progress upwards on the social ladder, they cannot seize these opportunities when they tend to find themselves at the bottom of the economic pile.

All states pass legislation against minorities, notably exclusive nationality laws. Immigration controls, aimed at keeping foreigners out, go hand in hand with nationality legislation. In addition, the instruments of the state, in the form of the police and judiciary – whether within a liberal democracy or an autocracy – have persecuted members of minority groups.

'Public opinion' helps to exclude minority groups in all nation states. The visual, aural and written media all play a central role in the perpetuation of images of minority groupings. All three media operate using national stereotypes which are ever present but vary according to the audience at which they are directed and the nation state in which they operate, as well as varying according to the minority under the spotlight. Thus, in post-War Britain, Afro-Caribbeans have received far more attention than Cypriots. Hostility towards minorities intensifies at times of perceived stress such as economic crisis, political upheaval, war and large-scale, uncontrolled immigration.

The perpetuation of ethnic stereotypes influences everyday hostility towards outgroups. This can simply take the form of refusal to enter into friendships, relationships or marriage with members of a minority community. Most seriously, discrimination exists in employment, experienced by minorities throughout the continent. Trade unions exclude immigrants as the example of early post-War Britain illustrates.

Racist political groupings help to whip up racism and have existed in all liberal democracies, both before and after the fall of communism. Virtually every western liberal state has a tradition of racist parties covering the entire post-War period with direct or less concrete (ideological) links with inter-war fascism. These groupings have usually arisen as a direct response to an increase in immigration as the British National Front, the French Front National and the German Republikaner would demonstrate. In all three cases, social, economic and political factors have played a role in the level of support which the groupings attracted. During the 1990s extreme political parties also sprang up in most of the new democracies of eastern Europe.

Finally, racist violence leaves its victims in no doubt that they are minorities. Physical attacks upon individuals of a different ethnic grouping have always been everyday occurrences, which are now measured in western liberal democracies. The perpetrators of such crimes, who may or may not have connections with extreme right-wing parties, aim either simply to injure the parties concerned or, in some cases, to murder them, an eventuality which has become common, especially affecting immigrants in Britain since the 1950s and Germany after reunification. With the liberalisation of the Soviet bloc, popular disturbances became xenophobic in their manifestations, focusing upon members of other competing minorities – illustrated most notably by events in Nagorno-Karabak and in riots against asylum seekers in eastern Germany. The most serious form of violence consists of ethnic cleansing. This took place on a small scale in Cyprus during the 1960s and, especially, during 1974, on both occasions accompanied by physical force. However, the phrase is most closely associated with Yugoslavia where the forced movement of populations has been accompanied by killing on a significant scale, which is regarded as genocide.

Ultimately, the exclusion of minorities seems inevitable as long as state control by dominant populations and their artificial cultures continues. All minorities in all nation states are subject to some sort of exclusionary practices as their position is ultimately incompatible with nationalism. Nation states make the existence of minorities certain. Both are inevitable products of modernity. In essence, minorities are an irritant to the system of industrialisation and its necessary ideology of nationalism because they cannot be standardised as easily as people who have the ethnic characteristics typical in the dominant population of a particular state. Nationalism has aimed at standardising all citizens in the territory which it controls and has victimised those which it cannot standardise. Inevitably, those who speak different languages or practise different religions will oppose such processes. The only way in which they can effectively do this is to politicise themselves by joining a national movement opposing the dominant state, although by creating such movements minorities inevitably lose some of their own distinct characteristics. The choices for minorities in post-War Europe have therefore consisted of becoming victims of assimilation and intolerance or, alternatively, politicising themselves. The nature of the excluding nation state leaves them with no other alternatives.

Minorities Within European Society and Economy

CHAPTER 2

Demography, Geography and Housing

The demography and geography of minorities determine their economic and political position, but generalisations are difficult to make and vary from one type of grouping to another. Jews represent the most advanced minority, often having a demographic structure ahead of the dominant grouping, with a lower birth rate and, consequently, an older population, as well as residing in some of the most respectable areas and best housing within individual nation states. In contrast, at the other extreme, Gypsies throughout Europe, especially in the east, live in the worst housing conditions, with demographic patterns which characterise poor and non-industrialised populations, more commonly found in Europe before the Second World War and outside the continent after 1945. In between these two extremes come other minority groupings in the form of localised populations and immigrants, the former more closely resembling Jews and the latter having more in common with Gypsies.

The demographic and geographic patterns of minorities play a central role in determining their economic and political position within individual nation states, as well as reflecting it. To take our two extremes again, the demographic and geographic evolution of Jews forms the basis of and reflects their position at the top of the social and economic scale as well as determining their ability to enter mainstream politics and to politicise themselves. In contrast, Gypsies, the ultimate outsiders in post-War Europe, have the most extreme demographic patterns and the worst housing conditions.

DEMOGRAPHY

Demographic patterns of minorities in European states vary enormously and are determined by a series of factors. In the first place processes of immigration and emigration have played a central role in the size of the populations of individual groups. Emigration to Israel, as well as to the USA, for instance, has fundamentally altered the size of the Jewish communities of Europe since the end of the Second World War, although some communities have increased in size as a result of immigration. Migration since 1945 has increased already existing minorities in individual locations, the best example consisting of internal movement within the Soviet Union, which led to the growth of the peripheral Russian populations, especially within the Baltic states. Migration has clearly played a central role in the evolution of immigrant minorities in western Europe, not just in terms of their size, but also in terms of their relative proportion of men, women and children because the capitalist states of western Europe initially imported productive young males (although, in the long run, their wives and children usually followed them).

Patterns of reproduction have been the other determining factor in the evolution of the demography of minorities since 1945. The more established and more prosperous groups, particularly Jews and some localised peoples, simply replicate the low birth rates characteristic of advanced states where the provision of state pensions and social security benefits lessens the need to have large numbers of children in the hope that one of them will look after the parents in old age. In contrast, groups such as Gypsies, who, particularly in eastern Europe, remain outside mainstream civil society, continue pre-modern demographic patterns of traditional societies, with high post-War reproduction rates which have resulted in an enormous expansion of the Gypsy populations of Europe, which many dominant populations in eastern Europe experienced in the hundred years before 1945. Immigrants, meanwhile, originating from less advanced areas of the globe, usually bring with them the reproductive patterns characteristic of their areas of origin, which means that they have large numbers of children in the initial phase, although, in the long run, they simply adapt to the norms of the states in which they reside.

The Jewish population demonstrates the ways in which both immigration and emigration have determined the size of that particular minority in locations throughout the continent. In June 1945 there were 53,000 Jewish displaced persons (DPs) in Germany,[1] a figure which increased to almost 200,000,[2] as people fled from 'post-War Polish anti-semitism',[3] although the number subsequently declined due mostly to migration to Israel and the USA. By 1990 the Jewish population in Germany stood at about 40,000. To add to the 15,000 survivors of the Holocaust another 15,000 who had fled from the Nazis returned, although a further increase, approaching 20,000, has occurred in numbers since the collapse of the Soviet Union as some Jews have moved from there to Germany.[4] Some reconstruction of the Jewish communities also

1 Frank Stern, *The Whitewashing of the Yellow Badge: Antisemitism and Philosemitism in Postwar Germany* (Oxford, 1992), p. 68.
2 Donald Webster, 'American Relief and Jews in Germany, 1945–1960', *Leo Baeck Institute Yearbook* 38 (1993), p. 293.
3 G. Goschler, 'The Attitude Towards Jews in Bavaria', *Leo Baeck Yearbook* 36 (1991), p. 445.
4 Lynn Rapaport, 'The Cultural and Material Reconstruction of the Jewish Communities in the Federal Republic of Germany', *Jewish Social Studies* 49 (1987), pp. 137, 141; Sergio Dellapergola, 'An Overview of the Demographic Trends of European Jewry', in Jonathan Webber (ed.), *Jewish Identities in the New Europe* (London, 1994), p. 64; Jeroen Doomernik, *Going West: Soviet Jewish Immigrants in Berlin Since 1990* (Aldershot, 1997).

took place in Austria after the end of the Second World War, consisting of those who had survived, DPs and returning Jewish refugees.[5]

Polish Jewry, along with the Jewish communities of several other European states, declined dramatically from the remnant which survived the Holocaust. Immediately after the end of the War anti-semitic pogroms took place in Poland, causing a first wave of emigration out of the country. These were followed by further emigration waves in 1949–50 and 1956–7, leaving between 25,000 and 30,000 Jews in Poland by the mid-1960s, about 8,000 to 9,000 of whom emigrated due to an anti-semitic campaign during the Arab–Israeli War of 1967.[6] In Bulgaria, the Jewish population which had remained almost intact during the Second World War left for Israel very shortly after the end of the conflict, meaning that by 1951 only 7,676 Jews lived in the country.[7] In Hungary the 200,000 Jews who had survived the Holocaust had fallen to about 100,000 forty years later, a major exodus of about 20,000 occurring after the failure of the 1956 Hungarian uprising, when Jews made up about 10 per cent of the 200,000 exiles.[8] Similarly, Czech survivors of the Holocaust also moved to Israel after the end of the Second World War, leaving just 16,000 by 1967.[9] An almost identical situation developed in Yugoslavia, which allowed the emigration of 7,500 Jews to Israel between 1948 and 1952, meaning that only about 6–7,000 remained by the early 1950s.[10] Jews also left the Soviet Union, totalling 256,446 between 1971 and 1981, 61.6 per cent of whom moved to Israel and 38.4 per cent of whom went to the West. Partly as a result of emigration and partly because of a fall in the birth rate, the 1989 Soviet census recorded 1,487,000 Jews, still easily the largest community in Europe. Since the collapse of the USSR further emigration has taken place, particularly to Israel.[11]

Outside the old Soviet bloc, France contains the largest number of Jews in Europe, partly due to the immigration of more than 260,000 North African Jews from the former French colonies of Tunisia, Algeria and Morocco.[12] After France comes England, whose Jewish population stood at 330,000 in

5 F. Wilder Okladek, *The Return Movement of Jews to Austria After the Second World War: With Special Consideration of the Return from Israel* (The Hague, 1969); Dellapergola, 'An Overview of the Demographic Trends of European Jewry', p. 64.

6 Kenneth C. Farmer, 'National Minorities in Poland', in Stephan M. Horak (ed.), *Eastern European National Minorities, 1919–1980: A Handbook* (Littleton, CO, 1985), p. 56; L. Dobroszycki, 'Restoring Jewish Life in Post-War Poland', *Soviet Jewish Affairs* 3 (1973), pp. 58–72.

7 Peter John Georgeoff, 'National Minorities in Bulgaria', in Horak, ibid., p. 284.

8 Laszlo Varga, 'The Image of the Jews in Hungarian Public Opinion', *Patterns of Prejudice* 27 (1993), p. 103.

9 H. Renner, 'The National Minorities in Czechoslovakia After the End of the Second World War', *Plural Societies* 7 (1976), p. 30.

10 Harriet Pass Freidenreich, *The Jews of Yugoslavia: The Quest for Community* (Philadelphia, 1979), p. 193; Paul Benjamin Gordiejew, *Voices of Yugoslav Jewry* (Albany, NY, 1999), pp. 68–9, 79.

11 V. Zaslavsky and R. J. Brym, *Soviet Jewish Emigration and Soviet Nationality Policy* (London, 1983), p. 53; Mikhail A. Chlenov, 'Jewish Communities and Jewish Identities in the Former Soviet Union', in Webber, *Jewish Identities in the New Europe*, p. 130; Yoram Gorlizki, 'The Jews', in Graham Smith (ed.), *The Nationalities Question in the Post-Soviet States* (London, 1996), p. 447.

12 Simon P. Sibelman, '"*Le Renouvellement Juif*": French Jewry on the Eve of the Centenary of the Dreyfus Affair', *French Cultural Studies* 3 (1992), p. 265.

1985.[13] Spain experienced an increase in its Jewish population, from 2,500 in 1950 to 12,000 by 1980 partly as a result of immigration, this time from South America during the 1970s, meaning that settlement expanded from the core centres of Barcelona, Madrid and Málaga.[14] In all approximately 1 million Jews live within western Europe.[15]

Amongst localised groupings, emigration has often taken place out of the main area of settlement, particularly where a minority has lived in a less economically advanced region, although in some cases the reverse is true, with an economically vibrant periphery attracting immigrants from the core. Lapland falls into the former category, so that many Sami have moved to the southern parts of Scandinavia. In Sweden, Stockholm had a Sami population of approximately 1,500 by the early 1980s while in Finland females have tended to migrate more than males, which has left a situation in some villages in which there are ten times as many single men as women.[16]

Both Brittany and Corsica have experienced migratory patterns similar to Lapland. Between 1831 and 1926 a total of 1,127,000 Bretons left their birthplace, followed by a further 17,000 per year between 1946 and 1954. Similar trends have continued until the present, which means that Brittany has an older population than France as a whole. A massive exodus has also taken place out of Corsica, involving as many as 400,000 people during the last two centuries, although, in this case, a large number of people has also moved into the area, so that just over half of the inhabitants of Corsica were born on the island. The rest include Sardinians, Moroccans, French Algerians and 60,000 people born on the French mainland. Furthermore, during the summer, '1 million tourists occupy the vast number of chain hotel beds which have replaced traditional Corsican small hostelries'.[17]

In Spain both the Basque land and Catalonia have a healthy economic growth rate which has attracted immigrants from the centre, a process which had actually developed from the late nineteenth century and, in the post-War period, meant that both peripheral regions had a faster rate of population growth than the rest of Spain. Immigration into these regions reached its peak in the years 1955–75, closely corresponding with the economic boom and years of labour migration which occurred in northern and western Europe.

13 Geoffrey Alderman, *Modern British Jewry* (Oxford, 1992), p. 323.
14 Haim Avni, *Spain, the Jews, and Franco* (Philadelphia, 1982), p. 205.
15 Dellapergola, 'An Overview of the Demographic Trends of European Jewry', p. 64.
16 Lars-Anders Baer, 'The Sami: An Indigenous People in Their Own Land', in Birgitta Jahreshog (ed.), *The Sami National Minority in Sweden* (Stockholm, 1982), p. 12; Helvi Nuorgam-Poutasuo, Juha Pentikäinen and Lassi Saressalo, 'The Sami in Finland: A Case Study', in *Cultural Pluralism and the Position of Minorities in Finland* (Helsinki, 1981), p. 86; Mervyn Jones, *The Sami of Lapland* (London, 1982), pp. 5, 9.
17 For Brittany see: David H. Fortier, 'Brittany: "Breiz Atao"', in C. R. Foster (ed.), *Nations Without A State: Ethnic Minorities in Western Europe* (New York, 1980), p. 147; Commission of the European Community, *Linguistic Minorities in Countries Belonging to the European Community* (Rome, 1986), p. 125. Corsica is briefly dealt with by: Georgina Ashworth, 'The Corsicans', in Ashworth (ed.), *World Minorities*, Vol. 1 (Sunbury, 1977), pp. 55–6; and Felipe Fernández-Armesto (ed.), *The Times Guide to the Peoples of Europe* (London, 1994), p. 177.

Consequently, in the period 1950–81 the share of Catalonia in the Spanish population went from 11.6 to 15.8 per cent while that of the Basque Country increased from 3.8 to 5.7 per cent.[18]

In the Soviet Union the most important movement consisted of the migration of Russians towards the Union republics, especially, in areas west of the Urals, towards the Baltics, the Ukraine and Belorussia, but also towards Central Asia in the form of Kazakhstan and Uzbekhistan. In addition, other ethnic groups made their way towards Russia while population movements also took place between other republics, especially contiguous ones. The movement of Russians outside their places of birth has long historic traditions linked with the expansion of Russia since the Middle Ages which, during the course of the centuries, had resulted in the migration of peasants, priests, professionals, industrialists and bureaucrats. Migration continued from Russia during the Soviet period encompassing party functionaries, people involved in economic growth and planning, members of the Red Army and students and academics. Russians played a major role in the development of cities in their new areas of settlement.

Ukraine, especially the industrially advanced area in the east, represented one of the main destinations for Russians, so that 11 million lived there at the end of the Soviet period, accounting for 22 per cent of the population.[19] All three Baltic Republics experienced significant Russian immigration after the Second World War. Latvia's Russian population increased from 9 per cent in 1935 to 34 per cent by 1989, with much of the growth occurring in the immediate post-War years. In 1989 a total of 905,500 Russians lived in Latvia, together with 119,700 Belorussians, 92,100 Ukrainians, and 1,387,800 Latvians, who, by this time, made up just 52 per cent of the population.[20] In the first decade after 1945 Estonia attracted 'ideological, economic, political, and military' bureaucrats from the Soviet Union. There then followed an immigration of overwhelmingly Russian workers to staff new industrial projects established by the Soviets in Estonia. By 1989 Estonians made up 61.5 per cent of the population, while Russians constituted 30.3 per cent, in contrast to the situation in 1945 when Estonians had constituted approximately 97.3 per cent of the local population.[21] In Lithuania the number of Russians increased from 2.5 per cent of the population in 1923 to 8.5 per cent in 1959 and 9.3 per cent in 1989; over both of these periods the proportion of Lithuanians had also risen, due mostly to the elimination of Jews during the Second World War.

18 Juan Díez Medrano, *Divided Nations: Class, Politics, and Nationalism in the Basque Country and Catalonia* (Ithaca, NY, 1995), pp. 119–20; Marianne Heiberg, *The Making of the Basque Nation* (Cambridge, 1989), p. 99.
19 Paul Kolstoe, *Russians in the Former Soviet Republics* (London, 1995), p. 170.
20 Julis Dreifelds, 'Immigration and Ethnicity in Latvia', *Journal of Soviet Nationalities* 1, pp. 43–57; Anatol Lieven, *The Baltic Revolution: Estonia, Latvia, Lithuania, and the Path to Independence*, 2nd edn (London, 1994), pp. 183–8.
21 Riina Kionka, 'Migration to and from Estonia', *Report on the USSR*, 14 September 1990, pp. 20–1; Rein Taagepera, 'Estonia and the Estonians', in Zev Katz, Rosemarie Rogers and Frederic Harned (eds), *Handbook of Major Soviet Nationalities* (New York, 1975), pp. 76–7.

The explanation for the lower level of Russian immigration lies in the fact that Lithuania was less industrialised than either Estonia or Latvia and also had a higher birth rate which meant that local labour reserves tended to be used to fuel economic growth.[22] Persecution of Russians in the post-Soviet Baltic states has forced many to migrate to Russia.[23]

The Russian Federation changed from a net exporter of population to a net importer. Thus, whereas the republic experienced a net loss of 598,000 people between 1966 and 1970, this had reversed to a net inflow of 725,000 from 1976 to 1980, to increase even further to 1,767,000 in the years 1979–88, when Muslims, especially from Kazakhstan, formed a substantial proportion of the immigrants moving to areas of greater economic opportunity.[24] Immigration has continued in the 1990s from the 'new abroad' of post-Soviet states, as well as from Asia and Africa.[25]

Clearly, migration represents the reason for the evolution of the immigrant communities of western Europe. Initially, most states accepted refugees from the fall-out of the post-War settlement, but subsequently looked further afield, either to the Mediterranean periphery or to colonies in the case of those states which possessed them. By the middle of the 1970s labour importation had ceased, but in the following two decades, new refugees from central and eastern Europe began to enter those European states with liberal asylum laws, notably Germany and, to a lesser extent, Sweden.

In the immediate post-War period Britain initially accepted just over 90,000 DPs from the European continent, as well as approximately 145,000 Poles. There then followed over 100,000 Italians and nearly a million Irish. Britain subsequently turned to its colonies and by the 1970s the country had been transformed by influxes of Chinese, West Indians, Cypriots, Indians, Pakistanis and East African Asians.[26]

France also initially accepted refugees wandering the European continent in the immediate post-War period, in this case mostly Germans, totalling about 150,000, including 110,496 former prisoners of war who wished to remain in the country.[27] The French state subsequently turned to the European periphery,

22 Vladis Gaidys, 'Russians in Lithuania', in Vladimir Shlapentokh, Munir Sendich and Emil Payin (eds), *The New Russian Diaspora: Russian Minorities in the Former Soviet Republics* (Armonk, NY, 1994), pp. 92–3; Saulius Girnius, 'Migration to and from Lithuania', *Report on the USSR*, 14 September 1990, p. 25.

23 See, for instance, United Nations High Commission for Refugees, *The State of the World's Refugees: A Humanitarian Agenda* (Oxford, 1997), pp. 237–8.

24 John Dunlop, 'Confronting the Loss of Empire', in Ian Bremmer and Ray Taras (eds), *Nations and Politics in the Soviet Successor States* (Cambridge, 1993), p. 47.

25 See Cristiano Codagnone, 'The New Migration in Russia in the 1990s', in Khalid Koser and Helma Lutz (eds), *The New Migration in Europe: Social Constructions and Social Realities* (London, 1998), pp. 39–59.

26 For more detail see, for instance, Panikos Panayi, *The Impact of Immigration: A Documentary History of the Effects and Experiences of Immigrants and Refugees in Britain since 1945* (Manchester, 1999).

27 'German Free Workers in France', *International Labour Review* 58 (1948), p. 230; James R. McDonald, 'Labour Immigration into France, 1946–1965', *Annals of the Association of American Geographers* 59 (1969), p. 119.

notably Italy, Spain and Portugal. By the early 1960s, it had begun to import people from its former colonies, including Algeria, Morocco and Tunisia, as well as from its West Indian possessions. By 1990 foreigners made up 6.35 per cent of the French population, including over 500,000 Portuguese, Algerians and Italians and more than 400,000 Moroccans and Spaniards. In addition, France also acted as home to 339,600 West Indians.[28]

Millions of ethnic Germans from eastern Europe, followed by refugees from the German Democratic Republic, flooded into western Germany immediately after the end of the Second World War, but – following the erection of the Berlin Wall in 1961 – the Federal Republic had to turn to southern Europe, Turkey and North Africa for labour supplies to feed its booming economy. By 1989 nearly 5 million foreigners lived in Germany, by far the largest group consisting of Turks, who totalled 1,612,623. Italians and Yugoslavs both numbered more than 500,000. Since the fall of the Berlin Wall the Federal Republic has witnessed a further influx of millions of ethnic Germans from eastern Europe and the former Soviet Union, as well as refugees, particularly from the wars in Yugoslavia.[29]

Because of the size of their economies, Britain, France and Germany have attracted the largest numbers of immigrants since the Second World War, but similar developments have taken place on a smaller scale throughout western Europe. In some cases, such as Holland, the immediate post-War years initially witnessed a net loss of population due to emigration. But economic growth from the 1950s meant labour importation. Initially, most states, in common with the British, French and German pattern, focused upon their hinterland, so that, for instance, Sweden attracted large numbers of Finns, while Switzerland recruited Italians. However, like the larger states the smaller ones subsequently recruited from further afield. Holland turned to both its East and West Indian possessions. Other countries imported people from the two major labour exporters of Turkey and Italy, with the result that communities from both of these states exist in many western European countries. Most western European states now have a foreign proportion of their population totalling between 5 and 10 per cent, although exceptions to this rule include Finland, Denmark and Norway.[30]

Since the 1980s several southern European states, notably Italy but also including Greece and Spain, have become countries of immigration, attracting economic migrants and refugees, especially from eastern Europe and Africa. Although precise numbers prove difficult to establish, because most newcomers remain illegal and unregistered, the figures for Spain and Greece nevertheless run into hundreds of thousands while those for Italy total millions.[31]

28 See Alec G. Hargreaves, *Immigration, 'Race' and Ethnicity in Contemporary France* (London, 1995), pp. 8–14.
29 See Hartmut Berghoff, 'Population Change and its Repercussions on the Social History of the Federal Republic', in Klaus Larres and Panikos Panayi (eds), *The Federal Republic of Germany Since 1949: Politics, Society and Economy Before and After Unification* (London, 1996), pp. 35–73.
30 An outline of migration to the whole of western Europe can be found in Panikos Panayi, *Outsiders: A History of European Minorities* (London, 1999), pp. 117–60.
31 See contributions to Russell King and Richard Black (eds), *Southern Europe and the New Immigration* (Brighton, 1997).

As well as migration, fertility rates have played a central role in the evolution of minority populations within Europe. Obviously, low birth rates have a negative impact upon any population within Europe, whether part of a majority or a minority, as they inevitably mean a reduction in the rate of increase, so that many of the peoples of Europe have now returned to the situation of the pre-industrial era with stable populations – as the classic example of the Jews, amongst minorities, illustrates. In contrast, the other quintessential European minority, the Gypsies, represent the very antithesis of the Jews in terms of reproduction rates, which determine all other aspects of their social and economic life.

Jewish minorities very much fall into the general patterns of declining re-production rates, characteristic of most 'indigenous' groups, both majorities and minorities, on the European continent. Jews, like Christians, now marry later, enter into unions which have a significant chance of failing, and, whether the marriages succeed or fail, they tend to produce few children, having fallen to 1.5 per Jewish woman in both France and Russia. About 15 per cent of Jews do not marry at all. The reasons for these changing fertility patterns are those which affect European populations as a whole, in the sense that increased prosperity has led people to spend the money which they earn on themselves rather than children. Similarly, an increasing participation of middle-class women in industry and the professions, caused by a combination of European industry's need for labour and the feminist movement (in which Jewish women played a large role), has further reduced the possibilities for child rearing, as mothers can spend limited amounts of time at home. Marriage with non-Jews, which may make up as much as 50 per cent of all unions, provides the final factor in this process of decline.[32]

The above patterns are illustrated in the largest European Jewish community, in the USSR. Between 1959 and 1989 the number of births to Jewish mothers fell by 65 per cent. In 1969 the Jewish birth rate in the Russian Federation stood at 6.7 per thousand while the rate for the non-Jewish population totalled 14.7 per thousand. Consequently, in the Soviet Union as a whole the proportion of Jews decreased from 1.1 per cent in 1959 to 0.5 per cent in 1989, although much of this coincides with the period when emigration progressed on a significant scale, so that demographic and migratory factors combined to lead to population decline.[33]

The falling fertility rates of Soviet Jewry, together with emigration, affecting mostly younger people, led to changes in its age structure, with a growth in the older age groups and a decline in the younger ones. The 1959 census revealed that 17 per cent of Soviet Jewry was under 15 years of age and that 8.8 per cent was over 65. By 1989 these figures had changed to 11.6 and 23.6

32 See Dellapergola, 'An Overview of the Demographic Trends of European Jewry', p. 69; Bernard Wasserstein, *Vanishing Diaspora: The Jews in Europe Since 1945* (London, 1996), p. 282.
33 Wasserstein, ibid., p. 181; Mark Tolts, 'Trends in Soviet Jewish Demography Since the Second World War', in Yaacov Ro'i (ed.), *Jews and Jewish Life in Russia and the Soviet Union* (London, 1995), p. 366.

respectively.[34] For most of the post-War period a serious imbalance in the gender division of Soviet Jews has existed, with, at differing times, either men or women forming the majority, and leading many Jews to choose non-Jewish partners. In 1970 there were 110 men to every 118 Jewish women, which is mostly explained by the uneven military losses during the Second World War. In the younger age groups, men outnumber women so that in 1989 the number of Jewish males between 25 and 29 exceeded by nearly one-third the number of Jewish women between 20 and 24. In 1988, 58.3 per cent of males and 47.6 per cent of females amongst Soviet Jewry married non-Jewish partners, fitting into the pattern of other ethnic groups within the USSR.[35]

Anglo-Jewry has also failed to reproduce itself. Whereas the average number of Jewish births in Britain totalled 5,100 during the 1950s, by the 1980s it had fallen to less than 3,500. The excess of deaths over births rose from 400 at the end of the 1970s to 954 in 1988. Similarly, synagogue marriages declined from nearly 3,000 in the late 1940s to 1,057 by 1989.[36] By the end of the twentieth century significant numbers of British Jews were, like much of the British population, marrying people from another religious group or not marrying at all, often involved in relationships out of wedlock.

The surviving German populations of eastern Europe have demographic characteristics which resemble those of the Jews. In Czechoslovakia, for instance, the German population has declined due to a combination of emigration, low fertility rates and marriage with non-German partners. Whereas in 1950 they numbered 165,000, making up 1.8 per cent of the population, by 1980 they had fallen to 56,796, making up 0.6 per cent of the population. An indication of the low rate of fertility is provided by the age structure of the German group. According to the census of 1961, almost half of the Germans in Czech lands were over 50 and only 12 per cent consisted of children. In this year the ratio of men to women stood at 1,000 to 1,321. This situation, as well as the fact that Germans lived in population centres where they made up a small percentage of the population, contributed to a high rate of mixed marriages.[37]

No group could contrast as greatly with the Jews and Germans as the Gypsies. In Czechoslovakia, for instance, between 1970 and 1980 the average yearly rate of population growth amongst the Gypsy population stood at 3.8 per cent in the Czech Republic, compared with 0.49 per cent amongst the rest of the population; in Slovakia the figure totalled 2.26 per cent for Romanies and 0.91 per cent for non-Gypsies. Consequently, the Gypsy population had quite a different age and sex pyramid in 1980, with 43.1 per cent of its population

---

34 Tolts, ibid., pp. 368–9.
35 Ibid., pp. 368–73; Thomas E. Sawyer, *The Jewish Minority in the Soviet Union* (Boulder, CO, 1979), p. 41.
36 Wasserstein, *Vanishing Diaspora*, p. 92; Alderman, *Modern British Jewry*, pp. 324–6.
37 Josef Kalvoda, 'National Minorities in Czechoslovakia, 1919–1980', in Horak, *Eastern European National Minorities*, pp. 125–6; Vlastislav Häufler, *The Ethnographic Map of the Czech Lands, 1880–1970* (Prague, 1973), pp. 76–8.

under 15 and 3.6 per cent over 60, compared with figures of 24.3 and 15.7 per cent respectively for the population of Czechoslovakia as a whole. Therefore the Gypsy share of the population of Czechoslovakia increased from 0.83 per cent in 1947 to perhaps 2.03 per cent by 1980. During the 1970s the state became so concerned about such developments that it carried out sterilisations of Gypsy women, often without their knowledge if they had abortions or births by caesarean section. Other women were offered financial incentives to accept sterilisation, a policy which continued for a short while after the 1989 revolution.[38] The following is the experience of one woman:

> I have a husband and six children. I have one grown-up son. I got pregnant with another man while my husband was in jail. He had raped another woman and was in jail for eleven years. I was young, I behaved like a whore, and so I slept with another man. I got pregnant. So I went to get an abortion, and they told me, 'Be so kind as to sign here before you go in for the abortion.' So I signed and went in for the abortion. They just gave me the paper to sign, folded it, and put it into an envelope. I didn't know anything. After the procedure, they told me that something went wrong, that they had to repeat the procedure. I was afraid that part of the fetus would stay in me, so they gave me an injection and brought me upstairs to the operating room. After the operation, when I went downstairs, the women asked me what was wrong and I told them about the badly-done abortion. They told me that I had been sterilized. But at that time I didn't know what sterilization was. The doctor had explained to me that there would be a period of time when I wouldn't be able to have children and that maybe after a while I'd be able to have children again. But the other women told me that I wouldn't be able to have any more children. I was shocked. I said, this is impossible, no. I cried, wept and then Dr Pavlini came in and slapped me across the face. He said 'Shut up! Be happy you won't have any more children! You fucking Gypsy gang!' I began to make a scene there and told him that he had no right to use this tone with me. Then he said, 'Be glad, you cunt, that you won't have any more children. How many Gypsies do you want to bring to this republic?' He said, 'Hitler was a prick because he didn't kill all of you. What, do you want to overwhelm the entire republic?' And I remained silent.[39]

The numbers of Hungarian Gypsies also rose, officially totalling 320,000 by 1971 and making up 3 per cent of Hungary's population. During the 1990s their birth rate could have been two or three times as high as that of the rest of the population, although they also experienced a higher death rate. By 1990 the Hungarian Gypsy population may have reached about 800,000.[40] In Bulgaria

---

38 Helsinki Watch, *Struggling for Ethnic Identity: Czechoslovakia's Endangered Gypsies* (New York, 1992), pp. 19, 30, 32; Kveta Kalibova, Tomas Haisman and Jitka Gjuricova, 'Gypsies in Czechoslovakia: Demographic Development and Policy Perspectives', in John O'Loughlin and Herman van der Wusten (eds), *The New Political Geography of Eastern Europe* (London, 1993), pp. 133–44.
39 Helsinki Watch, ibid., pp. 22–3.
40 Zoltan D. Barnay, 'Hungary's Gypsies', *Report on Eastern Europe*, 20 July 1990, p. 26.

TABLE 2

ESTIMATES OF GYPSY POPULATIONS IN EUROPEAN STATES

	Conservative	High
Ex-Yugoslavia	700,000	1,000,000
Romania	500,000	1,500,000
Hungary	400,000	800,000
Ex-Czechoslovakia	300,000	500,000
Poland	30,000	80,000
Ex-Soviet Union	300,000	1,000,000
Bulgaria	300,000	500,000
Spain	500,000	1,000,000
France	250,000	300,000
Italy	70,000	100,000
Germany	100,000	120,000
Great Britain	70,000	100,000
Greece	100,000	120,000

Source: Gérard Chaliand and Jean-Pierre Rageau, *The Penguin Atlas of Diasporas* (Harmondsworth, 1995).

the number of Romanies increased by about 550 per cent to 523,519 in the century after 1878, so that, by the early 1980s, they made up 6 per cent of the population. Their birth rate was 13 per thousand in 1974, compared with 6.2 for Bulgarians. By the start of the 1980s Gypsies made up 8.85 per cent of all Bulgarians under 25. However, they also had a far higher infant mortality rate, which, in the early 1990s, stood at 240 per thousand compared with 40 per thousand for Bulgarians, which explains the desire to have large numbers of children. The high death rate amongst children of Gypsies in Bulgaria is largely explained by the poor living conditions characteristic of eastern European Romanies.[41]

Demographic developments amongst the Gypsy communities in western Europe have resembled those in the eastern half of the continent (see Table 2). In Finland a government committee which carried out work in 1954 discovered that 50.3 per cent of Romanies were under 15.[42] In Britain, the total number of Gypsies is lower than the typical size of Gypsy populations in east European states, standing at about 60,000 in the middle of the 1970s, although a high fertility rate meant that this number was increasing by about 2,000 per year. Marrying at an earlier age than the general population, they tend to have children within a year or eighteen months of their wedding, with the absence of offspring regarded as sinful.[43]

41 Simon Simonov, 'The Gypsies: A Re-emerging Minority', *Report on Eastern Europe*, 25 May 1990, pp. 14–15; Luan Troxel, 'Bulgaria's Gypsies: Numerically Strong, Politically Weak', *RFE/RL Research Report*, 6 March 1992, p. 59.
42 C. H. Tillhagen, 'The Gypsy Problem in Finland', *Journal of the Gypsy Lore Society* 37 (1958), pp. 42, 44.
43 Judith Okely, *The Traveller-Gypsies* (London, 1983), pp. 105–24, 158.

TABLE 3

COMPARATIVE POPULATION GROWTH RATES OF MUSLIMS IN THE USSR, 1959–79

Nationalities	Numbers (millions)			Annual increase (%)	
	1959	1970	1979	1959–70	1970–9
Total USSR	209	242	262	1.34	0.90
Russians	114	120	137	1.12	0.70
Ukrainians	37	41	42	0.82	0.48
Muslims	24	35	44	3.19	2.37

Source: Alexandre Bennigsen and Marie Boxrup, *The Islamic Threat to the Soviet Union* (London, 1983), p. 126.

Many of the Muslim populations of Eastern Europe and the Soviet Union had demographic similarities to the Gypsies, especially where they remain very much distinct from the dominant grouping, or where they form the most important minority. In the USSR, the rate of population growth of all Muslims took off after the Second World War (see Table 3). Between 1926 and 1979 the number of Muslims in the Soviet Union grew from 17,292,000 to 43,000,000 or from 11.7 per cent of the population to 16.5 per cent, meaning that by the 1980s the USSR had become the fifth-largest Muslim state in the world after Indonesia, Pakistan, India and Bangladesh.[44]

The different groups of Muslims within Yugoslavia, which consisted of Bosnians, Albanians and Macedonians settled within their own political units, also had higher birth rates. The three groups lived in the least urbanised areas of the state and had higher fertility rates than the average for Yugoslavia as a whole. In the years 1950–64 Bosnia-Herzegovina had a natural increase of 22.8 per cent, compared with the Yugoslav average of 12.9 per cent. In 1977 the republic and national figures had declined to 12.6 and 9.3 per cent respectively.[45] In Macedonia, Muslims, consisting of ethnic Turks, Slavs who converted to Islam, and Albanians, formed a majority. In the early 1970s the population of Macedonia as a whole had a young structure, with 32.5 per cent of the population under 14 and just 5.8 per cent over 65, although for Turks and Albanians the former figure stood at 42.5 per cent and 43.1 per cent respectively.[46] In 1971 the mostly Albanian province of Kosovo had the youngest average population within Yugoslavia, at 23.2 years of age for males and 24 for females, while its natural increase in 1977 stood at 27.5 per cent, more than twice the figure for Bosnia. Albanians, both inside and outside Kosovo,

44 Alexandre Bennigsen and S. Embers Wimbush, *Muslims of the Soviet Empire* (London, 1985), p. 24; Nassrine de Rham-Azimi, *Soviet Muslim Populations* (Geneva, 1986), p. 55.
45 F. E. Ian Hamilton, *Yugoslavia: The Patterns of Economic Activity* (London, 1968), p. 36; Fred Singleton and Bernard Carter, *The Economy of Yugoslavia* (London, 1982), pp. 214–16.
46 Boro Pekevski, 'Demographic Situation and Ethnic Characteristics of the Population of Macedonia', in M. Apostolaki and H. Polenakovich (eds), *The Socialist Republic of Macedonia* (Skopje, 1974); Singleton and Carter, ibid., p. 215.

demonstrated the highest rate of natural increase so that between 1921 and 1986 their numbers multiplied five times, while that of the Yugoslav population as a whole simply doubled.[47]

Since 1945 the predominantly Orthodox and Catholic republics of Yugoslavia have had a lower fertility rate than that which existed in the Muslim areas. In the years 1950–4 Croatia and Slovenia had average natural increases of 11.5 and 11.9 per cent, while Serbia's stood at 14.8, although the lowest annual rise occurred in the Vojvodina, with 10.9. By 1977 all of these four regions had rates of natural increase below the Yugoslav average of 9.3.[48] Mixed marriages certainly took place in post-War Yugoslavia, leaving such couples in a crisis during the war of the early 1990s. Many marriages broke up, although more common was 'a pattern in the crisis areas of women assimilating the national consciousness of their husbands: Croat women espousing the Serb ideal of their partners and Serb women denouncing Serb aggression against the homeland of their lovers'.[49]

Certain fertility patterns clearly emerge amongst the pre-modern Muslim populations of Europe, which link them together and, as a group, make them as distinguishable as Jews or Gypsies. In virtually every state in which Muslims live, they have a birth rate higher than that of the surrounding population and, consequently, a younger age structure. This is at least partly explained by the fact that pre-War Muslim minorities in Europe tend to live in less industrialised areas of European states which have relatively low rates of urbanisation, particularly when compared with the advanced economies of north and west Europe. Demographic patterns form the basis of the status of Muslims as minorities.

Few localised groupings have fertility patterns characteristic of the dispersed Gypsies and Muslims. For instance, little variation exists between the English and the Welsh, Scots and Irish. In other instances, however, we can detect fairly significant differences, as indicated by the Slovak population of the Czech Republic, which increased from 0.4 per cent of the population in 1930 to 3.3 per cent – a total of 320,998 people – by 1980. Part of the reason for this increase lies in the migration of Slovaks into the Czech lands but just as important is the fact that the Slovaks living in the republic had a much higher birth rate than either the Czechs or even the Slovaks who lived in Slovakia. Nevertheless, an extremely high degree of intermarriage occurred between Czechs and Slovaks in the Czech Republic. During the 1950s less than a quarter of marriages involving Slovaks in the Czech republic consisted of two Slovaks. In 90 per cent of mixed marriages, children took Czech nationality. By the 1980s, Slovaks made up 31.3 per cent of the inhabitants of Czechoslovakia as a whole, consequently remaining the junior partner they always had been since this state emerged at the end of the First World War.[50]

47 Singleton and Carter, ibid., p. 216; 'Albanians in SFR Yugoslavia', in *Kosovo: Past and Present* (Belgrade, n.d.), p. 340.
48 Singleton and Carter, ibid.
49 Misha Glenny, *The Fall of Yugoslavia: The Third Balkan War* (London, 1993), p. 90.
50 Häufler, *Ethnographic Map of the Czech Lands*, pp. 72–5, 82.

Kurdistan has had higher fertility and mortality rates than Turkey as a whole, following the usual situation in an undeveloped area, although in this case we are referring to an undeveloped region within an underdeveloped state. Between 1945 and 1965 the average annual rate of population growth in Kurdistan stood at 2.88 per cent, compared with 2.65 per cent in Turkey as a whole.[51]

The total number of ethnic groups in the USSR declined during the course of its history from 200 in 1926 to 104.[52] The range in their size was striking. In 1979 Russians, as the largest, counted 137,397,089 whereas the smallest, the Negidal, who lived in northern Siberia, totalled a mere 504.[53] As a rule, the nationalities with their own Union political units tended to count the largest numbers while the smaller ones tended to be those with little political power.

Although the Soviet Union as a whole had a fertility rate and age structure characteristic of an industrialised economy during its last decades, regional variations – due again to the differential levels of industrialisation and urbanisation – also existed. The overall fertility rate for the Soviet Union began to decline during the 1960s, leading the government to pursue pro-natal policies. The actual birth rate fell from 26 per thousand in 1950 to 18 by 1975. The main reasons for this, as in the case of western societies, lay in increasing urbanisation, rising consumer expectations and use and availability of contraception, as well as, in this case, a shortage of housing which added to the desire to keep to small families.[54] The above facts particularly applied to the western republics of the RSFSR, Belorussia, the Ukraine and the Baltics, which, in 1975, had annual birth rates of around 15 per thousand while the Muslim average stood much closer to 30.[55] The decline of the birth rate meant a change in the Soviet age structure which had more old people and less young people from the 1960s, although, again, we need to recognise the regional variations which existed. Thus while the percentage of people under 15 averaged between 23 and 33 per cent for western republics, for some of the Muslim regions it came closer to 50 per cent.[56] The differential birth rates meant that the percentage of Slavs amongst the Soviet population declined during the post-War period.[57]

According to the 1959 census, out of a total of 50.4 million families, approximately 5.2 million or 10.2 per cent were ethnically mixed, a factor which plays a role in the decline of ethnic consciousness and often results in

51 Kendal, 'Kurdistan in Turkey', in G. Chaliand (ed.), *A People Without A Country: Kurds and Kurdistan* (London, 1980), p. 48; Majeed R. Jafar, *Under-Underdevelopment: A Regional Case Study of the Kurdish Area of Turkey* (Helsinki, 1976), p. 85.
52 Viktor Kozlov, *The Peoples of the Soviet Union* (London, 1988), p. 15.
53 James S. Olson (ed.), *An Ethnohistorical Dictionary of the Russian and Soviet Empires* (Westport, 1994), pp. 753–7.
54 Roger Munting, *The Economic Development of the USSR* (London, 1982), p. 169.
55 David Heer, 'Fertility and Female Work Status in the USSR', in Helen Desfosses (ed.), *Soviet Population Policy: Conflicts and Constraints* (London, 1981), p. 83.
56 Kozlov, *Peoples of the Soviet Union*, pp. 140–1.
57 Ralph S. Clem, 'Ethnicity', in James Cracraft (ed.), *The Soviet Union Today*, 2nd edn (Chicago, 1988), pp. 304–5.

assimilation into the majority Russian ethnicity. By 1979 the total number of mixed marriages had reached 7.9 million or 13.5 per cent of all families. However, variations certainly existed across the Soviet Union, according to geographical locality, in terms of whether individuals lived in a rural or urban environment, and with regard to their ethnic group. Thus the figure for 1970 breaks down to show that the mixed marriage rate in urban areas stood at 17.5 per cent, while that in rural areas totalled 7.9 per cent. This clearly ties in with the opportunities available in urban environments, which tend to have a greater mix of people than rural ones. Linked with this is the fact that non-European groups, living in less industrialised areas, tended to have lower rates of mixed marriage than those in the north and west of the Soviet Union.[58]

A series of factors has determined the fertility patterns of immigrants in post-War western Europe. Most of those who initially moved consisted of young males, meaning little reproduction with members of their own group could take place. In many cases, however, wives and children followed subsequently, introducing higher fertility rates from the European periphery or further afield. Nevertheless, in the long run, reproduction patterns have moved into line with those of natives.

Sweden actually had a fairly even gender ratio amongst its immigrants, although members of both sexes often left husbands or wives behind in their place of origin. In 1977 a total of 64 per cent of married women and 60 per cent of married men from Turkey had partners living outside Sweden, with the corresponding figure for Yugoslavs totalling 47 and 52 per cent. In Kulu, the area which provided many Turkish immigrants to Sweden, emigration led to a large number of divided families, which, however, gradually disappeared as family reunification occurred. Once within Sweden, immigrants tended to have a younger age structure with more children and those who were single tended to marry younger than Swedes. While only one-third of Swedish women in Stockholm between 16 and 65 had children under 11, the corresponding figure for Finnish, Greek and Yugoslav women reached 50 per cent and was even higher for Turkish women, who had the strongest fertility rate.[59]

European immigrants to Britain also had even sex structures.[60] However, during the 1950s South Asian immigrants tended to consist of single males. In 1956 an extraordinary 92 per cent of all Pakistanis and Bangladeshis in the UK

58 Ibid., p. 309; Kozlov, *Peoples of the Soviet Union*, pp. 188–203.

59 Christina Jonung, *Migrant Women in the Swedish Labour Market* (Stockholm, 1982), pp. 9, 16; British Refugee Council, London, QSW 85.2, Irene Palmgreen, 'Situation of Immigrant Women in Sweden', 1981; Sahlin Alpay and Halil Sariaslan, *Effects of Immigration: The Effects of Immigration on the Town of Kulu in Central Turkey of Emigration to Sweden* (Stockholm, 1984), p. 31; James Widgren, *Report to OECD (SOPEMI) on Immigration to Sweden in 1978 and the First Half of 1979* (Stockholm, 1979), p. 34.

60 See, for instance: Mary Kells, '"I'm Myself and Nobody Else": Gender and Ethnicity Among Young Middle-Class Irish Women in London', in Patrick O'Sullivan (ed.), *The Irish World Wide Series: History, Heritage, Identity*, Vol. 4, *Irish Women and Irish Migration* (London, 1995), p. 201; R. King, 'Italian Migration to Great Britain', *Geography* 62 (1977), p. 178; Robin Oakley, 'Family, Kinship and Patronage: The Cypriot Migration to Britain', in Verity Saifullah Khan (ed.), *Minority Families in Britain: Support and Stress* (London, 1979), p. 10.

were men, while the figure for Indians stood at 79 per cent. As the 1960s and 1970s progressed, changes took place in the ratio of men to women which, in the case of Indians, reached 56 to 44 per cent by 1974 although the figure for Pakistanis still stood at 65 to 35 per cent.[61] Some Bangladeshi wives did not move to Britain until the 1990s. One stated, in answer to a question as to why her husband had called her over:

> He'd lost all his strength and the English woman had left him. Now who was going to look after him? Earlier he cooked and fed that woman, but now he's housebound so I have to do it.[62]

The demographic structure of immigrants moving into France and its development since the 1960s falls into the classic pattern of an initial phase where young males significantly outnumbered females, followed by family reunification and a consequent reduction in the imbalance. At the same time, the young immigrant population of the 1960s has become older while the number of children produced has declined, although both figures still exceed the French totals.

In 1968 there were 1,547 males to every 1,000 females amongst all immigrants in France, although these figures hide variations between individual groups, so that the proportion for Moroccans stood at 3,551 to 1,000, while that for Algerians was 2,884 to 1,000. These figures have changed as family reunification has taken place so that whereas males made up 61.8 per cent of all immigrants in 1962, this figure had declined to 57.2 by 1982.

The age composition of immigrants has also changed. In 1968 a total of 67.7 per cent of immigrants were in the working age 15–64, compared with 62.5 per cent of the entire French population. The number of immigrants under 15 totalled 21.4 per cent compared with 25.2 per cent of the whole population of France. These statistics illustrate the fact that foreigners were imported as industrial fodder. As well as the ageing of the immigrant population since the 1960s, family reunification has also led to an increase in the number of children under 15, 70 per cent of whom were born in France according to the 1982 census. Thus while fertility rates may have fallen for foreign women, they still remain (especially for North Africans) much higher than the French rate, although that of southern European women was, in 1990, almost the same as the 1.8 children per French woman. In contrast, the figure for Algerian women stood at 3.2, having fallen from 4.2 in 1982 and 8.5 during the early 1960s. Overall, foreigners accounted for 11 per cent of all births in 1982, half of them North Africans.[63]

---

61 Vaughan Robinson, *Transients, Settlers and Refugees: Asians in Britain* (Oxford, 1986), pp. 224–5.
62 This quote is from Katy Gardner, 'Ethnicity, Age and Masculinity Amongst Bengali Elders in East London', in Anne J. Kershen (ed.), *A Question of Identity* (Aldershot, 1998), p. 169.
63 Stephen Castles and Godula Kosack, *Immigrant Workers and Class Structure in Western Europe* (London, 1973), pp. 50–1; Hargreaves, *Immigration, 'Race' and Ethnicity*, pp. 108–9; Philip E. Ogden, 'International Migration in the Nineteenth and Twentieth Centuries', in Ogden and Paul E. White (eds), *Migrants in Modern France* (London, 1989), pp. 49–52.

Immigrants in Germany have experienced similar demographic developments to those in France. During the late 1960s children under 16 made up around 15 per cent of the foreign population, while about 90 per cent of immigrants were under 45. An uneven sex structure also existed so that in September 1969 the Federal Republic housed 1,337,400 foreign men over 16 compared with 680,200 foreign women.[64] In the Turkish case the percentage of women increased from 6.8 per cent in 1960 to 26 per cent by 1975.[65] By 1981 there were 658 Turkish women to every 1,000 Turkish men in Germany – below the average for foreigners of 666 to 1,000, with Greeks, at 836 per thousand, and Portuguese, 832, having the most even sex structure. Following the typical pattern, the foreign population was younger than the German. Thus, while 17.9 per cent of Germans were under 15, the figure for foreigners stood at 26.3 due to family reunification and higher fertility rates. In 1981, while foreigners made up 7.5 per cent of the German population, they accounted for 13 per cent of births. At the other end of the scale only 2.1 per cent of foreigners were over 65, compared with 15.5 per cent of Germans.[66] More striking, only 211 of the 84,415 Turks in Berlin in 1976 were over 65.[67]

Family structures have changed as a result of migration to Germany, with a decline of extended units in favour of the nuclear family.[68] In some cases the original marriage in Turkey broke up as in the case of Fatma, who left behind her husband and children to work in Germany, but found that when she returned her husband was living with another woman, had spent her remittances and also lost his job.[69] Meanwhile, the uneven male-to-female ratio amongst immigrants in Germany has led to an increase in mixed marriages. By 1990 a total of 9.6 per cent of marriages – 39,784 out of 414,475 – involved a German and non-German partner.[70]

In Switzerland the foreign workers of the 1950s and 1960s had a dramatic impact upon demographic structures. In 1960 an amazing 66.9 per cent of aliens with temporary permits were aged 20–39, compared with just 25.7 per cent of the Swiss population which fell into this age group. The male-to-female ratio was also uneven, standing at 156.4 per 100 for the age group 20–39 and 191.6 per 100 for those between 40 and 64 years of age. By the end of the 1960s there had been an increase in children but also a normalisation in the sex ratios so that the figure for all foreigners in all age groups had declined

---

64 Castles and Kosack, *Immigrant Workers and Class Structure*, p. 51.
65 Nermin Abadan-Unat, 'Implications of Migration on Emancipation and Pseudo-Emancipation of Turkish Women', *International Migration Review* 11 (1977), p. 33.
66 Stephen Castles, *Here for Good: Western Europe's New Ethnic Minorities* (London, 1987), pp. 100–6.
67 Gabrielle Mertens and Ümal Ankipar, *Türkische Migrantenfamilien* (Bonn, 1977), p. 92.
68 Abadan-Unat, 'Implications of Migration', p. 54.
69 Ayşe Kudat, 'Structural Change in the Migrant Turkish Family', in R. E. Krane (ed.), *Manpower Mobility Across Cultural Boundaries* (Leiden, 1975), p. 82.
70 Harald Schumacher, *Einwanderungsland BRD: Warum die deutsche Wirtschaft weiter Ausländer braucht* (Düsseldorf, 1992), p. 144.

from 1,300 men for every 1,000 women in 1960 to 1,179 per thousand in 1969.[71]

The geographical location of minorities plays as important a role as their demography in their status. Their location is often determined by the political history of the state in which they live. Most minorities find themselves in an underprivileged position. The main exceptions consist of Jews who tend to concentrate in desirable environments. Gypsies and Muslims, at the other extreme, often live in rural areas, although Gypsies are ubiquitous. In the case of localised groupings, the patterns of state creation and evolution have often determined their position on the periphery of many countries. This peripheral position has often played a role in their relative economic backwardness as they tend to live in areas with worse economic conditions than the centre and, in instances where this is not the case, the centre often exploits the economic advantages of the periphery – through, for instance, mineral extraction, as the Ukraine would illustrate. Virtually all immigrant settlement in post-War western Europe has moved towards towns and cities, because of the economic reasons which have led most people to migrate there, so that they have basically become, most commonly, a labour force carrying out tasks shunned by natives. Little migration into western Europe since 1945 has moved into rural areas.

Jews in the Soviet Union were overwhelmingly concentrated in towns and cities, as they have been throughout the twentieth century. In 1970 only 50,000 Jews lived in rural areas. Moscow, Leningrad and Kiev contained the three largest Jewish communities, each counting more than half a million souls, making up 26 per cent of all Jews enumerated in 1970.[72] Jews further concentrated within particular Union republics although, in this sense, they have much in common with the rest of the Soviet population. Five of the republics (the RSFSR, the Ukraine, Belorussia, Uzbekhistan and Moldovia) contained 89.9 per cent of the Jewish population of the USSR, but also 83 per cent of the entire Soviet population according to the census of 1970. In fact, Jews were heavily concentrated in two republics in the form of the RSFSR, with 37.5 per cent in 1970, and the Ukraine, holding 36.1 per cent of the total in that year.[73]

Jews in Britain also focus on urban areas. London has always been the capital of Anglo-Jewry, counting about 210,000 Jews in 1992, making up 3 per cent of the metropolitan population. The other major focus consists of Manchester, although Jewish communities of around 1,000 people or less exist in most of the major British cities. During the early post-War years

---

71 Kurt B. Mayer, 'The Impact of Postwar Immigration on the Demographic and Social Structure of Switzerland', *Demography* 3 (1966), p. 73; Castles and Kosack, *Immigrant Workers and Class Structure*, p. 52.
72 Theodore H. Friedgut, 'Soviet Jewry: The Silent Majority', *Soviet Jewish Affairs* 10 (1980), p. 50.
73 Sawyer, *Jewish Minority in the Soviet Union*, p. 35.

some Jews settled in smaller towns such as Buxton, Hitchin and Penrith, but, with the decline in numbers, these disappeared, accompanied also by movement into the larger Jewish settlements, especially London and Manchester. Within these two cities, the working-class groupings which developed before the First World War have formed part of the unrelenting stream out of the early settlement areas in the city centre and into the suburbs. In the case of London this has meant migration from the East End towards those areas which had begun to attract Jews before 1939, particularly in north-west but also north-east London.[74]

Historical and political developments have played a role in the geographical evolution of the other diasporic communities since the end of the Second World War. In Bulgaria, Muslims have remained more rural than the rest of the population. In 1956 a total of 13.8 per cent of the Turks in that country lived in towns, compared with 33.6 per cent of the population as a whole.[75] During the 1950s the Muslims of Western Thrace in north-east Greece lived in both rural and urban settlements. The three main cities of this province, Xanthi, Komotini and Alexandroupolis, contained Muslim quarters, although other Muslims lived amongst Greeks. In the countryside, some Turks resided in purely Muslim villages, while others lived in settlements also inhabited by Greeks. Nevertheless, the Turkish minority was more rural than the Greek population. By the 1980s, while the urban-to-rural distribution of Greeks within the country stood at 56.2 to 43.8 per cent, that of the Muslim population of Western Thrace divided at 20 per cent to 80 per cent, indicating a far lower level of economic development.[76]

In Cyprus the geographic development of the Turkish and Greek communities is fundamentally dependent upon the political history of this state. During the 1950s, as the former ruling group, the Turks were slightly more urbanised than the Greek population, with 27 per cent of the former living in towns compared with 19 per cent of the latter, although Greeks formed a majority of the six recognised towns on the island (Nicosia, Limassol, Famagusta, Larnaca, Paphos and Kyrenia). In the rural regions, where the majority of people lived, Greeks made up 83 per cent of the population, while Turks constituted 16 per cent just after the Second World War. The Turkish minority formed between 13 and 24 per cent of the six districts of the island.

The 1974 invasion and its geographic consequences virtually began the history of Cyprus from scratch, resulting in one of the quickest and most

74 Alderman, *Modern British Jewry*, pp. 323, 329–30; Anne Kershen, 'The Jewish Community in London', in Nick Merriman (ed.), *The Peopling of London: Fifteen Thousand Years of Settlement from Overseas* (London, 1993), p. 138; Stanley Waterman and Barry Kosmin, 'Ethnic Identity, Residential Concentration and Social Welfare: The Jews in London', in Peter Jackson (ed.), *Race and Racism: Essays in Social Geography* (London, 1987), p. 263.
75 Firoze Yasemee, 'The Turkic Peoples of Bulgaria', in M. Bainbridge (ed.), *The Turkic Peoples of the World* (London, 1993), pp. 45–7.
76 K. G. Andreades, *The Moslem Minority in Western Thrace* (Thessaloniki, 1956), p. 9; Association of Western Thracians, *Human Rights and Documents on the Minority in Western Thrace* (Ankara, 1987), p. 7.

systematic acts of ethnic cleansing – although, admittedly, the separation of the two communities had begun before this time as the number of villages containing both Greeks and Turks had declined. As the Turkish army flooded into the country, 201,000 Greeks fled southwards. Simultaneously, about 40,000 Turkish Cypriots moved to the north of the island. Nevertheless, the ethnic cleansing was not perfect because 12,289 Greeks remained trapped on the Karpasia peninsula in the north-east of the island, although by 1990 about 11,700 had left. Five years later 486 Greek Cypriots lived in the north, while 343 Turks remained in the south.[77]

After the ethnic cleansing authorised by the Allies at the end of the Second World War, the largest concentration of Germans lived within the Soviet Union. As a result of their deportation authorised by Stalin in 1941, they became scattered in peripheral regions of the Soviet Union, having previously lived mainly in the western and central parts of Russia. Germans remained concentrated in the peripheral areas in 1989, with the largest numbers living in Russia and Kazakhstan. About 900,000 resided within the former, the majority concentrated in south-west Siberia. A similar number lived in Kazakhstan. A further 100,000 resided in Kyrgyzstan, focused upon its capital of Bichkek, as well as 30,000 to 40,000 in Uzbekhistan.[78]

The thoroughness of the process of eliminating Germans from eastern Europe during the late 1940s meant that far smaller numbers of this dispersed minority remained in states west of the Soviet Union. Nevertheless, for much of the post-War period, the German population of Romania stood at more than 300,000, although the opportunities to move to Germany following the death of Ceaucescu have resulted in a serious decline in numbers. The geographical concentration in the intervening decades lay within the districts which had evolved historically as German areas of settlement within this artificially created state, above all in Transylvania. In addition, smaller German communities resided in southern Bukovina and northern Dobruja, while a few thousand lived in Bucharest. The Germans in post-War Romania, especially Transylvania, had a significant urban concentration. Within Transylvania they made up 23 per cent of the population of Sibiu, 15 per cent of Timisoara, 23 per cent of Medias and 20 per cent of Resita.[79]

77 Alexander Melamid, 'The Geographical Distribution of Communities in Cyprus', *Geographical Review* 46 (1956), pp. 355–74; Robin Oakley, 'The Turkish Peoples of Cyprus', in Bainbridge, *Turkic Peoples of the World*, pp. 88, 94; Christos P. Ioannides, *In Turkey's Image: The Transformation of Occupied Cyprus into a Turkish Province* (New Rochelle, NY, 1991), p. 39; Keith Kyle, *Cyprus: In Search of Peace* (London, 1997), p. 34.
78 Anthony Hyman, 'Volga Germans', in Smith, *Nationalities Question*, pp. 465–74; Detlef Brandes, 'Die Deutschen in Russland und der Sowjetunion', in Klaus J. Bade (ed.), *Deutsche im Ausland: Fremde in Deutschland* (Munich, 1992), p. 132; Benjamin Pinkus, 'The Germans in the Soviet Union since 1945', in I. Fleischauer, B. Pinkus and E. Frankel (eds), *The Soviet Germans Past and Present* (London, 1986), pp. 103–12.
79 G. D. Satmarescu, 'The Changing Demographic Structure of the Population of Transylvania', *East European Quarterly* 8 (1975), pp. 433, 437; Brigitte Mihok, 'Minorities and Minority Policy in Romania Since 1945', *Patterns of Prejudice* 27 (1993), pp. 81, 82, 83, 90.

Perhaps one geographic characteristic which binds all localised groupings, as well as linking together all post-War European minorities, consists of concentration. In the United Kingdom, while the Welsh and Scots live mostly in their own countries, rural-to-urban settlement patterns do not play a significant role in distinguishing them from the English. While parts of Scotland may have some of the most sparsely populated areas in Europe, the bulk of its population lives in cities, which closely resemble those of England and Wales.

Northern Ireland, on the other hand, provides an example of ethnic differences on a local scale in a fairly unusual way amongst minorities on the European continent because of the acting out of cleavages between Roman Catholics and Protestants on a city scale, manifested through residential segregation more characteristic of immigrant groupings. In Northern Ireland Catholics make up about 38 per cent of the population. Segregated settlement patterns became more extreme from the late nineteenth century and especially after the 1960s, but it appears that Catholics and Protestants have always lived in separate communities: the growth of sectarian politics has made them conscious of their differences and willing to act upon these differences. This schism increased with industrialisation during the nineteenth century, leading to the migration of large numbers of Catholics into Belfast, where sectarian riots, with economic sparks, became a regular occurrence. The 1911 census demonstrated that 41 per cent of Catholics and 62 per cent of Protestants lived in streets which contained over 90 per cent of their own community. By 1972 70 per cent of Catholics and 78 per cent of Protestants lived in segregated streets.[80] One Catholic couple who refused to move were still resident in 1993 in a house which they had purchased in 1956. Their experience was not very pleasant, as described by the wife, Sue Murphy:

> We are stuck here. I am very frightened and I can't sleep any more.
>   I don't go out at night. Kids throw stones from both sides, they shout and light bonfires. I'm not sad *every day*, but you don't know what's going to happen next.[81]

Although ethnic cleavages have not resulted in the same level of political upheaval in France as they have in Britain, the regional political movements which exist in the former do rest at least partly on geographic differences. To take the examples of Brittany and Corsica: their obvious geographical similarity lies in their distance from Paris, the centre of French life, which results in economic underdevelopment, mostly due to lack of industrialisation, which has meant a greater preservation of rural employment. As late as 1975 a total

80 Frank Wright, *Northern Ireland: A Comparative Analysis* (Dublin, 1987), pp. 1–20; Frederick W. Boal, 'Segregating and Mixing: Space and Residence in Belfast', in Frederick W. Boal, J. Neville and H. Douglas (eds), *Geographical Perspectives on the Northern Ireland Problem* (London, 1982), pp. 249–53.
81 *Independent*, 9 November 1993.

of 46 per cent of the population of Brittany lived on the land, compared with 27 per cent for France as a whole.[82]

In Czechoslovakia the Hungarian minority continued to be concentrated in its historically evolved settlement area consisting of a 345 mile long strip on the Slovakian–Hungarian border, covering 3,516 square miles. This region contains 92.2 per cent of the Hungarian minority in Slovakia and they make up 61.7 per cent of its population. A total of 59.3 per cent of the Hungarian population live in villages with less than 5,000 people, while five cities house more than 10,000 Hungarians.[83]

In Romania Hungarians continued to form the largest minority grouping after the Second World War, focused upon the ethnically diverse region of Transylvania where about 90 per cent of them lived. According to an estimate from 1977, a total of 2,030,000 out of 2,200,000 Hungarians in Romania lived in Transylvania during that year, when they made up 22 per cent of the overall population. They predominated in three regions in the east of Transylvania, furthest away from Hungary: Harghita (84.5 per cent), Covasna (78 per cent) and Mures (43.7 per cent). Outside Transylvania the most important settlement of Hungarians lies in Bucharest. Historically, Hungarians, like Germans, have concentrated in the large cities within Transylvania. Since the Second World War increasing urbanisation within Transylvania has tended to make use of Romanians from other parts of the country, which has meant that the Hungarian proportion of many Transylvanian cities has declined.[84]

The minorities within Yugoslavia and its various republics had their own concentrations, which, as in the case of Romania, often had little to do with artificial boundaries and rested, instead, on historically evolved settlement patterns. Thus while some Serbs outside Serbia lived on the border between Serbia and Croatia, others found themselves in concentrations as far away as possible from Serbia in north-west and south-west Bosnia, as well as in a coastal strip in Croatia around Knin. In addition, many Yugoslav towns and cities, especially within Bosnia and Croatia, had mixed populations, including, of the best known, Sarajevo, Mostar and Knin (see Map 1).

In contrast to the heterogeneous nature of former Yugoslavia, the Turkish state contains just one substantial minority in the form of the Kurds, concentrated on the eastern underdeveloped borderlands of the country and spreading over the boundaries, especially into Iran and Iraq. The 8.5 million Kurds who make up 19 per cent of the population of Turkey live mostly in this region,

---

82 M. McDonald, *'We Are Not French!' Language, Culture and Identity in Brittany* (London, 1989), pp. 4, 320.
83 Kalvoda, 'National Minorities in Czechoslovakia', pp. 124–5; *Hungarian Minority in Czechoslovakia/Slovakia* (Bratislava, 1993), p. 7; 'Slovaks of Czechoslovakia', in Minority Rights Group (ed.), *World Directory of Minorities* (London, 1989), p. 122.
84 Rudolf Joó, *Report of the Situation of the Hungarian Minority in Rumania* (Budapest, 1988), p. 25; Joó, *The Hungarian Minority Situation in Ceaucescu's Romania* (New York, 1994), pp. 32–3; Bennet Kovrig, 'The Magyars in Rumania: Problems of a "Coinhabiting" Nationality', *Südosteuropa* 35 (1986), p. 478; Mihok, 'Minorities and Minority Policies in Rumania', pp. 82–3; George Schöpflin and Hugh Poulton, *Rumania's Ethnic Hungarians* (London, 1990), p. 11.

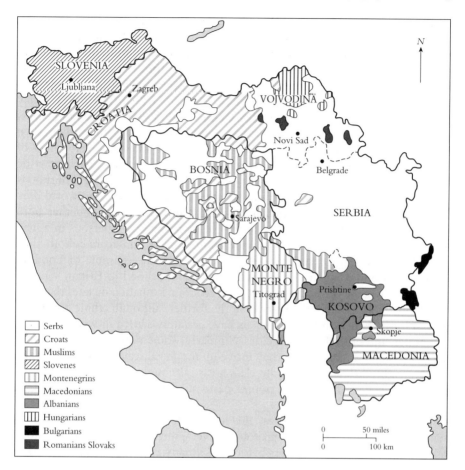

Map 1   National and Ethnic Distribution in Yugoslavia

although as many as a million Kurds may have moved out of the region between 1950 and 1980 because of its underdeveloped nature, many of them settling in Istanbul, which has over half a million Kurds, and other industrialised centres. In all, about 2.5 million Kurds residing in Turkey live outside the core area of concentration, although most of these had resided there before the migration of the post-War years. Furthermore, nearly 400,000 Kurds moved to western Europe as foreign workers between 1950 and 1980. However, Kurds are not the only group in Kurdistan. According to the census of 1970 the population of the area totalled 7,557,000 of whom 6,200,000 (83 per cent of the total) were Kurds. The rest were mostly Turks (including expellees from Bulgaria), Arabs and Armenians. In 1965 Kurds made up just 12.2 per cent of towns housing more than 10,000 people, while Turks constituted 80.4 per cent of the population of such settlements and Arabs made up 7.5 per cent. More recently, a rapid

43

urbanisation, caused by population growth and mechanisation in agriculture, has caused problems in the expanding towns surrounded by slums.[85]

The settlement patterns of immigrants in post-War western Europe are essentially beyond their own control. As an urban proletariat, at or near the bottom of the social and economic ladder, they have usually had no choice but to concentrate in the poorest parts of the cities to which they move. They prefer to live next to people of their own national or ethnic group, a process which facilitates the attempted reconstruction of activities from their own homeland such as the building of places of worship and the development of businesses which sell products – especially food and clothing – characteristic of the place of origin. The newcomers essentially create ethnic neighbourhoods in urban environments, as immigrants have done throughout the world during the nineteenth and twentieth centuries. They congregate together both because they wish to and because of fear of living amongst persons in a new environment with whom they cannot communicate and from whom they often face hostility. Of course they might, to take the example of London, *prefer* to settle in Mayfair – the wealthiest neighbourhood in Britain – rather than the East End – the poorest – but their economic situation dictates that they will more likely settle in the latter than the former, although ethnic communities of businessmen and professionals have certainly settled in wealthier parts of London and other European cities. Similarly, some minorities change their areas of residence if and when they move up the social scale so that they create ethnic neighbourhoods in middle-class areas, although these are not quite as well developed as those in the poorer parts of cities, with their more tightly packed housing patterns.

The impact of immigrants on the urban geography of many European states has been one of the most profound developments in the post-War history of Europe. Whereas in the years before 1945 many countries had little experience with immigrants, in several states (of which western Germany provides one of the best examples) it is impossible to visit a town of any size which does not have obligatory ethnic restaurants and a small area of immigrant settlement. Clearly, these patterns reveal themselves on a larger scale in the more substantial European cities, so that, in the case of Britain, its three largest urban concentrations – London, Birmingham and Manchester – have some of the highest percentages of immigrants. However, even somewhere like Leicester, with virtually no experience of immigration before 1945, now has a non-white population making up over a quarter of people living in the city.

The West Indian population in Britain has demonstrated some of the most classic immigrant settlement patterns in post-War Europe, with high concentrations in several inner-city areas, but especially London. In 1965, for instance, 101,385 out of 173,659 West Indians in Britain lived in London and the South-East.[86] Particular areas of London, especially within the inner city,

---

85 Kendal, 'Kurdistan in Turkey', pp. 47–9; David McDowall, *The Kurds* (London, 1989), pp. 7, 14.
86 Ceri Peach, *West Indian Migration to Britain: A Social Geography* (London, 1968), p. 65.

have developed West Indian communities since 1945. Upon their first arrival in the capital they found that they were moving to a metropolis which had lost 100,000 homes due to German bombing during the Second World War and which had further experienced a post-War boom in marriages and births, which meant that there were almost 500,000 more families in London than there were homes. This situation contributed to the development of colour prejudice against West Indians, so that they were forced to move into some of the poorest parts of London, one of the earliest consisting of the Colville area of Notting Hill, where they also faced exploitation from unscrupulous landlords charging them high rents in the knowledge that, because of their experiences of rejection elsewhere, the immigrants had no choice but to accept what these landlords offered them. By 1958 Notting Hill may have had a West Indian population of 7,000.[87] The 1961 census revealed that twelve local authorities, mostly in London, counted Jamaican populations of 2,000 or more.[88] Some dispersal has taken place since then but major areas of concentration in London continue to exist, including Notting Hill in the west, Tottenham in the north and Brixton in the south. One of the reasons for the continued concentration lies in the fact that West Indians still face discrimination in their search for accommodation, whether they want to rent or buy.

The South Asian populations of Britain have not focused upon the capital to quite the same degree as West Indians. In 1961 Greater London contained 37.05 per cent of the total Indian population of England and Wales, and 27.72 of Pakistani residents. They lived together in large inner-city Victorian houses, which meant that they could cushion themselves from the indignities of racism and rejection they would have to endure by mixing with white people. In addition, by remaining within an ethnic enclave this would assist in the process of saving money away from the temptations of spending hard-earned cash, especially in a situation where everyone in the same household had the goal of sending remittances to relatives back in the home country.

Major Indian and Pakistani communities have subsequently developed throughout the country. By the 1970s Bradford contained 30,000 Pakistanis out of a total population of about 300,000. These Pakistanis had originated from a few areas of the country, notably Mirpur, which accounted for 60 to 70 per cent of the newcomers. But even in a town like Gravesend, not known for its Asian concentration, the number of Sikhs increased from just over 100 in the late 1950s, consisting almost entirely of males, to several thousand within a few years. In Gravesend, as elsewhere, the racial prejudice of surrounding white people helped in the development of Asian enclaves because once one Asian bought a house in a particular area, white people all around moved, fearing that their house values would fall. This process was rapid and took place

87 Donald Hinds, *Journey to an Illusion: The West Indian in Britain* (London, 1966), pp. 83–5; Edward Pilkington, *Beyond the Mother Country: West Indians and the Notting Hill White Riots* (London, 1988), pp. 53–61.
88 E. J. B. Rose et al., *Colour and Citizenship: A Report on British Race Relations* (London, 1969), p. 102.

throughout the country. The East African Asians who moved to Britain during the late 1960s and early 1970s tended to gravitate towards the areas which already had ethnic concentrations, despite the state's attempts to prevent this. More recently, Asian suburban communities have also developed.[89]

European immigrants in post-War Britain have also settled in particular areas and – especially in the case of Italians and, more particularly, Greek Cypriots – have developed ethnic enclaves, although, because of the fact that they have slightly more in common with English people and consequently face less hostility, more dispersal takes place, particularly amongst the Irish and, to a lesser (but still significant) extent, the Italians. While ethnic neighbourhoods may not have developed to any great extent amongst the Irish in post-War Britain, they did tend to move towards particular areas of the country, notably London, as well as the west Midlands where the engineering and car industries offered them employment opportunities. Within London the Irish focused on particular boroughs, especially in the north and west of the capital.[90] One of the most important of these concentrations, representing an ethnic neighbourhood, lies in Kilburn:

> The impression on first arrival is that one might well be in Ireland – Irish papers, both local and national, are on sale, the main Irish banks have branches in the High Road, Irish names appear above shop fronts and Irish accents abound.[91]

Of the 97,848 Italian immigrants living in Britain in 1981, 31 per cent (or 30,752) resided in London, concentrated mostly in the central and northern boroughs, with an ethnic neighbourhood in Clerkenwell which has existed since the nineteenth century. Bedford acts as home to one of the major provincial Italian communities, totalling around 5,000 and originating overwhelmingly from the south of the country.[92] Of the approximately 100,000 Cypriots living in Britain in 1966, about three-quarters could be found in London.[93] Although they had initially concentrated in the inner London boroughs, forming ethnic neighbourhoods in Camden Town, they subsequently moved further north, first to Haringey (especially around Green Lanes), and then on to the middle-class suburb of Palmers Green where concentration has also developed. Nevertheless, in terms of residence patterns within London, Greek Cypriots are represented in all boroughs from Hackney, one of the poorest, to Barnet,

89 Robinson, *Transients, Settlers and Refugees*, pp. 226–8; Dilip Hiro, *Black British: White British* (London, 1971), p. 73; Rozina Visram, 'South Asians in London', in Merriman, *Peopling of London*, p. 174; Arthur Wesley, *Sikhs in England: The Development of a Migrant Community* (Calcutta, 1979), pp. 50–1; Verity Saifullah Khan, 'Migration and Social Stress: Mirpuris in Bradford', in Khan, *Minority Families in Britain*, pp. 40, 50.
90 Colin Holmes, *John Bull's Island: Immigration and British Society, 1871–1971* (London, 1988), p. 216.
91 Judy Chance, 'The Irish in London: An Exploration of Ethnic Boundary Maintenance', in Jackson, *Race and Racism*, p. 147.
92 Terri Colpi, *The Italian Factor: The Italian Community in Great Britain* (Edinburgh, 1991), pp. 166–7, 184–7.
93 Floya Anthias, *Ethnicity, Class, Gender and Migration: Greek Cypriots in Britain* (Aldershot, 1992), p. 6.

one of the richest. Outside the capital the only significant Greek Cypriot communities can be found in Birmingham, Manchester and seaside towns in south-east England, where they are heavily involved in the catering trade as restaurant owners.[94]

Geographical concentration of immigrants in France has developed in a similar way to that in England. However, as much as 8.1 per cent of the foreign population of the former lived in rural areas in 1990, although this remained far below the French percentage, which stood at 27.3 per cent in the same year. In fact, the larger the size of the city, the more over-represented were immigrants in comparison with the French population. Thus 30.5 per cent of immigrants lived in cities with between 100,000 and 200,000 inhabitants, compared with 15.1 per cent of French people. The greatest concentration of immigrants lies in and around the three major cities of Lyons, Marseilles and Paris, which, together, accounted for 59 per cent of the foreign population living in France in 1990.

In fact, 35.6 per cent of immigrants lived in Paris in 1990, where they formed 12.9 per cent of the population. This concentration on Paris has not always been so marked because during the late 1940s and early 1950s only 8.5 per cent of immigrant workers lived in the French capital, with a greater concentration to the north, east and south-west. Nevertheless, by the end of the 1960s the Paris area had become the home of between 35 and 40 per cent of permanent immigrants, a situation facilitated by the city's physical growth and the consequent creation of jobs in construction, public works and domestic service. Not all immigrant communities in France are equally concentrated in the capital. Whilst 44 per cent of Portuguese, 39 per cent of Tunisians and 37 per cent of Algerians lived here in 1982, at the other end of the scale Paris accounted for 28 per cent of Moroccans, 26.7 per cent of Spaniards and 18.5 per cent of Italians. Within the capital immigrants remained more focused in specific locations, notably the Ville de Paris and the surrounding areas of Hauts de Seine and Seine St Denis, with particular concentrations of North Africans, although this group remains under-represented in the capital compared with its proportion of the foreign population on a national scale.

Clermont Ferrand has the highest proportion of North Africans amongst its foreign population, standing at 72.2 per cent in 1982. In Roubaix North Africans made up 10.4 per cent of the entire population. Like Paris the major provincial cities have concentrations of foreigners. In Marseilles, for instance, where immigrants make up one in ten of residents, 69 per cent of whom are North Africans, there is a heavy concentration in the centre and north of the city.[95]

94 Robin Oakley, *Changing Patterns of Distribution of Cypriot Settlement* (Coventry, 1987).
95 Hargreaves, *Immigration, 'Race' and Ethnicity*, pp. 66–9; Xavier Lannes, 'Regional Aspects of Immigration into France', in Brinley Thomas (ed.), *Economics of International Migration* (New York, 1958), pp. 215–24; McDonald, 'Labour Immigration into France', pp. 128–30; Philip E. Ogden, 'Immigration into France Since 1945', *Ethnic and Racial Studies* 14 (1991), pp. 310–14.

Immigrants in the Federal Republic of Germany also focus on the larger industrial conurbations, to which they were recruited. The largest cities contain the greatest concentrations. In 1977 Frankfurt had a foreign population of 17.1 per cent, Munich 15.4 per cent, Cologne 11.3 per cent, West Berlin 8.6 per cent and Hamburg 6.9 per cent. At the other end of the scale the more rural German state of Schleswig-Holstein had a foreign population of just 2.9 per cent of the total.[96]

Within the cities of major concentration, again following classic patterns of settlement, immigrants have tended to focus on particular locations. In some instances this was due to initial proximity to the workplace, although the process has been further assisted by chain migration and prejudice within German neighbourhoods. One survey found that 60 per cent of Italians seeking accommodation could find somewhere to live in an immigrant neighbourhood within one month, whereas only 37.2 per cent seeking housing in German quarters found a flat so quickly.

In Duisburg the neighbourhoods closest to steel works, which imported immigrants, tended to have the highest concentrations of foreigners. The housing policies of firms, which provided accommodation for many of the newcomers, also helped in the process of inner-city concentration, as did the desire of the migrants to save and send remittances to relatives in the homeland where they eventually planned to return, which meant that young males were prepared to live in poor housing to save money. The settlement patterns in Cologne closely resemble that of Duisburg in the sense that concentration has taken place around some of the major firms which provided accommodation for the imported workers, including Ford and Deutsche Bundesbahn. In West Berlin, meanwhile, the heaviest concentration of Turks developed in Kreuzberg, one of the poorest districts of the city. At the other end of the social scale a predominantly professional group in the form of the Japanese in Düsseldorf – who totalled 3,372 people in 1983, the sixth-largest foreign grouping in the city, made up of people imported by Japanese companies – has also focused heavily in particular areas of Düsseldorf. In fact, this minority displayed the highest concentration of any immigrant group living in this metropolis, so that 61.3 per cent of the Japanese here live in six inner-city wards. In this case segregation is voluntary, rather than controlled by the cost of accommodation.[97]

---

96 Siegfried Bethlehem, *Heimatvertreibung, DDR-Flucht, Gastarbeiterzuwanderung: Wanderungsströme und Wanderungspolitik in der Bundesrepublik Deutschland* (Stuttgart, 1982), p. 121; Hans Heinrich Blotevogel, Ursula Müller-ter Jung and Gerald Wood, 'From Itinerant Worker to Immigrant? The Geography of Guestworkers in Germany', in Russell King (ed.), *Mass Migration in Europe: The Legacy and the Future* (London, 1993), p. 90.

97 Blotevogel, Jung and Wood, ibid., p. 92; John R. Clark, 'Residential Patterns and Social Integration of Turks in Cologne', in Krane, *Manpower Mobility Across Cultural Boundaries*, p. 63; Barbara von Breitenbach, *Italiener und Spanier als Arbeitnehmer in der Bundesrepublik Deutschland* (Munich, 1982), p. 98; Faruk Şen, '1961 bis 1993: Eine kurze Geschichte der Türken in Deutschland', in Claus Leggewie and Zafer Şenocak (eds), *Deutsche Türken: Das Ende der Geduld* (Hamburg, 1993), p. 23; Günther Glebe, 'Segregation and Intra-Urban Mobility of a High-Status Ethnic Group: The Case of the Japanese in Düsseldorf', *Ethnic and Racial Studies* 9 (1986), pp. 461–83.

The immigrant (as well as the native) population of the Netherlands is concentrated in the western provinces of Noord-Holland, Zuid-Holland and Utrecht.[98] At the end of the 1960s all of these urban agglomerations had immigrant populations approaching 5 per cent, although this figure has increased since then.[99] The Surinamese have two important concentrations in Amsterdam. Those who settled there before the large influx of this group (which occurred during the middle of the 1970s) tended to move to several inner-city locations, where they lived in lodging-houses. However, these inner-city concentrations could not cope with the new influx of the 1970s. Consequently, many of the new settlers moved to Bijlmermeer, the newly built south-eastern part of the city containing public housing, which the Surinamese obtained easily because they faced little competition from the native middle-class population, for whom the housing was intended. In 1982 this district housed 7 per cent of the population of Amsterdam, but 28 per cent of the city's Surinamese residents. The Surinamese constituted 20 per cent of Bijlmermeer's population of 50,000. Although this represents ethnic concentration, it has taken place in a manner different from the classic European pattern, because of the high quality of much of the housing. The other immigrant groups in the Netherlands, from southern Europe, Turkey and further afield, have tended to focus in areas of low-quality nineteenth-century housing. The reasons for this concentration are the temporary nature of the stay of many immigrants, chain migration and hostility from natives.[100]

The varying experiences of different groups do not make minorities in the Netherlands in any way unique, as diversity exists amongst foreign groupings in all European states. Often, as in the Dutch case, those which most closely follow the settlement patterns of the dominant population are those which are most akin to its norms, whereas immigrant groups who had no previous connection with a particular society find it more difficult to integrate. Another important factor in the Dutch case, as in all European states, is the earning power of different groups and their place in the labour market, as class clearly plays a role in determining choice of residence.

Switzerland reveals similar patterns. Some Swiss cities have immigrant shares of their population higher than virtually any other urban centres in Europe. In 1980, when foreigners made up 14.8 per cent of the population of the country

98 Ger Mik and Nia Verkoren-Hemelaar, 'Segregation in the Netherlands and Turkish Migration', in N. Abadan-Unat (ed.), *Turkish Workers in Europe* (Leiden, 1976), pp. 260–1.
99 Hans Kok, 'Labour Migration and Migration Policy in the Netherlands', in Abadan-Unat, *Turkish Workers in Europe*, p. 298.
100 Leo de Klerk and Hans van Amersfoort, 'Surinamese Settlement in Amsterdam, 1973–83', in Malcolm Cross and Hans Entzinger (eds), *Lost Illusions: Caribbean Minorities in Britain and the Netherlands* (London, 1988), pp. 147–63; Hans van Amersfoort, 'Ethnic Residential Patterns in Dutch Cities: Class, Race or Culture?', in T. E. Gerholm and Y. G. Litman (eds), *The New Islamic Presence in Western Europe* (London, 1988), pp. 234–5; Ceri Peach, *The Caribbean in Europe: Contrasting Patterns of Migration and Settlement in Britain, France and the Netherlands* (Coventry, 1991), p. 22; Mik and Verkoren-Hemelaar, 'Segregation in the Netherlands', pp. 259–83; Gideon S. Bolt and Ronald van Kempen, 'Segregation and Turks Housing Conditions in Middle-sized Dutch Cities', *New Community* 23 (1997), pp. 363–84.

as a whole, the proportion for Geneva reached 35.7 per cent, Lausanne stood at 23.2 per cent, Basle 18.2 and Zurich 17.7. Some residential segregation has taken place according to the countries of origin of the newcomers and the sort of employment pursued. In the case of Zurich, Germans and Austrians did not segregate themselves largely due to linguistic similarities. However, the predominantly middle-class English and French showed a high degree of segregation within wealthier districts. In contrast, at the other end of the scale, Turks, Spaniards and Italians resided in poorer areas of the city.[101]

In Sweden, during the first few years after the end of the Second World War, a few Estonians and Hungarians worked on farms, but the vast majority of immigrants to the country since 1945 have moved – following the normal pattern – to cities, above all to the Stockholm area, which attracted about 40 per cent of immigrants to Sweden between 1945 and 1970, although since then settlement has taken place in other centres, including Malmo and Göteborg. About 80 per cent of immigrants in Sweden live in eight of its 24 counties, concentrated, like the Swedish population, in the warmer southern part of the country. Foreigners make up about 8 per cent of the population of Stockholm, focused in particular districts of the city, especially Spånga. The main reason for this ethnic concentration is similar to that which attracted the Surinamese to Bijlmermeer in Amsterdam, in the sense that the immigrants collectively moved to newly constructed state housing.[102]

HOUSING

The housing patterns of minorities follow their demography and settlement. In other words, those with the highest birth rates, living in the worst areas, occupy the lowest-quality accommodation. Gypsies perfectly illustrate this process. In an ideal situation they try to wander, although, by the post-War period, the state has succeeded, using force or incentives, in trapping this nomadic group because of its non-adherence to the traditional settlement patterns of dominant populations. The freedom of the Gypsies essentially represents an irritant to post-War states.

In Czechoslovakia persecution from the eighteenth century had ensured that, by the twentieth, the majority of Gypsies had become sedentary. However, the early decades after 1945 resulted in attempts to settle those who still remained nomadic. Immediately after the end of the Second World War most Gypsies lived in Slovakia in 'dreadful . . . rural ghettoes . . . completely segreg-

---

101 Michael Arend, 'Housing Segregation in Switzerland', in E. D. Huttman, W. Blauw and S. Saltman (eds), *Urban Housing: Segregation of Minorities in Western Europe and the United States* (Durham, NC, 1991), pp. 155–67; Castles and Kosack, *Immigrant Workers and Class Structure*, pp. 271–5.
102 Harald Runblom, 'Immigration to Scandinavia After World War II', in Sven Tägil (ed.), *Ethnicity and Nation Building in the Nordic World* (London, 1995), p. 306; Anna-Lisa Lindén and Göran Lindberg, 'Immigrant Housing Patterns in Sweden', in Huttman, Blauw and Saltman, *Urban Housing*, pp. 92–107; British Refugee Council, London, QSW 85.2, Irene Palmgreen, 'Situation of Immigrant Women in Sweden', 1981.

ated from mainstream society and without adequate water, sewage, electricity, and navigable roads'.[103] Under these conditions a migration of thousands of Gypsies took place out of Slovakia, moving west towards industrial conurbations in North Moravia and North Bohemia to play a role in the general labour market on a mass scale as unskilled factory and construction workers, therefore representing a surplus labour supply for post-War Czech industrialisation.

However, the migration led to similar urban concentrations to those which developed amongst foreign immigrants in western capitalist states, as well as sparking a similar negative reaction from the dominant population and the state. Against this background the Czech government decided to launch a campaign against the nomadic habits of Gypsies, despite the fact that only one group – the Olach Roms, who numbered 6,000 – maintained a truly itinerant way of life, living in caravans and tents. In 1958 the Communist Party of Czechoslovakia cast doubt over whether Gypsies were a national group and there followed Law 74 which prevented nomadism. Enforcing this law could involve the brutal act of shooting horses and removing wheels from carts. The measure also attempted to control less nomadic Gypsies, showing particular concern for their instability in employment. The underlying objective consisted of a desire to assimilate Gypsies into a standardised type, although the economic motivation was a desire to provide reliable labour for the expanding Czech economy. Local authorities would play a part in the ending of nomadism as they had to assist Gypsies in their attempts to find permanent housing and employment. 'Nomads', as the 1958 Law labelled them, could not obtain employment unless they had their identity cards stamped by local authorities.

But this measure had limited success because both employers and local authorities put little effort into enforcing it. In 1965 the government therefore created the National Council for Questions of the Gypsy Population, with the aims of enforcing full employment amongst adult Romanies and of eliminating small Gypsy settlements in order to disperse their inhabitants amongst the rest of the population. Again, this programme achieved limited success, for similar reasons to the failure of the 1958 legislation. A development of Gypsy organisations following the Prague Spring led to a relaxation of the repressive resettlement policies, which still, however, continued for several years after the suppression of the 1968 revolution.

During the early 1970s Gypsies in Czechoslovakia lived in several types of accommodation. The most symbolic of the assimilationist tactics of the state were those caravans, with their wheels removed, which continued to house Olach Romanies. A second group consisted of those who, like some immigrants into western Europe, lived in temporary barracks. Others found homes in disused blocks of flats earmarked for demolition. Still others received low-quality flats provided by the local council or by their employers. Finally, a small group lived in modern, comfortable flats in new blocks.

103 Helsinki Watch, *Czechoslovakia's Endangered Gypsies*, p. 53.

The relocation programme continued during the 1970s and 1980s although Gypsies now moved into better accommodation, even if they may not always have wished to leave their original homes. Between 1972 and 1981 the government demolished 4,000 shanties and relocated 4,850 families, although in 1983 there still remained 400 Gypsy settlements in Slovakia, with 3,018 shanties providing accommodation for 21,622 people, or 10 per cent of the Gypsy population. According to the 1980 census the average number of persons in a Gypsy household totalled 5.6 while that for the rest of the population stood at 3.1. Despite the westward migration which had taken place, most Gypsies still lived in Slovakia. In the early 1990s the new Slovak Republic still had between 300 and 400 ghettos, unchanged for 200 years, without water, sewage systems, electricity and toilets.[104]

Few Hungarian Gypsies still pursued a travelling life after 1945. Again due to industrialisation, Gypsies have moved into the urban labour force. In the 1950s the overwhelming majority of Romanies were rural but by the 1980s about 40 per cent lived in towns, including 50,000 in Budapest. Gypsy housing conditions have remained poor throughout the post-War period. In the early 1960s about two-thirds of all Romanies 'lived in dilapidated houses in ghettoized shanty towns, with several generations sharing a room, usually with no indoor toilets, frequently without any running or at least potable water and with one third of dwellings lacking electricity'. The state responded to this situation by launching a housing development plan in 1964 which resulted in a fall in the number of slum dwellings from 50,000 to 5,000 by 1984, as well as a fall in their occupants from 250,000 (75 per cent Gypsies) to 40,000. However, ghettos redeveloped in some areas to which Gypsies moved.[105]

The above picture is repeated, with variations, elsewhere in eastern Europe. From the end of the 1950s the Bulgarian government dispersed Gypsies in blocks of flats amongst the rest of the population. Nevertheless, after the collapse of communism most Gypsies lived in ghettos, located in 160 of Bulgaria's 237 cities and 3,000 of its 5,846 villages, with poor sanitation and overcrowding.[106] For example:

> The city of Silven has the largest population of Gypsies in Bulgaria, some 50,000, or one quarter of the city's population. Gypsies live in several

104 Ibid., pp. 28, 53–9; Josef Kalvoda, 'The Gypsies of Czechoslovakia', *Nationalities Papers* 19 (1991), pp. 284–7; William O. McCagg, 'Gypsy Policy in Socialist Hungary and Czechoslovakia', *Nationalities Papers* 19 (1991), pp. 319–20; Otto Ulč, 'Gypsies in Czechoslovakia: A Case of Unfinished Integration', *Eastern European Politics and Societies* 2 (1988), pp. 306–15; Eva Davidóva, 'The Gypsies in Czechoslovakia: Part II: Post-War Developments', *Journal of the Gypsy Lore Society* 50 (1971), pp. 47–8; Willy Guy, 'Ways of Looking at Roms: The Case of Czechoslovakia', in Rehfisch Farnham (ed.), *Gypsies, Tinkers and Other Travellers* (London, 1975), pp. 213–15; Kalibova, Haisman and Gjuricova, 'Gypsies in Czechoslovakia', pp. 141–4.
105 Helsinki Watch, *Struggling for Ethnic Identity: The Gypsies of Hungary* (New York, 1993), pp. 3, 7; David M. Crowe, 'Hungary', in Crowe and J. Kolsti (eds), *The Gypsies of Eastern Europe* (Armonk, NY, 1991), p. 121; McCagg, ibid., p. 320.
106 Simonov, 'The Gypsies', p. 13.

crowded districts, on the outskirts of the city, and are mostly segregated from Bulgarians.

Peyo Daslev is Silven's most densely populated Gypsy district. In this ghetto, it is common for three or four families to live in one house, and for five or six people to sleep in the same room. Homes often lack toilets.[107]

In Romania assimilationist desires led to the resettlement of those Romanies who still pursued a nomadic way of life, resulting in the confiscation of wagons.[108] The Polish government successfully settled its Gypsy population by passing a stream of legislation from the early 1950s, culminating in a 1964 resolution which forbade Gypsies from travelling in caravans – which meant that they became a sedentary community, settled on state farms, working in manufacturing co-operatives, or absorbed by bigger industrial concerns.[109] The Soviet Union forbade Gypsies from wandering with the passage of a 1956 decree 'On Reconciling Vagrant Gypsies to Labour', although this proved only partially effective.[110]

Developments amongst the Gypsy communities in western Europe resemble those in the eastern half of the continent, although the state did not usually intervene as directly in a liberal democratic form of government, as it did under the old communist regimes, even though both types of rule may have had the same assimilationist desires. Gypsies in Britain have more successfully maintained their itinerant way of life, despite attempts by the state to control their movement. They follow travelling patterns dependent upon a variety of factors including availability of work, access to camping places, harassment by police and local authorities, and competition with other Romanies. After the Second World War they abandoned the horse-drawn caravan in favour of mechanised transport, so that as early as 1965 only 6 per cent of Gypsies still resorted to the former method of transport.

Although the state made attempts to control the movement of Gypsies from the end of the nineteenth century, a turning point came with the passage of the Caravan Sites Act of 1968 which required local councils to provide adequate accommodation for Gypsies residing in or moving into their territory. By 1974 just over one hundred sites had appeared, increasing to 142, with 2,254 pitches by January 1977. However, Gypsies regarded these with hostility, viewing them as an attempt to impose assimilation and permanent settlement. As one Gypsy stated: 'We had a grand time till talk of all these sites. Now we can't go anywhere. They've closed our old stopping places.'[111]

---

107 Helsinki Watch, *Destroying Ethnic Identity: The Gypsies of Bulgaria* (New York, 1991), p. 23.
108 Helsinki Watch, *Destroying Ethnic Identity: The Persecution of Gypsies in Romania* (New York, 1991), pp. 5, 17, 18.
109 Jerzy Ficowski, *The Gypsies in Poland: History and Customs* (Warsaw, 1989), pp. 50–2.
110 David M. Crowe, *A History of the Gypsies of Eastern Europe and Russia* (London, 1995), pp. 188–91.
111 Martin Smith, *Gypsies: Where Now?* (London, 1975), pp. 4, 8–10; Thomas Acton, *Gypsy Politics and Social Change* (London, 1974), pp. 46–7.

The underlying objective of the British state was to move Gypsies closer to the norms of English middle-class sedentary housing patterns. The arrival of wanderers into an area where the population cannot move so freely creates jealousies amongst those who feel trapped in their environment. The same is true of eastern European regimes, although in this case the various governments aimed at controlling the living conditions of Gypsies, which they – and 'enlightened', as well as assimilationist, opinion within their borders – found offensive.

Amongst localised minorities, who usually live in more deprived areas than the dominant population, housing conditions are most likely to be worse than those which characterise the dominant population. For instance, the traditional housing of the Sami consisted of mobile tents transported by this migratory people and strong enough to keep out wind, rain and snow, although more recently local authorities, under Sami and media pressure, have constructed modern accommodation.[112]

The condition of housing in Northern Ireland is worse than for the United Kingdom as a whole and better for Protestants than for Catholics. In the early 1970s one in five 'of the total dwelling stock' in Northern Ireland was 'statutorily unfit' compared with a figure of 7.3 per cent for England and Wales. In the middle of the 1980s the average number of people living in a Protestant household was 2.82, while the figure for Catholics stood at 3.62, mostly because members of the latter community tended to have more children. However, only 5 per cent of Protestants, compared with 16 per cent of Catholics, lived in overcrowded accommodation. Other indicators of housing conditions, such as the number of bedrooms per house, also demonstrate that Catholics have lived in poorer conditions, although, because of state policy reacting to Catholic political movements, differences have lessened and Catholics have gained greater access to public housing than previously.[113]

The settlement patterns of immigrants have tended to place them at the very bottom of the housing market, especially upon their first arrival. Accommodation was particularly bad in the French and German cases, partly because of the sheer weight of numbers during the 1960s and, in the latter case, the early 1990s. One of the solutions developed by immigrants in France during the 1960s, against the lack of housing available, the indifference of the state and discrimination against them, was simply to create shanty towns. German governments, meanwhile, have been more conscientious towards their newcomers but they have tended to offer a curious short-term solution of putting up foreign workers during the 1960s, and asylum seekers and ethnic Germans during the 1990s, into camps, although these minorities always move out in the long run to settle in towns and cities of all sizes throughout the entire country.

112 Israel Ruong, *The Lapps in Sweden* (Stockholm, 1967), p. 95; T. I. Itkonen, 'The Lapps of Finland', *Southwestern Journal of Anthropology* 7 (1951), pp. 52, 67.
113 David J. Smith and Gerald Chambers, *Inequality in Northern Ireland* (Oxford, 1991), pp. 330–67; Northern Ireland Housing Executive, *Housing Condition Survey, 1974: Principal Characteristics of the Northern Ireland Dwelling Stock by District* (Belfast, 1974).

Throughout the post-War period immigrants in France have lived in housing conditions worse than those of native-born French people, especially during the 1960s. The newcomers moved into a western capitalist state facing a severe housing crisis in which natives also endured extreme overcrowding due to a situation of rapid urbanisation combined with an ageing housing supply. In addition to the millions of foreign workers moving into the large French cities, these urban agglomerations also attracted natives from rural areas and small towns, as well as repatriates from Algeria.

Immigrants into post-War France had several possible choices of housing open to them, none of them especially appealing. In the first place, some employers provided accommodation, usually in prefabricated huts. Secondly, a small minority of immigrants lived in single furnished rooms, although few could actually afford this. The only exception consisted of Iberian maids working for the Paris bourgeoisie, who had an attic room provided for them, which sometimes also housed their husband and children.

Some unscrupulous landlords who owned cheap hotels exploited the newcomers, accommodating numerous people in one room and sometimes even selling beds in shifts. Immigrants rented a room by the day, week or month. The problems faced by people living in this type of housing included bad sanitation, overcrowding and a lack of cooking facilities. Some of these hotels had beds everywhere, including cellars and even the reception.

Speculators also converted old and unused buildings into so-called accommodation, including cellars, disused factories and houses usually in suburban areas. The following describes the situation in one of these buildings:

> In an old chocolate factory owned by a private speculator at Ivry (a suburb of Paris), 541 black Africans were sharing eleven rooms in 1969. Some of the dormitories – including one in which seventy people were sleeping – had no windows. The ground floor boasted two taps with drinking water, the other floors, two taps with non-drinking water. There were five wcs and one washbasin. The communal kitchen spread a revolting smell. No cleaning services for the rooms were arranged by the landlord. Each worker was entitled to one sheet, which was changed every forty days. The blankets had been cleaned once in the four years in which this 'clandestine hotel' had existed.

As an alternative to such accommodation, some immigrants simply built their own shanty towns or *bidonvilles* which appeared in the suburbs of major French cities, particularly Paris, constructed of any materials which immigrants could obtain, but usually consisting of wooden huts. Whatever they were made of, they inevitably had few amenities. They housed mostly single men but also some families. More than any other development they emphasised the exclusion of immigrants from French society, representing ghettos as detached from mainstream society as Black settlement areas in US cities. *Bidonvilles* existed in large numbers, totalling 225 official ones in a survey carried out by the French state in 1966, although the true number may have been three times as high. Paris contained 119 out of the official total of 225, housing 46,827 people concentrated mostly to the north-west of the city. The national total stood at 75,000 people.

The French census of 1968 revealed that 20 per cent of immigrant workers lived in inadequate housing, although 56.8 per cent resided in overcrowded conditions, of which 26.8 were critically overcrowded. Some groups fared worse than others, with Africans collectively living in the poorest housing. Nevertheless, the Portuguese represented 20.6 per cent of the inhabitants of the *bidonvilles* and also constructed and lived in the largest shanty town in Paris, which lay in Champigny-sur-Marne, to the east of the city. In contrast, few West Indians, as French citizens, lived in such accommodation or in the overcrowded hotels.

Since the 1960s the situation for immigrants has improved, mainly due to the actions of the state. In the first place, the *bidonvilles* and other slum housing had disappeared by the end of the 1970s. The main solution to the problem of poor accommodation lay in the movement of immigrants towards public housing, especially true for Africans. However, in many cases this has resulted in the creation of high-rise ethnic ghettos. In 1990 24 per cent of immigrant households lived in public housing, compared with 14 per cent of French families. The figure for Algerians and Moroccans exceeded 40 per cent. In contrast, the owner-occupier rate stood at 56.2 per cent for French people and 26.4 for foreigners, although within the latter figure the totals for individual groups varied from 8.4 per cent for Turks to 55.9 per cent for Italians.[114]

Upon their first arrival in Germany most foreign workers would find themselves living in communal accommodation provided by the firms employing them, city authorities, welfare associations, or even private individuals. In 1962 about two-thirds of newly arrived immigrants lived in such accommodation,[115] consisting of mass overcrowded quarters with minimum furnishing and poor cooking and sanitary provision, administered by house managers in an authoritarian manner. About one-third of the buildings had been constructed before 1948 and one-quarter were made of wood.[116] Conditions within some of these resembled those faced by immigrants in France in the same period, as the following description of communal accommodation in Düsseldorf in 1967 illustrates:

---

114 Hargreaves, *Immigration, 'Race' and Ethnicity*, pp. 66–76; Castles and Kosack, *Immigrant Workers and Class Structure*, pp. 285–304; Stephanie A. Condon and Philip E. Ogden, 'The State, Housing Policy and Afro-Caribbean Migration to France', *Ethnic and Racial Studies* 16 (1993), pp. 256–97; Joyce Edmond-Smith, 'The Immigrant Worker in France', in Nicholas Deakin (ed.), *Immigrants in Europe* (London, 1972), pp. 13–16; Edmond-Smith, 'West Indian Workers in France – II', *New Community* 2 (1973), pp. 74–5; Paul E. White, 'Immigrants, Immigrant Areas and Immigrant Communities in Post-War Paris', in Ogden and White, *Migrants in Modern France*, pp. 195–211. The 'old chocolate factory' extract is from Castles and Kosack, p. 286.
115 Ulrich Herbert, *A History of Foreign Labour in Germany, 1880–1980: Seasonal Workers/Forced Labourers/Guest Workers* (Ann Arbor, 1993), pp. 217–18.
116 Clemens Amelunxen, 'Foreign Workers in West Germany', in William A. Veenhoven (ed.), *Case Studies in Human Rights and Fundamental Freedoms*, Vol. 1 (The Hague, 1975), p. 123.

There are six Turkish and Greek guest workers living in a space no more than 15 square meters. The beds are stacked one on top of the other and crowded together. All the men are already lying in the bed, although it is only 8:30 in the evening. But what else do they do in this hole? There aren't even enough chairs. In the centre of the room, under a naked light bulb dangling from a crooked wire, there is a table covered by a 'tablecloth' made of old newspaper. The floor is bare and filthy, the walls are no different. You search in vain for a picture, some curtains . . .

You have to climb up a steep wooden stairway to get to the adjacent room. The room is held together only by thin plywood walls. There's a light still burning. A worker is kneeling on a small rug, saying his prayers. The other men are lying in their beds. They have made a makeshift lamp-shade from a paper bag from one of the large department stores. There is no heating oven for these people from the south, who miss nothing perhaps more here in Germany than sun and warmth.[117]

In time the foreign workers of the 1960s and 1970s moved out of such communal accommodation, especially when their families arrived, although this was a gradual process so that 34 per cent of foreign workers still lived in such buildings at the end of 1972. But even when they moved into the private market they inevitably found themselves in accommodation below the level of that enjoyed by Germans. In the first place their houses have been smaller, so that 84 per cent of foreign families lived in homes containing less than four rooms during the early 1970s. In North-Rhine Westphalia the living quarters of aliens were 36 per cent smaller than that of the population as a whole. In addition, accommodation for foreigners on a national scale was less likely to have conveniences, and foreigners were more likely to live in older buildings. Italians and Spaniards resided in the best conditions, followed by Greeks and – considerably worse off – Turks and North Africans. Immigrants are far less likely to own their accommodation than Germans, the figure for the former standing at just 3.5 per cent in 1965 and, in Hessen, reaching 7.9 per cent in 1987, compared with 42 per cent of Germans. Also in Hessen at this time – although the gap had narrowed between the situation of Germans and foreigners since the 1960s – the former still lived in larger and newer housing, a situation reflected in the Turkish population of Düsseldorf.[118]

Immigrants who have made their way to Sweden have, from a housing point of view, moved to one of the most advanced countries in Europe, where only 4 per cent of dwellings are not modern. Nevertheless, differences

117 This extract is from *Handesblatt*, 16 February 1967, and is translated and quoted in Herbert, *History of Foreign Labour in Germany*, pp. 218–19.
118 Amelunxen, 'Foreign Workers in West Germany', pp. 123–4; Helga Reimann, 'Die Wohnsituation der Gastarbeiter', in Helga and Horst Reimann (eds), *Gastarbeiter* (Munich, 1976), pp. 131–48; Heinz Sautter, 'Wohnsituation ausländischer Haushalte in Hessen', in Claudia Koch-Arzberger, Klaus Böhme, Eckart Hohmann and Konrad Schact (eds), *Einwanderungsland Hessen? Daten, Fakten, Analysen* (Opladen, 1993), pp. 30–48; Günther Glebe, 'Housing and Segregation of Turks in Germany', in Şule Özüekren and Ronald van Kampen (eds), *Turks in European Cities: Housing and Urban Segregation* (Utrecht, 1997), pp. 142–3.

exist between the accommodation of foreigners and Swedes. For instance, whereas only 3.6 per cent of Swedes live in overcrowded conditions, the corresponding figure for non-Nordic nationalities is 10.1 per cent, while that for southern Europeans totals 21.5 per cent.[119]

A large percentage of immigrants who made their way to Norway moved straight to Oslo. The city and its immediate vicinity contained about 25 per cent of Norway's foreigners in 1977, including 80 per cent of the country's Moroccans and 68 per cent of its Pakistanis. Living conditions for foreigners in Norwegian cities have been below those for natives, often by a long way. Employers had responsibility for the housing of immigrants during their first year of residence, although this often meant provision of communal accommodation in barracks with poor sanitation and little space per occupant. After this first year immigrants tended to move to the poorer parts of the city, sometimes into houses due for demolition, usually living in overcrowded conditions compared to the Norwegian population. Conditions were especially bad in Oslo, although in Kristiansand immigrants lived in similar conditions to Norwegians. Refugees tend to live in better accommodation than foreign workers.[120]

The recent immigrants to southern European states resemble those labour migrants who moved to northern and western Europe during the 1960s and 1970s. In the case of Portugal, for instance, where 52 per cent of the foreign population lived in Lisbon in 1989, many formed shanty towns around the city, taking over temporary accommodation previously used by people who returned from Portugal's African colonies.[121] In the case of Italy immigrants also live in poor accommodation in the form of sub-let rooms, rented beds or hostels. They have tended to consist of people who arrive in the country without their families.[122]

THE SIGNIFICANCE OF DEMOGRAPHIC AND RESIDENTIAL PATTERNS

The demography, geography and housing of minorities in post-War Europe play a central role in all other aspects of their lives, as well as reflecting them. At one extreme the Jewish populations of Europe, the most successful of all minorities, have demographic and geographic patterns which at least equal those of the dominant populations of the states in which they reside. They have low birth rates, low death rates and low marriage rates. They live in

119 Anna-Lisa Lindén and Göran Lindberg, 'Immigrant Housing Patterns in Sweden', in Huttman, Blauw and Saltman, *Urban Housing*, pp. 108–13; British Refugee Council, London, QSW 85.2, Irene Palmgreen, 'Situation of Immigrant Women in Sweden', 1981.
120 Laila Kvisler, 'Immigrants in Norway', in G. Ashworth (ed.), *World Minorities*, Vol. 2 (Sunbury, 1978), pp. 54–5; Eva Haagensen, *Young Immigrants in Norway: A Survey of Action Taken by the Authorities and Measures Proposed* (Oslo, 1986), pp. 7–9.
121 Martin Eaton, 'Foreign Residents and Illegal Immigrants: *Os Negros em Portugal*', *Ethnic and Racial Studies* 16 (1993), pp. 544, 551–4.
122 Claudio Calvaruso, 'Illegal Immigration to Italy', in *The Future of Migration* (Paris, 1987), pp. 310, 312.

high-quality accommodation, often in the most exclusive parts of capitalist cities. The reasons for this situation revolve around the length of time that they have lived in some European states, which has enabled them to move up the social scale and become ever more assimilated to the norms of the people around them.

In contrast, at the other end of the scale we have Gypsies. Of course, like Jews, they have also resided in European states for centuries. But Gypsies have the highest reproduction rates of virtually any population in Europe and live in the worst housing conditions. The reason for this lies in their refusal to assimilate. The basis of their whole existence as an ethnic group revolves, as much as anything else, upon their physical separation from the dominant groupings in the states in which they live.

Immigrants resemble Gypsies, although it seems likely that most new-comers will, in the long run, like Jews, move ever closer to the norms of the dominant populations in the states in which they reside. This was certainly not the case upon their first arrival. They tended to live in the worst housing conditions and had extremely uneven age and sex triangles, due to the fact that western European states had imported them for the purpose of exploiting their labour power. By the end of the twentieth century, many of these patterns have changed, so that the age/sex triangles have become more even, while initially high reproduction rates have fallen, especially for the children of the newcomers. Furthermore, their housing patterns have improved, although they could hardly fail to do so in the case of the inhuman conditions faced by those immigrants who moved to France and Germany. But we should certainly not overestimate the changes which have taken place, particularly the geographic ones, as immigrants still tend to reside in worse housing than the dominant population and still tend to concentrate in ghettos.

The reproductive rates and geographical patterns of all types of minorities fundamentally affect both their social and economic position and their ability to develop a political consciousness. Groups such as Gypsies, which have patterns reminiscent of the developing world, find themselves working in the worst employment, as do immigrants. Furthermore, their demographic, housing and consequent employment patterns affect their ability to succeed educationally and thus to develop a political consciousness which protects their status. At the other end of the scale we again find the Jews, with their closeness to the norms of dominant populations allowing them to prosper economically and to develop a rich ethnic consciousness.

The long-standing localised minorities fit into neither of the above patterns. Rarely do their demographic patterns show significant variations from the norm, although their geographic location often plays a central role in their status as minorities, as it has done since the nation states in which they live came into existence. This peripheral position again determines their position both economically and politically.

CHAPTER 3

Economic and Social Status

The geographic and demographic patterns of minorities on the European continent replicate themselves in their economic and social status. Indeed, all aspects of the socio-economic life of peoples throughout the European continent remain closely linked. In the classic pattern, the groupings residing in the worst housing conditions with the highest birth and mortality rates would find themselves employed in the least desirable occupations shunned by the dominant grouping. This is the most common pattern, but some European minorities have low birth rates and reside in predominantly urban environments, often of a high quality, and also have a superior occupational and economic position, notably Jews.

Assertions about social and economic differences may appear to apply more to capitalist societies than they do to the eastern European regimes which evolved under the Soviet model. Thus in the capitalist states which survived the Second World War, the social structure would consist of distinct classes. First, a residual aristocracy, which had intermarried with the bourgeoisie. The middle classes contain several groupings. In a classic Marxist sense the bourgeoisie consists of those who own the means of production, although this would exclude the professional bourgeoisie involved in the administration – in one sense or another – of modern states, employed as academics, bureaucrats, doctors and lawyers, groups which have increased enormously in size since 1945. Within the middle classes we need to recognise the existence of a petty bourgeoisie, differentiated from the higher echelons of this social grouping primarily by economic position and covering such occupations as clerical work and shopkeeping. The working classes would, in a Marxist sense, consist of those who do not own the means of production and therefore earn wages, although in the post-War period, as the professional bourgeoisie has grown, this definition proves problematic. A better description of the working classes for our own purposes would be those people involved in manual or, perhaps better still, low-paid labour. The other significant social grouping in capitalist society, which survives from pre-industrial times, consists of people involved in agriculture (many of whom own their land in post-War Europe), although their numbers vary significantly from one nation state to another. Finally, we also need to recognise the existence of an underclass in capitalist society, consisting of those who do not fit comfortably in the working class. Major groupings here consist of 'professional criminals' and the long-term unemployed.

Earning power represents a major factor differentiating social classes in capitalism. This consideration also played a determining role in Soviet-style society, which, however, contained a slightly different social structure, with three basic divisions. At the top, in terms of earning power and prestige, we can distinguish a white-collar elite, which included bureaucrats in the service of the party and the state, doctors, academics and factory managers. Secondly, we can point to workers, who varied from the highly skilled to general labourers. Finally, there were the peasants, some of whom continued to own land in some parts of eastern Europe.[1] Other groups which existed, at various times in Soviet-style society, included forced workers. The underclass has only really taken off after the collapse of the USSR. Clearly, variations existed in the relative sizes of the different social groupings from one eastern European state to another, depending upon the level of industrial development.

How do minorities fit into the above social structures? Does the experience vary from one category or group to another, between different nation states or between social and economic systems? It is extremely rare to find minorities represented in the aristocracy, except in the case of ruling houses which found themselves in exile. The case of the bourgeoisie or their equivalent group in eastern Europe proves more complicated. Both Soviet and western Jewry are over-represented in these social groupings, as are some localised minorities. Similarly, some immigrants move into this social category, either through social mobility, most typically by establishing a business, or because they were already part of the middle class before they entered a particular state, as the example of academics, students or businessmen moving from one capitalist state to another would illustrate. Nevertheless, minorities are under-represented in these social classes and over-represented in the less prestigious and economically less well-paid sections of society. In the case of localised groupings this largely reflects their peripheral geographic position, which influences the relative underdevelopment of the region in which they live. The overwhelming majority of immigrants into western Europe found employment in working-class occupations, although, when mass unemployment began to take off during the 1970s, they suffered particularly badly. Similarly, minorities in eastern Europe would tend to be concentrated outside the bourgeoisie, either within the industrial working class in the more advanced states, or in agricultural activity in those cases where a predominantly rural society continued to exist. In other cases minorities do not fit into the classic class structure of either eastern or western Europe, the best example consisting of Gypsies, who, in their traditional way of life, pursue similar activities throughout the

1 See David Lane, *Politics and Society in the USSR* (Oxford, 1978), pp. 404–6.

European continent – although since 1945 they have tended to fall more and more within the industrial working classes or the underclass of the states in which they live. Minorities, by the very nature of their existence, differ in their social and economic structure from dominant groupings throughout Europe, and tend to find themselves towards the bottom.

SUCCESSFUL GROUPINGS

The overwhelming majority of Jews are successful, but some localised minorities are also as rich as the dominant grouping, while some immigrants have made it good. Post-War European Jewish groups focus at the top of the social scale. Soviet Jewry underwent a significant social and economic transformation from the end of the nineteenth century, changing from a predominantly poor grouping involved in small-scale artisan trades, to a minority which became highly concentrated (in occupational terms) in the bureaucratic classes, as the most highly educated grouping in the Soviet Union. This situation is explained at least partly by the effects of the Nazi invasion in the west which wiped out most of the Jewish working classes, leaving people higher up on the social scale who demanded better education for their children. In 1973 about 16 per cent of Jews (343,000 people) had a university education. As a result of this they concentrated in occupations at the higher end of the Soviet social scale. In the first place, they found employment as scientific workers. In the early 1960s they also made up 14.7 per cent of all Soviet doctors, 8.5 per cent of writers and journalists, 10.4 per cent of judges and lawyers and 7.7 per cent of actors, musicians and artists. On the other hand, they remained under-represented in the various levels of the Soviet administration despite the fact that, by 1976, they had a higher ratio of Communist Party members than any other nationality.[2]

British Jews have also experienced upward mobility since 1945 due to the arrival of professional Jewish refugees from Nazism during the 1930s and the embourgeoisement of the descendants of poor Russian Jews who had entered Britain at the end of the nineteenth century. In 1961 the census revealed that 44 per cent of Jews were to be found in the top two social classes, compared with 19 per cent of the rest of the population, while 0 per cent of Jews fell into the lowest social class of the unskilled, compared with 8 per cent of the general population. Particular Jewish occupations included the running of businesses of all sizes so that in the mid-1970s 47 per cent of Sheffield Jewry was self-employed, compared with 5 per cent of the rest of the city's population. In addition, Jews continued to be over-represented in the professions, especially

2 Alec Nove and J. A. Newth, 'The Jewish Population: Demographic Trends and Occupational Patterns', in Lionel J. Kochan (ed.), *The Jews in Soviet Russia Since 1917* (Oxford, 1978), pp. 152–7, 165; Zev Katz, 'The Jews in the Soviet Union', in Zev Katz, Rosemarie Rogers and Frederic Harned (eds), *Handbook of Major Soviet Nationalities* (New York, 1975), p. 359; Thomas E. Sawyer, *The Jewish Minority in the Soviet Union* (Boulder, CO, 1979), pp. 42–7; Bernard Wasserstein, *Vanishing Diaspora: The Jews in Europe Since 1945* (London, 1996), pp. 182–3.

in the areas of law, medicine and higher education. Furthermore, Jews have featured prominently amongst the very rich in Britain.[3]

In view of its situation at the end of the Second World War, German Jewry has undergone one of the most dramatic social transformations of any ethnic group in Europe, although in the sense of building itself up from devastation, it does not differ from the German population as a whole at the end of the Second World War. Those Jewish displaced persons in 1945 were barely alive and had no interest in their social status, hardly able to work because of the physical and psychological trauma from which they had emerged. Nevertheless, in the long run, the Jewish community in Germany eventually developed a pattern approximating that of other European Jewish national groupings. By 1952 many Jews had become integrated into the German economy, involved either in legitimate retailing or in black marketeering, although others would never work again because of the physical or mental scars left by the War. Some returnees regained the administrative, legal and academic positions which they had held before 1933.[4] The movement of Soviet Jews into Germany at the end of the Cold War meant many of them found themselves at the lower end of the social scale, if only because of the initial difficulty in integrating and finding employment.[5]

Nevertheless, Jews throughout Europe generally represent a minority group distinguished by advantage rather than disadvantage, a situation essentially explained by the historical urban concentration of this minority throughout the European continent, meaning that when opportunities arose for social mobility, as a result of the economic advances of the post-War period, this group was in a better position to seize them than the rest of the population. In addition, the dedication to education central to the Jewish religion played a determining role in allowing Jews to take up professional positions. Finally, because of their social position, they did not, in the post-War period, endure the working-class hostility in their search for employment and social mobility which other European groupings would face, especially immigrants.

The Catalan and Basque minorities in Spain are localised groups in a better position than the dominant population because the periphery is more advanced than the centre. In the Basque land, which (together with Catalonia) was already economically more industrialised than the rest of Spain before 1945, a further upturn occurred during the 1960s revolving particularly around the production of steel, machinery and tools, automobiles, petrochemicals and fertilisers.[6] Both Catalonia and the Basque land experienced high annual rates

3 Geoffrey Alderman, *Modern British Jewry* (Oxford, 1992), pp. 331–5; Wasserstein, ibid., pp. 74, 242; W. D. Rubinstein, *A History of the Jews in the English-Speaking World: Great Britain* (London, 1996), pp. 401–6.
4 Lynn Rapaport, 'The Cultural and Material Reconstruction of the Jewish Communities in the Federal Republic of Germany', *Jewish Social Studies* 49 (1987), pp. 141, 142.
5 Madeleine Tress, 'Soviet Jews in the Federal Republic of Germany: The Rebuilding of a Community', *Jewish Journal of Sociology* 37 (1995), pp. 39–49.
6 J. Martín Ramirez and Bobbie Sullivan, 'The Basque Conflict', in Jerry Baucher, Don Landis and Arnold Clark (eds), *Ethnic Conflict: International Perspectives* (London, 1987), p. 124.

of economic growth in the boom of the late 1980s. The 1981 census revealed that 46.53 per cent of natives in Catalonia were employed in middle-class occupations in contrast to 26 per cent of Spanish immigrants. In the Basque country the figures for middle-class occupations amongst natives and immigrants respectively were 49.12 and 22.8 per cent.[7]

In post-War western Europe as a whole, immigrants have tended to concentrate at the lower end of the social scale. Imported for the purpose of filling the labour shortages which existed when the western European nation states needed to re-industrialise after 1945, the newcomers generally obtained occupations shunned by the population already present. In general, the above picture holds true but not all immigrants remain trapped at the bottom of the social ladder. This situation is less characteristic of newcomers who migrated with skills or those who face a low level of prejudice. Economic mobility – the accumulation of capital – represents the easiest way for immigrants to progress in western capitalist societies because, unlike social or political success, it requires less of a symbolic sacrifice. Assimilation is fundamental if one is to succeed in mainstream politics, while social progression usually requires the shedding of some traditional habits, even if they are as basic as changing clothing. In contrast, people who make money fit in with the western liberal ideal of working hard and progressing with limited aid from the state, and (in a capitalist system) face less barriers in their path. Furthermore, in many cases immigrant businessmen provide services and employment for their own communities, as ethnic economies have developed in numerous European cities which count substantial numbers of a particular group and therefore create a demand for food and other products from the homeland. But immigrant entrepreneurs certainly face some types of animosity, from the basic level of having their businesses attacked to hostility from established commercial interests. Many immigrant groups have seized the opportunities which have developed as a result of economic restructuring and the growth of small businesses from the 1970s, and in many cases – provided they have the right advantages and skills – have moved into self-employment on a significant scale.

For British West Indians one of the main opportunities for social advancement lies in sport, especially football and boxing, where ethnic clustering has occurred. In the former, West Indians made a breakthrough during the 1970s and are now present at all levels in the professional game. Clearly, for people like Sol Campbell, the earning potential is enormous but, for each Sol Campbell, there are probably hundreds or even thousands of Black youths who have aspired to be like him but have not succeeded.

Asians in Britain have moved into business on a significant scale since the end of the 1970s. In 1977 the ratio of self-employed Asian heads of household stood at about the same level as that for whites, but by 1982 a total of 18 per cent of Asian males in employment owned their own businesses, compared with

7 Juan Díez Medrano, *Divided Nations: Class, Politics and Nationalism in the Basque Country and Catalonia* (Ithaca, NY, 1995), pp. 120–1.

a figure of 14 per cent for whites and 7 per cent for West Indians. By 1988, while the proportion for whites remained the same, that for Indians had reached 24 per cent and for Pakistanis and Bangladeshis it stood at 22 per cent.[8]

Many of the Poles who moved to Britain had middle-class occupations. Some had more success than others in continuing their careers in Britain, including doctors, engineers and technicians; lawyers had difficulty because they required retraining. In the long run some Poles purchased their own businesses, counting 2,500 people by 1960, while by the mid-1970s around 20,000 had bought their own homes.[9] Of the other European groups in Britain, the Irish have developed a significant middle class which includes doctors, dentists, travel agents and, most notably, entrepreneurs working in the construction industry.[10] Greek Cypriots have experienced significant social mobility amongst both the first and second generations. However, even as early as 1966 as much as 19.6 per cent of Cypriots in London were self-employed, when the figure for the population as a whole totalled 7.1 per cent. The category of self-employed Cypriots tended to function by exploiting other members of the minority, especially in the field of clothing manufacture where women usually worked at home for meagre wages.[11]

Although some immigrants have established themselves as small businessmen in France, they count a lower proportion of their population in such activity than either the native population or immigrants in Britain. In 1990 the figures for self-employed people amongst immigrants totalled 6 per cent for foreigners and 18 per cent for French people. Nevertheless, as in the British case, much of the movement into self-employment took place from the 1970s. Furthermore, many immigrants opened grocery stores in areas containing heavy concentrations of their own ethnic group. Others established cafés and restaurants. The most entrepreneurial amongst the immigrant groups include the Chinese (consisting mostly of refugees from Indochina), North Africans (especially Tunisians), Spaniards, Italians and Portuguese.[12]

The West Indian immigrants into France find themselves with social and employment structures more favourable than most immigrants in the country, due to their linguistic command of French (as a result of attending a French-based education system), and to their status as French citizens. In 1982 80 per

8 Jochen Blaschke, Jeremy Boissevain, Hanneke Grotenberg, Isaac Joseph, Mirjana Morokvasic and Robin Ward, 'European Trends in Ethnic Businesses', in R. Waldinger, H. Aldrich and R. Ward (eds), *Ethnic Entrepreneurs: Immigrant Businesses in Industrial Societies* (London, 1990), p. 82.

9 Sheila Patterson, 'The Poles: An Exile Community in Britain', in James L. Watson (ed.), *Between Two Cultures: Migrants and Minorities in Britain* (Oxford, 1977), pp. 219–21.

10 Colin Holmes, *John Bull's Island: Immigration and British Society, 1871–1971* (London, 1988), p. 231; Seán Hutton, 'The Irish in London', in Nick Merriman (ed.), *The Peopling of London: Fifteen Thousand Years of Settlement from Overseas* (London, 1993), p. 121.

11 E. J. B. Rose et al., *Colour and Citizenship: A Report on British Race Relations* (London, 1969), pp. 154–8; Floya Anthias, *Ethnicity, Class, Gender and Migration: Greek Cypriots in Britain* (Aldershot, 1992), pp. 57–66.

12 Alec G. Hargreaves, *Immigration, 'Race' and Ethnicity in Contemporary France* (London, 1995), pp. 57–60; Blaschke, Boissevain, Grotenberg, Joseph, Morokvasic and Ward, 'European Trends in Ethnic Businesses', pp. 99–104.

cent worked in service industries. Although less than 3 per cent fell into the category of professionals and managers, and just over 1 per cent were self-employed, more than 10 per cent worked as 'intermediate professionals', employed as civil servants, nurses, social workers and technicians.[13] West Indians in France therefore have a much more balanced employment structure than either their British counterparts or the bulk of French immigrants, but do not have the same number of people as natives at the top of the social scale.

Some take-off has occurred in ethnic business participation in Germany, especially from the 1980s, when Turks began to involve themselves in this area. Italians have opened up ice-cream cafés and pizza restaurants, which now exist in virtually every settlement of any significance in Germany. Greeks, Spaniards, Portuguese and Yugoslavs have also opened restaurants, often simply serving their own specialities in the traditional German *Gaststätten* which already existed. Turks have also moved into the catering trade, specialising in take-aways. However, the size of the Turkish minority in the Federal Republic has provided the opportunity to develop businesses aimed at this grouping, especially grocers, dry-cleaners and travel agents. The number of Turkish businesses increased from 22,000 in 1985 to 35,000 in 1992.[14]

UNDERDEVELOPED REGIONS

Geographical factors play a central role in the differing levels of prosperity between the regions in which majorities and minorities live. The fact that the majorities control much of the economic and political power of states which contain peripheral minorities further aggravates the social and economic position of the latter. However, it would be untrue to suggest that all members of minorities within underdeveloped regions fall below the social and economic levels of the majority populations situated in the centre.

Many of the Balkan Muslims live in peripheral underdeveloped regions. In Bulgaria the Turkish minority essentially consists of a group which has not experienced the same level of economic change as the dominant population, even after Bulgarian industrialisation took off during the 1960s. When they worked in non-agricultural occupations, they tended to find themselves employed as unskilled labourers involved in the construction of roads, ports and other public works schemes.[15]

During the 1950s the Muslims of Western Thrace mostly found themselves working in agriculture, especially the cultivation of tobacco, which was not

13 Stephanie A. Condon and Philip E. Ogden, 'Afro-Caribbean Migrants in France: Employment, State Policy and the Migration Process', *Transactions of the Institute of British Geographers* New Series, 16 (1991), pp. 445–7; J. Edmond-Smith, 'West Indian Workers in France: II', *New Community* 2 (1972–3), pp. 76–9.
14 Faruk Sen, '1961 bis 1993: Eine kurze Geschichte der Türken in Deutschland', in Claus Leggewie and Zafer Şenocak (eds), *Deutsche Türken: Das Ende der Geduld* (Hamburg, 1993), p. 27.
15 Firoze Yasemee, 'The Turkic Peoples of Bulgaria', in M. Bainbridge (ed.), *The Turkic Peoples of the World* (London, 1993), p. 48; Kemal H. Karpat, 'The Turks of Bulgaria', in Syed Z. Abedin and Ziauddin Sardar (eds), *Muslim Minorities in the West* (London, 1995), pp. 60–1.

very lucrative. Those living in the towns and cities worked in commercial, industrial and artisan occupations but were under-represented in these areas. In the district of Xanthi Muslims made up 49 out of 458 merchants, 15 of 104 manufacturers, 45 out of 456 artisans and 104 out of 840 professional men.[16] Since the 1950s their position has further deteriorated, at least partly due to restrictions which they have faced in pursuit of their livelihood, especially after the Turkish invasion of Cyprus. These constraints have meant the following: they cannot buy real estate and can only sell it to Christians; they cannot construct or expand buildings; they have virtually no opportunity of obtaining loans; and they even have difficulties in renewing their driving licences. Furthermore, they find themselves excluded from careers in the civil service. Finally, Muslims in Western Thrace have also experienced confiscation of their land in the 'public interest' and have rarely received adequate compensation.[17]

Yugoslavian Muslim areas also found themselves towards the bottom of tables indicating economic progress. Apart from relative levels of urbanisation, these differences manifested themselves in other ways. Industrialisation in Yugoslavia as a whole began to take off during the 1950s so that in an index of industrial production, set at 100 in 1939, the figure had reached 391 by 1959. This process continued into the following decades, leading the United Nations to count Yugoslavia as one of ten newly industrialised states during the 1970s. But the national level of industrial production hid significant disparities between the different republics in this federated state, with the Muslim areas remaining economically backward compared with the national average and especially in relation to Catholic Croatia and Slovenia. Although part of the reason for these disparities lay in geographic and demographic factors, political manipulation by the more powerful republics, who gained more than their fair share of economic resources, aggravated the problem.

In demographic terms the faster rate of population increase in the poorer Muslim republics meant that any increases in wealth which did occur in these territories did not necessarily manifest themselves in a rise in individual income as they would have to be divided amongst a greater population, in contrast to the slower-growing populations of Slovenia, Croatia and Serbia. At the same time, Croatia had an additional geographical advantage in its Dalmatian coastline, whither western tourists with foreign currency flocked. Historically, those areas which had been under Ottoman rule lagged behind those which had experienced Habsburg control. Nevertheless, unequal distribution of investment in the early post-War decades aggravated any differences which existed. Bosnia, which had important reserves of coal and iron ore as well as significant potential sources of hydro-electric power, did not experience large-scale industrialisation within its borders. Instead, these raw materials went to already more developed areas in Croatia, Slovenia and around Belgrade. In

16 K. G. Andreades, *The Moslem Minority of Western Thrace* (Thessaloniki, 1956), pp. 25–6.
17 F. de Jong, 'The Muslim Minority in Western Thrace', in G. Ashworth (ed.), *World Minorities*, Vol. 3 (Sunbury, 1980), pp. 96–7.

addition, Bosnia's share of industrial investment declined in the first two five-year plans after the Second World War, from 19.4 per cent to 12.6 per cent, while Serbia's grew from 31.3 to 41.7 per cent. This counteracted the rhetoric of the Yugoslav Communist Party which aimed at the reduction of regional differences. Nevertheless, whatever measures of national wealth are used for measuring relative economic development, the differences between the richer and poorer Yugoslav republics remained large and – certainly in the early post-War decades – actually widened. In terms of national income per capita, the three poorest areas consisted of Bosnia-Herzegovina, Macedonia and (way behind these two) Kosovo. Thus, with an index for Yugoslavia which stood at 100, the figures for Bosnia and Macedonia declined, between 1965 and 1977, from 69.3 to 65.1 and 69.2 to 68.1 respectively, while that for Kosovo fell from 37.0 to 30.4. All of this occurred, of course, at the very time when the Catholic republics increased their wealth so that the gap between Kosovo and the richest territory of Slovenia increased from 1:4.7 to 1:6.5.

Such developments clearly caused resentment amongst the Muslim republics, which led to the development of plans to redress the differences. In turn, however, these resulted in further resentments amongst those republics who had to pay out money in order to bring the poorer areas up to their level of wealth. Croatia, for instance, particularly resented having to surrender funds gained through its tourist industry. Thus, in 1989 while the gross domestic product per capita in the richest republic, Slovenia, stood at an index of 196.80, that for Kosovo totalled just 25.66. The Communist Party had done little to resolve vast regional differences, although it seems difficult to see what any federal government could do in a situation in which history, geography and demography – together with nationalism within the individual republics – were against it.[18]

The Celtic fringe in the United Kingdom has lower standards of living, higher levels of unemployment and a smaller middle class than England as a whole, although Scotland and Wales are economically more advanced than some areas of England, especially Merseyside and the North-East, which in 1997, for instance, both had higher unemployment rates than Wales and Scotland.[19] A second cleavage within the United Kingdom occurs in Northern Ireland because, in addition to the fact that this province as a whole remains behind England, economic differences exist between the Catholic and Protestant populations.

18 Joel M. Halpern, 'Yugoslavia: Modernization in an Ethnically Diverse State', in Wayne S. Vucinich (ed.), *Contemporary Yugoslavia: Twenty Years of Socialist Experiment* (Berkeley and Los Angeles, 1969), p. 319; S. P. Ramet, *Nationalism and Federalism in Yugoslavia, 1963–1983* (Bloomington, IN, 1984), pp. 30–3; Fred Singleton, 'Objectives and Methods of Economic Policies in Yugoslavia, 1970–1980', in Alec Nove, Hans-Hermann Höhman and Gertraud Seidentecher (eds), *The East European Economies in the 1970s* (London, 1982), p. 301; Dragomar Vojnić, 'Disparity and Disintegration: The Economic Dimension of Yugoslavia's Demise', in Payam Akhavan and Robert Howse (eds), *Yugoslavia: The Former and the Future* (Washington, DC, 1995), pp. 78–82, 100; Robert J. Donia and John V. A. Fine Jr, *Bosnia and Herzegovina: A Tradition Betrayed* (London, 1994), pp. 180–1.
19 Office for National Statistics, *Social Trends 28* (London, 1998), p. 428.

A comparison of England and the UK as a whole with Wales and Scotland illustrates the economic differences between the Celtic fringe of Britain and its Anglo-Saxon core. Throughout the years 1965–73 average hourly earnings in Scotland stood at between 94 and 98 per cent of the UK rate. Unemployment in Scotland always exceeded the level for the UK by at least one-fifth between 1965 and 1977, with a level twice as high in 1965. Part of the reason for the higher unemployment rate lies in the fact that a greater proportion of people in Scotland were employed in the declining heavy industries, notably ship-building, steel production and coal mining. In terms of social class Scotland has had a lower proportion of its population situated in the higher groups and a larger percentage in the lowest classes. For instance, 19.1 per cent of the male working population of Scotland fell into the category of unskilled in 1971 compared with just 7.7 per cent for England. The figure for Wales was 9.9 per cent in the same year.[20] Other statistics for Wales indicate more significant differences with England. In 1973, for instance, weekly Welsh family income was £6.42 less on average than the level in Britain as a whole in a year in which Wales was the only region in Britain to experience a decline in family income.[21] Similar to the situation in Scotland, 19.2 per cent of the male work-force in Wales in 1973 was employed in the heavy industries of mining and metal manufacture, as opposed to 5.8 per cent for the UK as a whole, which again meant that Wales would experience a higher unemployment rate during the Thatcher years when these two industries suffered in particular. Another interesting statistic pointing to the economic dependence of Wales upon England demonstrates that, again in 1973, a total of 75 per cent of Welsh firms with 100 or more employees had their head offices outside Wales.[22]

This indicates another central reason for the social and economic differences between the Celtic fringe and the southern English core: the fact that economic and political resources are so heavily concentrated in England, and, more especially, in London and the South-East. Furthermore, the peripheral position of Scotland and Wales within the European continent means that they resemble other marginal parts of Europe which lie furthest away from the central area of economic productivity focused between Munich and Milan.

Northern Ireland's economic indicators point to a lower level of economic development than the rest of the UK. Most clearly this province has experienced higher unemployment and lower average incomes. Since the War unemployment has only rarely, and then for short periods, fallen below 6 per cent. Throughout the 1950s the level remained at 7 per cent, which was four or five times higher than in Great Britain. Much of the unemployment was concentrated in the greater Belfast area where decline in shipbuilding and

20 James G. Kellas, *Modern Scotland*, 2nd edn (London, 1980), pp. 22–6.
21 Gwynfor Evans, *A National Future for Wales* (Swansea, 1975), p. 33.
22 Charlotte Aull Davies, *Welsh Nationalism in the Twentieth Century: The Ethnic Option and the Modern State* (New York, 1989), pp. 64–5.

general engineering accounted for 68 per cent of unemployment and made up 57 per cent of the total for Northern Ireland. Wage rates, like unemployment, were also significantly different between Northern Ireland and the rest of the UK. For instance, in 1950–1 personal income per head in the province stood at £168 and by 1959–60 had risen to £284. Nevertheless, the corresponding figures for Great Britain had grown from £221 to £378 during the same period. In 1974 the average personal weekly income in Northern Ireland, which stood at £52.30, was not only much lower than the figure for the UK as a whole, but also significantly below the average for the poorest region in England (Yorkshire/Humberside), where the figure was £65.70.[23] These differences have continued to exist despite the financial support which Northern Ireland receives. In 1988/9 the province obtained a subvention of £1.9 billion. 'Since the population of the region is about one and a half million people each inhabitant of Northern Ireland in 1989/90 was therefore subsidized by the British state and the European Community to the tune of £1,500 per annum.'[24]

Numerous social and economic indicators point to the fact that Roman Catholics have done less well than Protestants. To begin with, members of the former grouping have always suffered higher rates of unemployment than those in the latter. In 1971 there were 2.62 Roman Catholics unemployed for every 1 Protestant, a figure which had declined slightly to a ratio of 2.44 to 1 by 1981 and 2.36 to 1 by 1985. Part of the explanation for this situation lies in direct discrimination faced by Catholic employees, as Protestants control two-thirds of industrial concerns in the province. Historically evolved social and employment patterns of Protestants and Catholics have also influenced the different levels of unemployment, with the latter concentrated in occupations where joblessness is more likely to occur. According to the 1971 census 52 per cent of Roman Catholics were classified as semi-skilled and unskilled, whilst the percentage for Protestants stood at 40. In addition, over one-fifth of the Catholic labour force was employed in the construction industry, which often experiences seasonal lay-offs. These statistics mean that Protestants are more likely to be concentrated at the higher end of the occupational and social ladder. According to the same census, 15 per cent of Protestants and 12 per cent of Catholics were in the top professional and managerial jobs. Thus the model Catholic male was unskilled manual while the model Protestant was skilled manual. Catholics are also under-represented in state employment. The most striking statistic is provided by the Royal Ulster Constabulary which, in 1969, had a Catholic 'work-force' making up just 11 per cent of the total. Similarly, Roman Catholics are far less likely to be found in senior grades of the Northern Ireland civil service, while they count large numbers in the lower grades. Thus, in 1991, even after state initiatives to rectify the

23 Sabine Wichert, *Northern Ireland Since 1945* (London, 1991), pp. 61, 64, 214; John Simpson, 'Economic Development: Cause or Effect in the Northern Irish Conflict', in John Darby (ed.), *Northern Ireland: The Background to the Conflict* (Belfast, 1983), p. 81.
24 See John McGarry and Brendan O'Leary, *Explaining Northern Ireland* (Oxford, 1995), pp. 72–6.

situation, Catholics made up 19 per cent of grade A posts and over 40 per cent of the three lowest levels, F, G and H.[25]

Celts are junior partners in terms of their social and economic position within the UK. The level of their underdevelopment, which is significant rather than extreme, and which is determined by historically evolved geographic, political and economic factors, is reflected amongst other marginalised populations in western Europe. Brittany, for instance, remained stagnant while the rest of France underwent its post-War boom. Thus, between 1954 and 1962 the number of farmers and fishermen in this industrially underdeveloped region declined by 25 per cent and 20 per cent respectively. Small industries were closed or bought up by Parisian companies and then run down.[26]

In Italy, in the area bordering Slovenia, Slovenian speakers have concentrated in agricultural employment. The discriminatory practices of Italian speakers who run the bureaucracy of the Italian state in the area have meant that Slovenian speakers have tended not to work in white-collar, entrepreneurial or professional jobs.[27] In contrast to the statistics for Slovenian speakers, those Italian speakers who moved to Italy from the Yugoslav side of Trieste after the Second World War have had significant concentrations in the liberal professions as doctors, pharmacists, lawyers and priests, although the refugees as a whole suffered unemployment on a significant scale during the 1950s.[28]

In Czechoslovakia the Czech areas were historically more industrialised than Slovakia, although, after the War – mostly as a result of Communist Party policy – some equalisation occurred between the two areas as the Slovak economy demonstrated a greater vitality than its Czech counterpart. Thus whereas in 1948 33.1 per cent of the population of the Czech Republic was engaged in agriculture, compared with 60.5 per cent in Slovakia, by 1989 these figures had almost equalised to 9.4 and 12.2 per cent respectively. Similarly, the percentage of people involved in manufacturing industry and construction had increased from 1948 figures of 38.8 per cent in the Czech Republic and 20.8 per cent in Slovakia, to 47.4 per cent in the former and 43.8 per cent in the latter in 1989.[29]

Inequalities between Kurdistan and the rest of Turkey reveal themselves in numerous ways, typical of a centre/peripheral relationship. Kurdistan produces various crops, particularly cereals, amounting to 15 per cent of the total for

25 David J. Smith and Gerald Chambers, *Inequality in Northern Ireland* (Oxford, 1991), pp. 16, 55–6; Tom Wilson, *Ulster: Conflict and Consent* (Oxford, 1989), pp. 110–11; Simpson, 'Economic Development', p. 102; Fair Employment Commission, *Monitoring Report No. 4* (Belfast, 1993), p. 1.
26 Meic Stephens, *Linguistic Minorities in Western Europe* (Llandysul, 1976), pp. 384–5; David H. Fortier, 'Brittany: "Breiz Atao"', in C. R. Foster (ed.), *Nations Without a State: Ethnic Minorities in Western Europe* (New York, 1980), p. 147.
27 Aleš Lokar and Lee Thomas, 'Socioeconomic Structure of the Slovene Population in Italy', *Papers in Slovene Studies* (1977), pp. 26–39.
28 Theodor Veiter, 'Soziale Aspekte der italienischen Flüchtlinge aus den adriatischen Küstengebieten', in T. Mayer-Maly et al. (eds), *Festschrift für Hans Schmitz zum 70. Geburtstag*, Vol. 2 (Vienna, 1967), pp. 288–9.
29 Václav Průcha, 'Economic Developments and Relations, 1918–1989', in Jiří Musil (ed.), *The End of Czechoslovakia* (Budapest, 1995), pp. 74–5.

Turkey and dominating production in the area. The importance of this area to Turkey's cereal production provides one example of exploitation of the periphery by the centre. The extraction of minerals from Kurdistan provides another. These include chrome deposits (amongst the world's largest), iron ore and oil. The development of road and rail links between Turkey and Kurdistan assisted in the exploitation of the latter's mineral resources. Despite investment from the Turkish centre during the 1980s, Kurdistan has remained poorer than the rest of Turkey, with the highest illiteracy rate in Turkey in the middle of the 1980s and a lower than average GDP.[30]

The Soviet Union provides a different picture from Turkey because of the countless groupings of enormously varying sizes which lived within its borders. The most westerly regions – notably the Ukraine, parts of Russia and the Baltic republics – were those with the most advanced economies, while the Asiatic periphery, bordering on to parts of the world which are equally underdeveloped, had lower standards of living.

The Soviet Union wanted to bring the less advanced nationalities up to the level of Russians from the beginning of its existence. The Communist Party Congresses of the early 1920s called for the planting of industries in the less developed regions of the Soviet Union. Thirty years later Nikita Kruschev called for equal funding for the republics. The 1977 Soviet Constitution endorsed the policy of convergence in socio-economic levels. Reforms under Gorbachev during the mid-1980s, promoting economic decentralisation, also had equalisation as their central aim. But did the reality match the rhetoric of Soviet leaders and their party from Lenin to Gorbachev? We can ask whether resources moved from the periphery to the Russian centre, characteristic of colonial exploitation (see Map 2).

Most economic indicators suggest that while some equalisation did take place there remained vast differences throughout the history of the Soviet Union, although Russia was, in the case of many statistics, not the most advanced republic. Historical and geographical factors have as much to do with the figures as Soviet policy, although, ultimately, we need to ask whether equalisation of the entire Soviet Union was ever a realistic goal and whether Soviet leaders seriously thought they could achieve this aim.

In terms of educational attainment, Russians were ahead of virtually all of the Muslim populations at all levels between 1959 and 1980, as well as having a higher index than Ukrainians and Belorussians, and being on a similar level to Estonians and Latvians. Nevertheless, Georgians and Armenians were ahead of Russians at most levels of education for much of this period, while the Jews were easily the most successful grouping of all. In terms of per capita income, the RSFSR had the third-highest level in the period 1960–5, behind Latvia and

---

30 Kendal, 'Kurdistan in Turkey', in G. Chaliand (ed.), *A People Without a Country: The Kurds and Kurdistan* (London, 1980), pp. 51–4; Majeed R. Jafar, *Under-Underdevelopment: A Regional Case Study of the Kurdish Area in Turkey* (Helsinki, 1976), p. 58; David McDowall, *The Kurds* (London, 1989), p. 5; Kemal Kirişci and Gareth M. Winrow, *The Kurdish Question and Turkey: An Example of Trans-State Ethnic Conflict* (London, 1997), pp. 122–6.

Estonia. Moldavia had the lowest index, standing at 39.4 compared with 100 for Russia, 48.4 for Azerbaijan and 77.9 for the Ukraine.

Statistics on investment within the individual Soviet republics give little indication that the central government matched its policies to its rhetoric in the desire to equalise levels of development throughout the USSR. In the period 1918–60 the average per capita investment in the non-Russian republics was two-thirds of that in the RSFSR, with Russia receiving by far the highest levels of cash injection. The gap narrowed over the following 25 years, although, overall, Russia remained ahead. Such statistics clearly suggest that Russia has taken more than it has given during the Soviet period, meaning that the colonial cycle of exploitation inherited from the Tsars was not actually broken.[31]

The economic history of individual republics reveals some of the above patterns, as well as pointing to other inequalities. Within the RSFSR, for instance, it becomes clear that the smaller populations did not have the same experience as the Russians. The numerically small minorities of the Russian far north, for example – who, through their traditional means of subsistence, lived by reindeer farming – simply became victims of economic exploitation for the sake of advancing the Soviet economy, which wreaked ecological destruction in order to get to the rich deposits of natural resources, including gold, timber, coal, oil and gas. Vast tracts of forest disappeared. By the 1980s some areas had rivers, traditionally used for fishing, with oil deposits two inches thick, killing all life within them. Worse still, nuclear tests during the 1950s and 1960s affected the health of the native populations, the local animals and the vegetation. People who lived in this part of Russia also lost rights to land which they had used for hundreds of years. Furthermore, during the 1960s reindeer herders were forced to give up their nomadic way of life and move into fixed villages.[32]

The Ukraine, the second-largest of the Soviet republics in terms of both population and geographical expanse, was one of the most exploited due to its vast mineral resources and agricultural productivity. 'In 1970, with 3 per cent of the area and 19 per cent of the population of the USSR, the Ukraine produced one third of the USSR coal output, 48 per cent of the steel, and 57 per cent of the iron ore', as well as 19 per cent of Soviet grain and 28 per cent of its vegetables. However, by the early 1990s, it had a serious energy problem, obtaining 90 per cent of its petroleum and natural gas from the

31 The facts and statistics for the above discussion come from: Vsevolod Holubnychy, 'Some Economic Aspects of Relations Among the Soviet Republics', in Erich Goldhagen (ed.), *Ethnic Minorities in the Soviet Union* (New York, 1968), pp. 50–120; Gertrude E. Schroeder, 'Nationalities and the Soviet Economy', in Lubomyr Hajda and Mark Beissinger (eds), *The Nationalities Factor in Soviet Politics and Society* (Boulder, CO, 1990), pp. 43–72; Donna Bahry and Carol Nechemias, 'Half Full or Half Empty? The Debate Over Soviet Regional Equality', in Rachel Denber (ed.), *The Soviet Nationality Reader: The Disintegration in Context* (Boulder, CO, 1992), pp. 287–304; Ellen Jones and Fred W. Grupp, 'Modernisation and Ethnic Equalisation in the USSR', *Soviet Studies* 36 (1984), pp. 159–64.
32 Nicolai Vakhtin, *Native Peoples of the Russian Far North* (London, 1992), pp. 24–6; Piers Vitebsky, 'The Northern Minorities', in Graham Smith (ed.), *The Nationalities Question in the Post-Soviet States* (London, 1996), pp. 97, 99–100.

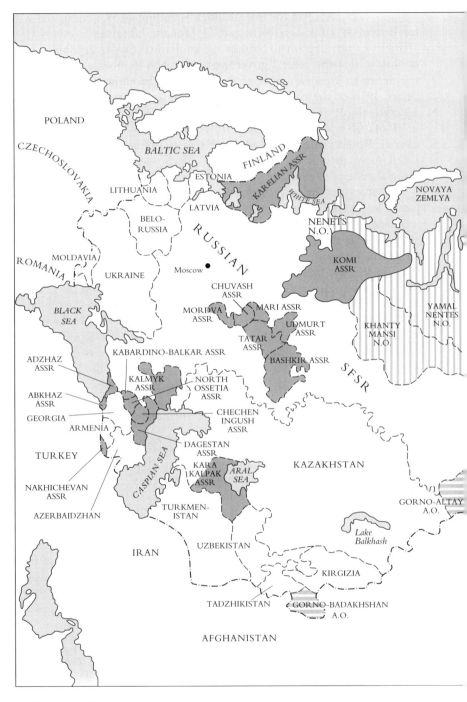

Map 2 The Soviet Union
Source: M. McCauley, *The Soviet Union 1917–1991* (London, Longman, 1993)

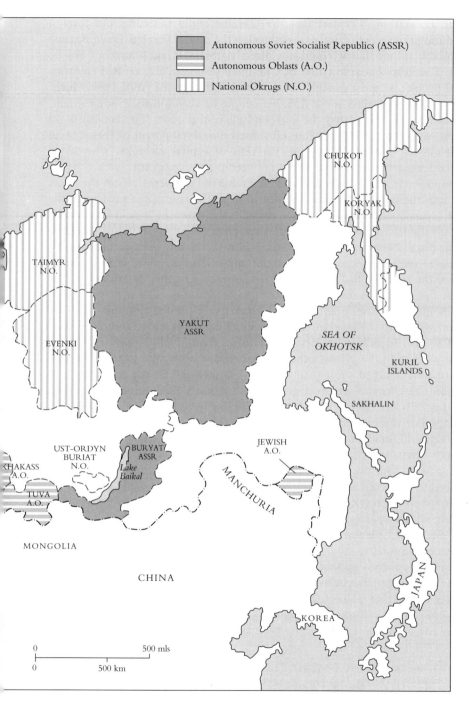

Russian Federation. The fact that the Ukraine could not carry out foreign trade during the Soviet period except through the central Foreign Trade Agency in Moscow meant that it could not directly obtain foreign currency for its goods. The years of exploitation of Ukrainian resources also created environmental problems, most notably the Chernobyl disaster of April 1986 which, in the short run, forced about 135,000 people to abandon their homes, and, in the long run, devastated the surrounding countryside. The consensus of opinion suggests that the Ukraine subsidised the development of Russia at an annual rate of between 10 and 20 per cent of capital earnings, whereas in imperial Russia the figure fluctuated between 3 and 5 per cent.[33]

Consequently, the population of the Ukraine did not benefit from the effort it put into the industrialisation and nutrition of the rest of the peoples of the USSR – particularly the Russians – to quite the extent it should have done, although significant economic progress and improvements in living standards did take place. Nevertheless, these would almost certainly have occurred under a capitalist regime, because of the economic resources available in the area, whether the republic had gained independence or remained politically tied to Russia.

Economic indicators point to the comparatively limited progress made by Ukrainians due to the level of economic exploitation practised by the Russian Soviet centre. In occupational terms statistics from 1960–1 show that more people worked in the primary than the secondary economic sector, although this situation changed subsequently. In 1970, although 52 per cent of people living in the Ukraine were categorised as working class, ethnic Ukrainians made up 73.6 per cent of this number. Similarly, while 23 per cent of the population of the Ukraine worked in white-collar occupations in 1970, only 16 per cent of Ukrainians laboured in this sector of the economy. Furthermore, although Russians accounted for 19 per cent of the population of the Ukraine, they made up 34.3 per cent of university students in 1970. Nevertheless, we also need to point out that educational levels increased in absolute terms in the Ukraine as in the rest of the Soviet Union. While the number of people with a higher education rose from 6.2 per cent to 18 per cent in the USSR as a whole between 1939 and 1959, the Ukrainian figure grew from 6.7 per cent to 17 per cent. Similarly, living standards also increased along with the rest of the Soviet population, so that between 1951 and 1958 the income of the average worker rose 23 per cent in the republic, while personal consumption increased by 1 per cent a year under Stalin and reached 4 per cent under Kruschev.[34]

33 Roman Szporluk, 'The Ukraine and the Ukrainians', in Katz, Rogers and Harned, *Handbook of Major Soviet Nationalities*, p. 22; 'Ukraine', in *Eastern Europe and the Commonwealth of Independent States: A Political and Economic History*, 2nd edn (New York, 1994), p. 683; Walter Dushnyck, 'Discrimination and Abuse of Power in the USSR', in Willem A. Veenhoven et al. (eds), *Case Studies in Human Rights and Fundamental Freedoms: A World Survey* (The Hague, 1975), p. 480; Orest Subtelny, *Ukraine: A History*, 2nd edn (Toronto, 1994), p. 534.
34 Subtelny, ibid., p. 505; Yaroslav Bilinsky, *The Second Soviet Republic: The Ukraine After World War II* (New Brunswick, NJ, 1964), pp. 60–3; Boris Lewytzkys, *Politics and Society in the Soviet Ukraine* (Edmonton, 1984), pp. 171–2, 189–90.

The Ukraine therefore represented a peripheral region of the USSR and not a Russian colony. It would be wrong to describe it in the latter terms, unless we accepted the same definition to describe Scotland's relationship with England. Both Scotland and the Ukraine, while they may be relatively under-developed, have made progress, although both may well have done better as independent political entities.

Other Soviet republics had a similar relationship with Moscow. Belorussia closely resembles the Ukraine in many ways. Between 1959 and 1970 the proportion of this republic's population employed in agriculture declined from 55 per cent to 30 per cent. By 1985 industrial production accounted for 60 per cent of the republic's GNP.[35] Like the Ukraine, it specialised in particular industrial goods and agricultural products. In 1987, although it had 3.6 per cent of the population of the USSR, it produced 14.2 per cent of its tractors, 22.5 per cent of motorcycles, 11.3 per cent of refrigerators and 18.2 per cent of fertilisers. Belorussia suffered a devastating blow from the Chernobyl disaster because of the wind direction. Over 2.2 million people, one in every five inhabitants, and 18 per cent of productive land lay in the zone of most severe long-term radiation. Nevertheless, in 1990 the republic still accounted for 16 per cent of its own meat products and 22 per cent of dairy produce.[36]

The three Baltic republics had similar experiences under Soviet control, facing economic exploitation and competition from the large, literate and more industrially advanced Russian populations within their borders. Estonia, for instance, was highly industrialised and its per capita gross industrial output in 1968 was higher than that of any other republic within the USSR. It produced 75 per cent of all the Soviet Union's oil shale, used for electricity and chemical products, although in the long run the mining of this product created disastrous ecological problems, so that by the middle of the 1980s protests began over the fact that some of the poorer-quality oil shale, which had been dumped, self-ignited. Fires had actually begun in 1965 and by 1987 about 50 million tonnes had been dumped, catching fire and polluting the ground water. During the 1960s Estonia, along with Latvia, had been given the role of socio-economic laboratory for the Soviet Union because of its advanced social, material and cultural development. In addition, Estonia, to-gether with the other two Baltic republics, played a leading role in pioneering the use of computers within the USSR, especially after the establishment of the Cybernetics Institute in Tallinn in 1960. The most important products in the republic included electrical energy, fertilisers, wool fabrics, meat and fish. The republic also concentrated on the production of consumer goods. Like the Ukraine, it exported much of its produce – 31 per cent of its 'material production', in fact, of which 88 per cent went to other parts of the Soviet

35 Steven L. Guthier, 'The Belorussians: National Identification and Assimilation, 1890–1970: Part 2, 1939–1970', *Soviet Studies* 29 (1977), p. 271.
36 Jan Zaprudnik, *Belarus: At the Crossroads of History* (Boulder, CO, 1993), p. 187.

Union. Nevertheless, by the 1970s Estonia, along with Latvia, had established itself as the wealthiest republic in the USSR.[37]

Latvia closely resembled Estonia in its economic relationship with Russia and the Soviet Union. Until 1990 it was completely integrated in the central-ised Soviet economic system. Although the area had begun to industrialise during the nineteenth century, this process took off after the Second World War and by the end of the 1960s it was the most heavily industrialised repub-lic in the Soviet Union.[38]

Lithuania industrialised later than either Latvia or Estonia, but after the Second World War it made up for lost time with the fastest growth rate in the manufacture of industrial products between 1940 and 1969. Its major products included machine tools, computers and radio and television sets.[39] A break-down of the social structure of the national groupings in Lithuania according to the 1989 census reveals that the titular majority of this republic lay behind Russians, in terms of relative levels of economic development, but ahead of the smaller Polish population. Thus, whereas 168 per thousand Russians had a university education, the figure for Lithuanians was 101 while that for Poles was just 45. Similarly, 40.9 per cent of Russians were involved in non-physical labour, but the percentage of Lithuanians was 33.4, while that of Poles was just 21.[40]

In terms of social and economic development there seems little reason to view the Soviet Union as any different from western states in the post-War period. Russia was not the most advanced republic as this status would apply to the Baltics, at least partly because of the influx of Russians into these areas. However, like England, it was the centre and most of the peripheral regions remained behind it in social and economic terms. The level of exploitation practised by Russia resembles a colonial political structure. Nevertheless, while the Russians may have gained more than other peoples of the Soviet Union from industrial advance, the movement forward took place throughout the Soviet Union. The Russians benefited due to historical and geographical factors and, above all, due to the fact that they dominated the instruments of political power.

---

37 Romuald Misiunas and Rein Taagepera, *The Baltic States: Years of Dependence* (London, 1993), pp. 233–5; Rein Taagepera, *Estonia: Road to Independence* (Boulder, CO, 1993), pp. 95, 121; Taagepera, 'Estonia and the Estonians', in Katz, Rogers and Harned, *Handbook of Major Soviet Nationalities*, pp. 75–6; 'Estonia', in *Eastern Europe and the Commonwealth of Independent States*, p. 293; Anatol Lieven, *The Baltic Revolution: Estonia, Latvia, Lithuania and the Path to Independence*, 2nd edn (London, 1994), p. 333.
38 Frederic T. Harned, 'Latvia and the Latvians', in Katz, Rogers and Harned, *Handbook of Major Soviet Nationalities*, p. 95; 'Latvia', in *Eastern Europe and the Commonwealth of Independent States*, p. 401.
39 Frederic T. Harned, 'Lithuania and the Lithuanians', in Katz, Rogers and Harned, *Handbook of Major Soviet Nationalities*, pp. 119–20.
40 Vladis Gaidys, 'Russians in Lithuania', in Vladimir Shlapentokh, Munir Sendich and Emil Payin (eds), *The New Russian Diaspora: Russian Minorities in the Former Soviet Republics* (Armonk, NY, 1994), pp. 94–5.

THE LABOUR COMMODITY CALLED IMMIGRANTS

Without the post-War capitalist boom which affected western Europe from the 1940s until the 1970s, millions of immigrants would not have made their way to the western half of the continent. They arrived as part of a conscious recruiting process involving state and industry for the purpose of carrying out menial industrial tasks which members of the native population increasingly avoided as they became ever more educated. The fact that they have a level of education lower than the native population – which, in some cases, may mean virtual illiteracy in the language of the state to which they have moved – makes social mobility difficult. In much of continental Europe they possess limited legal rights and cannot vote, which makes their economic exploitation easier than the exploitation of indigenous labour. The positions which they take at the bottom end of the social scale entail, in the short run, working the longest hours under the worst conditions for low rates of pay, often rewarded through the piece rate, sometimes employed by their own fellow nationals. However, this short-term exploitation does not prevent immigrants from, in the long run, defending themselves by joining trade unions. Nevertheless, initially at least, immigrants are prepared to accept whatever is directed towards them because, while their economic position may compare pitifully with that of the dominant population of a particular state, it is usually a significant improvement (certainly in terms of wages) on their earning potential in their country of origin. If the migrants intend to remain only temporarily, with the promise of economic improvement upon return with any money which they may have earned, they are even more prepared to accept bad working conditions in the same way as they accept poor housing. The level of exploitation which immigrants endured during the 1950s and 1960s was further driven by western capitalism's realisation of all of the above factors. This applied to both businesses and governments. The latter also realised that, in the short run, the newcomers had no social costs such as schooling of children, although this changed after family reunification and the development of entitlement to pensions. The children of immigrants also tend to find themselves towards the bottom of the social scale largely due to the continued existence of prejudice, which had affected the first generation. While all newcomers and their offspring face prejudice, those with dark skin face the greatest hostility of all.

Upon first arriving in Britain, West Indians found themselves heavily concentrated in employment at the lower end of the social scale. Although they may have had qualifications which demanded a better position than the one they actually obtained, the needs of the British economy, combined with British racism, dictated that they obtained some of the worst jobs. Prejudice against the employment of Black people in particular occupations was overwhelming during the 1950s, although it did not apply equally to all jobs, which meant that West Indians could find employment if they were prepared to work in the areas assigned to them. Thus they faced less hostility in factories than they did in jobs dealing with the public. Until the 1960s West Indians rarely served in shops because owners feared that shoppers might withdraw their custom. Similarly:

> One large dairy combine with extensive milk rounds in the London area said that they would not employ coloured milk roundsmen as this might prejudice sales. It was said that housewives would not like Negroes calling at their homes, and even if they did not mind, their husbands might object.[41]

Further examples of racial hostility against West Indians are endless. In 1963 the Bristol Omnibus Company turned down the application of one West Indian for employment solely on grounds of race, a decision which led to a high-profile campaign which forced this firm to change its mind.[42] Nevertheless, working 'on the buses' was actually one service industry where West Indians did make a breakthrough, revealing another fact about employment patterns of immigrants in that they tend to cluster in the same way that they form residential concentrations, again because they have made an initial breakthrough and because the dominant society allows them to concentrate in that particular occupation. Therefore by the end of 1958 London Transport employed about 4,000 Black workers, 1,000 of whom had been recruited directly in Barbados, while the rest had picked up jobs after arriving in London. They received just two days' training and started working on the lowest grades, hoping to obtain promotion – which some had done by 1960 – to positions as bus drivers, train guards and booking office clerks, as well as, in a few cases, station foremen.[43]

About 24 per cent of West Indians arriving in Britain had professional or managerial experience, while 46 per cent were skilled workers, 5 per cent semi-skilled and just 13 per cent consisted of unskilled manual workers.[44] Nevertheless, a survey carried out in 28 metropolitan London boroughs during the early 1960s, based on the 1961 census, indicated that the employment which they eventually obtained did not reflect their previous skill and training levels. This demonstrated that 54 per cent of West Indian males worked in semi-skilled and unskilled manual employment, while just 2 per cent worked in professional or managerial occupations. The other 43 per cent had jobs as skilled manual or non-manual employees. This compared unfavourably with English people who counted 12 per cent in professional or managerial occupations and 29 per cent in the semi-skilled and unskilled categories.[45]

Much of the prejudice faced by West Indians in the search for employment was also endured by Asians in Britain. Their socio-economic position partly depends upon the group concerned. Pakistanis and Bangladeshis have tended

41 Clifford S. Hill, *How Colour Prejudiced is Britain?* (London, 1965), p. 109.
42 Dilip Hiro, *Black British: White British* (London, 1971), p. 53.
43 Ron Ramdin, *The Making of the Black Working Class in Britain* (Aldershot, 1987), p. 197.
44 Edward Pilkington, *Beyond the Mother Country: West Indians and the Notting Hill White Riots* (London, 1988), p. 23.
45 R. B. Davison, *Black British: Immigrants to England* (London, 1966), p. 70.

to do worse than Indians and refugees from East Africa. According to the 1971 census, 78.84 per cent of Pakistanis worked in manual occupations.[46] Those Asians in employment also continued to be more heavily concentrated in manual occupations than white people, the figures standing at 46 per cent for native British, 75 for Indians and 82 for Pakistanis and Bangladeshis.[47]

Most of the European immigrant minorities in post-War Britain also reveal, initially at least, a significant concentration at the lower end of the social scale. The overwhelming majority of Polish immigrants, about 80–90,000 people, 'entered the post-war British economy as unskilled workers, irrespective of their education and occupational background. They were for the most part directed to the heaviest, least attractive, least secure or lowest paid sectors of industry, where local labour shortages were most acute.'[48] The Ministry of Labour, War Office, Trades Union Congress and British Employers Federation all played a part in this process. The areas of employment counting the largest numbers of Poles – more than 5,000 each in February 1949 – consisted of construction, agriculture, coal mining and hotel and restaurant work.[49]

Those workers imported into continental states during the period of labour migration also went towards specific occupations, in which they were legally obliged to work under the terms of their work permits. The vast majority of immigrants in France have consisted of manual workers. This trend began with the Europeans who entered immediately after the end of the Second World War. In the years 1948–54 agriculture employed more foreigners than any other economic activity, an unusual situation within the economic history of both post-War France and Europe as a whole, but partly explained by an intensification of the movement of people from the countryside to urban areas immediately after 1945. Mining also accounted for a significant number of immigrants in early post-War France. In addition, foreigners began to find employment in the sectors in which they would come to play a large role in the following decades, most notably construction.

In fact, building work became the major area of employment for immigrants from 1954[50] and in the period 1956–67 accounted for 37.5 per cent of all foreign workers in France, assisting in a post-War building boom. In this same period 16.5 per cent of foreign workers found employment in manufacturing – notably in textile, motor-car and steel production – while 14.1 per cent worked in services and 3.5 per cent in mining.[51] Those immigrant women who lived

46 Muhammad Anwar, *The Myth of Return: Pakistanis in Britain* (London, 1979), p. 97.
47 Muhammad Anwar, 'Muslims in Britain', in Abedin and Sardar, *Muslim Minorities in the West*, p. 40.
48 Patterson, 'The Poles', pp. 220–1.
49 Keith Sword with Norman Davies and Jan Ciechanowski, *The Formation of the Polish Community in Great Britain, 1939–1950* (London, 1989), p. 470.
50 Cicely Watson, 'Recent Developments in French Immigration Policy', *Population Studies* 6 (1962), pp. 22–7; J. R. McDonald, 'Labour Immigration in France, 1946–1965', *Annals of the Association of American Geographers* 59 (1969), p. 121.
51 James F. Hollifield, *Immigrants, Markets, and States: The Political Economy of Post-War Europe* (Cambridge, MA, 1992), pp. 144, 149–59.

in France during the 1960s also worked in particular occupations, especially domestic service, which accounted for 46.1 per cent of Spanish women and 37.2 per cent of Portuguese females in 1968.[52] As late as 1976 a total of 89.2 per cent of foreigners worked in unskilled, semi-skilled or skilled manual work, including 54.4 per cent in the first two categories, meaning that less than 11 per cent of foreigners in France worked in non-manual employment, compared with a figure of 45 per cent for French people.[53]

Immigrants and their children have experienced a shift away from the areas in which they found employment during the 1960s and early 1970s so that the 14.1 per cent of foreigners working in services in the period 1956–67 had increased to 49.8 per cent by 1990 which, at the same time, meant a fall in the number of people involved in construction and manufacturing to 20.6 and 26.2 per cent respectively. Nevertheless, the service sector of the economy covers a wide range of activities and those in which foreigners counted large numbers tended to be those which French people shunned, such as garbage collection and bus driving.[54] It 'is relatively rare to see Frenchmen wielding the roadsweeper's broom, cleaning the bus shelters and underground shelters or manning France's dustcarts'. In 1988, despite any occupational mobility which may have taken place amongst immigrants in France, 78.8 per cent of them still worked as 'labourers', 13.3 per cent found employment in offices and shops, 4.2 per cent as qualified technical staff and 3.7 per cent as executives.[55]

The bulk of immigrants in Germany, imported as uneducated industrial fuel to stoke the fires of the German economic miracle, have employment experiences similar to those of Europeans and North Africans in France, labouring in manufacturing, construction and metallurgy. Particularly during the phase before the arrival of families, foreign workers in Germany, like immigrants throughout Europe, played a large role in the expansion of the economy, because of their various advantages. In the first place, their demographic structure meant they had not cost anything to rear, as the state had not paid for their schooling. Upon first arrival foreign workers, because of their age, were at the peak of their economic activity. Furthermore, as they tended to receive lower wages, this proved beneficial to German employers. Since 1970 immigrants have always formed more than 8 per cent of the labour force,[56] and without their concentration in manual employment it is difficult to see how the growth rates of the German economy could have been sustained since the 1950s, especially in view of the desire for social mobility of Germans.

52 Stephen Castles and Godula Kosack, *Immigrant Workers and Class Structure in Western Europe* (London, 1973), p. 64.
53 Carliene Kennedy-Brenner, *Foreign Workers and Immigration Policy: The Case of France* (Paris, 1979), p. 35.
54 Hollifield, *Immigrants, Markets, and States*, pp. 144, 158–9; Hargreaves, *Immigration, 'Race' and Ethnicity*, p. 45.
55 Brian Fitzpatrick, 'Immigrants', in J. E. Flower (ed.), *France Today*, 7th edn (London, 1993), pp. 105–6.
56 Hartmut Berghoff, 'Population Change and Its Repercussions on the Social History of the Federal Republic', in Klaus Larres and Panikos Panayi (eds), *The Federal Republic of Germany Since 1949: Politics, Society and Economy Before and After Unification* (London, 1996), p. 53.

The only serious argument which questions the benefit of foreigners to the German economy suggests that rationalisation and increases in efficiency would have taken place without immigration, meaning that growth rates could have been sustained, although this would still not solve the problem of who would carry out some of the most menial of tasks where working with hands is crucial.

The social structure of immigrants in Germany has always differed from that of the native population, as they have always concentrated in particular areas of economic activity. Those foreigners already in the Federal Republic by the early 1960s focused upon metallurgy, construction and manufacturing, although some changes took place in the distribution between these three major areas. In 1963 the percentage of the total foreign population employed in the metal trades, manufacturing and construction stood at, respectively, 22.2, 20.1 and 11.2.[57] Despite the last figure, by this time immigrants constituted over 8 per cent of employees in the building trades, compared with 5 per cent in the metal trades and 4.43 per cent in manufacturing.[58] By the middle of the 1970s 38 per cent of foreigners worked in iron and metallurgical industries, 24 per cent in other manufacturing industries and 18 per cent in construction.[59] They have continued to play a large part in these areas and have also moved into other sectors of the economy, so that in 1980 they made up 12.9 per cent of employees in building, 20 per cent in textile production, as well as 8.5 per cent of people involved in the primary industries of agriculture, forestry and fishing.[60]

Inevitably, foreign workers tend to work in jobs which require a lower amount of skill and education. In 1972 the total proportion of immigrants in Germany working as unskilled labourers stood at 38 per cent, while the percentages for semi-skilled and skilled were 41 and 20.[61] By 1980 some change had taken place when 30 per cent of foreign males worked in skilled and supervisory employment, 42 per cent in semi-skilled and 27 per cent in un-skilled, although the proportions varied from one group to another, with Turks counting the highest proportion of unskilled and Yugoslavs, Spaniards and Portuguese having the largest percentages of skilled and supervisory staff.[62] Nevertheless, a significant level of promotion proved much more difficult to achieve and those who did move tended to progress up just one category, from, say, unskilled to semi-skilled.[63]

57 'Die Beschäftigung ausländischer Arbeitskräfte in Deutschland 1882 bis 1963', *Wirtschaft und Statistik* 27 (1965), p. 94.
58 Hans Stirn, 'Ausländer Beschäftigung in Deutschland in den letzten 100 Jahren', in Stirn (ed.), *Ausländische Arbeiter im Betrieb* (Cologne, 1964), p. 18.
59 Clemens Amelunxen, 'Foreign Workers in West Germany', in Veenhoven, *Case Studies in Human Rights*, p. 115.
60 Jürgen Fijalkowski, 'Gastarbeiter als industrielle Reservarmee', *Archiv für Sozialgeschichte* 24 (1984), p. 406.
61 Gerald Kühlewind, 'The Employment of Foreign Workers in the Federal Republic of Germany and their Family and Living Conditions', *German Economic Review* 12 (1974), p. 361.
62 Stephen Castles, *Here for Good: Western Europe's New Ethnic Minorities* (London, 1984), p. 134.
63 Ibid., pp. 137–8.

In practice, guest workers perform the most menial and dirtiest tasks. They drag tar spreaders, carry pig iron, clean toilets, and cart away the garbage of affluence. The public service departments of most West German municipalities would collapse were the guest workers to disappear overnight.[64]

Those working in factories have occupied 'places in the assembly line of mass production'.[65]

Foreign workers inevitably face the worst working conditions and receive the lowest wages. In the early 1970s immigrants had an accident rate at work two and a half times as high as Germans, due both to a lack of knowledge of accident-prevention rules and to the fact they laboured in more dangerous employment.[66] Furthermore, during the 1970s 'wages for male foreign workers were more than 75 per cent, in the case of women 60 per cent below the average for comparable jobs' performed by Germans. In addition, immigrants 'continued to work more frequently than their German counterparts in piece-work and on shifts'.[67]

Those immigrants who made their way to the Netherlands from other European states during the 1960s consisted, like their counterparts migrating to Germany, of people moving into areas with a shortage of labour. Between 1960 and 1966 they represented about 12 per cent of the increase in the Dutch labour force. The largest concentration lay in metal manufacture, where foreign workers made up 37 per cent of the work-force. Overall, three-quarters of these newcomers were employed in manufacturing. The vast majority (72.6 per cent) also worked in unskilled occupations, compared with just 14 per cent of the male work-force of the country as a whole.[68] By 1981 all minorities made up 4.9 per cent of the labour force, a lower level than most of the other western European industrialised states.[69]

Foreign workers moving into Belgium in the immediate post-War years found themselves heavily concentrated in mining, a sector of the economy which employed 69.7 per cent of males who migrated there between 1950 and 1954, while manufacturing accounted for 42.7 per cent of foreign female employees.[70] Those who followed in the 1960s also moved into these areas, as well as into the construction industry and the domestic service sector, but again – following the typical European pattern – heavily concentrated at the lower end of the social and occupational ladder. The second generation has not found it easy to progress upwards, at least partly because they tend to be

64 Amelunxen, 'Foreign Workers in West Germany', p. 119.
65 Ibid., p. 120.
66 Ibid.
67 Ulrich Herbert, *A History of Foreign Labour in Germany, 1880–1980: Seasonal Workers/Forced Laborers/Guest Workers* (Ann Arbor, 1990), p. 241.
68 Adriane Julieta Marshall-Goldschvartz, *The Impact of Labour: The Case of the Netherlands* (Rotterdam, 1973), pp. 34–5, 77, 88.
69 Castles, *Here for Good*, p. 128.
70 Xavier Lannes, 'International Mobility of Manpower in Western Europe', *International Labour Review* 73 (1956), p. 9.

less successful at school than Belgian children – in some cases, during the 1970s and 1980s, not even obtaining a primary school diploma.[71]

By 1964 foreigners in Switzerland counted 880,000 employees out of a total work-force of 2,500,000 concentrated particularly heavily in mining, manufacturing and construction – in line with the typical European pattern – as well as in the hotel sector, where foreigners made up 33 per cent of employees.[72] In Austria those foreigners who moved into the country during the early 1960s found themselves working in the typical immigrant sectors. In 1964 construction counted 32 per cent of them, while metal industries attracted 16 per cent and textile manufacture accounted for 10 per cent. Nevertheless, by the beginning of the 1980s these three sectors employed only about one-third of foreigners, as a large number had moved into the service sector, although not necessarily on to a higher skill level.[73] Similarly, immigrants in Sweden have worked in most occupations but are more likely to be found in mining and industry than Swedes and have been 'more often exposed to very high noise levels and very dirty tasks, run a greater risk of accidents, and have more stressful jobs'.[74] Particular sectors of concentration for foreigners in Sweden (both men and women) have included engineering, hotel and restaurant work, and cleaning.[75]

The immigrants who have arrived in southern European states from the 1970s have also worked at the bottom end of the occupational ladder. In 1981, for instance, 47.6 per cent of Tunisian immigrants in Italy laboured in seasonal occupations connected with fishing, while a further 14.3 per cent were employed in agriculture. Immigrants in Piedmont have worked in 'the least skilled jobs in the tertiary sector' – particularly as domestic servants and hotel and restaurant employees – therefore occupying 'the lowest and most precarious positions in the labour market'.[76] Their position as illegal immigrants, unregulated by state labour practices, further adds to the wretchedness of their position and the extent to which they face exploitation. In the classic pattern they push Italians upward socially but can also depress local wage levels, although they probably carry out jobs which Italians no longer want to do anyway. Very similar developments have occurred in Greece where immigrants, especially from Poland, Albania, Egypt and the Philippines, work in domestic service, cleaning, tourism, construction and harvesting, often on a seasonal basis. One such worker was Christos, an ethnic Greek Albanian from the village of Vouliarotes in southern Albania:

71 Eugeen Roosens, 'Migration and Caste Formation in Europe: The Belgian Case', *Ethnic and Racial Studies* 11 (1988), p. 211.
72 Anne Sue Matasar, 'Labor Transfers in Western Europe: The Problem of Italian Migrants in Switzerland' (Columbia University PhD thesis, 1968), pp. 18, 20.
73 G. Biffl, 'Structural Shifts in the Employment of Foreign Workers in Austria', *International Migration* 23 (1985), pp. 47–9.
74 David Schwarz, *Sweden, An Immigrant Country – As I See It* (Stockholm, 1979), pp. 6–7.
75 British Refugee Council, London, QSW 85.2, Irene Palmgreen, 'Situation of Immigrant Women in Sweden', 1981, pp. 11–12.
76 Claudio Calavaruso, 'Illegal Immigration to Italy', in *The Future of Migration* (Paris, 1987), pp. 311–12.

I'm living with my uncle now and I'm working as a builder. I earn about 2,500 drachmas a day, it's not much – Greek builders are better paid – but what can I do? It's the first time I've worked on a building site. I have no papers and no work permit. The Greek government hasn't the slightest idea of my arrival here, or of my existence. I'm an illegal alien.[77]

OUTSIDERS AND OUTCASTS

Within European society and economy there exists a series of groups which do not fit comfortably into the predominant social and economic system or have dropped out of it because they have suffered long-term unemployment. Gypsies fall into the former category, having striven as long as possible to escape from the regularised wage labour which managed to devour most of the population of Europe as capitalism began to take control of the continental economy during the nineteenth century. Similar to the Gypsies are the Lapps, who also pursued their own specific economic activities. But during the course of the twentieth century industrialisation has succeeded to an increasing extent in eating up the independence of these groups, leaving them at the bottom of the economic scale. Different from Gypsies and Lapps are the remnant populations of Germans and Hungarians in several eastern European states who previously held a privileged position as representatives of ruling empires, but lost this during the course of the twentieth century, a situation where the stigma of being political outcasts affected their social and economic position. Finally come those immigrants and their offspring who suffered disproportionately when unemployment took off during the 1970s and so fell into the underclass.

Vastly under-represented throughout the whole of Europe at the bottom end of the social scale, Gypsies – in their traditional way of life and economic activity, suspicious of education – remain a class apart, outside the traditional social structure of European industrial states. Even when they become part of the unskilled work-force of a particular society, they still remain apart from the equivalent section of mainstream society, perhaps constituting part of an underclass, or, more accurately, retaining their own distinctive social characteristics. This means that, ultimately, they always remain – to a greater or lesser extent – socially separate (as they desire), so that industrialisation cannot standardise them completely.

In England, Gypsies have fairly successfully continued their traditional economic activity since the end of the Second World War. 'In Britain's industrialised capitalist economy, the Travellers are one of the few groups who have remained independent of one of its fundamental features: wage-labour',[78] the

---

77 Theodoros Iosifides, 'Immigrants in the Athens Labour Market: A Comparative Survey of Albanians, Egyptians and Filipinos', in Russell King and Richard Black (eds), *Southern Europe and the New Immigration* (Brighton, 1997), pp. 26–50. The quotation comes from Russell King, Theodoros Iosifides and Lenio Myrivili, 'A Migrant's Story: From Albania to Athens', *Journal of Ethnic and Migration Studies* 24 (1998), p. 160.
78 Judith Okely, *The Traveller-Gypsies* (London, 1983), p. 53.

main factor which keeps them apart from the capitalist class structure. This does not mean that they never work as employees for firms, but simply that they do not become tied to a particular employment for any length of time, as this would clash with their travelling life and the concept of their independence from mainstream society. Their main activities can be seen as supplying goods and services where gaps exist in the market. In essence, they 'use their mobility to advantage in exploiting the dominant system'.[79]

Their economic activity divides into a number of categories. Scrap-metal dealing has been an important source of income, as has rag collection from houses and estates, an activity in which most women found themselves employed to a greater or lesser extent. Tarmacking on a small scale by wealthier Gypsies, who could afford to buy the necessary equipment, took off in the post-War period, usually providing services for householders who required work on their drives. In addition, the more traditional Gypsy occupations continued after 1945, including fortune telling, horse trading, the hawking of flowers and knife grinding, although all of these have declined. Gypsies also found casual employment as agricultural labourers, usually at harvest time, especially the picking of soft fruits in the Fenland and the West Midlands, as well as the gathering of potatoes. In essence, the Gypsies of Britain ultimately remain 'self-employed' and while they may not earn as much as mainstream society (although there are variations between families), they remain contented because they do not have the same material needs.[80]

In Scandinavia, some of the above patterns are repeated. One travelling group in Norway, the tartars (which lives in the east of the country and may not be descended from the wanderers who entered medieval Europe from further east), has similar occupations which have allowed its members to remain distinct from mainstream society, including working in metal and buying and selling of goods, road building and working on farms, as well as begging and stealing.[81] Similarly, one survey in Finland from the 1950s revealed that 26 per cent of adult Gypsies were listed on the books of the criminal police as people suspected of offences, over half of them theft from property.[82] In Sweden Gypsies switched from selling handicrafts in the immediate post-War period to hawking goods which were more attractive to the dominant society, as well as changing the forms of entertainment they performed for the same reason.[83]

In eastern Europe maintenance of economic distinctiveness has proved more problematic for Gypsies because of the energy which several states expended in attempts to bring Gypsies under their control. Czechoslovakia perfectly

79 David Sibley, *Outsiders in Urban Societies* (Oxford, 1981), pp. 55–6.
80 Ibid., pp. 56–66; Barbara Adams, Judith Okely, David Morgan and David Smith, *Gypsies and Government Policy in England* (London, 1975), pp. 116–25.
81 Fredrik Barth, 'The Social Organization of a Pariah Group in Norway', in Farnham Rehfisch (ed.), *Gypsies, Tinkers and Other Travellers* (London, 1975), pp. 285–6.
82 C. H. Tillhagen, 'The Gypsy Problem in Finland', *Journal of the Gypsy Lore Society* 37 (1958), p. 48.
83 Ingrid and Arne Trankell, 'Problems of the Swedish Gypsies', *Scandinavian Journal of Educational Research* 12 (1968), p. 157.

illustrates this process in action. Before the communist take-over of 1948 many Romanies worked as blacksmiths, tinsmiths, basket weavers and wood-cutters, as well as collecting and repairing household appliances. Furthermore, others continued to work as musicians. Some of these employments survived for several decades, particularly in Slovakia. In Bratislava door-to-door selling continued into the 1960s, while almost all of the cafés and restaurants in Slovakia had Gypsy musicians. Even after migration to Czech and Moravian cities, Romanies continued in this activity, performing in coffee houses, as well as at weddings and dances. Similarly, the occupations of horse dealing and fortune telling continued into this period.[84]

Nevertheless, in the attempt to push forward Czech industrialisation, the state made efforts to bring Gypsies into the mainstream. In 1970 66.3 per cent of males and 41.2 per cent of females of economically active ages were 'employed', figures which had risen to 87.7 per cent and 54.9 per cent by 1980. Consequently, in contrast with their English brethren, the Gypsies of Czecho-slovakia did become proletarianised, serving as a surplus labour force carrying out tasks shunned by other sections of the population in the post-War indus-trialisation process: in 1980 a total of 75.5 per cent of them were employed as manual labourers, overwhelmingly in construction.[85]

However, Gypsies have also fallen into criminality on a significant scale, a development which leads to much resentment and exaggeration of figures. During the 1960s the rate of crimes committed by them stood at twice the level for the rest of the population and they were particularly heavily involved in theft and burglary.[86] This may be partly a reaction against the attempts of the dominant society to force Gypsies to fit into their norms, reflecting the distance between Romanies and Czechs and Slovaks.

The social situation of Gypsies in Czechoslovakia ties in with their failure in education, although, as this is a major form of state standardisation, it is not surprising that Gypsy children – encouraged by their parents, who view it in a hostile manner – should rebel against being forced to learn. On the other hand, of course, people cannot obtain their just share of any state system without literacy and the communicating and campaigning skills which it brings. Although all Romany children were attending school by the 1980s, their rate of truancy was twice as high as that for the rest of the population. The illiteracy rate had dropped to 10 per cent by this time, while Czechs and

---

84 Helsinki Watch, *Struggling for Ethnic Identity: Czechoslovakia's Endangered Gypsies* (New York, 1992), p. 75; Anna I. Duirchova, 'Glimpses of the Rom: Excursions in Slovakia', *Journal of the Gypsy Lore Society* 50 (1970), pp. 27, 39; Eva Davidóva, 'The Gypsies of Czechoslovakia: Part II: Post-War Developments', *Journal of the Gypsy Lore Society* 50 (1971), pp. 42–3.
85 Otto Ulč, 'Gypsies in Czechoslovakia: A Case of Unfinished Integration', *Eastern European Politics and Societies* 2 (1988), pp. 321–2; David J. Kostelancik, 'The Gypsies of Czechoslovakia: Political and Ideological Considerations in the Development of Policy', *Studies in Comparative Communism* 22 (1989), pp. 314–15; Josef Kalvoda, 'The Gypsies of Czechoslovakia', *Nationalities Papers* 19 (1991), p. 285.
86 Ulč, ibid., pp. 322–3; Ulč, 'Communist National Minority Policy: The Case of Gypsies in Czechoslovakia', *Soviet Studies* 20 (1969), p. 429.

Slovaks had been completely literate since the end of the nineteenth century.[87] Furthermore, only 25.6 per cent of Gypsies had completed nine years at school in 1981, while a grand total of just 191 attended university in that year.[88] As Gypsy children were far less successful at school than the rest of the population, large numbers of them were sent to 'special schools' for the mentally handicapped. This policy indicates that the authorities did not bother with Gypsy children if they did not fit into the system which they provided. As late as 1991, out of 59,284 students attending schools for the mentally handicapped, 24,126 came from Gypsy families. Part of the problem lies in the fact that some children cannot speak the language of the majority population. The post-communist regimes have not changed their attitude to any great extent so that in Slovakia segregation has survived in some classrooms, where children face hostility from their teachers because of their origins.[89] Gypsies and the Czech and Slovak education systems are therefore caught in a vicious circle in which traditional Gypsy hostility to education is heightened by the brutal methods used. Consequently, Romanies in Slovakia and the Czech Republic would appear to be trapped in their social position as an underclass, forced upon them by state policies consequent upon industrialisation and the need for cheap labour after the Second World War.

Similarly, in Hungary, the traditional employment patterns of Gypsies followed those elsewhere on the European continent, so that during the early post-War years they were employed as musicians, brick and basket makers, horse dealers and casual labourers. However, Hungarian economic growth during the 1960s resulted in the recruitment of thousands of Romanies in the mining, heavy industry and agricultural sector, performing the most difficult and dangerous tasks with the lowest rates of pay. Consequently, 90 per cent of men and 40 per cent of women amongst the Gypsy population were fully employed by 1971. The end of communism was catastrophic for the Gypsies of Hungary who experienced a national unemployment rate of between 60 and 70 per cent, and which reached 100 per cent in some areas. Gypsies also face educational difficulties in Hungary. As late as 1971 only 39 per cent of Romanies over the age of 14 were literate, although the Hungarian state did not pursue the same ruthless policies as its Czechoslovak neighbour. Nevertheless – equally disturbing – there existed from the 1970s a special 'department for miscellaneous crimes' which tried to establish whether Gypsies were genetically criminal.[90] Even those Gypsies who did have some success in education still faced difficulties in securing employment, as one mother recalled:

> I taught my daughter that as a Gypsy she would have to work hard to get results. She wanted to go to technical school or become a nurse but they

87 Ulč, 'Gypsies in Czechoslovakia', p. 319.
88 Kostelancik, 'Gypsies of Czechoslovakia', p. 315.
89 Helsinki Watch, *Czechoslovakia's Endangered Gypsies*, pp. 39, 40.
90 Francis S. Wagner, 'The Gypsy Problem in Postwar Hungary', *Hungarian Studies Review* 14 (1987), pp. 37, 40; Helsinki Watch, *Struggling for Ethnic Identity: The Gypsies of Hungary* (New York, 1993), pp. 6, 8, 11, 28.

would not take her. Her school mistress said as a Gypsy she shouldn't even think of going to the gymnasium [high school] because she couldn't cope and would only be crushed . . . well, I yelled and screamed till she got her recommendation . . . and she went to the gymnasium . . . and she worked hard and got good grades . . . and now? Now nothing. She is sitting at home, crying her eyes out because there is no work, though she's been looking for six months now.[91]

In Romania Gypsies traditionally made a living as tinsmiths, brick makers and wood carvers, fitting in with their itinerant way of life which the socialist regime allowed them to pursue, to a limited extent. Nevertheless, under the economic system that came into operation they could not practise one of their other traditional occupations in the form of buying and selling, and they became widely associated with the black market. Other Gypsies had worked on the soil, but had to labour upon state farms after collectivisation took place. A larger number found themselves employed as workers as a result of post-War industrialisation. A total of 47.3 per cent of Gypsies were workers in 1966, while 30.4 per cent were employed as collective farmers. As we might expect, only 0.5 per cent worked in professions, again linked with their educational backwardness. Very few Gypsies managed to progress beyond even the primary school level during the 1960s, meaning that few ever made it to secondary schools and, according to the census, only one Gypsy was enrolled at university in 1966. Rates of illiteracy remained high, standing at 37.7 per cent in 1956. After the fall of Ceaucescu most Gypsies found themselves in a situation of poverty, illiteracy and unemployment – a legacy of centuries of discrimination.[92]

The traditional Bulgarian Gypsy occupations of selling copperware and wooden spoons, as well as street entertainment, declined with the ban on travelling introduced in 1958, while some local authorities specifically prohibited the playing of street music. Nevertheless, a few of the traditional occupations survived into the early 1990s, although during the previous four decades and more many Gypsies had been pushed into unskilled factory work. Because of both the rise of unemployment following privatisation and their lack of education, Gypsies often became the first to face periods without work. In 1997 Bulgarian dailies carried reports of the death of three Romany children due to starvation. On the positive side some Gypsies established their own small businesses, although they faced hostility because of their image as black marketeers.[93]

In the rest of eastern Europe similar patterns of economic deprivation amongst Gypsies as the result of failed attempts at assimilation also emerge,

91 Helsinki Watch, ibid., p. 13.
92 Helsinki Watch, *Destroying Ethnic Identity: The Persecution of Gypsies in Rumania* (New York, 1991), pp. 24–8, 36; Trond Gilberg, 'Ethnic Minorities in Romania Under Socialism', in B. L. Faber (ed.), *The Social Structure of Eastern Europe* (New York, 1976), pp. 199, 201, 203, 205; David M. Crowe, *A History of the Gypsies of Eastern Europe* (London, 1995), p. 138.
93 Helsinki Watch, *Destroying Ethnic Identity: The Gypsies of Bulgaria* (New York, 1991), pp. 40–2; Crowe, ibid., pp. 26, 28; *Roma Rights* (Spring 1997), p. 10.

although (probably because they do not exist in such large numbers) the effort expended on attempting standardisation of the Gypsies has not been so great. In Poland the traditional methods of securing a livelihood declined as Gypsies moved into factories and collective farms, although fortune tellers still managed to survive and may even have increased in number. Similarly, Gypsy music playing received state support in 1952.[94] The multinational nature of Soviet and Yugoslav society also meant that the Gypsies in these two states did not endure the same level of economic deprivation as their brethren in Czechoslovakia, Romania and Bulgaria, although similarities exist. In the USSR ten Gypsies belonged to the Soviet Writers Union. In Yugoslavia, meanwhile, Romanies had great difficulty in progressing beyond primary school – partly due to the attitudes of their parents – which meant that they obtained the lowest-quality jobs, and hardly ever made it into the professions.[95]

Ultimately, whatever system of government has existed in Europe, it has failed the Gypsies simply by attempting to bring them into the dominant economic system and, in many cases, eliminating ways of making a living which evolved over hundreds of years. Similarly, attempts at educational assimilation have resulted in almost complete failure. The situation of the Gypsies encapsulates the inability of the modern nation state to allow minorities to continue with ways of making a living which do not fit into dominant norms.

The Lapps have certain similarities to the Gypsies, although they have not faced the level of overt persecution directed towards the Romany populations of eastern Europe. In their traditional way of life – where it has continued to survive – they live outside the conventional social and economic structure. This old-fashioned way of living in a hostile environment pre-dates sedentary agriculture and involved herding reindeer or fishing as a means of subsistence. Nevertheless, this method of livelihood has declined in importance as Lapps have moved into mainstream occupations and the mainstream socio-economic structure, in many cases at the very bottom of it, as Lapp areas have experienced high levels of unemployment since the 1970s.

Reindeer breeding involves a migratory way of life. In the classic lifestyle the reindeer provided 'food from its flesh, blood and milk, clothing from its skin, sewing-thread from its sinews, glue and material for many small objects from its horns and bones, and containers or holders from its intestines'.[96] During the summer the animals wander over pastures in the high land of northern Norway, Sweden and Finland. In September and October the reindeer are reclaimed by their owners and sorted into those who will be slaughtered, mostly for meat, and those who will survive for another year. These then move further south, giving birth between April and June and then returning to their summer pastures. In the early 1980s about 3,000 (800 households) of the 17,000 Swedish Sami made a living by farming about 21,000 animals. In Finland in the same period 1,425 out of 3,484 Lapp families were involved in

94 Jerzy Ficowski, *The Gypsies of Poland: History and Customs* (Warsaw, 1989), pp. 50–3.
95 Crowe, *History of the Gypsies*, pp. 191, 229, 230.
96 T. I. Itkonen, 'The Lapps of Finland', *Southwestern Journal of Anthropology* 7 (1951), p. 38.

reindeer herding, while another 134 practised both reindeer herding and fishing. In Norway about 607 households owned about 200,000 animals. Since the early 1970s reindeer herders have become reliant on snowmobiles. This activity is no longer a subsistence livelihood, but can be, with large herds, quite profitable. In addition, permanent settlements have developed.[97]

As outcasts, many of the German populations of eastern Europe witnessed a significant deterioration in their social and economic position after the Second World War, as a result of the reaction against Nazism. In Romania about 40,000 Germans faced relocation from the Banat to the Bragan Steppe in 1951 in order to carry out forced labour, although they subsequently returned in the years 1954–6. However, during land reforms which took place immediately after the War, many Germans lost their farms.[98]

The German population of the Soviet Union started the immediate post-War years in the position of complete outcasts, facing a difficult economic situation – especially those deportees who 'arrived in waste lands with no dwellings, sanitation or other basic necessities'. Germans who moved into already inhabited regions fared slightly better, although working conditions for all of them remained brutal so that they had to carry out up to fourteen hours of hard physical work per day on very low food rations. As many as 100,000 Germans may also have been employed in the labour army which carried out public works schemes throughout the Soviet Union. The situation of Germans began to improve after the lifting of restrictions against them in 1955: they moved out of labour camps and obtained employment in industrial centres or on collective farms, progressing rapidly up the economic ladder from a situation of extreme poverty to one of relative comfort. They have become heavily concentrated in the categories of manual and specialised workers. Their living conditions from the 1960s compared favourably with the population of the areas in which they found themselves after deportation, but they remained behind the levels of prosperity of the Slav populations. At the end of the Soviet Union, as unemployment rose with the deteriorating economic situation, hundreds of thousands of Germans decided to move to Germany.[99]

The Hungarian minority in Romania resembles that of the Germans of eastern Europe, as representatives of a political enemy which previously controlled the region. All population groupings in Romania experienced a social

97 Lars-Anders Baer, 'The Sami: An Indigenous People in Their Own Land', in Birgitta Jahreshog (ed.), *The Sami National Minority in Sweden* (Stockholm, 1982), p. 16; Helvi Nuorgam-Poutasuo, Juha Pentikäinen and Lassi Saressalo, 'The Sami in Finland: A Case Study', in *Cultural Pluralism and the Position of Minorities in Finland* (Helsinki, 1981), pp. 59–60; Israel Ruong, *The Lapps in Sweden* (Stockholm, 1967), pp. 29–38; Mervyn Jones, *The Sami of Lapland* (London, 1982), pp. 7–9; Tom Ingold, *The Skolt Lapps Today* (Cambridge, 1976), p. 116; John L. Irwin, *The Finns and the Lapps: How They Live and Work* (Newton Abbot, 1973), pp. 150–4.
98 Leo Paul, 'The Stolen Revolution: Minorities in Romania After Ceaucescu', in John O'Loughlin and Hermann van der Wusten (eds), *The New Geography of Eastern Europe* (London, 1993), p. 159.
99 Benjamin Pinkus, 'The Germans in the Soviet Union Since 1945', in I. Fleischauer, B. Pinkus and E. Frankel (eds), *The Soviet Germans Past and Present* (London, 1986), pp. 116–25; Adam Giesinger, *The Story of Russia's Germans: From Catherine to Kruschev* (Battleford, Saskatchewan, 1974), p. 323; Anthony Hyman, 'Volga Germans', in Smith, *Nationalities Question*, pp. 465, 471.

and economic transformation after the end of the Second World War due to industrialisation. At the same time Romanian policy deliberately aimed at reducing the numbers of members of minorities in positions of economic and administrative responsibility, particularly in the regions in which minorities are concentrated. Furthermore, Hungarians who do hold senior positions have been dispersed towards areas which do not have Hungarian majorities. Consequently, those Hungarians who progress up the economic ladder find that, in a classic situation applicable to immigrants, they have to sacrifice their original ethnic consciousness in order to move upwards.[100]

Many of the immigrants who moved to Europe from the 1950s and who initially worked in manual occupations would find that, as a result of the economic crisis of the 1970s and 1980s, they would become over-represented in the unemployment statistics due to both the sectors of employment in which they laboured and the continued existence of prejudice against them. This prejudice has also affected their children who have been unprepared to move into the sort of menial tasks carried out by their parents, leading to a situation in many European cities in which an immigrant underclass has developed, living off welfare benefits or criminality.

Some British West Indians have fallen into this trap. The problem of unemployment has affected the West Indian minority in Britain to a greater extent than most other groupings in the country due primarily to the prejudice against employing Black people. Although the second generation has suffered particularly, this problem began to manifest itself from the early days of West Indian immigration. A sample from the 1961 London census revealed that 6 per cent of West Indians were unemployed, compared with 3.2 per cent of English people.[101] The experience of Aaron Donane, who eventually committed suicide, may be typical, even if the way his life ended is not:

> For almost ten years, Aaron Donane told his wife that if no job turned up, he would kill himself. The talk of suicide began on his fifty-fifth birthday, almost ten years to the day from his arrival in England from the West Indies. During the period following his residence in London, he worked jobs, then he was unemployed. Then more jobs then more unemployment. By the time he was fifty, he and his brother Prince were almost always out of work. Both had become angry and depressed. They needed one another badly in these times, but their conversations together invariably ended in bitter quarrelling. Each, apparently, reminded the other of his own sadness, frustration, and sense of total failure. Yet they deeply cared for one another and had no one closer, not even their wives and children. For those who knew them or heard them fighting, especially when they had drunk too much, it almost seemed better that both were out of work. If one had been

---

100 Bennet Kovrig, 'The Magyars in Rumania: Problems of a "Coinhabiting" Nationality', *Südosteuropa* 35 (1986), p. 481; George Schöpflin and Hugh Poulton, *Rumania's Ethnic Hungarians*, 2nd edn (London, 1990), p. 15; Gilberg, 'Ethnic Minorities in Romania', pp. 203–5, 220–3.
101 Davison, *Black British*, p. 89.

able to find a job and not the other, there was no telling what this might have done to their friendship. Their wives argued this point, however. Both insisted that a job for either one would have been far better than no jobs. Competition, the women agreed, may well lead to death. But unemployment practically guarantees it![102]

The experience of the children of the West Indian immigrants in their search for employment has been even more bitter than that of their parents. From the middle of the 1960s youth employment officers throughout Britain reported that 'they experience little difficulty in placing coloured school-leavers in unskilled work, but there is considerable difficulty in placing them in skilled occupations, clerical positions and in occupations where a service is given to the public, such as that of shop assistant'.[103] A study of equally qualified applicants for apprenticeships to 300 West Midland firms during the 1980s demonstrated that while whites had a success rate of 44 per cent, only 15 per cent of Afro-Caribbeans managed to obtain positions.[104]

A lower rate of success at school influences the relative labour market position of West Indians in their search for employment, although discrimination again plays a central role here. In the first place, as many Afro-Caribbean populations have remained in the inner city, they consequently attend the most underfunded schools in the country in the poorest local authorities with the worst academic records. In addition, especially during the early decades of settlement, West Indian children faced hostility or indifference from their teachers, the overwhelming majority of whom were white and who taught a white curriculum. One survey in 1979 revealed that only 0.15 per cent of teachers in Britain were of Caribbean origin.[105]

Despite these factors, second-generation West Indians aspire to better employment than their parents, although this issue needs to be kept in perspective. There 'is always an expectation that the second generation of any migrant group will attain a more equal starting point in comparison with the young indigenous population'.[106] It is hardly as if Black school-leavers are asking for senior management positions with salaries to match. A survey from the late 1970s demonstrated that only 14.2 per cent of West Indians even aspired to non-manual employment,[107] but, because of the discrimination which they have faced, they have had difficulties in achieving even that limited aim.

---

102 Thomas J. Cottle, *Black Testimony: The Voices of Britain's West Indians* (London, 1978), p. 89.
103 Hill, *How Colour Prejudiced is Britain?*, p. 138.
104 John Wrench and John Solomos, 'The Politics and Processes of Racial Discrimination in Britain', in Wrench and Solomos (eds), *Racism and Migration in Western Europe* (Oxford, 1993), p. 164.
105 Ramdin, *Making of the Black Working Class*, p. 250.
106 Shirley Dex, 'The Second Generation: West Indian Female School Leavers', in Annie Phizacklea (ed.), *One Way Ticket: Migration and Female Labour* (London, 1983), pp. 53–4.
107 Malcolm Cross, 'Ethnic Minority Youth in a Collapsing Labour Market: The UK Experience', in C. Wilpert (ed.), *Entering the Working World: Following the Descendants of Europe's Immigrant Labour Force* (Aldershot, 1988), p. 76.

The above combination of factors has guaranteed that Black youth in Britain has experienced higher rates of unemployment than their white counterparts. Thus, while 18 per cent of white men and 15 per cent of white women between the ages of 16 and 25 were unemployed in 1985, the corresponding percentages for Afro-Caribbeans were 32 and 34 respectively. For all age groups, the percentage of Afro-Caribbeans without employment is also higher.[108] In inner-city areas the figures are even worse. In 1985 in the Lozells area of Handsworth in Birmingham, only 3 per cent of Afro-Caribbean summer school-leavers had found a job by November of that year.[109]

Asian youths have had similar experiences to those of West Indians, especially if they lived in the inner city. By 1985 the unemployment rate for Pakistani and Bangladeshi males had reached 28 per cent while the percentage for males between 16 and 24 stood at 39 – 5 per cent higher than for West Indians. In addition, 28 per cent of Indian males in this age group were not working.[110]

Immigrants and their children in France are also more likely to find themselves unemployed, especially as a result of the general decline in manual employment since the 1970s. Nevertheless, again like Britain, immigrants had actually begun to experience unemployment not long after their movement into France, so that 40 per cent of Africans and 18 per cent of Algerians were unemployed in 1969 compared with a virtually non-existent rate of between 1 and 2 per cent for the French population.[111] By 1990, when the unemployment rate for French people stood at 10.4 per cent, the figure for foreigners averaged out at 19.5 per cent, although this hides significant deviations between different minorities, with Portuguese, Italians and Spaniards experiencing percentages of 10.2, 12.2 and 12.5 respectively, while over a quarter of Africans found themselves unemployed.[112] Young people tended to experience especially high rates of unemployment: in 1982, for instance, an amazing 50.7 per cent of foreign women between 15 and 19 found themselves out of work.[113]

The unemployment experience of immigrants in Germany closely resembles that of their British and French counterparts due to their concentration in sectors of the labour market which have seen rationalisation and to their lack of education and knowledge of German. Before 1974, because of the specific recruitment of foreigners for particular jobs, they had a lower unemployment rate than Germans, but since that date a greater proportion of foreigners than Germans has been affected, reaching 11.9 per cent in 1982 when the rate for Germans stood at 7.5 per cent.[114]

108 Ibid., p. 72.
109 John Rex, 'Life in the Ghetto', in John Benyon and John Solomos (eds), *The Roots of Urban Unrest* (Oxford, 1987), p. 106.
110 Cross, 'Ethnic Minority Youth', p. 72.
111 Joyce Edmond-Smith, 'The Immigrant Worker in France', in Nicholas Deakin (ed.), *Immigrants in Europe* (London, 1972), p. 12.
112 Hargreaves, *Immigration, 'Race' and Ethnicity*, p. 41.
113 Salvatore Palidda and Marie-Claude Muñoz, 'The Condition of Young People of Foreign Origin in France', in Wilpert, *Entering the Working World*, p. 99.
114 Castles, *Here for Good*, p. 145.

This difference also applied to young people, due to discrimination and problems with language experienced by foreign children at school. In many cases the children of foreigners were at a disadvantage from the start because when they first attended school they had little or no knowledge of the language of tuition – in obvious contrast to Germans – although since the middle of the 1970s the individual German states have made efforts to provide language classes to such pupils. In some cases this proved counter-productive because some local governments established an apartheid-style education system, with children of the same nationality attending their own classes. At the secondary-school level, immigrant children tended to go to the lowest level of *Hauptschule*, which limited their employment opportunities when they left. They were under-represented in *Gymnasium* or *Realschule*, which would pre-pare them for university or white-collar occupations. Once they entered the labour market, ethnic minority youths were also less likely to obtain an apprenticeship than their German counterparts, demonstrating that they have continued in the disadvantaged social position of their parents. This is further indicated by the higher unemployment rates experienced by the children of foreign workers.[115] Many of these inevitably drifted into crime, such as the Turkish rap singer Durmuş, who grew up in the underprivileged Berlin quarter of Kreuzberg. In answer to a question about how he moved into crime, he answered:

I only need to say Kreuzberg. I grew up in an international environment with Germans, Italians, Turks and others. And when one became involved in shit, we all followed. We were only children. We didn't realise the consequences of our actions. We fell into shit without realising. Everyone I know has a criminal record.[116]

By the late 1980s in the Netherlands, while ethnic minorities made up 5.5 per cent of the population, they constituted 15 per cent of all of those out of work.[117] In 1979, unemployment amongst the Dutch labour force stood at 5.5 per cent, but for the Surinamese it had reached 25 per cent. By 1984 the figures had reached 13 per cent and between 40 and 45 per cent for Dutch and Surinamese people respectively. The percentage for Antilleans stood at 43 per cent in 1984.[118] From the early days, West Indians moving to the Netherlands – like their counterparts migrating to English cities – faced discrimination in employment, which played a role in confining them to the lower end of the

115 Thomas Faist, 'From School to Work: Public Policy and Underclass Formation Among Young Turks in Germany during the 1980s', *International Migration Review* 27 (1993), pp. 306–31; C. Wilpert, 'Work and the Second Generation: The Descendants of Migrant Workers in the Federal Republic of Germany', in Wilpert, *Entering the Working World*, pp. 111–49.
116 *Spiegel*, 14 April 1997.
117 Helma Lutz, 'Migrant Women, Racism and the Dutch Labour Market', in Wrench and Solomos, *Racism and Migration in Western Europe*, p. 132.
118 Theo Reubsaet, 'On the Way Up? Surinamese and Antilleans in the Dutch Labour Market', in Malcolm Cross and Hans Entzinger (eds), *Lost Illusions: Caribbean Minorities in Britain and the Netherlands* (London, 1988), pp. 108–10.

labour market, as did their less advanced education and training levels compared with the native Dutch population.[119]

In Scandinavia foreign workers have also experienced a higher unemployment rate than Swedes, standing at 9.9 per cent in 1979, in comparison with
their share of the labour force in the country, which totalled 5.3 per cent.[120]
Those refugees who entered Sweden during the 1980s experienced difficulty
in finding suitable jobs. By 1990 the unemployment rate of non-Nordic
nationals had reached 6.3 per cent, much lower than the experience of immigrants in other European states, but higher than the Swedish average of just
1.8 per cent.[121] In Norway immigrants have generally been employed 'in the
lowest paid jobs, constituting the unskilled labour force'.[122] Refugees moving
into Norway during the 1970s have had enormous problems in finding
employment, so that 65 per cent of asylum seekers were unemployed in 1987,
compared with a figure of just 2 per cent for the country as a whole, although
the state did spend large amounts of money in attempting to integrate these
newcomers into the work-force.[123] In Denmark foreign workers have also
experienced higher unemployment rates than the native population, standing
at 31.8 per cent in 1989, compared with 12.4 per cent for Danes. For Turks
the percentage reached 44.3 per cent. The classic factors of structural changes
in employment from the 1970s and prejudice created this situation.[124]

MINORITIES IN EUROPEAN ECONOMY AND SOCIETY

Wherever they have moved in western Europe, immigrants and their children
find themselves concentrated towards the lower end of the social and economic
ladder, carrying out the most difficult and worst-paid tasks required by advanced
economies in sectors such as manufacturing, construction, mining, domestic
service and agriculture. Since the middle of the 1970s many immigrants and
their children have faced long-term unemployment. Both economic factors
and prejudice contributed to this position of immigrants. The progress which
has taken place amongst some immigrants in western Europe – most clearly
illustrated by the development of ethnic businesses – does not change the
general situation.

119 Jeremy Boissevain and Hanneke Grotenberg, 'Culture, Structure and Ethnic Enterprise: The
Surinamese of Amsterdam', *Ethnic and Racial Studies* 9 (1986); Blaschke, Boissevain, Grotenberg,
Joseph, Morokvasic and Ward, 'European Trends in Ethnic Business', p. 93.
120 James Widgren, *Report to OECD (SOPEMI) on Immigration to Sweden in 1978 and the First
Half of 1979* (Stockholm, 1979), p. 35.
121 British Refugee Council, London, QSW 36, Ministry of Labour, 'Immigrant and Refugee
Policy in Sweden', 1991, p. 24.
122 Laila Kvisler, 'Immigrants in Norway', in G. Ashworth (ed.), *World Minorities*, Vol. 2
(Sunbury, 1978), p. 36.
123 British Refugee Council, London, QNO 44.2, 'Norway's Challenge: Asylum Seekers and
Refugees, 1985–88', 1988, pp. 23–55.
124 Jan Hjarnø, 'Migrants and Refugees on the Danish Labour Market', *New Community* 18
(1991), pp. 77–85.

Nevertheless, it may be too early for immigrants to reach the same level of prosperity as those minorities who have resided in western Europe for longer periods of time. After all, if we examine the history of French or British immigration during the past century, many of those who moved into these two states before the Second World War have done extremely well, as the history of late nineteenth-century Jews demonstrates. However, we can equally point to countless minorities in European history who have not had such a positive experience. The Gypsies offer the most extreme examples. What will happen to the post-War immigrants? Will they be future Gypsies, or will they progress up the social and economic ladder?

The answers to these questions are not easy. It may be that some groups can assimilate more easily than others. Those with economic backgrounds closer to the ones which prevail in western Europe may find it easier to succeed. Indeed, the history of Italians in France or Germany, or Greek Cypriots in Britain, suggests that this is the case. In contrast, Turks have had greater difficulty in succeeding wherever they have settled, as have West Indians in Britain and Holland, or North Africans in France. In the last two cases strong colour prejudice plays a part.

Economic power is inextricably linked with literacy and the development of political strength. An underlying reason for the failure of the Gypsies lies in their low literacy rates, caused by their hostility towards education which they see as standardisation and a threat to their ethnicity. However, the teaching of Gypsy children in eastern Europe in languages which they do not understand does not help their situation. In contrast, the most advanced minority in Europe, the Jews, also has the highest rates of literacy – a fact deeply rooted in Jewish history, with the requirement of literacy forming part of their Jewishness.

Ultimately, of course, Jews have always remained outsiders in Europe because, however literate they may have become and however much economic muscle they may have built up, they have never held political power for themselves. In the era of the nation state, as well as before that, they have been a political outgroup. The state controls power and rules primarily for people with the right 'national' credentials. However, if minorities of whatever type are prepared to take up the norms of the ruling group they can succeed. If not, they remain outside the body politic.

Ethnicity

CHAPTER 4

The Basis of Difference

Ethnicity comes from the Greek word, *ethnos*, which simply means 'nation': no difference exists between an ethnic group and a nation, in the true sense of the meaning of the latter word, applying to a group of people with shared characteristics. This relates equally to immigrants, dispersed groups and local-ised minorities, who share the same characteristics. In the first place their geographical concentration keeps them together, whether as immigrants in an inner-city area of London, Gypsies in a slum on the outskirts of Prague, or Albanians over a wider expanse in Kosovo. Similarly, marriage to members of their own grouping also perpetuates the ethnicity of minorities as they will have children who share those same characteristics. In situations in which ethnic groups dominate a particular geographical location, the chances of endogamy are higher.

Nevertheless, residence and marriage patterns simply perpetuate ethnic dif-ferences and they do not represent their basis, which can be divided into three categories, in the form of appearance, language and religion. These all rest, ultimately, with origin, although we need to recognise that myth-makers have perpetuated the significance of origin during the last two centuries in the case of both dominant groupings and minorities. The root of origin lies in the first known area of settlement of a particular group: no people of Europe is indigenous if we trace their history back far enough.

Appearance represents the most controversial signifier of difference, usually referring to physiognomy or skin colour. Clearly, Asian, Arab and Black immigrants in contemporary Europe look different from the fairer settlers who have lived on the continent for thousands of years. Similarly, differences in physical appearance exist between most Germans born in the north German plain and most Turks born in Anatolia.

But it is wrong to suggest that any group in Europe has a claim to ethnic purity. The constant population movements during the whole course of the continent's recorded history and the intermixing of peoples which has taken place make this impossible. Similarly, Black or Asian people clearly do not constitute the same ethnic group because of the colour of their skin. Only racists would make this claim, or, contradicting them, anti-racists, who develop Black ethnicity as a reaction against the slurs of racists. Ethnicity based on colour is completely artificial, although it might be inevitable in situations of potent and omnipresent racism. Black people in a particular part of Europe usually have a wide range of origins. While Africans in France may all look the same to French racists – or to much of the white population of France as a whole – the range of their countries of origin, from the equator to the Mediterranean, makes it impossible for them to constitute the same ethnic group, if only in terms of the enormous range of languages they speak. In fact, they would only be able to communicate in French, which means that if they did constitute an ethnic group it would be a completely artificial one like all others.

The appearance of groups also manifests itself in other ways – notably dress, which once again makes recent newcomers conspicuous. A middle-aged Muslim woman in a Parisian street in the middle of summer wearing traditional clothing, is clearly different from a scantily clad 20-year-old fair French girl. However, dress may not signify very much in distinguishing two long-established groups in Europe, say Czechs and Slovaks, especially in an urban environment. We might suggest that in the long run all people in Europe will wear similar western-style clothes. But this assertion is disproved if we consider the difference between a white English middle-class male working in the City of London and, just a few miles away in Brixton, a working-class Afro-Caribbean. Dress does matter in ethnic difference. Clearly, manufacturers of clothing are aware of ethnic differences and, in industrial societies, exploit them. Nevertheless, we need to distance ourselves from national costumes, which are completely artificial creations in the same category as national anthems.

Food, which can be regarded as another aspect of appearance, also differentiates one ethnic group from another. Again the variation is greater between Europeans and post-War arrivals from overseas. A Manichean difference exists between a Pakistani in Bradford during the early 1960s feasting upon a hot curry and his English neighbour plodding away at boiled potatoes, steak and kidney pudding and tinned peas. However, it would again be more difficult to distinguish the diet of long-established populations who have lived next to each other and have developed similar cuisines which have often involved a mixing of ideas. All areas of the Balkans and eastern Mediterranean, for instance, use a tomato-based flavouring. Religion would further play a role in the diet of other European ethnic groups, including Jews, Muslims, Hindus and Jains.

Appearance, encompassing dress and food, represents a basis for difference, but the last two are not built upon to any great extent by ethnic ideologues. However, this cannot be said to hold true of language – perhaps the most important basis for the development of political ethnicity. Nevertheless, we need to recognise the fact that all modern literary languages are artificial constructs of the age of industry and nationalism. Pre-literate societies communicate in dialects which thousands rather than millions of people speak. The act of creating a literary language in a particular area destroys the sum of its parts. Such an action represents a move towards a politically based ethnicity because no group can regard itself as a nation unless it possesses its own language. Once this has happened, the literate middle classes of a particular area can persuade the government of a state to grant them language rights in their area, which can encompass anything from putting up road signs in the literary language to allowing its use in education. In the case of the latter, minority language use can vary from a few hours a week in a primary school to the establishment of universities which teach in a particular language. Nation states are often more willing to grant language rights before any other form of autonomy to indigenous minorities. But they do not act so generously towards immigrants, which means that such newcomers consequently establish schools to preserve their own language amongst their children, even if tuition takes place after normal school hours. Such measures clearly represent a staking of autonomy against the dominant language, as do all manifestations of linguistic independence.

While language is central to the claim of most ethnic groups which wish to describe themselves as distinct entities, religion is only slightly less important. It may have represented an attempted act of standardisation in centuries past when the major religions first developed, but attending a religious service in many parts of (especially western) Europe today is the most important way for members of some groups to display their difference from the dominant population in the state in which they live. For some minorities (including Jews and Balkan Muslims), religion is more important than language as many now speak the tongue of the populations which surround them, most notably in Yugoslavia. However, many more ethnic groups differentiate themselves from the dominant population by their religion in some way or other, again especially true with regard to immigrants into Europe who have brought into the western half of the continent religions which hardly existed there before 1945, notably Islam, Hinduism and Buddhism. In other instances, notably Northern Ireland, historically evolved religious adherence forms the basis of difference, although in these cases religion has been superseded by politics.

Several basic differences clearly exist between European peoples which form the basis of ethnicity. However, we need to ask how consciously individuals, as opposed to groups, feel this difference. An immigrant certainly notices the change between his or her former place of residence and his or her new surroundings. In post-War Europe this is especially true for individuals who migrate from a village in a developing country to a large industrialised city, virtually moving from one world to another. Such people are profoundly conscious of their difference, which becomes more apparent if they try to move into the dominant society, during which they would face varying degrees of rejection, often because of their inability to speak the national language. Such uneducated immigrants value the opportunity to use their own tongue with people of their own sort – which represents one reason for ethnic clustering – or to practise their own religion in such a time of obvious spiritual need, a fact which leads to the construction of temples or churches. For such individuals the continuance of their traditional way of life, no matter how mutated it may become in the western surrounding, is really a question of psychological survival. Their level of difference makes it virtually impossible for them to become part of the dominant grouping.

For the children of immigrants the situation should be different. They have spent most or all of their lives in a western European state and consequently speak the language of the dominant community and have become acculturated to their surroundings. However, while their school life may revolve around their country of residence, their home experience focuses upon the language, religion and homeland of their parents. In such a situation, the children of immigrants are deeply conscious of their difference. This consciousness becomes reinforced by the snubs they face from the dominant society, especially in employment. The combination of upbringing and prejudice forces them back on to their own group, whether in terms of choice of marriage partner, religion, residence, eating, use of language, or dress, the last of which often has little to do with the clothing of parents.

Indigenous minorities almost represent a direct contrast to immigrants in the sense that they only become conscious of their difference when the dominant grouping, and its nationalist ideology, moves into their area. The spread of literacy often occurs in the language of the nation state in which a particular people live, which gives rise to demands for language provisions in schools amongst politically active members of a region. The spread of a national culture also makes a local population realise its difference, because of difficulties it has in relating to images on a television screen or to information in a newspaper. The arrival of transportation can also have an effect, as it can allow outsiders to move into an area, whether as administrators or immigrants working in new industries in a particular region. In such situations, the local population becomes conscious of its difference.

In other instances, especially in the case of dispersed minorities, awareness of difference has existed for centuries – in the case of Jews, for over two millennia, due, above all, to the perennial persecution which they have faced, which reinforced their distinctiveness rather than lessened it. Similarly, Gypsies in post-War Europe are deeply conscious of their difference both because of their food, clothes, religion, language, occupation and residence patterns and because of the hostility which they have faced from European states since the Middle Ages.

Ethnicity therefore becomes an issue when people are faced with new situations, either because they themselves have moved into an area, because a dominant national ideology has encroached on their space, or because they face hostility from the populace and government in a particular state. In essence, ethnicity is a reaction to these new situations. Food, dress, language and religion do not represent difference except in a situation in which people do not do the same. Only then do people become conscious of their difference and only then can political ethnicity develop. In such a situation a movement can evolve which attempts to unify these different people but, in unifying, simply standardises the differences which exist, so that political ethnicity is simply nationalism under another guise. In an age of internationalisation due to industrialisation, migration and television, individuals face countless choices about who they are and make a series of decisions about their identity. Ethnicity as a political phenomenon is forced – as forced as nationalism. Difference is not, even though standardisation exists in language, religion, food and clothing.

APPEARANCE

In terms of the different aspects of appearance, variations clearly exist between minorities and dominant populations within Europe. Any attempt to tackle basic difference, without reference to clothing or food – in other words, focusing just on physiognomy and physical characteristics – proves politically sensitive, but one cannot deny that variations exist between some minorities and majorities. This is especially true of immigrants who may have moved into Europe from thousands of miles away. They are different from most western Europeans in terms of skin colour, especially if they originate in Africa or Asia, but sometimes also in terms of physiognomy or even height. Nevertheless, pure physical appearance plays less of a role in determining other types of minorities in Europe. Only a racist would insist that all Jews look different, especially when in all other respects – such as clothing and accent – they have become fully assimilated into the populations which surround them. Gypsies in eastern Europe prove more distinctive because a lack of intermarriage in some areas has meant that they appear far darker in terms of skin colour. Similarly, the Muslim populations of the Soviet Union look different from Slavs. Nevertheless, distinguishing Serbs, Croats and Muslims in former Yugoslavia, or Greeks and Turks in Cyprus, merely in terms of physical appearance proves difficult.

Most problematic of all – and essentially futile – would be an attempt to differentiate many of the localised minorities of Europe from the dominant populations simply in terms of physical appearance. If we took the British case, we cannot distinguish between the Scots, Welsh and English or between Catholics and Protestants in Northern Ireland in this way. The same could be said of, for instance, Czechs and Slovaks, or Bretons and the rest of the French population. The explanation for this lies both in the similar origins of these varying groups and in intermarriage between them.

The function of dress similarly varies from one type of minority to another. With few exceptions, most of the long-standing populations of Europe, whether majorities or minorities, wear clothing originally designed in London, New York, Paris or Milan, which filters its way through to most of the population of Europe. Scottish traditional highland dress, for instance, has clearly declined in importance, except on artificial ceremonial occasions. The reasons for the disappearance of such clothing in everyday situations have much to do with the English elimination of traditional Scottish ethnicity in the eighteenth century, but it is unlikely that such dress would have survived industrialisation. The last point also applies to the Balkans. Historically, dress played a part in distinguishing the Greeks of Albania, for instance. During the nineteenth century Greek Albanian women wore 'a distinctively embroidered chemise or shift and a thick white woollen sleeveless coat called *sigouni*' while men wore 'a short full skirt known as the *foustanella*'.[1] In Macedonia, women wore long shirts, which sometimes reached their feet, over which was an apron. Scarves covered their heads. Men wore shirts with collars turned upwards and embroidered round the sleeves and neck, over which they wore waistcoats, and also wore mostly white trousers.[2]

Some minorities have continued to wear different clothing from dominant societies until more recently. The Gypsies provide one example. For instance, while English Gypsies wear similar clothes to gorgios, they regard short skirts, tight trousers and low-cut tops as too revealing. In contrast, they view the wearing of large amounts of gold jewellery positively.[3] Gypsies in Czechoslovakia still wore, until the 1970s, distinctive, if not traditional, clothing. The difference 'is seen in the special choice of clothing styles and colours available in the town, and in how they are worn, giving interesting contrasts and combinations with more traditional garments. Their love of ornaments and striking colours continues undiminished.'[4]

One of the most distinctive of all minorities in Europe, as well as in their land of origin in India, consists of Sikhs. The basis of their difference lies in their religion, which developed during the fifteenth century from the impact of Islam on Hinduism in the Punjab. Ten Gurus founded the religion, the last of whom, Guru Gobind Singh, established the *Khalsa*, the Sikh brotherhood, an identity symbolised by the five Ks: the *Kesh* (unshorn hair), the *Kacha* (short drawers), the *Kanga* (comb), the *Kirpan* (steel dagger) and the *Kara* (iron bangle).[5] In fact, the turban is now 'the most notable feature of men's clothing' and its function 'has to do wholly with religious and social identity and cohesion'. In India some women wear the *salwar kamiz* (trousers and tunic), which is common in the Punjab, or the more common Indian female dress, the Sari, covering the midriff in the case of Sikhs. They also wear a scarf over their heads.[6]

---

1 Linda Welters, 'Ethnicity in Greek Dress', in Joanne B. Eicher (ed.), *Dress and Ethnicity: Change Across Space and Time* (Oxford, 1995), p. 59.
2 Galaba Palikrusheva, 'Ethnographic Conditions in Macedonia', in M. Apostolski and Haralampie Polenakovich (eds), *The Socialist Republic of Macedonia* (Skopje, 1974).
3 Barbara Adams, Judith Okely, David Morgan and David Smith, *Gypsies and Government Policy in England: A Study of the Travellers' Way of Life in Relation to the Policies and Practices of Central and Local Government* (London, 1975), p. 7.
4 Eva Davidóva, 'The Gypsies in Czechoslovakia: Part II: Post-War Developments', *Journal of the Gypsy Lore Society* 50 (1971), pp. 48–50.
5 This information was provided by Professor Gurharpal Singh of the University of Hull.
6 W. Owen Cole and Piara Singh Sambhi, *The Sikhs: Their Religious Beliefs and Practices* (London, 1978), pp. 109–11.

To what extent have these traditions continued in Europe? With regard to dress, many males abandoned their homeland appearance upon first arriving in Britain during the 1950s by shaving off their beard and hair and dispensing with their turbans. But when their wives made the journey to the new country they continued to wear the *salwar kamiz*, which embarrassed the husbands into growing their hair and beards again and using their turbans. The trend developed further with the arrival of Sikhs from East Africa. In fact, some Sikh males continued to wear turbans despite facing outright hostility from transport authorities which employed them in Wolverhampton, Manchester and Leeds. Furthermore, some motorcyclists wore them instead of crash helmets, despite the illegality of this act, which eventually led to a change in the law allowing Sikh motorcyclists to maintain their turbans.[7]

For the second generation, changes have taken place so that it is unusual to see either men or women born in England wearing traditional clothing. Nevertheless, there have certainly been exceptions, as one girl growing up in Gravesend recalled:

In the early years before hordes of Punjabis arrived, my mother dressed us like the English. My brother and I associated with English friends. As our parents did not want to be different in any way, they assured our learning the language properly. When our relatives came, everything changed drastically. The women would come to our house and say 'Don't you think Nimi's hair should be braided now that she is ten' or 'Nimi should not go to school with bare legs, otherwise she will grow up to be immodest'. Immediately my mother's attitude changed. I was no longer to be like the English, but was to dress and be like the Punjabi villagers, whom I began to abhor.[8]

When this girl grew up she had, no doubt, to make choices – like all children of immigrants throughout Europe – between pursuing the same way of life as her parents, or adopting the one which surrounded her, which has often resulted in the second generation picking elements of both. Sikh women born in Britain are as much influenced by their locality within England as by English fashions as a whole. Thus Sikh women in Birmingham appear 'Brummie' in their clothing and accents, just as women from Camden in London look Camdenian.[9]

Greek Cypriots in London are even more westernised than Sikhs in their appearance. Young Greek Cypriot male immigrants invariably wore westernised clothes before migrating to Britain, and often adopted the most fashionable styles shortly after their arrival. But even middle-aged males would never

7 Ibid., p. 110; Roger Ballard and Catherine Ballard, 'The Sikhs: The Development of South Asian Settlements in Britain', in James L. Watson (ed.), *Between Two Cultures* (Oxford, 1977), pp. 36–7.
8 Quoted in Arthur Wesley Helweg, *Sikhs in England: The Development of a Migrant Community* (Calcutta, 1979), pp. 54–5.
9 Parminder Bhachu, 'Culture, Ethnicity and Class Among Punjabi Sikh Women in 1990s Britain', *New Community* 17 (1991), pp. 408–9.

have worn the traditional Cypriot peasant dress in England. This consisted of a white shirt, black waistcoat, black *vraka*, a sort of baggy trousers, and black knee-length boots. In contrast, Greek Cypriot widows would wear black.

In France, the issue of immigrant dress reached centre stage in political and media debate following the expulsion of three girls by the principal of a college in Creil on 18 September 1989 simply for wearing a headscarf. The principal justified his decision by pointing to regulations from the 1930s which forbade the wearing of religious and political insignia. The Right inevitably supported the stand taken. But some sections of the Left, including leading intellectuals, also believed that the principal of the college had taken the right decision, basing their views on the secular nature of the French education system. Feminists, meanwhile, claimed that the headscarf enslaved women. The issue was resolved by the end of October 1989 when Prime Minister Lionel Jospin said that scarves could be worn in schools as long as proselytising did not occur, which was hardly likely to have happened in the first place.[10] From the point of view of second-generation Muslim girls in France, the issue highlights their position as they are trapped between two completely contrasting norms. On the one hand, French society is overtly sexual, meaning that both men and women can have partners before they marry. On the other, Muslim society still prizes the virginity of women before marriage.[11]

Like clothing, food varies as a distinguishing factor from one group to another. Again, differences exist between localised long-standing minorities and more recent arrivals, with the latter more likely to continue eating foods from their homeland, which have vast differences from what the local population consumes. We need to distinguish here between the reality of immigrant food, available because of the importation of provisions to support large immigrant communities, and the existence of restaurants for members of mainstream society, which sometimes have a limited connection with foods eaten by minorities. Ethnic food may well survive minorities themselves and can even be present in a particular location without representatives of a group, especially true with the Chinese. Furthermore, as minorities become assimilated their identification with their food becomes weaker. In such a situation individuals are prepared to sample all varieties of food, including that eaten by other ethnic minorities.

In their traditional way of life, Gypsies eat particular delicacies, partly guided by a taboo system. In Poland, the favourite food of the Gypsies has been chicken, but they also enjoyed hedgehogs and mushrooms.[12] In England, Gypsies prefer to buy packaged food when they go shopping because it has not so obviously been touched, and possibly poisoned, by gorgio hands.[13] In

10 Cathie Lloyd and Hazel Waters, 'France: One Culture, One Race', *Race and Class* 32 (1991), pp. 49–50; David Beriss, 'Scarves, Schools, and Segregation: The *Foulard* Affair', *French Politics and Society* 8 (1990), pp. 1–13.
11 R. D. Grillo, *Ideologies and Institutions in Urban France: The Representation of Immigrants* (Cambridge, 1985), pp. 152–4.
12 Jerzy Ficowski, *The Gypsies of Poland: History and Customs* (Warsaw, 1989), pp. 61–2.
13 Judith Okely, *The Traveller-Gypsies* (London, 1983), pp. 83–4.

Czechoslovakia the food of most Gypsy families 'can be regarded as some form of Slovak or sometimes Hungarian cooking'. However, 'most of the food is either boiled or cold; baking and frying are rare and have started to spread only recently. Most popular and common are boiled meat, especially pork (*balano mas*), potatoes (*phaba*, *gruli* or *bandurky*) and various kinds of "non-powder" soups (*zumin*).' In addition, most families eat noodles, cabbage, pigs' blood, cheap salami 'or their gypsy food (*goja*, stuffed intestines)'.[14]

In the traditional way of life the basis of the Lapp diet rested on the reindeer, which provided meat and milk for the whole year. Husbands prepared food when it involved meat 'due to the old idea that the woman is unclean and must not touch game', although this situation no longer existed by the early post-War years. Reindeer milk formed an important part of the Sami diet. Some of it was drunk, some was used for cheese and some of it buried underground or left in cold springs for later consumption. However, by the 1960s the milking of reindeer had almost ceased. The Lapps also ate numerous other animals which they hunted, including elk, squirrel, beaver, bear and ptarmigan. 'Those Lapps who have few or no reindeer live chiefly on fish in summer, when the Reindeer Lapps also fish if they have the opportunity.'[15]

Some differences in the diet of the English and Scots have survived into the late twentieth century, although 'haggis, neeps, brose, stovies, porridge and other traditional foods washed down with malt whisky hardly constitute an habitual diet in Scotland'. However, subtle variations exist between the diet of the average Scot and that of the average citizen of south-east England. In 1973, for instance, Scots ate 30 per cent less fruit and 20 per cent more cereal products than people in south-east England.[16] Nevertheless, this hardly constitutes the basis of difference between England and Scotland.

With increasing secularisation Muslims find it more and more difficult to adhere to the dietary requirements of their religion, whether this consists of avoiding pork or fasting at Ramadan. In the Soviet Union, observance of fasting during the feast of Ramadan became highly problematic because of the difficulties created by not eating between sunrise and sunset while people had to work. Some employees of state institutions were offered food or drink by their superiors. Refusal to accept proved that they were fasting and could lead to dismissal. Muslims further faced pressure to eat pork in government restaurants and in the army.[17] In western capitalist states it has proved easier for Muslim immigrants to continue their dietary practices as the state has not intervened directly to control the dietary habits of minorities, although some children had problems with standardised school dinners, which paid little attention to the requirements of Muslims.

14 Davidóva, 'Gypsies in Czechoslovakia', p. 51.
15 T. I. Itkonen, 'The Lapps of Finland', *Southwestern Journal of Anthropology* 7 (1951), pp. 36, 46–9, 56–8; Israel Ruong, *The Lapps of Sweden* (Stockholm, 1967), pp. 29–30.
16 Kenneth Blaxter, 'The Scottish Diet', in Robert Underwood (ed.), *The Future of Scotland* (London, 1973), pp. 75–6.
17 Richard Pipes, 'Muslims of Soviet Central Asia: Trends and Prospects, Part I', *Middle East Journal* 9 (1955), pp. 149–50, 157.

Most immigrants have brought their food with them. In Switzerland, for instance, the arrival of Italians meant an increase in the importation of tomatoes, which form a basis of the Italian diet.[18] Another group in Switzerland, Tibetan refugees, continued to eat their own food, such as ragbay (which resembles ravioli), as best they could – although obtaining yak butter, a staple of the Tibetan diet, proved problematic in view of the absence of yaks in Switzerland.[19]

LANGUAGE

The various aspects of appearance play a tertiary role in determining ethnicity, when compared with the importance of language and religion. The continued survival of languages depends to a great extent on the attitude of the state and the organisational ability of individual groups. If the state recognises a language, usually by granting educational rights, the perpetuation of the minority which uses it becomes more assured. Most minority groupings in Europe have their own language, although this does not necessarily consist of one which they alone use. By the end of the twentieth century those languages in use by minorities have usually evolved through several stages including their creation into a literary medium, which ignores many of the dialects contributing to the whole. In addition, many languages borrow some of the words in use by the dominant grouping.

Language has represented the central factor differentiating Germans from the populations which have surrounded them in the post-War period, although in some areas, such as Kazakhstan, physical appearance continued to play a role. The German minority of Denmark has experienced a high rate of exogamy due to the similarities and consequent lack of social distance between Danes and Germans. However, because of the continuance of language teaching in German, the proximity of the German border and the political activity of the *Bund Nordschleswiger*, the German-speaking minority has not disappeared – now counting between 15,000 and 20,000 people who identify themselves as Germans – as a result of legal guarantees for education. In 1989 the German minority maintained 18 private schools attended by 1,184 pupils. Despite the schools, most members of the minority communicate in Danish.[20]

The German linguistic group has had greater success in surviving in the South Tyrol than in Denmark, due to the fact that it forms the majority of the population in the area, which the Italian state has recognised by granting

18 Lucio Boscardin, *Die italienische Einwanderung in die Schweiz mit besonderer Berücksichtigung der Jahre 1946–1959* (Basle, 1962), pp. 82–3, 121–2.
19 Lauri Pilarski, 'Little Tibet in Switzerland', *National Geographic* 134 (1968), pp. 711–27.
20 Jørger Elklit, Johan Peter Noack and Ole Tonsgaard, 'A National Group as a Social System: The Case of the German Minority in North Schleswig', *Journal of Intercultural Studies* 1 (1980), pp. 5–18; Meic Stephens, *Linguistic Minorities in Western Europe* (Llandysul, 1976), p. 237; Lorenz Rerup, 'National Minorities in South Jutland/Schleswig', in Sven Tägil (ed.), *Ethnicity and Nation Building in the Nordic World* (London, 1995), pp. 276–7; Minority Rights Group, *Minorities and Autonomy in Western Europe* (London, 1991), p. 18.

language rights. The Autonomy Statute of 1948 allowed the establishment of German-language schools and permitted the use of German in government offices. At the primary level the Italians and Germans have had their own schools, but at secondary level parents have had the choice of sending their children to either a German or Italian school.[21]

In some eastern European states the German minorities received similar language rights, although the situation has varied from one location to another. In Poland the old order relegated German to the status of a foreign language. Rapid changes took place after the end of communism so that German had been introduced in 157 schools in Silesia by the end of 1990.[22] Similarly, the German grouping in Czechoslovakia faced a denial of language rights but this also changed after 1989.[23]

In Hungary the state nationalised all schools in 1949 and two years later Edict No. 15 proposed to introduce mother-tongue education throughout the country. In the academic year 1960–1 a total of 2,223 children attended minority kindergartens, 2,517 went to language schools and 25,540 were enrolled in bilingual institutions. However, by 1968–9 these figures had fallen, respectively, to 1,340, 1,991 and 18,240, with the Germans (as well as Slovaks) experiencing the most dramatic decrease in numbers. During the 1970s German was taught more and more as a foreign language and the special schooling arrangements gradually disappeared. Industrialisation and urbanisation, leading to German migration to urban centres, and consequent subtle pressure to assimilate, helped the government to pursue this policy. More positive developments occurred after the fall of communism, although by this time the number of people who could actually still speak German had rapidly declined. Two secondary schools adopted German as their language of instruction in most subjects, while a third offered the choice of tuition in German. In addition, training for teachers of German also returned.[24]

In Romania minority schools came under state control in 1948. Their number increased from 2,289 in the 1948–9 academic year to 2,534, including 412 German ones, by 1958–9. Following the normal pattern, a larger number of German and other foreign-language schools existed at the primary and junior level than at the secondary standard. Over the following decades, especially under Ceaucescu, provision for foreign-language schools declined.[25]

21 Minority Rights Group, ibid., p. 8; Stephens, ibid., p. 531.
22 Agnieszka Rochowicz, 'National Minorities in Poland', in John Packer and Kristian Myntti (eds), *The Protection of Ethnic and Linguistic Minorities in Europe* (Turku/Åbo, 1993), pp. 108–9.
23 H. Renner, 'The National Minorities in Czechoslovakia After the Second World War', *Plural Societies* 7 (1976), p. 26; Minority Rights Group and TWEEC (eds), *Minorities in Central and Eastern Europe* (London, 1993), p. 39.
24 Frances S. Wagner, 'Ethnic Minorities in Hungary Since World War II', *Central European Forum* 2 (1989), pp. 74–6; David M. Crowe, 'Minorities in Hungary Since 1948', *Nationalities Papers* 16 (1988), pp. 26–7; Minority Rights Group and TWEEC, *Minorities in Central and Eastern Europe*, pp. 39–40.
25 Wilhelm Reiter, 'Die Nationalitätenpolitik der Rumänischen Volksrepublik im Spiegel Ihrer Staitistik', *Osteuropa* 11 (1961), pp. 189–91; Brigitte Mihok, *Ethnostrazifikation im Sozialismus, aufgezeigt auf den Bespielländern Ungarn und Rumänien* (Frankfurt, 1990), p. 110.

In the Soviet Union the Second World War experience of deportation had various effects on ethnic consciousness amongst Germans. Some 'sought to lose their ethnic identity and merge into Soviet society, while others reasserted their national consciousness more resolutely, some of them even joining the dissident movements. Still others sought to leave the USSR by emigrating to West Germany.'[26] German schools could no longer function because of a ban on German as a language of instruction, and German children could not even study the tongue of their parents as a foreign language. The situation began to improve after Chancellor Konrad Adenauer's visit to Moscow in 1955, by which time most young Germans had become illiterate in their mother tongue while some could not even speak it. In the following year German became available as a foreign language in Siberia and Kazakhstan. From 1957 Germans could also establish their own schools in areas in which they formed a majority, although this did not happen quickly. By the middle of the 1970s the vast majority of German children did not receive instruction in their mother tongue. Between the 1926 and 1989 censuses the number of Germans who gave their own language as their main means of communication decreased from 95 per cent to 49 per cent.[27]

Localised minorities have a greater chance of maintaining their language than dispersed peoples due to their concentration and larger numbers. These two facts mean that the language has a greater chance of surviving in everyday situations and also that the state has to pay attention to the desires of the minority because of its potential political power, which could destabilise the area in which they live.

Since the War language has developed into the fundamental basis of Sami distinctiveness, an issue which has become politicised and which the state has accepted by allowing minority language teaching in schools. The Lappish language has four main dialects but in a crude act of standardisation they became one in Norway and Sweden in 1979.[28] Between one-third and one-half of Lapps can actually speak some form of their own language. The proportion is higher amongst those working in reindeer farming than amongst those who are involved in other, more mainstream, forms of economic activity. In Finland about 16 per cent of Lapps used Lappish as their principal means of communication in the 1970s, while another 16 per cent used it together with Finnish. The rest spoke only Finnish.[29] Amongst the Sami living in the

26 Sidney Heitman, 'The Soviet Germans', *Central Asian Survey* 12 (1993), p. 75.

27 Detlef Brandes, 'Die Deutschen in Russland und der Soviet Union', in Klaus J. Bade (ed.), *Deutsche im Ausland: Fremde in Deutschland* (Munich, 1992), pp. 131–2; Adam Giesinger, *The Story of Russia's Germans: From Catherine to Kruschev* (Battleford, Saskatchewan, 1974), pp. 325–32; Karl Stumpp, *Die Russland Deutschen: Zwei Hundert Jahre Unterwegs*, 3rd edn (Munich, 1966), pp. 38–9; Benjamin Pinkus, 'The Germans in the Soviet Union Since 1945', in I. Fleischauer, B. Pinkus and E. Frankel (eds), *The Soviet Germans Past and Present* (London, 1986), pp. 125–8.

28 Lars-Anders Baer, 'The Sami: An Indigenous People in Their Own Land', in Birgitta Jahreshog (ed.), *The Sami National Minority in Sweden* (Stockholm, 1982), p. 19; Mervyn Jones, *The Sami of Lapland* (London, 1982), p. 10.

29 Erkki Asp, Kari Rantanen and Aila Munter, *The Lapps and the Lappish Culture* (Turku, 1980), pp. 15–19.

Norwegian fjords, about 40 out of 50 households spoke it as their domestic language in the early 1970s. Outside the home people used it according to the situation in which they found themselves, at least partly due to hostility which they faced from Norwegians. Language behaviour is such 'that Lappish must be regarded as a secret language or code, regularly used only in situations where Lappish identities are involved'. In shops, for instance, people used Norwegian because of the presence of people who spoke that language only. Sami-speaking parents thought that it was 'necessary' and 'right' to speak Norwegian to their children, in order to help them in their social and economic progression, so that they 'shall not have the same handicaps as we have had'.[30]

The Scandinavian states began to allow the teaching of Lappish in schools before 1945. By the 1980s Sami children in Norway received their first three years of school instruction in their own language, during which time they also learned Norwegian.[31] In Sweden the 1913 Education Act established elementary nomadic schools, which would migrate with the movements of the reindeer. A total of six of these existed by the early 1980s covering school years 1–6, while another went from years 7–9. Children remained at the schools for the course of the week and returned home at weekends. They received instruction in both Swedish and Sami.[32] In Finland Sami was taught in 22 primary schools in the Lappish area in 1989–90.[33]

The language of the Swedish minority in Finland, which is concentrated in the south and west of the country, has had a longer history of recognition than Lappish, both because of the existence of an external protecting state and because of its status as a literary language. In addition, as the language of a former colonial power, Swedish was widely spoken before Finnish independence. Furthermore, the language also has an economic use because of the dependence of the Finnish economy upon Sweden. It has enjoyed legal protection almost from the beginning of Finnish independence in 1917. In fact, the Constitution Act of 1919 declared that 'Finnish and Swedish are the national languages of the Republic', and that either could be used in any situation. Swedish-speaking schools have also received protection, making up 321 out of the 4,466 primary schools in Finland and 31 out of the 447 secondary schools in 1990. In addition, a Swedish-language university also exists in Turku/Åbo. Nevertheless, even in bilingual areas people tend to speak Finnish in mixed company.[34]

30 Harald Eidheim, *Aspects of the Lappish Minority Situation* (Oslo, 1977), pp. 55, 57.
31 Jones, *Sami of Lapland*, p. 12; Laila Kvisler, 'The Sami: The Lapps of Scandinavia', in G. Ashworth (ed.), *World Minorities*, Vol. 1 (Sunbury, 1977), p. 138.
32 Jones, ibid.; Baer, 'The Sami', p. 20.
33 Asp, Rantanen and Munter, *Lapps and Lappish Culture*, p. 21; Kristian Myntti, 'National Minorities and Minority Legislation in Finland', in Parker and Myntti, *Protection of Ethnic and Linguistic Minorities*, pp. 90–3.
34 Karmela Liebkind and Roger Broo, 'The Swedish-Speaking Finns: A Case Study', in Finnish National Commission for UNESCO, *Cultural Pluralism and the Position of Minorities in Finland*, 2nd edn (Helsinki, 1981), pp. 24–5; Anne Marie Beaurain, 'Ethnic Problems of Swedish Finns and Finnish Finns', *Plural Societies* 7 (1976), pp. 65–6; Myntti, ibid., pp. 87–8, 90; Max Engman, 'Finns and Swedes in Finland', in Tägil, *Ethnicity and Nation Building*, p. 210.

In the United Kingdom, language plays less of a role in underpinning Scottish than Welsh ethnicity. In Scotland the native language has virtually disappeared, a process hastened by events in the second half of the eighteenth century, although Gaelic had already declined in importance before that time. The major British Education Acts of 1872, 1918 and 1980 virtually ignored the provision of the language. The Education (Scotland) Act of 1980 made some progress by requiring local education authorities to provide Gaelic at all stages in Gaelic-speaking areas. But the language has declined during the last century. The 43,738 Gaelic monoglots of 1891 had fallen to 2,178 in 1951 and 477 in 1971, while the numbers of people who spoke both Gaelic and English declined from 210,677 in 1891 to 93,269 in 1951 – although since that time something of a stabilisation has taken place so that the figure stood at 79,307 in 1981, or 1.64 per cent of the Scottish population. The major concentration lay in the Western Isles, where 79.5 per cent of the population could speak Gaelic in 1981, while just 0.57 per cent of the population of Glasgow could use the language.[35]

More people speak Welsh than speak Gaelic due to the absence of genocidal policies against the Welsh during the second half of the eighteenth century and also due to the successful campaigns of Welsh nationalists in the nineteenth century in favour of their country and language, which have resulted in the educational and political acceptance of Welsh as a medium of communication to a much greater extent than Gaelic. Furthermore, 34 per cent of Welsh non-conformist and Anglican churches used Welsh in their services during the 1980s. The pressures against Welsh have come mainly from the movement of English people into the country throughout the nineteenth and twentieth centuries and from the advance of the English language, whose influence has spread even further with the growth of television since 1945. Children actually received instruction in Welsh by the end of the nineteenth century. Welsh has gained further recognition since the Second World War, both within schools and as a language of bureaucracy. Nationalists have played a role in pushing the Westminster government in their direction. Following legislation from London, scores of primary schools teaching some measure of Welsh came into existence. In addition, there were eleven bilingual secondary schools which taught a total of 7,680 pupils in 1980. The 1967 Welsh Language Act authorised the issue of government documents in both English and Welsh. Bilingual road signs also appeared and businesses began using the Welsh language. Despite the successes scored by Welsh nationalists, the use of their language has continued to decline: the total number of people who could speak Welsh decreased from 880,000 people in 1891, making up 54 per cent of the population, to 508,207, or 19 per cent, in 1981. The more rural areas of north and west Wales had a higher concentration of Welsh speakers than the industrialised south.[36]

35 Glanville Price, *The Languages of Britain* (London, 1984), pp. 52–9; Commission of the European Community, *Linguistic Minorities in Countries Belonging to the European Community* (Rome, 1986), pp. 172–9.
36 Commission of the European Community, ibid., pp. 185–9; Price, ibid., pp. 102–11.

In the middle of the 1980s nearly 4 million people in France spoke regional languages. The Basques (80,000 speakers), Catalans (200,000), Flemish (100,000) and Germans (1,260,000) all represent border minorities with the bulk of their populations on the other side of French boundaries. The populations who use these languages also speak French. In the typical pattern the languages have survived to a greater extent amongst the rural population than amongst the working classes and the bourgeoisie. The dialects spoken, in the case of Germans in Alsace for instance, do not always correspond to the standardised national language on the other side of the French border. In 1951 the Deixonne Law allowed the teaching of many of the above languages in the areas where speakers lived and since that time further provision has followed from the centre, although the extent to which they are taught varies from one region to another. Corsican is spoken by about half of the 300,000 inhabitants of Corsica but the 1951 language law did not allow its teaching in schools.[37] Breton is as healthy as any of the above languages due to the strength of the nationalist movement connected with it, which points to the medieval status of Brittany as an independent state. About 500,000 people use Breton – mostly peasants, fishermen and their families – although this represents a 62 per cent decline in the number of people speaking the language during the last century. The 1951 law allowed the teaching of Breton at all levels of instruction, and subsequent legislation has strengthened its position in schools.[38]

Language has historically played the central role in ethnicity in Belgium. Although both Flemish and French had obtained official recognition during the nineteenth century, further reforms have followed since 1900 mainly due to the fear of Flemish nationalists about the spread of French. Linguistic laws during the 1930s created two language areas in the country, a Flemish one in the north and a French one in the south, within which the respective languages would be the main ones used in education, although the other would be available after four years of schooling. Official communications would be written in both languages, but public officials would 'respond to matters in the language in which they were addressed'. The legislation essentially created a situation of bilingualism with regard to state officials, as well as establishing unilingual regions to satisfy Flemish nationalists.

Nevertheless, the laws did not achieve the aims of the Flemish nationalists because slightly more students were studying French-speaking courses at university, and Brussels was becoming more and more French, while people who progressed upward on the social ladder tended to speak French. Consequently, there followed further language laws in 1962 and 1963 which fixed the language frontier by law and transferred some territories from one side of the division established during the 1930s to the other. In addition, top civil service jobs would only be open to people who could speak both languages.

37 Stephens, *Linguistic Minorities in Western Europe*, pp. 295–402; Commission of the European Community, ibid., pp. 119–57.
38 M. McDonald, *'We Are Not French!' Language, Culture and Identity in Brittany* (London, 1989), pp. 7, 58.

In 1970 revisions to the Belgian constitution divided the country into four linguistic regions consisting of a northern Flemish one, a southern French one, a bilingual Brussels and a small German-speaking district in the east.[39]

Few other states in continental western Europe have quite the same language split as Belgium. A more typical example of linguistic division exists in the Netherlands, where the population of Friesland, of more than half a million, has its own Frisian language, spoken by about 400,000 people in the area, as well as a further 300,000 who have migrated to other parts of the Netherlands. Since the Second World War the Dutch state has accepted nationalist demands in the area to implement teaching in Frisian. As a result of a 1955 measure, all instruction has taken place in Frisian during the first two years of school, where the parents and school board agree that this should happen. Transition subsequently takes place to Dutch. Five Dutch universities have chairs in Frisian and offer the language as a subject of study. Legislation in 1975 further strengthened the position of Frisian within schools. Frisian is spoken throughout the rural areas and smaller settlements of Friesland, especially at home. In many cases people in the area speak a dialect which combines elements of Dutch and Frisian.[40]

Linguistic differences represent the major basis of ethnicity in Spain. Use of the unique Basque language, Euskera, has declined during the twentieth century, partly as a result of the immigration of people from other parts of Spain who could not speak it. In 1986 only 24.65 per cent of people in the Basque country could speak and understand Euskera, while 57.15 per cent had no comprehension at all. The language is used in rural areas, fishing villages and towns, but very few people speak it in the cities of Bilbao and San Sebastian. Euskera became established in schools during the late 1970s and early 1980s, and by 1990 around 12 per cent of children in the region received the bulk of their education in the language.

More people speak Catalan than Euskera. In 1986 less than 10 per cent of people living in Catalonia could not understand the language. It is spoken throughout the region in both rural and urban areas, although Spanish immigrants could generally not comprehend it. It is the official language of Catalonia, along with Spanish. Over 30 per cent of children in Catalonia received instruction in Catalan at the end of the 1980s.

In Galicia only 6 per cent of the population could not understand Galician in 1986. Peasants and fishermen speak the language while the upper and middle classes use Spanish. As in the case of the Basque land and Catalonia, the local language, along with Spanish, is the official means of communication,

---

39 Minority Rights Group, *Minorities and Autonomy in Western Europe*, pp. 20–2; R. E. M. Irwing, *The Flemings and Walloons of Belgium* (London, 1980), pp. 10–13; Aristide R. Zolberg, 'Splitting the Difference: Federalization Without Federalism in Belgium', in Milton J. Esman (ed.), *Ethnic Conflict in the Western World* (London, 1977), pp. 112–28; Alexander B. Murphy, *The Regional Dynamics of Language Differentiation in Belgium* (Chicago, 1988), pp. 114–19, 125–52.
40 'On the History and Situation of the Frisians in the Netherlands', *Europa Ethnica* 21 (1964), pp. 56–7; Meic Stephens, 'The West Frisians', in Ashworth, *World Minorities*, Vol. 1, pp. 150–1.

although less provision is made for teaching in Galician in schools than in the case of Basque and Catalan.[41]

In Germany and Austria language has again represented the main basis of difference between the dominant populations and the minorities which survived into the post-War period. In North Friesland, in Schleswig-Holstein for instance, about 60,000 people consider themselves to be of Frisian origin, of whom 10,000 have a knowledge of North Frisian, a dialect incomprehensible outside the region. It has no standardised form and no legal status, so that it is, in many ways, a completely natural language.[42] In this way it differs from Danish, which has protection from an external state, leading to the establishment of Danish-minority schools in South Schleswig.[43] The Sorbs, who live on the Czech border, represent the most distinct minority in Germany, due to the fact that they are a Slavonic group. The German Democratic Republic offered much support to the Sorbs which meant that almost the entire population of Lusatia was bilingual. Rural areas, which experienced little resettlement of Germans expelled from eastern Europe after the War, speak mostly Sorbian but elsewhere a much more mixed situation has existed. After the collapse of the GDR questions arose about the economic viability of protecting the linguistic rights of the Sorbs.[44]

In Austria the Slovenians of Carinthia have faced a series of threats to the survival of their language since the Second World War, most notably industrialisation and migration to the towns and the indifferent – if not negative – attitude of the state towards them. As Carinthia is the least industrialised region of Austria, the main way of gaining material success lay in moving to industrial areas which, in most cases, 'is tantamount to Germanization, if not sooner then later'. Marriage to a monolingual German 'is of course a death-blow'. German-speaking industrialists, meanwhile, have deliberately discriminated against Slovene speakers and firms, which has further deterred people from speaking the language.

The attitude of the state has not always favoured the use of the Slovenian dialect, although legal guarantees exist for the protection of the language. The Austrian State Treaty, signed by Austria and the Allied war powers in 1955, protected the rights of Slovenians, as well as the Croats of Burgenland, to use their own language in the areas in which they lived. Along with German, Slovenian and Croatian became the official languages. Elementary schools would carry out instruction in the minority languages and some provision would be made at secondary level. Furthermore, road signs would appear in

41 Manuel Medina, 'Spain: Regional, Linguistic and Ideological Conflict', in W. A. Veenhoven et al. (eds), *Case Studies in Human Rights and Fundamental Freedoms: A World Survey*, Vol. 1 (The Hague, 1975), pp. 138, 143, 144–5; Miguel Siguan, *Linguistic Minorities in the European Economic Community: Spain, Portugal, Greece* (Luxemburg, 1990), pp. 11–15, 27–31, 39–41.
42 Meic Stephens, 'The North Frisians', in G. Ashworth (ed.), *World Minorities*, Vol. 2 (Sunbury, 1978), pp. 84–7.
43 Minority Rights Group, *Minorities and Autonomy in Western Europe*, p. 18.
44 Gerald Stone, *The Smallest Slavonic Nation: The Sorbs of Lusatia* (London, 1972), pp. 161–72; Minority Rights Group and TWEEC, *Minorities in Central and Eastern Europe*, p. 33.

both German and Slovenian or Croatian. Further measures aimed at protecting the linguistic rights of the two minorities were passed at either the local or national level. Some of the educational provisions were implemented, but the number of pupils attending Slovenian bilingual schools declined from the end of the 1940s, and by the early 1980s only about 50,000 people still spoke Slovenian. The state did very little to put up bilingual road signs in Carinthia until 1972, but as soon as they went up German nationalists defaced or removed them, which resulted in the federal chancellor, Bruno Kreisky, ordering the uprooting of those which remained. The Croats of Burgenland, who have not been so assertive of their linguistic rights, have endured similar experiences to the Slovenes, with a decline in consciousness due to both economic and political reasons.[45]

In Czechoslovakia, Czechs and Slovaks spoke mutually intelligible languages, but the other main minorities had more distinct ones. In 1952 Hungarian became a second official language, along with Slovak, in areas of Slovakia with mixed populations. The number of Hungarian schools increased from 609, teaching 50,463 pupils in 1950, to reach a peak of 559, catering for 76,754 children in 1961, although this fell back to 257 institutions providing instruction for 48,405 individuals in 1990.[46] The Rusyns of north-eastern Slovakia represent a confusing group because they lack standardisation. This minority converses in its own dialect, which consists of western Ukrainian with differing degrees of Slovak influence in individual villages. Children learn standardised Ukrainian in minority schools.[47]

Shortly after the end of the War, in response to pressure from ethnic Hungarians in the state, the Hungarian minority in Romania enjoyed instruction in its own language from nursery to university level. But after the Hungarian uprising of 1956 the Hungarian school system in Romania came under threat, which meant that the proportion of children attending Hungarian-language schools declined from 8 per cent in 1955–6 to 5.5 per cent by 1974–5. A further decrease occurred during the 1980s, so that the number of Hungarian students educated in their own language fell from 171,924 in 1976 to 60,613

45 Österreichische Rektorenkonferenz, *Bericht der Arbeitsgruppe Lage und Perspektiven der Volksgruppen in Österreich* (Vienna, 1989), pp. 70–1; David F. Stermole, 'Some Factors Affecting the Maintenance of Bilingualism in Carinthia', *Papers in Slovene Studies* (1977), pp. 41–8; Drago Druškovic, *Carinthian Slovenes: Some Aspects of their Situation* (Ljubljana, 1973), pp. 27–34; Borut Bohe, 'International Law Aspects of the Position of the Slovene Minority in Austria', in Institute for Ethnic Problems (ed.), *Actual Questions of the Slovene and Croat Minorities in Austria* (Ljubljana, 1976), p. 10; Toussaint Hočevar, 'The Slovene and Croat Minorities in Italy and Austria', in Stephan M. Horak (ed.), *Eastern European National Minorities, 1919–1980: A Handbook* (Littleton, CO, 1985), pp. 259–60; Thomas M. Barker, *The Slovene Minority of Carinthia* (New York, 1984), pp. 241, 262, 265, 268.
46 SOS Transylvania, *Hungarian Minority in Czechoslovakia/Slovakia* (Bratislava, 1993), p. 9; Renner, 'National Minorities in Czechoslovakia', pp. 27–8; Josef Kalvoda, 'National Minorities Under Communism: The Case of Czechoslovakia', *Nationalities Papers* 16 (1988), p. 7.
47 Mykola Mušynka, 'The Postwar Development of the Regional Culture of the Rysyn-Ukrainians of Czechoslovakia', in Paul Robert Magocsi (ed.), *The Persistence of Regional Cultures: Rusyns and Ukrainians in Their Carpathian Homeland and Abroad* (New York, 1993), pp. 53–78; Magocsi, *The Rusyns of Slovakia: An Historical Survey* (Boulder, CO, 1993), pp. ix, 1.

ten years later. A limited improvement in this situation has taken place since the fall of Ceaucescu.[48]

In Yugoslavia, Serbo-Croat, which was standardised at the end of the nineteenth century, represented the dominant language. In addition, two further Slavic languages, Slovene and Macedonian, were used by large minorities, together with lesser ones: Ukrainian, Slovak, Czech, Bulgarian, Italian, Romanian, Albanian, Hungarian, Vlach and Turkish. Some of these had become highly standardised and literary, while others were used only on a local level and not written.[49] The language of Macedonia was created at the end of the Second World War, based upon spoken dialects in the area. The alphabet was ready in May 1945 and the first printer in the new language appeared in 1946.[50] All of the post-War Yugoslav constitutions recognised the equality of languages, although Serbo-Croat inevitably dominated.[51]

Language plays a large role in the basis of difference of Kurds in Turkey. Like the Greeks of Istanbul, the Kurds live in a state which displays hostility to their very presence. As a group without a nation state, spread over several already existing states, the Kurds are not standardised in terms of their language. They speak five major groups of dialects, which divide into regional sub-dialects, so that people from different parts of Kurdistan often cannot understand each other. The Turkish state banned the teaching of Kurdish in schools,[52] which has meant that many Kurds in Turkey can only speak Turkish.[53] Those Kurds who have moved westwards within Turkey have lost knowledge of whatever command they may have had of their own language and have become 'fully assimilated into Turkish society', recognised potentially only by a 'guttural accent' and a 'darker skin'.[54]

In the Soviet Union language represented the main signifier of difference. Not only did linguistic command form the basis of many of the ethnic groups identified by the Soviet censuses, the USSR had a great concern with literacy and virtually created new languages, often infused with Russian words. Together with the concern for minority languages went the spread of Russian, which became by far the most widely spoken language in the Soviet Union, pointing to a process of linguistic assimilation, as clear in this state as in any other within Europe.

---

48 Z. Michael Szaz, 'Contemporary Educational Policies in Transylvania', *East European Quarterly* 11 (1978), pp. 493–501; George Schöpflin and Hugh Poulton, *Romania's Ethnic Hungarians*, 2nd edn (London, 1990), pp. 12–13, 17, 20–1; Bennett Kovrig, 'The Magyars in Rumania: Problems of a "Coinhabiting" Nationality', *Südosteuropa* 35 (1986), pp. 481–3.

49 Albina Nečak Luk, 'The Linguistic Aspects of Ethnic Conflict in Yugoslavia', in Payam Akhavan and Robert Howse (eds), *Yugoslavia: The Former and the Future* (Washington, DC, 1995), pp. 112–20.

50 Hugh Poulton, *Who Are the Macedonians?* (London, 1995), p. 116.

51 K. Jancic, *The Relations Between Nationalities in Yugoslavia* (Belgrade, 1967), pp. 58–64.

52 Kendal, 'Kurdistan in Turkey', in G. Chaliand (ed.), *A People Without A Country: The Kurds and Kurdistan* (London, 1980), pp. 49–50; David McDowall, *The Kurds* (London, 1989), p. 7.

53 Michael Ignatieff, *Blood and Belonging: Journeys into the New Nationalism* (London, 1993), p. 137.

54 Jonathan Rugman and Roger Hutchings, *Atatürk's Children: Turkey and the Kurds* (London, 1996), p. 23.

The late Tsarist Empire operated on the principle of 'One emperor, one religion, one language'.[55] Only areas with limited local autonomy could use their own languages, including Poland, Finland and the Baltic provinces. Some languages were actually forbidden, including Ukrainian between 1876 and 1905.[56] However, the position of the Russian language remained weak within the Tsarist Empire because of the absence of educational provision capable of transferring it to minority peoples. In 1897 only 24 per cent of the population over the age of 9 were literate.[57] Consequently, vast numbers of people within the Russian Empire simply communicated in languages which they and their forefathers had used for hundreds or thousands of years.

The Bolsheviks believed in the equality of all languages and opposed the dominance of Russian. Lenin did not want to see any single state language. Instead, everyone would have the right to use their own language in both the private and public spheres, and would also receive education in this language. Consequently, on 31 October 1918 the Commissariat of the Enlightenment established a special section in order to develop schools using non-Russian languages.[58] The Soviet regime made great strides in this direction during the 1920s and 1930s. For instance, in 1927 93.9 per cent of Ukrainian pupils in the Ukraine attended elementary schools which taught in their own language, and by the middle of the 1930s native-language schools had opened in all regions of the USSR.[59]

However, at the same time as native languages were extended, so was Russification, a process actively pursued from the late 1930s and continued after the Second World War. In fact, Russification actually began in more subtle ways from the 1920s, caused by the absence of literary forms of some languages and by the transfer of some languages from an Arabic to a Roman or Cyrillic script, as well as the planting of Russian words in some of the old languages. Commissions of experts actually held congresses to decide linguistic matters. By the end of the 1930s, in keeping with a growing centralisation, a campaign had begun with the aim of introducing Russian-language teaching throughout the Soviet Union. Although Article 121 of the 1936 Soviet Constitution guaranteed citizens the right of school instruction in their own language, two years later the Council of People's Commissars passed a decree 'On the Obligatory Study of Russian Language in Schools in the National

---

55 Uriel Weinreich, 'The Russification of Soviet Minority Languages', *Problems of Communism* 2 (1953), p. 46.

56 Bernard Comrie, *The Languages of the Soviet Union* (Cambridge, 1981), p. 21.

57 Yaroslav Bilinsky, 'Education of the Non-Russian Peoples in the USSR, 1917–1967: An Essay', *Slavic Review* 27 (1968), p. 413.

58 Comrie, *Languages of the Soviet Union*, p. 22; Barbara A. Anderson and Brian D. Silver, 'Equality, Efficiency, and Politics in Soviet Bilingual Education Policy, 1934–1980', in Rachel Denber (ed.), *The Soviet Nationality Reader: The Disintegration in Context* (Boulder, CO, 1992), p. 355; Simon Crisp, 'Soviet Language Planning, 1917–53', in Michael Kirkwood (ed.), *Language Planning in the Soviet Union* (London, 1989), p. 23.

59 Bilinsky, 'Education of the Non-Russian Peoples', p. 418; Anderson and Silver, 'Equality, Efficiency, and Politics', p. 355.

Republics and Provinces', making the study of Russian compulsory in all non-Russian schools.[60]

After the Second World War the Soviet state basically pursued a policy of bilingualism, with an emphasis on Russian. The Education Law of 1959 allowed parents to choose their children's language of instruction and even to decide if they should receive tuition in their own language at all. In some instances this resulted in the disappearance of minority languages, such as Karelian. Some of the major languages, on the other hand, benefited from the 1959 legislation. Under Breshnev there developed the concept of Russian as the language of the Soviet people which would assist in the integration of minorities, a policy continued into the Gorbachev years.[61]

Soviet language planning had two clear but inevitable and contradictory results. On the one hand, minority languages survived and thrived in many cases, despite the disappearance of some. On the other hand, use of Russian clearly expanded. According to the census of 1970 the Soviet Union had 130 ethnic groupings who spoke 130 different languages, but with significant variations in the level of their development and the numbers of people who used them. Russian was the most advanced both in terms of the number of people who spoke it and with regard to its status as a literary language, forming the basis of a high culture which had developed over hundreds of years. In 1970 a total of 76 per cent of the population of the Soviet Union spoke Russian, Ukrainian or Belorussian. At the other extreme were more than 25 languages with less than 10,000 speakers, including over ten which counted less than a hundred. Only 96 people spoke Aleut while just one used Kasmar. Between 1934 and 1980 a total of 83 languages had been used in schools at some stage of the educational process. Those groupings which did not receive instruction in their own tongue lived either in the Far North or the Caucasus.[62]

Russian dominated: in 1970, although Russians themselves made up 53.7 per cent of the total population, 58.6 per cent classed it as their native language, which meant that 13 million Soviet citizens viewed themselves as having non-Russian ethnic origin but used Russian as their main means of communication.[63] They included migrants to urban areas who had adopted Russian, individuals who had married a Russian and their children, and those whose parents had sent them to a Russian rather than a native-language school.[64] The

60 Crisp, 'Soviet Language Planning', pp. 24–41; Anderson and Silver, 'Equality, Efficiency, and Politics', p. 356; Anderson and Silver, 'Some Factors in the Linguistic and Ethnic Russification of Soviet Nationalities: Is Everyone Becoming Russian?', in Lubomyr Hajda and Mark Beissinger (eds), *The Nationalities Question in Soviet Politics and Society* (Boulder, CO, 1990), pp. 46–54.
61 Isabelle T. Kreindler, 'Soviet Language Planning Since 1953', in Kirkwood, *Language Planning in the Soviet Union*, pp. 46–59; Anderson and Silver, 'Equality, Efficiency, and Politics', p. 356.
62 E. Glyn Lewis, *Multilingualism in the Soviet Union: Aspects of Language Policy and Its Implementation* (The Hague, 1972); Comrie, *Languages of the Soviet Union*, pp. 1, 10, 15, 279–81; Anderson and Silver, 'Equality, Efficiency, and Politics', p. 365.
63 Comrie, *Languages of the Soviet Union*, p. 1.
64 Brian D. Silver, 'The Status of National Minority Languages in Soviet Education: An Assessment of Recent Changes', *Soviet Studies* 26 (1974), p. 38.

1989 census also revealed that 48.1 per cent of Soviet citizens claimed Russian as their second language. In contrast, in both 1970 and 1979 only 3 per cent of people who claimed fluency in a second language did so in anything other than Russian.[65]

In a situation typical of the whole of Europe, different languages were used in particular circumstances. In the case of languages such as Aleut, spoken by small numbers of people, with no literary form, these are simply used in social situations. Most languages spoken by a significant number of people have a literary form.[66] The larger languages, with some sort of ethnic political units connected to them, tended to dominate in these particular areas.[67] In 1970 most of the republics counted over 85 per cent of their populations claiming the ethnic language of their territories as their main means of communication.[68] This applied right up to university level in republics with a tradition of higher education in their native tongue, although in some subjects and republics Russian played a significant role at this level.[69] Only Russian amongst Soviet languages 'has the additional function of being a lingua franca between speakers of a sizeable number of different languages, and of being used in relations with countries other than the USSR'.[70]

Language clearly played a central role in perpetuating difference in the Soviet Union. While Russification of languages took place to some extent and while Russian may have come to dominate as the main means of communication between different groupings, Soviet linguistic policy had at least as many positive as negative effects for the minority languages within its borders. Individual examples illustrate these processes. Ukrainian was the second most widely spoken language in the Soviet Union. Like many European languages, it did not actually emerge in a literary form until the nineteenth century. When the Bolsheviks came to power, they found that the population of the Ukraine tended to speak dialects and that various forms of literary Ukrainian existed according to geographical location. In 1925 the Council of People's Commissars of the Ukrainian Republic issued a decree for the standardisation of the spelling system.[71] By the 1979 census 89.1 per cent of the 36,488,951 Ukrainians living within their own republic declared Ukrainian as their mother tongue, with a further 10.9 per cent regarding Russian as their main means of communication. In contrast, of the 10,471,602 Russians living in the Ukraine, just 1.3 per cent described Ukrainian as their native language. Furthermore, as

65 J. Pool, 'Soviet Language Planning: Goals, Results, Options', in J. R. Azrael (ed.), *Soviet Nationality Policies and Practices* (New York, 1978), p. 223; Anderson and Silver, 'Some Factors in Linguistic and Ethnic Russification', p. 96.
66 Comrie, *Languages of the Soviet Union*, p. 27.
67 Viktor Kozlov, *The Peoples of the Soviet Union* (London, 1988), p. 179.
68 Lewis, *Multilingualism in the Soviet Union*, pp. 132–4.
69 Rasma Karklins, 'Ethnic Politics and Access to Higher Education: The Soviet Case', *Comparative Politics* 16 (1994), pp. 285–6.
70 Comrie, *Languages of the Soviet Union*, p. 28.
71 David Saunders, 'What Makes a Nation a Nation? Ukrainians Since 1600', *Ethnic Studies* 10 (1993), p. 115; James Dingley, 'Ukrainian and Belorussian: A Testing Ground', in Kirkwood, *Language Planning in the Soviet Union*, pp. 174–85.

early as 1959, out of 5.1 million Ukrainians who resided outside their own republic, 3.3 million (or 53.3 per cent) viewed Russian as their native language, due to a lack of Ukrainian language provision outside their titular republic. The language of instruction in schools within the Ukraine reflected the inroads made by Russian during the last decades of the Soviet Union, due to a combination of economic, demographic and political factors.[72] Even by 1996, five years after independence, the Russian language had not been undermined in the new Ukrainian state.[73]

In the Soviet Far North, the use of native languages declined. Following the Soviet pattern, some education occurred in native languages during the interwar years, but the post-War period witnessed an increasing tendency towards Russification. During the 1950s a growth occurred in the number of hours of Russian-language teaching. In areas with small class sizes or in cases where no literary language existed, native teaching ceased. Furthermore, pupils were punished if they used their own language at school and parents were told to speak Russian with their children at home. By 1970 only one out of 26 languages of the north, Nenets, was used for instruction in schools. The situation did not improve under Gorbachev and Yeltsin due to the lack of people available to teach some of the languages.[74]

Immigrants usually speak a different language from the citizens of the states into which they move. They strive to maintain their own language, but they are really fighting a losing battle. They have greater difficulties in obtaining concessions than the longer-standing minorities, because their more recent arrival means that they have less of a power base. Living in an urban environment, newcomers are forced to use the language of their new country in order simply to communicate in everyday matters. Ethnic ghettoisation can help to preserve the original language, especially in the case of women who often do not venture out of their area of residence.

Even if the first generation manages to preserve the use of their own language (which usually happens), problems arise for the second generation. While they probably continue speaking their parents' language when conversing with them, the use of their mother tongue may stop at the boundaries of the parental home. Once they enter the surrounding streets they find themselves confronted by a foreign language, which provides the means of instruction in the schools they attend, as well as the means of communication with their friends, either of their own ethnic group, the dominant society, or of other minorities. With the progression of time, more and more phrases of the surrounding national language move into the minority tongues – destined, eventually, to wipe them out, unless the state displays a willingness to support

72 Borys Lewytzkys, *Politics and Society in the Soviet Ukraine, 1953–1980* (Edmonton, 1984), pp. 179–90.
73 *Independent on Sunday*, 28 April 1996.
74 Nikolai Vakhtin, *Native Peoples of the Far North* (London, 1992), pp. 18, 31–2; K. E. Kuoljok, *Revolution in the North: Soviet Ethnography and Nationality Policy* (Uppsala, 1985), pp. 59–61, 142–3.

them. The provision of privately financed language schools by the minority community provides some support for the immigrant language.

Most migrants in Germany during the 1960s had a poor command of German and continued to use their own language. In the early 1970s only 7 per cent of Turks and 5 per cent of Portuguese described their command of German as 'very good'. Ten years later over 50 per cent of Turks, Spaniards and Italians still spoke bad German. As with all immigrants, those in Germany used their own language in their 'ghettos' and with their families, but conversed in German when dealing with Germans or members of other minority groups.[75] In addition, 'the Turkish language in Germany has incorporated many German terms', so that problems may arise when a Turk born in Germany converses with a native of Turkey. For example:

> On bidding farewell and on concluding a telephone conversation, many Turks now use the German 'Tshcüß' (bye-bye) instead of the Turkish 'hoscakal' or 'allahaismarladik'. This can cause friction. If for instance the custom of saying 'Tshcüß' is adopted at the end of a telephone call to Turkey, it may be understood to mean 'Tscüsch' – 'you donkey' and cause offence.[76]

Amongst Greek Cypriots in Britain everyday discourse, involving the first generation speaking with each other or with their children, takes place in the Greek Cypriot dialect, but when dealing with people from Greece, of which small numbers reside in Britain, the immigrants speak Standard Modern Greek, the national language of Greece and Cyprus. Similarly, newspapers and radio broadcasts use the latter language. In many cases the second generation has difficulties in conversing in Standard Modern Greek and often find themselves having spoken command of the Cyprus dialect and speaking English with a London accent. The Greek Cypriot dialect in London also adopts English words and phrases. For instance, *'ennen to kapof tinmou'*: a person from mainland Greece would never understand this, which is a corruption of the English phrase, 'he isn't my cup of tea'. These developments have taken place despite the provision of evening and Saturday schools for the children and grandchildren of Greek Cypriot immigrants, which would only teach Standard Modern Greek. By the middle of the 1960s Cypriot evening schools existed in every area of London, and a decade later over half the parents in the small Cypriot community in Manchester sent their children to Greek school. Such schools, which still survive, are usually run by churches or parents' organisations.[77]

75 Clemens Amelunxen, 'Foreign Workers in West Germany', in Veenhoven, *Case Studies in Human Rights*, pp. 121–2; Barbara von Breitenbach, *Italiener und Spanier als Arbeitnehmer in der Bundesrepublik Deutschland* (Munich, 1982), pp. 61–7.
76 Darsun Tan and Hans-Peter Waldhoff, 'Turkish Everyday Culture in Germany and its Prospects', in David Horrocks and Eva Kolinsky (eds), *Turkish Culture in German Society Today* (Oxford, 1996), pp. 146–7.
77 Evienia Papadaki and Maria Roussou, 'The Greek Speech Community', in Safder Allandina and Viv Edwards (eds), *Multilingualism in the British Isles: The Older Mother Tongues and Europe* (London, 1991), pp. 189–201; Vic George and Geoffrey Millerson, 'The Cypriot Community in London', *Race* 8 (1967), p. 291; Vasoulla Psarias, 'Greek Cypriot Immigration in Greater Manchester' (University of Bradford PhD thesis, 1979), p. 210.

RELIGION

The ethnicity of most groups in Europe evolves from a combination of appearance, language and religion, but in some cases the latter of these factors proves more important than the others. Jews and Muslims fit into this category. In the case of Islam this applies to both long-established settlers in Europe, as well as post-War arrivals. The former often speak the language of the population which surrounds them, while the latter usually do not. Religion plays a large role in particular areas of Europe, notably the Balkans and Northern Ireland, although in both of these cases it has become completely politicised.

Clearly, all major religions in Europe are, to a greater or lesser extent, institutionalised. Their survival depends upon two major factors: first, the extent to which twentieth-century secularisation undermines them; and, second, the attitude of the state, especially under the old order in the eastern bloc, and, even in the west, the freedom given to instruction in minority faiths in schools, also plays a role in this process.

Jewish survival has been threatened in numerous ways during the course of the twentieth century. Apart from the consequences of Nazi anti-semitism, Jewish numbers have also lessened due to low fertility rates and marriage with gentiles. In addition, in an increasing age of secularism, Jews have moved away from their religion at the same rate as the dominant populations. Finally, in some cases, more direct pressure – especially in overtly atheist eastern Europe – has also led many Jews to abandon their religion.

The experiences of the largest post-War European Jewish community, in the Soviet Union, best illustrate the above processes in action. The Bolsheviks viewed Judaism as a set of irrational beliefs rooted in the pre-socialist period which had made life tolerable for those who had to live in class society, whether feudal or capitalist. Religion 'must disappear in the conditions of the rational society which will provide fully for the needs of the human personality'.[78] Although the Soviet Union pursued various policies to hasten the disappearance of Judaism, it continued to recognise the Jews as a minority until its collapse, when just under 1.5 million people declared themselves as part of this group. Many of these viewed themselves as Jews in a 'technical' sense rather than necessarily in a religious one, although all of those who declared themselves Jewish would have Jewish ancestry. However, many other people, such as the children of mixed marriages, tended not to declare themselves Jews. In traditional Jewish communities, the 'calendar, foods, dress, sexual mores, business ethics, leisure time activities and values of Jews were regulated by religious law, one that encompasses all aspects of life'.[79] In this situation, which prevailed in the Tsarist period and into the years after 1917, Jews

---

78 Jacob Miller, 'Soviet Theory on the Jews', in Lionel Kochan (ed.), *The Jews in the Soviet Union* (Oxford, 1978), p. 48.
79 Zvi Gitelman, 'Power, Culture and Ethnicity: The Soviet Jewish Experience', in Pierre L. van den Berghe (ed.), *State, Violence and Ethnicity* (Niviot, CO, 1990), p. 75.

clearly practised their religion, attended their own schools and spoke their own Yiddish language. After 1917, Judaism also became more of a cultural phenomenon, with a development of theatre, writing and newspapers.

In purely religious terms, Judaism certainly declined under the Soviet Union due to secularisation, anti-semitism and exogamy. The decrease in the number of synagogues, due mostly to the anti-religious policies practised by the state, best indicates the decline in religious observance. 'Before 1917 there were religious institutions in every little *shtetl*: synagogues and prayer houses, religious schools, Talmudic academies, rabbinical courts and so on.' But from 1918, 'the Soviet authorities began a campaign aimed at closing synagogues and suppressing Jewish religious life'.[80] By the late 1940s around 200 synagogues operated in the Soviet Union and by the end of the Stalin period this had fallen to about 130. In addition, believers would also pray together in unofficial *minyanim* in private apartments in smaller towns.[81] Only 92 synagogues survived until 1976, together with 'several score' unofficial communities. By this time only 50,000 religious Jews may have lived in the USSR.[82] Religious adherence increased under Gorbachev, indicated by the importation of kosher food supplies. More importantly, the all-Union law on religion of October 1990 allowed freedom of worship outside specified locations,[83] a situation which has continued in the post-Soviet states – although, as well as releasing religious feeling, the collapse of the USSR has also witnessed a rise in anti-semitism.

Negative attitudes also faced post-Holocaust survivors elsewhere in eastern Europe. In Poland, strong state and popular anti-semitism, combined with increasing secularisation, made the survival of the Jewish religion difficult. Many of the 10,000 Jews who remained in the country after 1970 were Jewish more in terms of their nationality than their religion. Nevertheless, immediately after 1945, when the Jewish community reached its largest post-War extent of over 200,000, local Jewish committees developed in 235 cities, towns and villages, including Lodz, Cracow, Warsaw, Bialystock, Wroclaw and Sceczin. Many of these had schools offering instruction in Yiddish or Hebrew, or providing religious teaching. Furthermore, Polish Jewry constructed facilities for orphans, the aged, the sick and the homeless. Nevertheless, anti-semitic violence immediately after the War, as well as the temptations of Israel and the memory of the Holocaust, caused Jews to stream out of Poland, so that the 235 Jewish committees of 1945–6 had declined to 135 by 1947.[84] More recently,

80 Zev Katz, 'The Jews in the Soviet Union', in Zev Katz, Rosemarie Rogers and Frederic Harned (eds), *Handbook of Major Soviet Nationalities* (New York, 1975), p. 369.

81 Yaacov Ro'i, 'The Jewish Religion in the Soviet Union After World War II', in Ro'i (ed.), *Jews and Jewish Life in Russia and the Soviet Union* (London, 1995), pp. 264–8.

82 Lukasz Hirszowicz, 'Jewish Cultural Life in the USSR: A Survey', *Soviet Jewish Affairs* 7 (1977), p. 11.

83 Yoram Golozki, 'The Jews', in Graham Smith (ed.), *The Nationalities Question in the Post-Soviet States* (London, 1996), p. 445.

84 Lucjan Dobroszycki, 'Restoring Jewish Life in Post-War Poland', *Soviet Jewish Affairs* 3 (1973), pp. 65–6.

those Jews who survived into the 1980s organised themselves into eighteen religious organisations.[85]

For most of the post-War period, Hungary had the largest Jewish population in eastern Europe outside the Soviet Union, with a figure which totals around 100,000.[86] Although anti-semitism has surfaced since 1945, Hungarian minority policy during the communist era ensured that Jewish life continued. In 1948 the Jewish community leaders signed an agreement with the Hungarian government which allowed Jews freedom of worship, the right to operate a small number of schools with government support, as well as the right to maintain synagogues and to train rabbis. In return, the Jewish leaders pledged their loyalty to the state and the constitution. The more general policy of the Ministry of Education toward minorities also assisted the formation of Jewish schools. Hungary had the only rabbinical college in the Soviet bloc countries in the form of the National Theological Seminary.[87] Thirty synagogues held services in Budapest during the 1970s and the city also contained ten kosher butchers, a Jewish high school, a hospital and an orphanage.[88] However, large-scale assimilation occurred due to a combination of demographic, economic and political factors. Many Hungarian Jews took measures such as name changing in an attempt to deny their Jewish origins. One survey revealed that only 7 out of 117 Hungarian Jews interviewed had maintained Jewish traditions during the 1980s.[89]

The Jewish communities of Yugoslavia also continued to practise their religion after the Second World War, even though they became more and more secular. By the late 1970s less than 7,000 Jews lived in the country within 36 Jewish communities. Although Jewish weddings did not occur and religious practices were played down, the major Jewish holidays and customs were observed, especially by the older generation, who also attended synagogue services. In addition, the Jewish community carried out the traditional aid to the sick and poor members of its community. Its most significant body in this context consisted of a Home for the Aged in Zagreb.[90]

The two major Jewish minorities in the west, in France and Britain, have had slightly more success in maintaining their religious and educational activity than their brethren in the eastern half of the continent, despite the economic

---

85 Kenneth C. Farmer et al., 'National Minorities in Poland', in Horak, *Eastern European Minorities*, p. 57.
86 Thomas Tucker, 'Political Transition and the "Jewish Question" in Hungary Today', *Ethnic and Racial Studies* 19 (1996), p. 291.
87 Crowe, 'Minorities in Hungary Since 1948', pp. 25–8.
88 Bernard Wasserstein, *Vanishing Diaspora: The Jews in Europe Since 1945* (London, 1996), p. 208.
89 András Kovács, 'Changes in Jewish Identity in Modern Hungary', in Jonathan Webber (ed.), *Jewish Identities in the New Europe* (London, 1994), pp. 153–60.
90 Daniel Elazar et al., *The Balkan Jewish Communities: Yugoslavia, Bulgaria, Greece and Turkey* (Lanham, MD, 1984), pp. 12, 16–17, 41; Hariet Pass Freidenreich, *The Jews of Yugoslavia: A Quest for Community* (Philadelphia, 1979), pp. 194, 197–201. For an updated account see Paul Benjamin Gordiejew, *Voices of Yugoslav Jewry* (Albany, NY, 1999), who brings out the above themes and devotes much attention to 'secular' and 'submerged' Jewishness.

and demographic assimilatory pressures which they face. France has both Sephardic and Ashkenazi communities. The former is slightly more devout than the latter, partly because of its regeneration with new blood as a result of immigration from North Africa. These newcomers re-established Jewish communities in southern France which had disappeared two centuries previously, as well as founding new ones in other cities in the south of the country. An increase has occurred in enrolment in Jewish primary and secondary schools. In addition, during the 1980s adults also attended reading classes led by rabbis in increasing numbers. However, Jewish attendance at religious services has been low since the end of the Second World War. During the 1970s nearly one-third of Jews never attended synagogues at all, while only one-third did so on Yom Kippur, the holiest day in the Jewish calendar. Only 10.5 per cent went to synagogues on a regular basis. Sephardic Jews scored higher percentages than their Ashkenazi counterparts in these figures.[91] Some very devout Jews continue to live in France as the example of the following 40-year-old school teacher, interviewed in the late 1970s, indicates:

> On Shabbat we don't drive, we don't light fires, we don't turn on the lights, and we don't drive. On Friday we have a family dinner. We may play chess or checkers. For me it's really a family holiday. The next day we go to services, which last two and half or three hours. When we come back we have lunch. In the afternoon the children go to school. They go to Bar Yohiai. Then we all meet again at afternoon services. We may also go to what is called seder, a community meal where problems are discussed. In the evening we return home. So you see, on Shabbat life is quite full, both in family and in the community – speaking of course, about those who want to participate in Shabbat activities.[92]

The Jewish community in England also has divisions within it, from the conservative Orthodox to the reform and liberal communities. About 90 per cent of Jewish households are actually affiliated to a synagogue, although this does not reflect the levels of attendance. Surveys carried out in the London areas of Edgware in 1969 and Redbridge in 1983 revealed that only 10 and 13.6 per cent respectively of mainstream Orthodox Jews attended synagogues on a regular basis. By the end of the 1980s synagogue affiliation was increasing for extreme Orthodox Jews and decreasing for the Central Orthodox and Sephardic communities, leading to the development of a polarised Jewish population in Britain, in which the mainstream and Sephardic communities declined in their religious observance, while the extreme Orthodox increased in theirs.[93]

91 Dominique Schnapper, 'Israelites and Juifs: New Jewish Identities in France', in Webber, Jewish Identities in the New Europe, pp. 173–4; Wasserstein, Vanishing Diaspora, pp. 246–7.
92 Dominique Schnapper, Jewish Identities in France: An Analysis of Contemporary French Jewry (Chicago, 1983), p. 5.
93 V. D. Lipman, A History of the Jews in Britain Since 1858 (Leicester, 1990), pp. 240–1; Stephen H. Miller, 'Religious Practice and Jewish Identity in a Sample of London Jews', in Webber, Jewish Identities, pp. 192–204.

European Jewry, faced by a combination of assimilatory pressures, has clearly witnessed a decline in its basic religious values, most clearly indicated in a fall in religious observance. While this may have been most obvious in the overtly atheist society in the Soviet Union, the secular western European states experienced similar developments in terms of a decline in the level of Jewish devoutness. While we must bear in mind the economic pressures for assimilation, as well as declining birth rates, the lack of overt discrimination has also assisted in the process. Before the Nazis, the level of anti-semitism actually assisted in the survival of Jewish life in Europe. Apart from anything else, Judeophobia forced people back on to their own religion. In contrast the more subtle methods of conformity expected in post-War Europe, especially in the western liberal democracies, has assisted in the assimilation process. By assimilating, Jews have not disappeared altogether but have, instead, imitated the dominant grouping in the states in which they live.

In many ways, despite the basic theological difference, a devout Muslim resembles a devout Jew in the sense that a true adherence to that religion requires more than simply attending a mosque, but further involves controlled eating, wearing particular types of dress, leading family life according to Muslim law – which would influence all aspects of life – and following the five pillars of Islam, consisting of the profession of faith, praying five times a day, almsgiving, fasting during Ramadan and making a pilgrimage to Mecca. As in the case of Jews and Christians, Muslims have, over the centuries, divided into different sects, which lay varying degrees of stress on adherence to the above principles. In reality, in any part of post-War Europe, including Islamic areas of the Soviet Union, strict adherence to all aspects of the Muslim religion has been rare – if not impossible – especially with increasing secularisation and despite religious revival. However, the various Islamic communities in the Balkans and the Soviet Union have, to varying degrees, maintained many aspects of their formalised religion, despite (or perhaps because of) the negative and often hostile attitudes of the Christian or atheist states in which they live.

Bulgaria provides a good illustration of the dependence of Muslims upon the state. The 1947 constitution guaranteed all citizens freedom of conscience and religion. According to government sources, in 1951 the country contained 1,460 mosques with 1,850 imams. In 1952 the Bulgarian authorities banned the teaching of the Koran. During the 1960s and 1970s the state further forbade the printing or importation of the Koran, as well as prohibiting religious instruction in schools and outlawing circumcision. Furthermore, Islamic funerals were prohibited on 'health grounds' and some Turkish graveyards were destroyed. The number of imams had declined to 500 by 1985, while mosques had also decreased in number since the 1940s. Some improvements did occur in the position of the Bulgarian Turks and their religion during the 1990s. The 1991 constitution declared Eastern Orthodox Christianity as the traditional religion but also guaranteed freedom of religion to minorities, which meant the opening of new Islamic schools. The Muslim population emerged as more devout than other Bulgarians in the post-communist order.[94]

Religion formed the basis of politics throughout the history of Yugoslavia, with some spiritual foundation, as the case of Islam illustrates. All of the post-War Yugoslav constitutions guaranteed the right of religious freedom, although the state went down the path of increasing secularisation. In 1992 Hadji Jakub Effendi Selimovski, the spiritual leader of Yugoslav Muslims, as head of the Yugoslav Islamic Community, pointed to widespread absenteeism from mosques, affecting two-thirds of the Muslim population.[95] Yugoslavia did in fact have large numbers of mosques and other religious buildings in its Muslim areas throughout its history. While some of these existed before the Second World War, 400 new mosques were built between 1945 and 1985, while a further 380 underwent renovation. According to the 1981 census the country contained 1,985 mosques, 715 medžids (or smaller places of worship), 439 places for religious instruction and 3 religious schools. In 1980 approximately 120,000 children received Islamic religious instruction at primary-school level. In addition, every Muslim town or village had a separate graveyard for Muslims. Islam was more revisionist in Yugoslavia than in other states, evidenced by the appearance of female imams during the 1980s.[96]

The position of the Turkish minority in Western Thrace – in terms of its ability to practise its own religion and carry out the education of its children – has depended upon the attitude of the Greek state since the signing of the Treaty of Lausanne in 1923, the provisions of which applied equally to the Muslims in Western Thrace and the Greek communities in Constantinople, Imbros and Tendos. Article 38 guaranteed freedom of religion and movement.[97] During some periods, such as 1930–55, the Greek state has generally respected these terms,[98] but since then the position of the Turkish minority in Western Thrace, like that of Greeks in Turkey, has progressed on an irreversible downward path, closely connected with the deterioration of relations between the two states over the Cyprus issue.

The early 1950s therefore represent a healthy period for the Muslims of Western Thrace. During this time 259 mosques existed in the area. They were administered by about 400 officials of various types, while the number of active preachers stood at 30. A total of 279 Muslim primary schools existed

94 *The Turkish Minority in the People's Republic of Bulgaria* (Sofia, 1951), pp. 53–5; Helsinki Watch, *Destroying Ethnic Identity: The Turks of Bulgaria* (New York, 1986), pp. 12, 13, 14; Firoze Yasemee, 'The Turkic Peoples of Bulgaria', in M. Bainbridge (ed.), *The Turkic Peoples of the World* (London, 1993), pp. 48–50; Farzana Shaikh, *Islam and Islamic Groups: A Worldwide Reference Guide* (Harlow, 1992), p. 39; Wolfgang Höpken, 'From Religious Identity to Ethnic Mobilization: The Turks of Bulgaria before, under and since Communism', in Hugh Poulton and Suha Taji-Farouki (eds), *Muslim Identity and the Balkan State* (London, 1997), pp. 65, 75.
95 Shaikh, ibid., p. 282.
96 S. P. Ramet, 'Islam in Yugoslavia Today', *Religion in Communist Lands* 18 (1990), pp. 228–9, 233.
97 J. M. Wagstaff, 'The Turkish Speaking People of Greece', in Bainbridge, *Turkic Peoples of the World*, p. 137.
98 Tozun Bahcheli, *Greek–Turkish Relations Since 1955* (Boulder, CO, 1990), p. 171.

by the middle of the 1950s, as well as two religious schools and a gymnasium. During the 1954–5 school year 13,478 pupils attended the primary schools, 145 went to the religious schools and 137 were pupils at the gymnasium. A total of 385 teachers taught the Turkish language while 190 Greek teachers also worked in them. But few Turks made it to university in Greece and in many instances had to find a place in higher education in Turkey.[99]

By the 1980s the religious and educational life of Muslims in Western Thrace had witnessed a deterioration from the relatively secure position of the 1950s, although in terms of the numbers of mosques and schools little change had actually taken place in the intervening three decades. For instance, 250 mosques still existed. While a few had actually been pulled down, many others had simply fallen out of use. In addition, 279 primary schools had survived as well as two private gymnasia and two theological colleges. The Turks of Western Thrace have lived in a state which is reluctant to make even paltry concessions. This minority, like the Greek minority of Constantinople, is a political football in diplomatic relations between Greece and Turkey.[100]

The institutions of Muslims in the Soviet Union had faced devastation under inter-war Stalinism. After that time some rebuilding of formal religion occurred. From 1941 four territorially organised Spiritual Directorates controlled the lives of Soviet Muslims. These covered the following: the Sunni Muslims of European Russia and Siberia; Sunni Muslims of Central Asia and Kazakhstan; Sunni Muslims of the Northern Caucasus and Dagestan; and Sunni and Shiite Muslims of Transcaucasia. These bureaucratic bodies essentially acted as intermediary organisations controlling relations between the Muslim populations and the Soviet state. Religious education was forbidden in state schools. In addition, during the early post-War period, only one institution for the training of functionaries existed in Bukhara in Uzbekistan, which, having faced closure during the inter-war years, re-opened in 1952. By 1992 about twelve seminaries were functioning under the Tashkent Spiritual Directorate. The number of mosques in the Soviet Union totalled around 2,000 in 1947 and in 1955 the Spiritual Directorates had a record 8,052 registered mullah. By 1976 only about 300 mosques still existed, although a further 700 may have functioned unofficially. Their number increased subsequently and in 1986 a total of 751 Muslim communities were active in the USSR. In addition, the last decades of the Soviet Union also saw the growth of unofficial secret Sufi brotherhoods, which opposed both the Soviet Union and the Spiritual Directorates.

In concrete terms, the practice of Islam for Muslims in the Soviet Union lessened. Praying five times a day became a problem because it clashed with working hours, while attendance at Friday worship declined for the same

---

99 K. G. Andreades, *The Moslem Minority in Western Thrace* (Thesaloniki, 1956), pp. 11, 18; Isma'il Balic, 'Muslims in Greece', *Islamic Review* 40 (1952), pp. 35–6; Ümit Halûk Bayülken, 'Turkish Minorities in Greece', *Turkish Yearbook of International Relations* 4 (1963), p. 155.
100 International Affairs Agency, *The Western Thrace Turks Issue in Turkish–Greek Relations* (Istanbul, 1992), pp. 58, 80–1; Wagstaff, 'The Turkish-Speaking People of Greece', pp. 138–41; Bahcheli, *Greek–Turkish Relations Since 1955*, pp. 180–1; F. de Jong, 'The Muslim Minority in Western Thrace', in G. Ashworth (ed.), *World Minorities*, Vol. 3 (Sunbury, 1980), p. 98.

reason, meaning mostly old people went to the religious gatherings. Pilgrimage to Mecca became virtually impossible so that only about 500 Soviet citizens made this journey between 1945 and the middle of the 1960s. The Soviet authorities further prohibited almsgiving. Profession of faith could be made in private away from the eyes of the state.[101]

Of the individual Muslim groups in the Soviet Union, the Tatars managed to preserve traces of their religion from the birth of the Soviet Union until its death. Despite the anti-religious propaganda which circulated and the more direct state policies, up to '50 per cent of them practised their religion in one way or another, in spite of the proportion of firm believers being only 20 per cent'. Religion became less important for those Tatars who had moved into urban environments, especially in Slavic areas.[102] After the collapse of the Soviet Union, organised religion reasserted itself. In the Crimea, for instance, the Tatar community restored some of the mosques destroyed during the Soviet period – despite a shortage of funding – and also elected a traditional Muslim leader, or mufti.[103]

The post-War immigrants into western Europe have established Islam in this half of the continent for the first time. In Britain, as in most other western European states, they divide into a series of groups. The largest of these in terms of geographical origin arrived from South Asia – more specifically Pakistan, Bangladesh and India, especially Gujarat. The 1991 census, which counted 1,133,000 Muslims, gave a figure of 476,000 Pakistanis, 160,000 Bangladeshis and 134,000 Indians. In addition, it also pointed to 43,000 Muslims from Malaya, 134,000 of Arab origin, 26,000 Turks, 45,000 Turkish Cypriots and 115,000 Sub-Saharan Africans.

Muslims in Britain, wherever they have originated, have continued to practise their religion, although some groups are more devout than others. The first mosque in England actually appeared in Woking in 1889, but the post-War immigration has led to an increase in numbers from just 5 in 1966 to 452 by 1990, with different Muslim sects responsible for individual buildings, although, in addition, groups of people often hold religious services in houses.

After settling into the country for several decades, Muslims began to demonstrate concern about the education of their children, especially after the passage of the 1988 Education Reform Act. This re-introduced Christian assembly and Christian religious education into schools. Muslim parents had to write to the headteacher informing him or her that they did not wish their children to attend such assembly and education. Muslim organisations quickly established fifteen independent Muslim schools. The first two attempts to set up state-funded Muslim schools – like the 4,500 Jewish and Christian schools in

101 The above account comes from: Alexandre Bennigsen and Chantal Lemercier-Quelquejay, *Islam in the Soviet Union* (London, 1967), pp. 171–95; Bohdan R. Bociurkiw, 'Nationalities and Soviet Religious Policies', in Hajda and Beissinger, *Nationalities Question*, p. 157; Pipes, 'Muslims of Soviet Central Asia', pp. 148–58; Shaikh, *Islam and Islamic Groups*, p. 58.
102 Alexandre Bennigsen and S. Embers Wimbush, *Muslims of the Soviet Empire: A Guide* (London, 1985), p. 238.
103 Edward J. Lazzerini, 'Crimean Tatars', in Smith, *Nationalities Question*, pp. 432–3.

the same position – resulted in failure, although another change in the law meant that Muslim schools began to receive central government support in 1998.[104]

Birmingham contains the second-largest Muslim population in Britain after London, originating mostly in Pakistan and counting 55 mosques in the middle of the 1980s, 45 of which were, naturally, concentrated in the main areas of immigrant settlement. Most of them consisted of converted terraced houses. As well as acting as centres for prayer, the larger ones also attracted up to 500 children to classes.[105] In Bradford, Muslim children had attended mosque schools after normal school hours from the early days of Pakistani immigration into the city.[106]

Because of the origin of its immigrants, France contains a greater number of Muslims than Britain, totalling about 3 million by the middle of the 1980s, which meant that Islam had become the second-largest religion in the country. By this time at least a thousand mosques existed in France, although because of the size of some of these places of worship and their location, the true figure might be considerably larger. Like British Muslims, French ones divide further into language, religion and nationality. Inevitably, because of the hostility they face and the increasingly secular society in which they live, some Muslims – especially those of the second generation – have felt ambivalent about their religion and have stopped practising it.

By the end of the 1980s the education of Muslim children had become a central issue on the French political scene. Although about a fifth of pupils in France attended schools jointly funded by the state and one of the other three large religions in France (Catholicism, Protestantism or Judaism), not a single Islamic institution of this type existed in the country at the start of the 1990s. Instead, schools situated in areas with heavy concentrations of immigrants usually offered some Arabic teaching as well as introducing pupils to the Islamic religion in classes often conducted by a local imam. By the early 1980s some children, both Muslim and non-Muslim, received instruction in their mother tongue in accordance with agreements signed between the French government and eight other states, whereby the latter provided funding for the teaching of their languages in French state primary schools. In addition, mosques also provided religious instruction for immigrant children.[107]

---

104 Jürgen S. Nielsen, *Muslims in Western Europe* (Edinburgh, 1995), pp. 39–59; Muhammad Anwar, 'Muslims in Britain', in Syed Z. Abedin and Ziauddin Sardar (eds), *Muslim Minorities in the West* (London, 1995), p. 40; Mohammad S. Raza, *Islam in Britain*, 2nd edn (Leicester, 1993), pp. 37–47; *The Times*, 10 January 1998.
105 Daniele Joly, 'Making a Place for Islam in British Society: Muslims in Birmingham', in Tomas Gerholm and Yngve Georg Lithman (eds), *The New Islamic Presence in Western Europe* (London, 1988), pp. 34–6.
106 Verity Saifullah Khan, 'The Pakistanis: Mirpuri Villagers at Home and in Bradford', in Watson, *Between Two Cultures*, pp. 83–5.
107 Alec G. Hargreaves, *Immigration, 'Race' and Ethnicity in Contemporary France* (London, 1995), p. 101; Olivier Roy, 'Islam in France: Religion, Ethnic Community or Social Ghetto?', in Bernard Lewis and Dominique Schnapper (eds), *Muslims in Europe* (London, 1994), p. 55; Rémy Leveau, 'The Islamic Presence in France', in Gerholm and Lithman, *New Islamic Presence*, pp. 111, 117–21; Nielsen, *Muslims in Western Europe*, pp. 15, 20–1.

Islam made its first significant appearance in Germany as a result of the post-War labour importation, especially of Turks. By the middle of the 1990s about 1.7 million Muslims lived in the country, of whom 75 per cent consisted of Turks. Arabs and people from former Yugoslavia each counted more than 100,000 adherents of Islam. About 30 per cent of the total Muslim population regularly practises its religion, but only 22 per cent attends mosques. About half of the Muslims in Germany are indifferent to their faith.[108] Mosques were established in Germany from the 1950s, but those connected with the foreign worker influx only began in the 1960s, often in flats; since then minarets have been constructed. A city like Duisburg had 30 mosques in 1987. By this time these places of worship divided along national and religious lines throughout the country.[109]

In 1991 the Netherlands contained about 405,000 Muslims, made up mostly of Turks, Moroccans and Surinamese. The Dutch government actually constructed the first mosque in the country for Muslim Moluccans in Balk, in Friesland, in 1953. When foreign workers arrived from Turkey and Morocco during the 1960s they usually set aside a room in their boarding-houses for worship up to five times a day and would assemble there on Fridays as long as working hours allowed them to do so. These workers also obtained halal meat and fasted during Ramadan, even while they worked. After the arrival of families during the 1970s, children received religious instruction from an imam, financed, in the Turkish case, by the homeland government. People also began praying in halls, of which about 160 existed in the country by 1983, although only four properly constructed mosques functioned by this time. By 1989 the number of mosques and prayer halls had reached about 300, spread over 100 urban locations throughout the country.[110]

In addition to the two major non-Christian minority religions in Europe, various types of Christians have found themselves as minorities throughout the continent, some of long standing and others who have arrived since 1945. They have faced the same problems as Islam and Judaism in the form of increasing secularisation as well as indifference and even hostility from the state.

Northern Ireland represents one area where differing forms of Christianity represent the fundamental basis of difference – although it has become so politicised that the concepts of Protestant and Catholic seem to have developed into simply symbolic phrases in a struggle for the north-eastern corner of Ireland. Nevertheless, religious attendance in the province has remained at a much higher level than it has in the rest of Europe. In 1968, 95 per cent of Catholics went to church at least once a week, three times higher than Catholics in France or Austria, while 46 per cent of Protestants attended services on

108 M. Salim Abdullah, 'Muslims in Germany', in Abedin and Sardar, *Muslim Minorities in the West*, pp. 68–70.
109 Nielsen, *Muslims in Western Europe*, pp. 27–33.
110 Ibid., pp. 61, 62; J. Waardenburg, 'The Right to Ritual: Mosques in the Netherlands', *Nederlands Theologische Tijdschrift* 37 (1983), pp. 253–65.

a similarly regular basis, a rate twice as high as for Protestants in Great Britain. During the 1980s 70 per cent of adults in Northern Ireland still went to church once a week. Religion has come to control all aspects of the life of the two communities, so that 98 per cent of pupils went to segregated schools during the middle of the 1990s. In addition, exogamy is rare so that 96 per cent of people who responded to one survey in 1968 revealed that they had parents of the same religion. Much of the social and political life of Northern Ireland revolves around events directly or indirectly connected to the Catholic or Protestant churches.[111] The summer marches offer a good example, although they further illustrate the inextricable nature of religion, nationalism and politics in Northern Ireland.

Christianity also represents the basis of difference for minorities in Muslim states which emerged from the Ottoman Empire, although language also has much to do with differentiating peoples here, as the example of Greekness illustrates. Baptism into the Greek Orthodox religion as a baby plays as large a role as speaking a dialect of modern Greek in identifying a Greek person in the post-classical and post-Byzantine world. Greek ethnicity has faced hostility in Albania and Turkey.

The Orthodox religion in Albania, which served both Greek and Slav minorities, faced eradication following the declaration of the country as the first atheist state in the world in 1967. In April of that year 40 Orthodox priests were taken from prison to the city of Delvino, shaved in public and had their vestments removed and spat upon. Nevertheless, despite acts such as this, Greeks retained their belief in their God.[112]

The Greeks of Constantinople have faced a level of hostility similar to their brethren in Albania, as the Turkish Muslim state has attempted to eradicate the Greek Orthodox Church and its schools from its historical centre on Turkish soil – in contravention of the Treaty of Lausanne and the Helsinki Convention. In 1933–4 the Greek community maintained 54 churches and 44 schools with 7,667 students. Following improvements in diplomatic relations between Greece and Turkey during the late 1940s, by 1951 the Greek community maintained '6 *lycées*, 7 secondary schools, 1 theological academy, 51 primary schools and 5 nursery schools'.[113] Since that time, however, the position of the Greek minority in Constantinople has simply followed a continual downward slide, most clearly illustrated by the anti-Greek riots in the city in 1955 and the subsequent exodus of the population. This left just 2,000 people by the early 1990s, including 350 elderly or disabled people living in institutions supported by the community, 410 children and students, and 55 priests. The

111 The statistics come from John McGarry and Brendan O'Leary, *Explaining Northern Ireland* (Oxford, 1995), pp. 173–4, 186.
112 Wolfgang Höpken, 'Erste Ergebnisse der Bevölkerungszahlung in Albanien', *Südost Europa* 38 (1989), pp. 545–6; Cristodoulos Stavrou, *Die Griechische Minderheit in Albanien* (Frankfurt, 1993), pp. 104, 116, 125–6, 133–5; Hugh Poulton, *The Balkans: Minorities and States in Conflict*, 2nd edn (London, 1993), p. 196.
113 Alexis Alexandris, *The Greek Minority of Istanbul and Greek–Turkish Relations, 1918–1974* (Athens, 1983), pp. 191, 249.

410 pupils still remaining cannot study Greek history, they are not encouraged to speak Greek and they have outdated textbooks. An indication of the Turkish state's determination to eradicate the Patriarchy from Constantinople is provided by the fact that the Patriarch must be a Turkish citizen, which severely limits the choices available.[114]

Greek Cypriot immigrants in Britain have practised their religion unhindered, helped by the establishment of a significant number of churches. In London a Greek Orthodox church financed by Greek merchants opened in Bayswater in 1878 and served as the main focus for the Cypriot immigrants in the immediate post-War years. There quickly followed other churches in Camden Town in 1948, Kentish Town in 1959, Camberwell in 1963 and Hammersmith in 1965. In addition, there were thirteen Greek Orthodox churches outside London in 1965 and five others were being established.[115] By the early 1990s the number of Greek Orthodox churches in London and its suburbs had increased to 32.[116] With few exceptions they simply developed in vacated English churches. Easter represents the central event in the Greek Orthodox calendar. Greek Cypriots with any level of devoutness abstain from eating meat for a period of time varying between 1 and 50 days. The main service takes place on Easter Saturday when Greek Orthodox churches in London are packed to the rafters, with people also standing outside, usually on a cold or wet English April evening.

In Yugoslavia in the same way that the Muslim religion managed to survive, so did Catholicism and various types of Orthodox churches, in accordance with the provisions granting religious freedom in the post-War constitutions. Immediately after the end of the War, the Roman Catholic Church actually faced victimisation but its position improved again from the 1960s. By 1970 about 60 per cent of adults in Slovenia described themselves as religious, with about half of them attending church on a regular basis. In addition, the number of Catholic schools had doubled from the pre-War level. The Serbian Orthodox Church was also in a healthy position, although it had little appeal for younger people.[117]

Religion has played a significant role in distinguishing Ukrainians. Despite the persecution carried out by the Soviet state, the Orthodox Church and the Greek Catholic or Uniate Church managed to survive. The latter endured extreme hostility and faced dissolution at the end of the Second World War because of accusations of collaboration with the Nazis. This resulted in the liquidation of five dioceses, the murder or deportation of eleven bishops and about half of the 2,951 lay priests. Of the rest, 20 per cent escaped abroad and the remainder were forced into the Orthodox Church. In addition, a quarter

114 Helsinki Watch, *Denying Human Rights and Ethnic Identity: The Greeks of Turkey* (New York, 1992), pp. 2, 7.
115 George and Millerson, 'Cypriot Community in London', p. 290.
116 Sav Kyriacou and Zena Theodorou, 'Greek-Cypriots', in Nick Merriman (ed.), *The Peopling of London: Fifteen Thousand Years of Settlement from Overseas* (London, 1993), pp. 102–4.
117 Fred Singleton, *Twentieth-Century Yugoslavia* (London, 1976), pp. 200–7.

of the 4,400 churches and chapels became Orthodox, while the rest faced closure or destruction. Persecution continued after Stalin, but by the early 1980s the Church worked unofficially, claiming about 350 priests with allegiance to Rome and carrying out services in private, rather like Jews and Muslims in the Soviet Union. In 1989 Ukrainian Catholics took control of many churches in the western Ukraine, where this religion had been strongest. The Orthodox Church in the Ukraine endured less hostility, but the Autocephalous Ukrainian Orthodox Church (established just after the Revolution) had faced dissolution during the 1930s. The Ukraine appears to have been the most religiously devout area of the Soviet Union because in 1976 it counted 64 per cent of all open Orthodox churches in the USSR. In 1990 the Russian Orthodox Church here opportunistically changed its name to the Ukrainian Orthodox Church while the Autocephalous Orthodox Church re-emerged, at a time of religious revival. Disputes developed between the rival sects over loyalties and confiscated property.[118]

Appearance, religion and language represent the basis of difference amongst all types of minorities in post-War Europe. In themselves, they would not necessarily pose any sort of threat to other groupings. However, in an age when dominant nationalisms try to control all aspects of the lives of all their citizens, appearance, language and religion represent the springboard from which conscious, full-blown culture and political bodies can emerge.

118 Lewytzkys, *Politics and Society in the Soviet Ukraine*, pp. 190–4, 197–8; Walter Dushnyck, 'Discrimination and Abuse of Power in the USSR', in Veenhoven et al., *Case Studies in Human Rights*, pp. 475–80; Peter J. S. Duncan, 'Ukraine and The Ukrainians', in Smith, *Nationalities Question*, p. 196; Saunders, 'What Makes a Nation a Nation?', p. 113; Orest Subtelny, *Ukraine: A History*, 2nd edn (Toronto, 1994), pp. 578–9.

CHAPTER 5

The Politicisation of Difference

The leaders of peoples which do not conform to the dominant real and created values of individual nation states manufacture their own alternative sub-nationalism. No grouping of any sort, whether ethnic or otherwise, can obtain recognition of its position unless it can organise and publicise itself. The politicisation of difference takes place in a variety of ways, and not all groups have the same level of development. A difference exists between, at one extreme, a newly arrived immigrant grouping in an inner-city area of a western European state and, at the other, the long-settled Slovak or Croatian people within the countries where they formed large groupings.

Any minority which wants to get itself noticed needs to create a counter-culture. But by doing this, it is, like a nation state, involved in an artificial process which pays limited attention to the individual wishes of its component parts. But the exclusiveness of the dominant state makes this process inevitable. The development of a counter-culture represents the first step towards politicisation. Large minorities which have visions of becoming nation states create their own history, pointing to the difference in origin between themselves and the people who rule them. All minority groupings must develop their own media, especially newspapers. Immigrant communities of any size have done this, as well as importing newspapers from the homeland. Most long-established peoples also have their own press, unless the state prohibits them from publicising themselves – as happened under the old order in eastern Europe. Minorities have developed their own radio broadcasts and even stations, as well as television programmes and channels, a situation which has become easier with the advent of satellite, cable and digital television. Along with the development of media, especially in the case of large minorities creating their own form of nationalism, come more symbolic aspects of ethnicity in the form of museums, national costumes and even national anthems.

Counter-cultures form the basis for political activism by ethnic groups, which can take a variety of forms, in common with all types of modern political manoeuvring. The most direct methods involve demonstrating, especially in cases where groupings feel that no other options are open to them. This can result in peaceful protests, such as anti-racist marches (which, invariably, bring more than one ethnic minority together), or demonstrations by individual groups demanding recognition of their status as ethnic minorities. More potently, violence can result, especially in instances in which individual communities feel that they have remained ignored and persecuted. Such disorder is predominantly perpetuated by young people.

Violence is a primitive form of political activity carried out by the disenfranchised. In order to succeed, ethnic minorities have to create their own political groupings, some of which become advanced enough to hold seats in the national assembly, although others remain more elementary. Immigrants rarely form their own political parties but, more commonly, develop their own groups campaigning for a particular issue. This applies especially to refugees who have fled a particular state and continue their activity from their exile. In addition, political groupings representing long-established minorities can also campaign for their rights within particular nation states without developing into full-blown political parties.

The level of cultural and political development which a particular minority reaches depends upon a series of factors. Size obviously plays an important role, although it is not always the central one. The relative strength of the nationalist movements in Estonia and the Ukraine during the Gorbachev years would help to prove this point. The levels of literacy of a particular group also prove fundamental. This factor has seriously affected the ability of the Gypsies to organise themselves effectively. Similarly, immigrant and refugee groupings would need command of the language in the country in which they live to make themselves heard. Historical traditions of organisation also play a role. Thus, in the case of the Baltic republics, the fact that they faced annexation by the USSR in 1940 meant that they had recent memories of independence upon which to draw, while no such traditions exist in the case of the Gypsies.

CULTURE

In essence, culture is a product of modernity, building upon appearance, language and religion. Whether the culture consists of the development of a literary tradition or simply the establishment of ethnic newspapers, the entire process is artificial, bringing together diverse elements to form a justification for difference, which can then be stressed in various types of political activity. Culture amongst minorities has several facets. At its most basic, it covers the development of press organs and – more recently – radio and television, which represent a way of disseminating information, with a particular ethnic message. Clearly, literacy and organisational ability underlie the possibility of an ethnic media emerging, as does – especially in the case of radio and television broadcasts – the support of the state. Bureaucratic skills are also necessary for the establishment of ethnic cultural organisations, which can vary from local community centres in the case of immigrants, to the development of national museums in the case of some of the largest localised minorities in Europe. Finally, and closely connected with the growth of advanced ethnic organisations (especially theatres and museums), a high culture develops encompassing history, literature, art and music.

Different groupings have succeeded in developing an ethnic culture to varying extents, depending upon the duration of settlement, the size of the minority, the level of literacy and the attitude of the state. In this sense, groupings such as Gypsies and Vlachs remain relatively underdeveloped, as do recently arrived immigrants, while, at the other extreme, minorities such as Scots and Ukrainians managed to reach an advanced level of cultural development after 1945.

Although Gypsies have their own music, in terms of cultural organisational ability they represent some of the least advanced minorities in Europe, largely explained by a lack of literacy. In Czechoslovakia some developments took place at the end of the 1960s with the launch of magazines and festivals connected with the establishment of the Union of Gypsy Romanies. After the fall of the old order in eastern Europe a series of cultural groupings emerged, totalling 30 by 1992, including an association of Rome Writers.[1] Similarly, in Romania after 1990, under the auspices of the Ministry of Culture, Gypsy periodicals and radio broadcasts came into existence, although Gypsies have remained weak in these areas compared with the advances made by other minorities in the country. In Britain, formal Gypsy culture has been organised from above, by gorgios, as evidenced by the *Journal of the Gypsy Lore Society*, established in 1888 and published by that Society.

Due to the short spell of time they have spent in their new environment and their generally small size, immigrants also have a fairly limited cultural development. But they can create their own organisations and even their own culture, although the latter would consist of an artificial imitation of what they remember from their homeland when they left it, imbued with elements from their new surroundings. This new culture would manifest itself in a number of ways, especially through the media, particularly newspapers but also, more recently, radio and even television.

Immigrants in Britain illustrate these processes. For instance, early West Indian settlers in Brixton set up associations devoted to cricket, drinking and dancing, as well as informal groups focusing upon unlicensed drinking, gambling and ganja smoking.[2] In addition, by the early 1960s there also existed a London-based Black monthly newspaper in the form of the *West Indian Gazette*, founded in March 1958 with a circulation of 15,000.[3] Since that time the weekly *Voice* has become the main press organ of the West Indian community in Britain. In addition, Black broadcasting has also developed so that,

---

1 David M. Crowe, *A History of the Gypsies of Eastern Europe and Russia* (London, 1995), pp. 64–5.
2 Sheila Patterson, *Dark Strangers: A Sociological Study of the Absorption of a Recent West Indian Migrant Group in Brixton, South London* (London, 1963), pp. 348–9, 364–7.
3 Edward Pilkington, *Beyond the Mother Country: West Indians and the Notting Hill White Riots* (London, 1988), p. 143.

for instance, several Black radio stations exist in London devoting attention to different types of music.

The Greek nationalist Cyprus Brotherhood, established in 1934, and the Cypriot Communist Party, set up in 1931, acted as social clubs for London Greek Cypriots, arranging dances, excursions and lectures. In addition, there also existed two newspapers in London during the 1960s in the form of the Communist *Vema* and the nationalist *Helleniki*.[4] Both had disappeared by the middle of the 1980s although the former had reached a circulation of 8,500 in 1982. In total about 30 newspapers have come and gone for Greek Cypriots in Britain, the most important of which by the end of the 1980s was *Parikiaki*, containing an English section for second-generation Greek Cypriots with a poor reading ability in Greek.[5] By the 1990s numerous new associations had developed amongst the Cypriot community in London. These included community centres (which received some public funding), educational and youth associations, village societies, professional groupings, women's organisations, a Thalassaemia Society and at least one theatre group, Theatron Technis.[6] London Greek Radio broadcasts from Haringey, receiving advertising revenue predominantly from some of the numerous Greek Cypriot businesses which exist in London. It devotes attention to news from Cyprus, popular music from Cyprus and Greece, Greek cookery, quizzes, radio plays (usually in the Cypriot dialect), and current affairs.

Polish immigrants in Britain developed a wide range of organisations almost immediately after their entry into the country. By the middle of the 1950s this minority had established an umbrella organisation called the Federation of Poles in Great Britain to which were affiliated eleven social organisations, twelve occupational groupings, five religious associations, nine scientific, cultural and educational bodies and five relief organisations. In addition, the Polish community in Britain has also published its own newspapers and information bulletins, the best known of which is *Dziennik Polski*. Further organisations came into existence during the 1960s, many of them aimed at the second generation.[7]

Close similarities exist between the cultural life of immigrants in France and those in Britain. In the first place, most groups of newcomers of any size have developed their own organisations. According to government figures from 1982, a total of 402 immigrant organisations officially existed in France. The

4 Vic George and Geoffrey Millerson, 'The Cypriot Community in London', *Race* 8 (1967), pp. 285–9.
5 Floya Anthias, *Ethnicity, Class, Gender and Migration: Greek Cypriots in Britain* (Aldershot, 1992), p. 130.
6 Sasha Josephides, 'Associations Amongst the Greek Cypriot Population in Britain', in John Rex, Daniele Joly and Czarina Wilpert (eds), *Immigrant Associations in Europe* (Aldershot, 1987), pp. 42–61.
7 Jerzy Zubrzycki, *Polish Immigrants in Britain: A Study of Adjustment* (The Hague, 1956), pp. 102–19; Sheila Patterson, 'The Poles: An Exile Community in Britain', in James L. Watson (ed.), *Between Two Cultures: Minorities and Migrants in Britain* (Oxford, 1977), pp. 225–30; Keith Sword, 'The Poles in London', in Nick Merriman (ed.), *The Peopling of London: Fifteen Thousand Years of Settlement From Overseas* (London, 1993), pp. 158–61.

Portuguese counted the largest total: 69.[8] However, a Portuguese government source listed 850 in 1985, which means that 'if one relates the number of associations to the size of the immigrant population in France, there are nearly 1,230 potential members per association'. The range of activities catered for included politics, sport, dancing, folk songs and youth.[9] Italians in France developed in a similar way, often with support from organisations in Italy. For instance, between 1960 and 1970 Italian political parties all created offshoots in France. Subsequently, associations began to develop based upon particular localities in Italy, from village level upwards. Other types of groupings included those revolving around religion, sport, war veterans and culture.[10]

All of the major European minorities in Germany have developed their own associations. In 1986 the Spaniards counted about 120 local associations with interests including schooling and youth, concerns which have also attracted the attention of Greek immigrants.[11] The size of the Turkish community in Germany has facilitated a wide range of cultural developments. Eleven newspapers existed by the early 1990s; the oldest of these, with the largest circulation, was *Hürriyet*, which sold 110,000 copies, followed by *Türkiye*, with 35,000, and *Milliyet*, selling 25,000. Since 1964 the German regional radio station, WDR, based in Cologne, has broadcast radio programmes in Turkish which, in 1990, were listened to by 52 per cent of Turks in the city on a daily basis. Turks also watched television programmes provided for them by the regional broadcasting companies and, with the development of satellite television, many tuned in to TRT-International, a station broadcasting from Turkey for Turks settled abroad, which made a third of its programmes in Germany.[12] In addition, a high culture has developed amongst Turks in Germany, epitomised by the work of Ermine Sergi Özdamar, born in Malataya in eastern Anatolia in 1946 but moving to Germany as a migrant worker in 1965. After returning to Turkey, she moved back to Germany in 1976 and has produced (in German) several plays and novels, with the experience of Turks in Germany playing a major theme in her work. Özdamar represents just one prominent figure amongst many German Turks writing in German.[13] The opening to her short story, *Mutterzunge*, indicates the themes and experiences covered by her work:

8 Patrick Ireland, *The Policy Challenge of Ethnic Diversity: Immigrant Politics in France and Switzerland* (London, 1994), p. 64.
9 Marie-Antoinette Hily and Michel Poinard, 'Portuguese Associations in France', in Rex, Joly and Wilpert, *Immigrant Associations in Europe*, pp. 126–65.
10 Giovanna Campani, Maurizio Catani and Salvatore Palidda, 'Italian Immigrant Associations in France', in Rex, Joly and Wilpert, *Immigrant Associations in Europe*, pp. 176–83.
11 Barbara von Breitenbach, *Italiener und Spanier als Arbeitnehmer in der Bundesrepublik Deutschland* (Munich, 1982), pp. 109–26; Jürgen Fijalkowski, 'Conditions of Ethnic Mobilisation: The German Case', in John Rex and Beatrice Drury (eds), *Ethnic Mobilisation in a Multi-cultural Europe* (Aldershot, 1994), pp. 126–7.
12 Gülay Durgut, 'Tagsüber Deutschland, abends Deutschland: Türkische Medien in Deutschland', in Claus Leggewie and Zafer Şenocak (eds), *Deutsche Turken: Das Ende der Geduld* (Hamburg, 1993), pp. 112–22.
13 See the first four chapters of David Horrocks and Eva Kolinsky (eds), *Turkish Culture in German Society Today* (Oxford, 1996).

I sat with my twisted tongue in the city of Berlin. In a Black café, with Arabs as guests, the stools were too high and feet were swinging. An old tired croissant sat on my plate, which I still paid for to save the waiter from embarrassment. If only I knew where I had lost my mother tongue. My mother and I spoke in our mother tongue. She said to me: 'Do you know, you speak so, you think you explain everything, but suddenly you skip over unspoken words, then you explain calmly, I skip that with you, and then I breathe in calmly.' She then said: 'You half left half your hair in Germany.'[14]

Finnish immigrants in Sweden have developed a large variety of cultural associations, whose total number increased from just 14 in 1960 to 218 by 1985, counting 45,000 members. The proximity of Finland and Sweden clearly assisted in this process. An extremely wide range of organisations has existed, catering for groups ranging from communists to librarians. Some of the bodies also have Swedish members. As in the case of other advanced minority groups, the Finnish immigrants have also developed a literary culture focusing upon the problems of immigration.[15]

Because of the longevity of their residence in many parts of Europe and often their larger size, as well as the high level of literacy in the case of Jews and Germans, three of the dispersed minorities have evolved advanced cultures. The Jews represent the most developed of all. The largest European Jewish community, in the Soviet Union, while constrained by the state, also developed its own ethnic institutions. The patterns of Jewish cultural and political activity in the USSR follow those of their educational and religious development, with a successful period during the 1920s followed by Stalinist repression, which lasted beyond the Second World War with the existence of overt anti-semitic campaigns pursued by both Stalin and his successors into the 1970s.

During the early days of the Soviet Union, a secular Jewish culture developed with the establishment of Yiddish writers' organisations, theatrical groups, newspapers and periodicals.[16] But between 1949 and 1959 no Yiddish books or literary journals appeared at all in the Soviet Union. Just one Yiddish-language newspaper officially existed in 1970, together with one magazine, while only four books appeared in Yiddish. An increase in such publications occurred after the middle of the 1970s, although the number had only reached 22 for the whole of 1981. Nevertheless, other unofficial publications also appeared which focused purely upon cultural activity. *Sovietish Heymland*, an

---

14 My translation of Ermine Sergi Özdamar, *Mutterzunge* (Berlin, 1990), p. 7.

15 Magdalena Jaakkola, 'Informal Networks and Associations of Finnish Immigrants in Sweden', in Rex, Joly and Wilpert, *Immigrant Associations in Europe*, pp. 201–18; Rütta Yletyinen, *Sprachliche und kulturelle Minderheiten in den USA, Schweden und der Bundesrepublik* (Frankfurt, 1992), pp. 123–6.

16 Zev Katz, 'The Jews in the Soviet Union', in Zev Katz, Rosemarie Rogers and Frederic Harned (eds), *Handbook of Major Soviet Nationalities* (New York, 1975), pp. 373–7; Laurie P. Salitan, *Politics and Nationality in Contemporary Soviet-Jewish Emigration, 1968–89* (London, 1992), p. 14.

official journal of the Soviet Writers' Union, which started publication in 1961, represented the major Yiddish-language publication in the Soviet Union after the War, carrying stories on a wide range of subjects, but closely following the Communist Party line. In 1979 it had a circulation of just 7,000. Jewish theatre and music also witnessed a limited renaissance in the post-Stalin years, especially in the Baltic republics. Such developments intensified under Gorbachev. There followed, for instance, the founding of a club in Bukharu in Uzbekhistan in May 1987 to study the history of the Jewish quarter of the city, while the authorities in Kiev decided to establish a Jewish Theatrical Studio. In Lithuania the Jewish community set up a Society for National Reawakening as well as a sports organisation. September 1988 witnessed the first meeting of the Association for Jewish Culture, and in December of the following year there occurred a national meeting of representatives of Jewish organisations from all over the USSR. The momentum of these years has continued into the post-Soviet period as Jews have had greater opportunities to organise themselves in the less repressive regimes of the post-Soviet states. In Russia, for instance, a newspaper entitled the *Jewish Herald* had a circulation figure of 100,000 by the middle of the 1990s, while, on the other hand, the *Sovietish Heymland* had closed down.[17]

The state played a central role in the cultural life of Jews elsewhere in eastern Europe. In the German Democratic Republic the community of just a few hundred had its own library and newsletter during the 1980s,[18] while in Hungary the Jewish minority had its own media and organisations. After the collapse of communism the Union of Hungarian Jewish Communities became the central organisation of Hungarian Jewry. Even before the political changes had taken place, a body called the Hungarian Jewish Cultural Federation had come into existence in 1988, organising lectures on Jewish topics and publishing a journal called *Szombat*.[19] In Poland traces of Jewish culture survived the Second World War and its aftermath, as well as the anti-semitic campaign of the middle of the 1960s. A Jewish Social and Cultural Society, established in 1945, still existed into the 1980s. By that time a Yiddish publishing house printed less than ten titles a year, and a Yiddish newspaper, *Folks Shtyme*, and a literary monthly, *Yiddishe Schriften*, had a tiny circulation.[20]

17 Katz, ibid., p. 373; Lukasz Hirscowicz, 'Jewish Cultural Life in the USSR: A Survey', *Soviet Jewish Affairs* 7 (1977), pp. 3–21; Zvi Gitelman, 'What Future for Jewish Culture in the Soviet Union?', *Soviet Jewish Affairs* 9 (1979), pp. 20–8; Nora Levin, *The Jews in the Soviet Union Since 1917: Paradox of Survival*, Vol. 2 (New York, 1988), pp. 757–85; Mordecai Altschuler, 'Soviet Jewry: A Community in Turmoil', in Robert S. Wistrich (ed.), *Terms of Survival: The Jewish World Since 1945* (London, 1995), pp. 202–8; Eitan Finkelstein, 'Jewish Revival in the Baltics: Problems and Perspectives', *Soviet Jewish Affairs* 20 (1990), p. 5; Yoram Gorlizki, 'The Jews', in Graham Smith (ed.), *The Nationalities Question in the Post-Soviet States* (London, 1996), p. 451.
18 Monika Richarz, 'Jews in Today's Germanies', *Leo Baeck Institute Yearbook* 30 (1985), pp. 269–70.
19 Thomas Tucker, 'Political Transition and the "Jewish Question" in Hungary Today', *Ethnic and Racial Studies* 19 (1996), pp. 306–9; Janusz Bugajski, *Ethnic Politics in Eastern Europe: A Guide to Nationality Policies, Organizations and Parties* (Armonk, NY, 1995), p. 421.
20 Kenneth C. Farmer et al., 'National Minorities in Poland, 1919–1980', in Stephan M. Horak (ed.), *Eastern European National Minorities, 1919–1980: A Handbook* (Littleton, CO, 1985), p. 57.

Anglo-Jewry has developed extremely sophisticated cultural activities. Indications of this include newspapers, the most successful and longest running of which is the weekly *Jewish Chronicle*, and a Jewish Historical Society of England, which dates from the end of the nineteenth century. The various divisions of Anglo-Jewry have also established their own cultural bodies, most notably the Association of Jewish Refugees, founded in 1941.[21] The existence of Jewish societies at most British universities provides one indication of the continuance of Jewish culture amongst young Jews. However, this goes hand in hand with a long-term process of cultural assimilation.

Although lagging behind the Jews in levels of literacy and economic advancement, the Muslim populations of Europe have also developed a cultural life in many locations. Unlike the Jews, this sometimes forms the basis for the emergence of a fully developed nationalism. The existing state has often played a central role in the level of cultural development reached by these Muslim groups, especially under the old order in the Soviet bloc.

In Bulgaria, for instance, newspapers appeared in Turkish until the repressive campaign pursued by that state in the 1980s. In the early 1950s a total of five Turkish-language publications had a combined circulation of over 100,000. In addition, there also existed amateur art groups, which offered performances of Turkish folk songs and dances. However, by 1986 the various Turkish newspapers appeared in Bulgarian only and not one word of Turkish was published in the country. Furthermore, Turkish-language radio broadcasts ceased.[22]

Within the Soviet Union both the Muslim Azerbaijanis and their Christian Armenian neighbours developed a national consciousness, which manifested itself in the development of culture and media. Azerbaijan had its own composers, writers and artists working within Soviet traditions. In 1971 a total of 115 newspapers appeared in the republic, with a combined circulation of 2,192,000; 91 were published in Azerbaijani. In the same year, 29 magazines appeared, 23 of them in Azerbaijani, together with 430 Russian and 802 Azerbaijani books. Furthermore, television and radio had also taken off, while there also existed an Azerbaijani Academy of Sciences, together with 38 museums, 12 theatres and 2,004 public libraries.[23] Armenia also had its own art galleries, opera, ballet, cinema and Academy of Sciences.[24]

German culture and German organisations existed in most of the European states which they inhabited after 1945, however small their numbers in individual locations, as the example of Denmark illustrates. In this instance, the

---

21 Marion Berghahn, *Continental Britons: German-Jewish Refugees from Nazi Germany* (Oxford, 1988), pp. 150–67.
22 *The Turkish Minority in the People's Republic of Bulgaria* (Sofia, 1951), pp. 13, 36; Helsinki Watch, *Destroying Ethnic Identity: The Turks of Bulgaria* (New York, 1986), p. 13; Firoze Yasemee, 'The Turkic People of Bulgaria', in M. Bainbridge (ed.), *The Turkic Peoples of the World* (London, 1993), p. 49.
23 All of these statistics are from: Frank Huddle, Jr, 'Azerbaidzhan and the Azerbaidzhanis', in Katz, Rogers and Harned, *Handbook of Major Soviet Nationalities*, pp. 194–204.
24 Christopher J. Walker, *Armenia: The Survival of a Nation*, 2nd edn (London, 1990), p. 371.

German minority has had its own newspaper, *Der Nordschleswiger*, and, because of geographical proximity, has managed to obtain radio and television transmissions from Germany. Sporting activity has links with German national organisations, while a sporting festival has taken place on the last Sunday of June.[25]

In the German areas of Belgium the only newspaper existing after 1945 was the *Grenz Echo*, with many people reading the *Aachen Volkzeitung*, published on the other side of the German border. Belgian state radio has actually provided three hours of programmes for German speakers, although the proximity of Germany once again makes reception from the homeland straightforward. In addition, cinemas in eastern Belgium have also shown mostly German films.[26]

Under the communist regime in Poland, the German minority did not develop to any great extent because of restrictions upon the formation of associations and the publication of newspapers in their own language. This situation changed dramatically in the early 1990s, when over a dozen organisations came into existence (many of which counted several thousand members), together with two German minority newspapers.[27]

In Romania, despite immediate post-War persecution, the German grouping developed a vital cultural life. In 1949 a German Anti-Fascist Committee was created which published its own newspaper, *Neuer Weg*, with a circulation of 60,000. In addition, 285 German cultural institutes existed by 1952. By the early 1970s several other German newspapers had developed, while two German theatre companies had also been founded. The position of the German minority deteriorated under the repressive Ceauşescu regime of the 1970s, but in the early 1990s it had its own theatres, newspapers and museums, and broadcasting provision.[28]

After the easing of restrictions during the middle of the 1950s, German cultural life in the Soviet Union developed to a considerable extent. The first newspaper, *Neues Leben*, a state organ, began publication in 1957, although by the 1970s only three German newspapers in all were published in the USSR. The state made provision for broadcasts in German on both the radio and television, while German drama groups, choral societies and orchestras gave regular performances during the 1970s. In addition, a Soviet German literature developed in the post-War period, helped by the existence of groups such as the Congress of Soviet Writers of the Russian Republic and the Kazakhstan

25 Jørgen Elklit, Johan Peter Noack and Ole Tonsgaard, 'A National Group as a Social System: The Case of the German Minority in North Schleswig', *Journal of Intercultural Studies* 1 (1980), p. 6; Meic Stephens, *Linguistic Minorities in Western Europe* (Llandysul, 1976), pp. 237–8; Manfred Straka, *Handbuch der europäischen Volksgruppen* (Vienna, 1970), pp. 322–7.
26 Stephens, ibid., pp. 46–8; Straka, ibid., pp. 332–6.
27 Bugajski, *Ethnic Politics in Eastern Europe*, pp. 379–82; Agnieszka Rochowicz, 'National Minorities in Poland', in John Packer and Kristian Myntti (eds), *The Protection of Ethnic and Linguistic Minorities in Europe* (Turku/Åbo, 1993), pp. 108–9.
28 Georges Castellan, 'The Germans of Rumania', *Journal of Contemporary History* 6 (1971), pp. 70–3; I. Zlatescu-Moroiann and I. Oancea, *The Legislative and Institutional Framework for the National Minorities of Romania* (Bucharest, 1994), pp. 82–92.

German Writers' Section, although the decline in the use of German jeopardised the continuance of this literary tradition. In the Perestroika period several Soviet German organisations emerged, including *Widergeburt*, which aimed at re-establishing the Volga Republic.[29]

Because of their often large numbers, as well as their concentration in particular regions of individual nation states, localised minorities have had some of the greatest success in developing a cultural ethnicity, usually from the basis of their own language. Sometimes this culture – often of a literary and artistic nature – may have evolved over the course of hundreds of years and, more recently, may have received assistance from the controlling nation state.

In Scandinavia a Lapp culture has origins dating back hundreds of years, but it spread during the twentieth century due to the growth of literacy. A written Lapp language began in the seventeenth century; the New Testament was translated into Lapp in 1755, followed by the whole Bible in 1811. By the second half of the twentieth century Sami writers were producing considerable numbers of novels, short stories and poems, and have formed a series of organisations either within individual states or crossing national boundaries. Such bodies have included the Lapland Education Society and the Sami Writers' Union. Newspapers and magazines also appear in Lappish throughout Scandinavia, although Lapps have limited time devoted to them in national radio and television broadcasting partly due to the existence of different Lapp dialects. Since the 1970s some development has taken place in Lapp music, both in the traditional 'yoik' style and in a westernised fashion, although, in view of the size of the Sami population, such music cannot develop to any great extent. Finally, some Lapp handicraft productions, such as cooking utensils and basket work, have made their way to Scandinavian museums, with at least one Sami museum in existence.[30]

The Swedish-speaking minority in Finland has a culture dating back over several hundred years. In fact, because of the control of Finland by Sweden the first newspapers in Finland, beginning in 1714, appeared in Swedish and by the middle of the 1970s a total of 22 newspapers in Finland were published in Swedish, including 8 dailies. The most important of these, *Hufvudstadsbladet*, had a circulation of 70,000. Five Swedish theatres existed in Finland at this time. Many early literary works in Finland appeared in the Swedish language and several authors continued to write in Swedish after 1945, meaning the survival of a Finland-Swedish literature, which included novels,

29 Adam Giesinger, *The Story of Russia's Germans: From Catherine to Kruschev* (Battleford, Saskatchewan, 1974), p. 329; Anne Sheehy, *The Crimean Tatars and the Volga Germans: Soviet Treatment of Two Minorities* (London, 1971), pp. 26–8; Benjamin Pinkus, 'The Germans in the Soviet Union Since 1945', in I. Fleischauer, B. Pinkus and E. Frankel (eds), *The Soviet Germans Past and Present* (London, 1986), pp. 113–14, 128–35; Anthony Hyman, 'Volga Germans', in Smith, *Nationalities Question*, p. 468.

30 Lars-Anders Baer, 'The Sami: An Indigenous People in Their Own Land', in Birgitta Jahreshog (ed.), *The Sami National Minority in Sweden* (Stockholm, 1982), pp. 19–20; Israel Ruong, *The Lapps in Sweden* (Stockholm, 1967), pp. 50–5, 68–72; Mervyn Jones, *The Sami of Lapland* (London, 1982), pp. 10–12; Erkki Asp, Kari Rantanen and Aila Munter, *The Lapps and the Lappish Culture* (Turku, 1980), pp. 25–6.

poems and dramatic works. In broadcasting, some provision has been made for the transmission of programmes in Swedish. Furthermore, the Swedish-speaking Finns have also counted hundreds of youth organisations, song societies, sporting organisations and cultural groupings in the post-War period.[31]

In the United Kingdom all three of the peripheral states, over a period of hundreds of years, have developed their own culture. Sir Walter Scott and Robert Burns played a key role in creating a cultural vision of Scotland in the early nineteenth century. The images which they conjured, appealing to middle-class city dwellers in Scotland, gave the impression of 'a romantic, rural and largely imaginary place'.[32] The following extract from Scott's *Rob Roy*, as he returns to Scotland, makes the contrast with the English countryside:

> I approached my native north, for such I esteemed it, with that enthusiasm which romantic and wild scenery inspires in the lover of nature. No longer interrupted by the babble of my companion, I could now remark the difference which the country exhibited from that through which I had hitherto travelled. The streams now more properly deserved the name, for, instead of slumbering among the willows, they brawled along beneath the shade of natural copsewood; were now hurried down declivities, and now purled more leisurely, but still in active motion, through little lonely alleys, which, opening on the road from time to time, seemed to invite the traveller to explore their recesses. The Cheviots rose before me in frowning majesty; not, indeed, with the sublime variety of rock and cliff which characterizes mountains of the primary class, but huge, round-headed, and clothed with a dark robe of russet, gaining, by their extent and desolate appearance, an influence upon the imagination, as a desert district possessing a character of its own.[33]

Such imagery was perpetuated during the course of the nineteenth and into the twentieth century by writers such as Robert Louis Stevenson. At the end of the twentieth century, the existence of Scottish newspapers – notably the *Daily Record* and the *Scotsman* – plays a large role in Scottish culture. On a more popular level, sport has been just as important in galvanising the Scottish working classes together against the mythical English foe, illustrated most clearly in the establishment of an independent Scottish Football Association at the end of the nineteenth century and epitomised by the rivalry of England versus Scotland matches, which, more than any other occurrence in Scottish life, have brought vitriolic Scottish nationalism to the fore.

Contemporary Welsh culture, like its Scottish equivalent, also has its virulent manifestation in sport. In this instance rugby union is more important, giving rise to an independent league. Like the Scottish football team, the Welsh

---

31 Anne Marie Beaurain, 'Ethnic Problems of Swedish Finns and Finnish Finns: Present Situation', *Plural Societies* 7 (1976), pp. 66–7; Ragnar Meinander, 'Die Schwedische Bevölkerung in Finnland', in Pressabteilung des Finnischen Aussenministeriums (ed.), *Finnland: Geschichte und Gegenwart*, 2nd edn (Helsinki, 1964), pp. 309–13.
32 Jack Brand, *The National Movement in Scotland* (London, 1978), p. 93.
33 Sir Walter Scott, *Rob Roy* (London, 1973; originally 1817), p. 39.

rugby union side provides the main focus for outbursts of overt nationalistic pride when it enjoys victory. Welsh newspapers exist, of which the most important, the English-language *Western Mail* (published in Cardiff), had a circulation of 100,000 in the middle of the 1970s. In contrast, relatively few books appear in Welsh, totalling just 157 in 1967 and consisting mostly of religious works, volumes for children and poetry, although the situation has improved since then.[34] Provision has also been made for Welsh-language broadcasting on BBC, HTV and Channel 4.

In cultural terms the difference between the two communities of Northern Ireland is based simply upon allegiance to either the British Protestant or Irish Catholic 'way of life'. The adherence to the traditions and rituals of the marching season led by the Protestant Orange Order and the Catholic Ancient Order of Hibernians perfectly illustrates this difference. To an outsider rationally analysing these events, they represent a completely artificial attempt at re-creating traditions. The festivities are rooted in the present with, in the case of the Orange Order, people marching through Catholic areas wearing bowler hats and carrying long umbrellas to stress allegiance to imagined British ideals.[35] In the middle of the 1970s as much as 40 per cent of the adult male population of some rural communities were members of Orange Lodges.[36]

Many eastern European regimes under the old order offered their minorities a large degree of support which allowed significant cultural development, as the example of the Sorbs within the German Democratic Republic illustrates. During the 1960s and 1970s almost 2,000 books appeared in Wendisch (the Sorb language), all subsidised and usually published by the state. Common themes included resistance to the Nazis and the way of life in the Sorbian village. In addition, one daily newspaper, *Nowa doba*, also existed, together with several other Wendisch periodicals on a less regular basis, many of them for particular interest groups. The Sorbian People's Theatre came into existence in 1948, subsequently developing into the German-Sorbian People's Theatre. The main Sorbian organisation consisted of the Domowina, originally founded in 1912 and re-established in 1945, working under the Communist Party. It acted as both a cultural and political organisation. The Domowina disappeared immediately after reunification, to be replaced by the Sorbian National Assembly and several other cultural associations.[37]

The Hungarian minority in Czechoslovakia had a well-developed, officially recognised culture under the old regime. In 1949 the Cultural Union of

---

34 Alan Butt Philip, *The Welsh Question: Nationalism in Welsh Politics, 1945–1970* (Cardiff, 1975), pp. 64–7; Kenneth O. Morgan, *Rebirth of a Nation: Wales 1880–1980* (Cardiff, 1981), pp. 368–9.
35 For a description of festivities during the marching season see Michael Ignatieff, *Blood and Belonging: Journeys into the New Nationalism* (London, 1993), pp. 170–89.
36 Hastings Donovan and Graham MacFarlane, 'Informal Social Organisation', in John Darby (ed.), *Northern Ireland: The Background to Conflict* (Belfast, 1983), pp. 123–4.
37 Meic Stephens, 'The Sorbs', in G. Ashworth (ed.), *World Minorities*, Vol. 1 (Sunbury, 1977), p. 122; Gerald Stone, *The Smallest Slavonic Nation: The Sorbs of Lusatia* (London, 1972), pp. 85–9, 172–82; Minority Rights Group and TWEEC (eds), *Minorities in Central and Eastern Europe* (London, 1992), p. 33.

Hungarian Working People in Czechoslovakia came into existence, with the aim of promoting cultural, artistic and civic activities for ethnic Hungarians. During the 1980s it counted 517 organisations with 60,000 members. In addition, professional Hungarian theatre companies existed in Komárno and Košice. Furthermore, the Madach Publishing House printed about 50 Hungarian titles per year, while there were also 18 periodicals together with a daily newspaper, *Uj Szo*. Some broadcasting also took place in Hungarian on radio and television.[38]

The Rusyn minority of Czechoslovakia reached a level of cultural development similar to that of the Hungarians. A series of newspapers and periodicals appeared in Ukrainian from the 1950s, most importantly *Nove Žyttja*, the Communist Party organ. The Ukrainian National Theatre based in Prešov had given thousands of performances by 1990, which included between five and ten premières every season. Furthermore, a song-and-dance ensemble was established, while a Ukrainian literature developed in Czechoslovakia from the 1950s, leading to the establishment of a Ukrainian writers' section in the Czechoslovak Writers' Union. Ukrainians also had television and radio broadcasts in their language. One of the most important cultural developments consisted of the Museum of Ukrainian Culture, founded in 1956. Clearly the cultural development which had taken place under the old regime had received much support from the state. After 1989 the old bureaucratic structures collapsed and new ones succeeded them, notably the Rusyn Renaissance Society. Most of the cultural activity continued with a liberal democratic rather than a communist slant.[39]

In Romania, Hungarian culture developed to a great degree although it became ever more tightly controlled under the old regime. Hungarian newspapers and other publications appeared throughout the communist period. A single national newspaper in Hungarian was published in Bucharest from the 1950s, together with local organs and publications for particular sectors of society, including young people, women and the rural population. However, by the late 1970s the government cut down the number of newspapers and periodicals due to an apparent paper shortage. At the same time those organs which did continue often simply translated stories which had appeared in the Romanian press. Broadcasting in Hungarian occurred on both radio and television. The Kriterion Publishing House, established in 1969, controlled scientific and literary publications of national minorities in Romania. A total of 217 of the 315 titles issued in 1977 appeared in Hungarian. Other forms of Hungarian cultural expression in Romania included ten theatre or music groups

38 Josef Kalvoda, 'National Minorities Under Communism: The Case of Czechoslovakia', *Nationalities Papers* 16 (1988), p. 7; SOS Transylvania, *Hungarian Minority in Czechoslovakia/Slovakia* (Bratislava, 1993), pp. 6, 11.
39 Mykola Mušynka, 'The Postwar Development of the Regional Culture of the Rusyn-Ukrainians of Czechoslovakia', in Robert Magocsi (ed.), *The Persistence of Regional Cultures: Rusyns and Ukrainians in their Carpathian Homeland and Abroad* (New York, 1993), pp. 60–78; H. Renner, 'The National Minorities in Czechoslovakia After the Second World War', *Plural Societies* 7 (1975), pp. 28–30.

in the late 1970s. A series of Hungarian cultural organisations also emerged, although they often had a Romanian as their head. The repressive policies of the Ceaucescu regime during the 1970s even went as far as abolishing theatre groups and folklore study circles, indicating the dependence on the state of much ethnic cultural activity in the communist regimes of eastern Europe.[40] The cultural life of Hungarians in Romania has improved during the 1990s. Numerous newspapers have appeared in Hungarian and the minority also gained increased broadcasting time, while Hungarian theatre companies gave 857 performances in 1992.[41]

The Soviet Union had a schizophrenic policy towards the development of national cultures. While it ultimately aimed at assimilating all Soviet citizens within a unified Soviet culture, in the short run – partly in an attempt to win over minority groupings at the start of the Revolution – local cultures developed along with the languages created or standardised by the Soviet Union from the 1920s, which involved the growth of media, music, theatre, dance, literature and museums.

In the Ukraine, despite the elimination of virtually all traces of nationalism during the Stalin era, the continued importance of the Ukrainian language meant the survival of a literary culture within this republic. A Ukrainian cultural revival occurred during the 1950s with the appearance of standard works on Ukrainian history, language and literature. Kiev represented the centre of Ukrainian newspaper and periodical publishing and was the second-largest publishing centre in the USSR. In 1971 a total of 99 out of the 103 journals which appeared in the Ukraine were based in Kiev. The publications catered for a wide range of readerships based, for instance, on geographical location, occupation, age group and cultural activity, while some were mass-circulation dailies. However, 30 per cent of newspapers published in the Ukraine in 1971 appeared in Russian, while the share of books in the Ukraine which were written in Russian had reached 70 per cent of all titles in 1975. In addition, a significant proportion of programmes on Ukrainian television appeared in Russian.[42]

In Belorussia persecution of supposed bourgeois nationalists in literature, the arts and social sciences occurred under Stalin. However, the thaw of the Kruschev period resulted in the rehabilitation of writers who had been victims in the 1930s, while new literary works of the 1950s began to bring national themes to the surface and to criticise Stalin. However, many of the new

40 N. M. Goodchild, *Hungarian Minorities in Rumania* (London, 1980), pp. 18, 81; Rudolf Joó et al. (eds), *Report of the Situation of the Hungarian Minority in Rumania* (Budapest, 1988), p. 104; Rudolf Joó (ed.), *The Hungarian Minority Situation in Rumania* (New York, 1994), pp. 60–1; Bennett Kovrig, 'The Magyars in Rumania: Problems of a "Coinhabiting" Nationality', *Südosteuropa* 35 (1986), pp. 483–4.
41 Moroiann-Zlatescu and Oancea, *Legislative and Institutional Framework for the National Minorities of Rumania*, pp. 81–91.
42 Orest Subtelny, *Ukraine: A History*, 2nd edn (Toronto, 1994), p. 501; Roman Szporluk, 'The Ukraine and the Ukrainians', in Katz, Rogers and Harned, *Handbook of Major Soviet Nationalities*, pp. 31–4; Bohdan Krawchenko, *Social Change and National Consciousness in Twentieth Century Ukraine* (London, 1985), pp. 237–41.

works still tended to focus upon subjects favoured by the Communist Party such as the positive consequences of collectivisation and friendship between different Soviet peoples, although actors, writers and film producers in Belorussia spoke against the standardisation forced upon them by the Soviet authorities. In addition, a large proportion of publications by the 1960s appeared in Russian rather than Belorussian, totalling 80 per cent of all books and pamphlets issued in the republic in 1965, although 87 newspapers appeared in Belorussian compared with 35 in Russian. By 1970 Belorussia had 14 professional theatres, 49 museums and 7,199 public libraries. Out of the theatres only three performed in Belorussian, although numerous amateur groupings used the language.[43]

POLITICAL ACTIVISM

The existence of a minority culture often represents the first step towards the growth of some form of political activism, which in the case of post-War Europe has taken a variety of forms. At its most primitive, it can consist simply of rioting, an option pursued by second-generation immigrants, most notably within Britain during the 1980s. Immigrants, like other types of minorities, have also participated in the already existing mainstream political parties, in the hope of securing an improvement in the position of their grouping. Other forms of political activism have included emigration, as practised by Soviet Jewry. The emergence of pressure groupings, which may or may not develop into full-blown political parties, also represents a fairly basic form of political activity. Such options are usually open to some of the smallest and least advanced groupings in Europe.

Immigrants and refugees can politicise themselves in various ways. In the first place they can join mainstream political parties in their land of settlement, although this is not always an option either because of restrictions on voting for people without citizenship or because of hostility towards newcomers amongst party activists and hierarchies. In many instances – especially in the case of refugees – newcomers simply continue their pre-exile activities. Finally, in post-War Europe, the children of immigrants have found that the state and the media will pay attention to them if they are prepared to riot.

Political consciousness amongst Blacks and Asians in Britain has had a series of aspects since the Second World War. In the first place they have established their own organisations which have focused upon a variety of issues. Some of these political groupings have brought all Black immigrants together – in other words Afro-Caribbeans, Africans and Asians – on an anti-racist platform,

43 U. Hłybinny, 'Belorussian Culture After World War II', *Belorussian Review* 6 (1958), pp. 45–59; P. Urban, 'Belorussian Opposition to the Soviet Regime', *Belorussian Review* 6 (1958), pp. 30–44; Nicholas P. Vakar, 'The Belorussian People Between Extinction and Nationhood', in Erich Goldhagen (ed.), *Ethnic Minorities in the Soviet Union* (New York, 1968), p. 222; Jan Zaprudnik, 'Belorussia and the Belorussians', in Katz, Rogers and Harned, *Handbook of Major Soviet Nationalities*, pp. 63–4.

while others have involved individual ethnic groups. Amongst Asians in Britain, one of the most important early organisations was the Indian Workers' Association (IWA) which came into existence in Coventry in 1938 and held its first national conference in 1958. Despite the name of the organisation, the IWA has essentially been a Punjabi working-class group. The national organisation aimed at improving the life of its members in Britain, fighting racial discrimination and working with the British trade union and Labour movement. It is not particularly militant, playing little role in the disputes involving Asian workers at Imperial Typewriters in Leicester in 1974 and Grunwick in 1978, although it did have much to do with the anti-racist movement which developed during the 1960s.[44]

More recently, Islam has acted as a major political focus for Asians in Britain, especially after the Rushdie affair and the Gulf War, although obviously for a different religious sect from those attracted by the IWA. Several reasons can be given for the rise of Muslim political consciousness from the 1980s, linked to the spread of Islam as the ideology of the persecuted after the Iranian revolution, which struck a chord in the case of British Muslims because of their position on the social and economic ladder. This feeling intensified after attacks occurred upon mosques during the Gulf War in 1991, leading to the formation of a Supreme Council of British Muslims. At its first meeting in Bradford, which began on 20 January 1991 (shortly after the start of the Gulf War), the 200 imams and other religious leaders present unanimously supported the Iraqi invasion of Kuwait, declaring:

> The Muslim community in the United Kingdom is outraged at this savage, destructive war being waged by the United States, Britain and their allies against the Muslims of Iraq. We totally condemn this aggression. It must stop immediately in order to end further destruction of Muslims, their resources and land.

Young British Muslims, meanwhile, declared that they would fight for Saddam Hussein when interviewed on television.[45]

More generally, from the 1960s various organisations developed in Britain with the specific aim of fighting racism. The first major grouping consisted of the Campaign Against Racial Discrimination (CARD), established in December 1964 by a coalition of Black groups and white liberals. It had collapsed by 1967 but during its existence it had helped to bring the issue of racism to the attention of the white media as well as consequently playing a role in the passage of legislation which attempted to tackle prejudice.[46] The other major anti-racist organisation, the Anti-Nazi League, was established in 1977 as a

44 John DeWitt, *Indian Workers' Associations in Britain* (London, 1969); Ron Ramdin, *The Making of the Black Working Class in Britain* (Aldershot, 1987), pp. 396–410; Dilip Hiro, *Black British White British* (London, 1971), pp. 156–66.
45 *Guardian*, 21 January 1991; Akbar S. Ahmed, 'The Next Test for British Muslims', *TLS*, 15 February 1991.
46 John Solomos, *Race and Racism in Britain*, 2nd edn (London, 1993), p. 203; Ramdin, *The Making of the Black Working Class*, pp. 415–37.

reaction to the rise of the National Front. It remained particularly active until 1979. Its supporters came from the Labour Party and groups further to the left of it – most notably the Socialist Workers Party – and essentially aimed at eliminating the National Front from the British political scene. It had limited support from Blacks and Asians, many of whom regarded the amount of energy spent upon the National Front as pointless in view of the existence of inherent long-standing structural racism practised by the British state and British society.[47]

The perennial victimisation of Black youth led to the urban inner-city riots which broke out in locations throughout England during the 1980s. The consequences of the racism which they faced, forcing them to the bottom of the social scale, the creation of media stereotypes about them as a threat to white British citizens – especially as muggers – and the consequent stop-and-search tactics carried out against Black youth by the police during the 1970s and early 1980s meant that they felt they had only one means of making themselves heard – common to all dispossessed sections of any society – in the form of rioting. Although disturbances occurred in Bristol in 1980 and 1986 and in Brixton and Tottenham in 1985, the major nationwide outbreaks of violence took place in the summer of 1981, when most of the major inner-city areas of Britain with Black populations experienced disorder as a 'copycat' scenario developed whereby youths in one city, who suffered the same forms of social injustice as those in areas reported on the television the previous evening, simply carried out similar riotous activities in their own locations. Major areas affected included Moss Side in Manchester, Toxteth in Liverpool and Brixton in south London. Rioters consisted not simply of Afro-Caribbean youths but also members of other ethnic groups living in the inner city, as well as young whites experiencing the same deprived social and economic conditions.

Nevertheless, only a few members of immigrant minorities in Britain have resorted to violence as a means of political expression, as other options have allowed them to take part in mainstream processes. In the first place the ability of post-War newcomers from the Commonwealth to vote has meant that, in contrast to several other European states, they can play exactly the same role in the democratic process as autochthonous Britons. Blacks and Asians made up more than 15 per cent of voters in 51 constituencies in 1981, by which time the two major political parties had recognised the potential importance of ethnic minority votes and began to devote attention to them. However, Black and Asian voters have tended to participate in the electoral process to a lesser extent than white people. Those members of ethnic minorities who have voted have overwhelmingly elected Labour Party candidates. Polls carried out during the 1987 election campaign indicated that 67 per cent of Asians would vote Labour, while the figure for Afro-Caribbeans stood at

47 Solomos, ibid., pp. 211–12; Paul Gilroy, *'There Ain't No Black in the Union Jack': The Cultural Politics of Race and Nation* (London, 1987), pp. 131–5; Gideon Ben-Tovin and John Gabriel, 'The Politics of Race in Britain, 1962–79: A Review of the Major Trends', in Charles Husband (ed.), *'Race' in Britain: Continuity and Change*, 2nd edn (London, 1987), p. 159.

more than 85 per cent. The 1987 general election also saw the first four post-War non-white MPs – all of them representing the Labour Party – enter the House of Commons.[48] Nine ethnic minority MPs were elected in the 1997 election.

North African immigrants in France have also become involved in a variety of organisations. In the first place their homeland governments established associations for the immigrants. The Algerian state set up the Amicale de Algériens en Europe (AAE), with the aim of preventing the assimilation of those of its citizens who had gone overseas. By the early 1980s the AAE had established about 400 centres of Arabisation and also issued two publications, the twice-monthly *L'Algerien en Europe* and a monthly cultural review entitled *Afraq Arabyu*. The Moroccan government established a group called the Amicale des Travailleurs et Commerçants Moroccans en France, with the aim of maintaining the loyalty of immigrants. More recently, a series of Islamic organisations aimed at North African immigrants has developed in France, including the National Federation of French Muslims and the Union of Islamic Organisations in France. Nevertheless, Islamic Fundamentalism has attracted few North African Muslims in France who remain overwhelmingly hostile to the Front Islamique du Salut in Algeria.[49]

Of other minorities in post-War France, Antillean immigrants during the 1960s developed the Regroupement De l'Emigration Antillaise, which had close connections with political groupings in the West Indies struggling for independence from France.[50] Similarly, those Latin American refugees who moved to France during the course of the 1970s continued the activity which had caused their expulsion from their native lands. The political bodies which they established also had *peñas*, social clubs, attached to them, where friends could meet one another and listen to music. In the long run the proletarian exiles would organise themselves into social and sports clubs while the bourgeoisie tended to associate with people of their own occupational group.[51]

Immigrants in France have combined in an attempt to improve aspects of their economic, social and political status. During the late 1960s and early 1970s, demonstrations and riots took place over housing and working conditions. For instance, in 1968 some immigrants protested *against* attempts to destroy the *bidonvilles*. In 1972 foreign workers staged wildcat strikes as a protest against their employment conditions and in the following year held

48 Zig Layton-Henry, *The Politics of Immigration: Immigration, 'Race' and 'Race' Relations in Post-War Britain* (Oxford, 1992), pp. 100–23; Muhamad Anwar, 'Ethnic Minorities and the Electoral Process: Some Recent Developments', in Harry Gouldbourne (ed.), *Black Politics in Britain* (Aldershot, 1990), pp. 33–47; Shamit Saggar, *Race and Politics in Britain* (London, 1992), pp. 122–71.
49 Mark J. Miller, *Foreign Workers in Western Europe: An Emerging Political Force* (New York, 1981), pp. 37–8; Farzana Shaikh, *Islam and Islamic Groups: A Worldwide Reference Guide* (Harlow, 1992), pp. 77–8; Alec G. Hargreaves, *Immigration, 'Race' and Ethnicity in Contemporary France* (London, 1995), p. 125.
50 Joyce Edmond-Smith, 'West Indian Workers in France – III', *New Community* 2 (1973), pp. 308–10.
51 Ana Vasquez, 'The Process of Transculturation: Exiles and Institutions in France', in D. Joly and R. Cohen (eds), *Reluctant Hosts: Europe and its Refugees* (Aldershot, 1989), pp. 125–32.

similar protests against French racism, which had begun to manifest itself in the murder of immigrants. In fact, since the early 1970s protests against racism in France, especially racist violence and the rise of the National Front, have played a large role in uniting diverse immigrant communities, most clearly indicated by the creation of SOS-Racisme in 1984, which was actually supported by the governing Socialist Party. This appealed especially to young second-generation North African immigrants, or *beurs*, as did a number of alternative groupings, notably France-Plus. Inevitably, because of their socio-economic status, intimidations and murders by the police and militant racists, *beurs* have also protested by rioting on numerous occasions.[52]

In Germany immigrants played a large role in industrial disputes during the 1960s, the early 1970s and the aftermath of reunification in the 1990s.[53] Turks have organised themselves across the entire political spectrum. One of the largest groupings consists of Turkish Social Democrats. The mainstream Turkish Conservative parties established the Freiheitliche deutsch-türkische Freundschaftsverein. In addition, parties on the extreme left and right have resorted to violence. One of the best known of these is the Kurdistan Communist Party (PKK), which may have up to 50,000 members in Germany according to some estimates. The organisation has carried out bomb attacks against Turkish targets in Germany and has also organised numerous demonstrations where some protestors set themselves alight.[54]

As a result of racist violence which followed reunification in 1990, an anti-racist movement also developed in Germany. Its largest demonstration involved over 300,000 people in Berlin in November 1992, including the German President, Richard von Weizäcker. Tens of thousands of people attended the funeral of three victims of a petrol-bomb attack in Mölln near Hamburg at the end of November 1992, including the German foreign minister Klaus Kinkel. On 29 May 1993 a fire-bomb attack in Solingen killed five Turks and led to more demonstrations by their compatriots, which, on this occasion, turned violent in Solingen, Bremen, Duisburg and Augsburg. Civil disobedience also occurred in the form of the blocking of motorways around Solingen, Hamburg, Bonn and Cologne. The protests had died down somewhat by 2 June. On the following day a memorial service took place for the victims of Solingen in Cologne, attended by President von Weizäcker and several government ministers. On the same evening violence broke out in Bremen, Cologne and, more seriously, in Hamburg, where several million Deutschmarks' worth of damage resulted. The last outbreaks of violence occurred on Saturday 5 June, the most serious in Solingen, Berlin and Stuttgart.[55]

52 Miller, *Foreign Workers in Western Europe*, pp. 85–104; Ireland, *Policy Challenge of Ethnic Diversity*, pp. 81–93; Alec G. Hargreaves, 'The Political Mobilization of the North African Immigrant Community in France', *Ethnic and Racial Studies* 14 (1991), pp. 350–67.
53 Miller, *Foreign Workers in Western Europe*, pp. 104–13.
54 *Focus* 7, 28 June 1993; Bundesministerium des Innern, *Verfassungsschutzbericht, 1992* (Bonn, 1993), pp. 146–53.
55 See Panikos Panayi, 'Racial Violence in the New Germany, 1990–93', *Contemporary European History* 3 (1994), pp. 274–5, 279.

Turks in Germany, in many ways, have had no choice but to resort to civil disobedience because of their virtual exclusion from all democratic political processes due to the difficulty of obtaining German citizenship, which means that they cannot vote. The Netherlands, in contrast, resembles Britain because immigrants who entered the state from overseas territories have voting rights. As in Britain, the Dutch parties have made special efforts to appeal to immigrants although – once again resembling Britain – the newcomers have tended to vote heavily in favour of the social democratic Partij van de Arbeid. When Surinamese and Antilleans began to stand as candidates in both local and national elections during the 1980s, most represented this grouping.[56]

Because of their social status, lack of literacy and concentration in eastern European totalitarian states, Gypsies also remained fairly primitive in terms of political organisation. In Czechoslovakia the Gypsy population does not seem to have had any formal organisation until the period of liberalisation within this state at the end of the 1960s. In January 1968 the government allowed – as well as funded – the establishment of the Union of Gypsy-Romanies. The initiative for the body had come from a group of Gypsy intellectuals in Bratislava. It aimed at alerting the majority populations about the position of the Gypsies and the prejudice which they faced, as well as celebrating Gypsy distinctiveness. The Union organised a wide range of activities and aroused much pride and interest amongst Gypsies in Czechoslovakia. By the time it held its first national conference in 1969 it had attracted 5,000 members. However, following the Soviet invasion of Czechoslovakia in 1968 the Union became superfluous and disappeared in 1973.[57] New Gypsy organisations did not appear until after the Czechoslovak revolution at the end of 1989, which resulted in the birth of countless associations representing all manner of interests. The first Gypsy groupings included the Party of the Democratic Romany Union and the Party of the Integration of the Romany People in Slovakia. The most important was the Romany Civic Forum, which had over 70,000 members by the time of its first national meeting in Prague in the spring of 1990.[58]

In Hungary several Gypsy organisations existed with state support, usually for short periods, before the 1990s. These groups included the Hungarian Gypsies Council Federation, which lasted from 1957 until 1961, and the National Council for Gypsy Affairs, which survived for several decades. In 1985

56 See: Martin Custers, 'Muslims in the Netherlands', in Syed Z. Abedin and Ziauddin Sardar, *Muslim Minorities in the West* (London, 1995), pp. 87–8; and three articles by Jan Rath: 'Mobilization of Ethnicity in Dutch Politics', in Malcolm Cross and Hans Entzinger (eds), *Lost Illusions: Caribbean Minorities in Britain and the Netherlands* (London, 1988), pp. 267–84; 'Political Action of Immigrants in the Netherlands: Class or Ethnicity', *European Journal of Political Research* 16 (1988), pp. 623–42; 'Voting Rights', in Zig Layton-Henry (ed.), *The Political Rights of Migrant Workers in Western Europe* (London, 1990), pp. 137–9.
57 Josef Kalvoda, 'The Gypsies of Czechoslovakia', *Nationalities Papers* 19 (1991), pp. 277–8; Eva Davidóva, 'The Gypsies of Czechoslovakia: Part II: Post-War Developments', *Journal of the Gypsy Lore Society* 50 (1971), pp. 53–4; David J. Kostelancik, 'The Gypsies of Czechoslovakia: Political and Ideological Considerations', *Studies in Comparative Communism* 22 (1989), pp. 317–18.
58 Kalvoda, 'Gypsies of Czechoslovakia', pp. 290–1; Crowe, *History of the Gypsies*, pp. 64–5.

the government established the National Roma Council, followed by regional councils in 1986. Such bodies essentially represented 'extensions of the ruling Hungarian Workers Party' but they gave Gypsies political experience, which they used to open new groups, especially after the collapse of the old order. In 1990 there existed seven Gypsy parties and within three years 230 Roma groups of all types in Hungary. The most important of these, founded in 1989 and 1990, included the Democratic Alliance of Hungarian Gypsies, the Nationality Council of Gypsies in Hungary, the Hungarian Gypsy Party and the Hungarian Gypsies Social Democratic Party. Two of the major Hungarian political parties, the Association of Free Democrats and the Hungarian Democratic Forum, came to agreements with Gypsy organisations and declared their support for their aims. In addition, a Roma Parliament articulated the demands of the Gypsies to the government and National Assembly.[59]

In Bulgaria, a deliberate policy pursued during the 1950s had eliminated almost 200 Romany organisations but new ones developed after 1989. The largest of these consisted of the Democratic Union of Gypsies, whose leader, Manush Romanov, became a member of parliament under the banner of the Union of Democratic Forces in the 1990 election. However, the 1990 Law on Political Parties prohibited the registration of political parties based upon ethnicity, which meant that all such groupings had disappeared by 1991 and could therefore not participate in the election of that year.[60]

In western Europe Gypsies have fared little better in terms of their political development, even though they may not have faced direct state suppression. In Britain the formation of the Gypsy Council in 1966 represented a major development. This came into existence at a meeting held in St Mary Cray in Kent, attended by both Gypsies and their supporters. The latter clearly played a central role in politicising the Gypsies, with Gratton Puxon, the English writer and campaigner on their behalf, becoming the first secretary of the Gypsy Council. The organisation aimed to unify Gypsies, protecting their right to self-determination and preserving their traditional way of life. It played a large role in the campaign against the Caravan Sites Act of 1968.[61] In Germany the *Verband Deutscher Sinti* made efforts to gain compensation for the persecution which Gypsies had faced during the Second World War, again assisted by Gratton Puxon.[62]

---

59 Zoltan D. Barany, 'Hungary's Gypsies', *Report on Eastern Europe* (20 July 1990), pp. 28–30; Amnesty International Archive, London, M. Kovats, 'The Political Development of the Hungarian Roma Since the Change of System'; Bugajski, *Ethnic Politics in Eastern Europe*, pp. 417–20; Crowe, *History of the Gypsies*, p. 102.

60 Helsinki Watch, *Destroying Ethnic Identity: The Gypsies of Bulgaria* (New York, 1991), pp. 42–5; Luan Troxel, 'Bulgaria's Gypsies: Numerically Strong, Politically Weak', *Radio Free Europe/Radio Liberty Research Report* (6 March 1992), pp. 60–1; Simon Simonov, 'The Gypsies: A Re-Emerging Minority', *Report on Eastern Europe* 1 (25 May 1990), p. 14.

61 See: Thomas Acton, *Gypsy Politics and Social Change* (London, 1974); and Barbara Adams, Judith Okely, David Morgan and David Smith, *Gypsies and Government Policy in England* (London, 1975).

62 Gratton Puxon, 'Gypsies Seek Reparations', *Patterns of Prejudice* 15 (1981), pp. 21–5.

In some of the states containing small, persecuted Muslim minorities, the level of political development has not progressed beyond that of the Gypsies. In Bulgaria, a resistance movement against repression emerged amongst Turks during the 1980s. Mass protests occurred in many cities in the Turkish part of Bulgaria in 1989; on several occasions the authorities reacted by opening fire and killing demonstrators. In the middle of June 1989 about 1,000 Turks who had faced arrest went on hunger strike. In January 1988 six Turks joined the Independent Association for the Defence of Human Rights in Bulgaria and by February 1989 about 50 out of 300 members of the organisation consisted of Turks. In addition, two Turkish associations came into existence in the form of the Democratic League for the Defence of the Rights of Man, formed at the end of 1988, and the Association for the Support of Vienna, established in January 1989.[63] In the post-communist period the Movement for Rights and Freedoms, an overwhelmingly Turkish organisation, has been the most important body representing the Turks of Bulgaria.[64]

The Turks of Western Thrace enjoyed freedom of association in the first few decades after the Treaty of Lausanne, but organisations formed in this early period faced curtailment after the deterioration of relations between Greece and Turkey over the Cyprus issue. The Western Thrace Turks have had representatives in the Greek Parliament, whose number stood at three during the 1950s but had declined to two by the end of the 1980s, when one of the two MPs elected, Sadik Ahmet – together with one of his campaigners, Ibrahim Şerif – faced imprisonment for allegedly spreading slanderous information about the major Greek parties. Turkish resistance to the actions of the Greek state has included demonstrations, but one such event in Komotini, in 1988, was followed by bomb explosions in the central mosque and a Muslim cemetery.[65]

Amongst Muslim minorities in the Soviet Union, the Crimean Tatars represented one of the best organised of dissident groups. After facing deportation during the Second World War, their position did not improve for several decades after the conflict. In 1946 a statement by the Presidium of the Supreme Soviet of the Russian Republic declared that they had committed treason, after which they virtually became non-persons. Limited improvement occurred during the 1950s, when Crimean Tatars began to publish in their own language. But their position did not recover as significantly as other peoples deported during the Second World War. Consequently, in 1957 the Crimean Tatars launched a campaign for political rehabilitation, repatriation and restoration of the Crimean ASSR. The campaign began with petitions and escalated into

63 Hugh Poulton, *The Balkans: Minorities and States in Conflict*, 2nd edn (London, 1993), pp. 153–7.
64 Bugajski, *Ethnic Politics in Eastern Europe*, pp. 249–52; Wolfgang Höpken, 'From Religious Identity to Ethnic Mobilisation: The Turks of Bulgaria before, under and since Communism', in Hugh Poulton and Suka Taji-Farouki (eds), *Muslim Identity and the Balkan State* (London, 1997), pp. 72–81.
65 K. G. Andreades, *The Moslem Minority in Western Thrace* (Thessaloniki, 1956), p. 27; Isma'il Balic, 'Muslims in Greece', *Islamic Review* 40 (1952), p. 36; International Affairs Agency, *The Western Thrace Turks Issues in Turkish–Greek Relations* (Istanbul, 1992), pp. 42–8, 101; Shaikh, *Islam and Islamic Groups*, p. 85.

mass demonstrations, which resulted in arrests of the leaders of the Crimean Tatar movement. Nevertheless, by the middle of the 1960s the Crimean Tatars had established a permanent lobby in Moscow and founded 'Action Groups' in all of the areas in which they lived.

Although repression continued, the Soviet authorities eventually gave in to the pressure and, in 1967, issued a decree recognising the mistake made in deporting Crimean Tatars during the Second World War and restoring their full political rights – but not their autonomous republic, which meant that only limited resettlement occurred in the Crimea. Consequently, activity continued for the attainment of this final aim after 1967, in the form of petitions, demonstrations and political groupings, with no concrete results other than continued arrests and trials by the Soviet authorities. However, Tatars continued to return to the Crimea. Campaigning intensified under Gorbachev and into the post-Soviet period. Despite the fact that return had become easier, the Crimean Tatars had not regained their autonomous status, although they had developed their own political parties and gained representatives on both a local and national government level in the new Ukrainian state.[66]

Some of the localised minorities of Europe have only achieved limited political organisation because of their size, as the example of the Lapps illustrates. A series of groupings have developed concerned with both the preservation of the newly created Lapp culture and the rights of the Sami population. The leadership consists of either Lapps or members of the dominant populations interested in the Sami. Such bodies began to develop in the first half of the twentieth century, but only really established themselves after 1945.

The most important grouping in Sweden, the Svenska Samernas Riksförbund, came into existence in 1950 with the aim of overseeing and working for the improvement of the economic, social, political and legal position of the Sami population in the state. In Finland the first major Sami organisation, the Samii Litto, came into existence in 1945 through the efforts of Finnish liberals and Lapps. Other bodies have grown up revolving around particular groups of Finnish Lapps focused, for instance, on particular occupations or geographical locations. Furthermore, in 1972 a 20-member Lappish parliament came into existence working for the rights of the Finnish Lapps; elections regularly attract an 80 per cent turn-out. In Norway the major organisation is the Norska Samers Riksforbund, created in 1969 as a unifying body for all of the Norwegian groupings. The more radical ones have included the Sami Movement, which managed to mobilise Norwegian Lapps in the late 1970s and 1980s in order to protest against the construction of a dam in Masi in Sami territory in northern Norway.

In 1956 a conference in Karasjok in northern Norway established the Nordic Lapp Council which aimed at guarding the economic, social and cultural

66 V. Stanley Vardys, 'The Case of the Crimean Tatars', *Russian Review* 30 (1971), pp. 101–10; Sheehy, *Crimean Tatars and the Volga Germans*, pp. 9–24; Alan W. Fisher, *The Crimean Tatars* (Stanford, CA, 1978), pp. 172–200; Edward J. Lazzerini, 'The Crimean Tatars', in Smith, *Nationalities Question*, pp. 420–33.

interests of the Sami people throughout Scandinavia. It has succeeded in obtaining fairly equal rights for Lapps by playing the Scandinavian states off against each other. The other major transnational organisation is the Nordic Lapp Institute, established in 1973, working with the Nordic Lapp Council and organising research on the Lapps.[67]

NATIONALIST POLITICAL PARTIES

The most populous, advanced and concentrated minorities in Europe potentially have the ability to develop full-blown political parties which could obtain independence – or, at least, autonomy – an eventuality which has happened in many cases, especially in eastern Europe after communism, where rising nationalism played a large role in the collapse of the old order. In other instances, such as Cyprus and Yugoslavia, the nationalist movements have simply clashed with each other, which has often resulted in war. In yet other cases, such as Britain or Turkey, the ruling elites regard the peripheral areas as too fundamental a part of the body politic to let them go.

Several areas of western Europe have contained nationalist movements which have managed to improve the political position of the people which they represent. In the South Tyrol, the German speakers who form the majority of the population have become completely politicised. At the end of the Second World War they expected to rejoin Austria, but the Allies decided against this. Instead, the German population has attempted to gain autonomy, supported by the Austrian state. The German speakers of the South Tyrol pursued various methods in their attempts to achieve greater autonomy than that granted in the Autonomy Statute of 1948. The most popular has consisted of voting for the Südtiroler Volkspartei (SVP), established in 1954, which has regularly taken over 90 per cent of the German vote. During the late 1950s some members of the German minority resorted to violence, so that in 1961 47 bombs exploded on government property, usually frontier posts or pylons, which resulted in several deaths. As well as the SVP, various other parties representing the Germans have developed in the South Tyrol, usually lasting for only a few years (such as the South Tyrolean Social Democratic Party, which existed between 1945 and 1948).[68]

In both the Basque land and Catalonia nationalist groups have a history dating back to the nineteenth century and, despite the repression practised by

67 Ruong, *Lapps in Sweden*, pp. 100–4; Jones, *Sami of Lapland*, pp. 12–14; Asp, Rantanen and Munter, *Lapps and the Lappish Culture*, pp. 53–61; Harald Eidheim, *Aspects of the Lappish Minority Situation* (Oslo, 1977), p. 45; Helvi Nuorgam-Poutasuo, Juha Pentikäinen and Lassi Saressalo, 'The Sami in Finland: A Case Study', in Finnish National Commission for UNESCO (ed.), *Cultural Pluralism and the Position of Minorities in Finland* (Helsinki, 1981), pp. 91–2; Rowland G. P. Hill (ed.), *The Lapps Today in Finland, Norway and Sweden* (Paris, 1960).

68 Peter J. Katzenstein, 'Ethnic Conflict in the South Tyrol', in Martin J. Esman (ed.), *Ethnic Conflict in the Modern World* (London, 1977), pp. 300–23; Minority Rights Group, *Co-Existence in Some Plural Societies* (London, 1986), pp. 4–5; Straka, *Handbuch der europäischen Volksgruppen*, pp. 373–5.

Franco after his victory in the Civil War, this nationalism had resurfaced again by the end of the 1950s. In the Basque region the two most important parties consisted of the Partita Nacionalista Vasco (PNV), which had survived Franco, and its militant offshoot, Euskadi ta Askatasuna (ETA). Most of the PNV supporters initially went into exile and they began returning during the 1950s when the PNV started recruiting members from a series of cultural organisations such as climbing clubs and folk-dancing societies. Although the PNV lost membership and influence to ETA during the 1960s and early 1970s, it emerged stronger than ETA in the liberal democratic state which succeeded the death of Franco, with middle-class business support and a moderate non-racist programme stressing cultural and linguistic difference. However, its ultimate aim remained the creation of an independent Basque state. Since the middle of the 1970s the group has developed very much into a political movement with local branches, women's organisations, peasant associations and youth and cultural groups. It has also been the most successful Basque party in electoral terms.

ETA came into existence in 1959, growing out of a student group, Ekin, which had founded an eponymous magazine. It had entered the PNV's activist youth branch, Euzko Gastedi, and complete separation from the PNV occurred in 1959. The new organisation had a more left-wing outlook and was prepared to use violence to achieve its aims. It modelled itself on the national liberation movements in Cuba, Algeria and Vietnam. ETA aimed at protecting the Basque language and culture. The level of its activity was intense and included kidnappings and attacks upon policemen and suspected police informers. During 1975–6 the group carried out between one and two assassinations per week, although its biggest prize had been gained in 1973 when it killed Admiral Carrero Blanco, Franco's heir apparent. ETA also demanded 'revolutionary taxes' and other extortions on threat of death, as well as carrying out armed robberies. ETA split into several factions during the 1970s, one of which played a large role in forming a party called the Herri Batasuna, which was second to the PNV in terms of parliamentary representation amongst Basque nationalist parties by the early 1980s. In addition, ETA continued to exist as a military group carrying out acts of violence, reaching a peak in 1980 when it killed 80 people.[69]

Many Catalan political activists went into exile during the early years of the Franco regime. The opposition which did take place within Catalonia tended to focus on universities, the Church, or the remnants of the socialist and

69 The above account of Basque nationalism is based upon: Marianne Heiberg, *The Making of the Basque Nation* (Cambridge, 1989), pp. 103–29; J. Martín Ramirez and Bobbie Sullivan, 'The Basque Conflict', in Jerry Boucher, Dan Landis and Arnold Clark (eds), *Ethnic Conflict: International Perspectives* (London, 1987), pp. 128–33; Cyrus Ernesto Zirakzadeh, *A Rebellious People: Basques, Protests and Politics* (Reno and Las Vegas, 1991), p. 186; John Sullivan, *ETA and Basque Nationalism: The Struggle For Euskadi, 1890–1986* (London, 1988), p. 22; Juan Díez Medrano, *Divided Nations: Class, Politics, and Nationalism in the Basque Country and Catalonia* (Ithaca, NY, 1995), pp. 134–51; Daniele Conversi, *The Basques, The Catalans and Spain: Alternative Routes to Nationalist Mobilisation* (London, 1997), pp. 80–108, 222–56.

communist movement which often manifested itself in the form of industrial action. Major groupings included the Socialist Movement of Catalonia (MSC) and the Workers' Front of Catalonia (FOC). Unlike the Basque case, radical nationalist organisations had less of a role to play in Catalonia, with the main organisations including the Catalan National Front (FNC). The groups which survived into the post-Franco period had three demands: 'Freedom, Amnesty and Statute of Autonomy'. However, in contrast to the situation in the Basque land, nationalist parties in Catalonia have had limited success so that the major groupings are those which dominate Spanish politics.[70]

Rising nationalist movements in post-War eastern Europe would play a large role in the ultimate collapse of several states. Slovaks played a major part in the liberalisation period of the 1960s leading up to the Prague Spring of 1968, with a cultural grouping called the Matica Slovenska demanding the same rights as the Hungarian minority. The dissent against the state during the 1970s and 1980s actually had little to do with Slovak nationalism but focused upon civil rights. This changed after the 'Velvet Revolution' of 1989 when a series of Slovak parties quickly developed, demanding autonomy or independence. The first of these was the Slovak Nationalist Party which came into existence in March 1990 and gained 14 per cent of the vote in the general election in June of that year. The most important group, the Movement for a Democratic Slovakia (MDS), was formed in March 1991, when it split away from Public Against Violence, the group which had overthrown the communists from power. The MDS negotiated the peaceful 'Velvet Divorce', which came into operation at the start of 1993.[71]

The Soviet authorities did everything to eradicate traces of political nationalism, using methods such as deportation and the elimination of political elites. But the vitality of local cultures, the education of elites, recent memories of nation states and the existence of political nationalism in the west could not prevent similar developments occurring in the Soviet Union, aided by the implementation of the liberalisation programme of Gorbachev and the economic crisis of the Soviet Union during the 1970s and 1980s. Perestroika simply allowed the peripheral elites of the Soviet Union to turn to liberalism and its twin ideology of nationalism, meaning that, in a situation in which the Soviet authorities would not use violence, independent states would emerge. In this sense the death of the Soviet Union resembles the collapse of the European empires earlier in the post-War period. Britain and France could

70 Albert Balcells, *Catalan Nationalism: Past and Present* (London, 1996), pp. 125–201; Hank Johnston, *Tales of Nationalism: Catalonia, 1939–1979* (Brunswick, NJ, 1991); Medrano, ibid., pp. 152–73.
71 H. Gordon Skilling, 'Ferment Amongst Czechs and Slovaks', *International Journal* 19 (1964), pp. 496–512; Ferdinand Durcansky, 'Czech-Slovak Relations – CSSR's Unsettled Issue', *Central European Journal* (March 1968), pp. 891–5; G. Ashworth and R. Fegley, 'Czechoslovakia: Nationalities and "Normalisation"', in G. Ashworth (ed.), *World Minorities*, Vol. 3 (Sunbury, 1980), pp. 29–30; Miroslav Kusy, 'Slovak Exceptionalism', in Jiří Musil (ed.), *The End of Czechoslovakia* (Budapest, 1995), p. 143; Bugajski, *Ethnic Politics in Eastern Europe*, pp. 324–5, 333–4; Stanislav J. Kirschbaum, *A History of Slovakia: The Struggle for Survival* (New York, 1995), pp. 251–79.

hold on to their territorial possessions only as long as the process did not involve a loss of blood on a large scale. But once this became a condition, the imperial powers withdrew, although in most cases they continued to maintain a presence of some sort, either economic, political, military or through a residual population. The Soviet Union followed the same process. As Gorbachevism was not Stalinism there was never any question of killing non-Russian peoples on a large scale. Similarly, the Russians continued to maintain a presence in the areas which they had formerly controlled. Finally, the collapse of the Soviet Union created as many ethnic problems as it solved because – inevitably in any process of state creation – the new political entities have minority populations with minority cultures and minority nationalisms.

Political nationalism in the Soviet Ukraine remained weaker than it did in other republics, due mostly to Stalin's draconian policies here – but it did exist. For instance, between 1945 and 1950 the Ukrainian Insurgent Army, which had survived the Second World War, may have killed up to 35,000 Soviet security troops.[72] The movement managed to continue due to a series of factors including the favourable terrain, the almost unanimous support of the rural population and a fanatical ideology and closely controlled organisational structure.[73]

A second phase of Ukrainian nationalism developed after the death of Stalin and the thaw which followed in the Kruschev era. Many of the millions of Ukrainians deported to Siberia were allowed to return home. The manifestations of Ukrainian nationalism took various forms. For instance, in 1964 a group called the Ukrainian National Front came into existence and published a journal in 1965 and 1966 called *Fatherland and Freedom*. At the end of the 1960s a dissident movement developed in the Republic, consisting mostly of white-collar staff, especially academics. About 1,000 active dissidents lived in the Ukraine during the 1960s, although there were more sympathisers. Their concerns focused upon nationality as well as civil rights and religious issues. A new dissident publication, the *Ukrainian Journal*, began to appear both in the Ukraine and abroad, as Ukrainians in North America played a large role in perpetuating Ukrainian national consciousness. In 1975 the Soviet Union signed the Helsinki Accord, formally agreeing to respect civil rights, and in the following year 37 dissidents formed a Ukrainian Helsinki group in Kiev. However, by 1980 the organisation had disappeared, with its members either in prison or in exile.[74]

Repression continued in the early 1980s but by this time Ukrainian nationalism had begun to gain support from other sources. For instance, North American universities had founded two chairs and two institutes in Ukrainian

72 Walter Dushnyck, 'Discrimination and Abuse of Power in the USSR', in Willem A. Veenhoven et al. (eds), *Case Studies in Human Rights and Fundamental Freedoms: A World Survey* (The Hague, 1975), p. 469.
73 J. A. Armstrong, *Ukrainian Nationalism*, 3rd edn (New York, 1990), p. 224.
74 Subtelny, *Ukraine*, pp. 514–18; Szporluk, 'The Ukraine and the Ukrainians', pp. 44–6; Krawchenko, *Social Change and National Consciousness in Twentieth Century Ukraine*, pp. 250–4; Armstrong, ibid., pp. 229–33.

studies. In addition, a Ukrainian Patriotic Movement had come into existence within the Republic in 1980. By the second half of the 1980s, under the influence of Gorbachev, a Ukrainian cultural and political movement had developed apace. Mass meetings occurred in Lvov before the Moscow Communist Party Conference of June 1988, while much public attention in the Republic focused upon the Chernobyl disaster. By the end of 1989 about 30,000 national or cultural organisations had developed in the Ukraine, the most important of which included the Popular Movement for Restructuring in Ukraine. In the following year it began calling for Ukrainian independence, and by the end of 1991 this had become a reality, following demonstrations by miners and the formation of a Democratic Bloc – which won the elections in 1990 – and the adverse reaction to the communist coup in August 1991. However – inevitably in the new state – simultaneously with the development of Ukrainian nationalism during the late 1980s, movements had also developed amongst the various minorities which existed within the borders of the Ukraine, including the Tatars.[75]

Because of the lateness of incorporation in the Soviet Union and their history as independent states for two decades before their annexation by Stalin – as well as their advanced economic development – the Baltic states became extremely vociferous in demanding independence during the last decade of the Soviet Union. In fact, nationalist movements had survived into the immediate post-War period. For instance, in Estonia a group called the Armed Resistance League aimed at the restoration of that country's independence, which it hoped to achieve 'at such a time when England and the United States go to war against the Soviet Union, or when a political coup occurs in the Soviet Union itself'. Although the organisation had widespread support and was tightly controlled, the Soviet security services had wiped it out by the early 1950s. Similar movements also developed in Lithuania and Latvia during the early post-War period.[76]

Nationalist movements in the Baltic republics took off during the 1980s but there had been other stirrings after the 1950s. For instance, in Estonia two groups in 1972 – the Estonian National Front and the Estonian Democratic Movement – sent a joint memorandum to the United Nations calling for UN-supervised elections in Estonia as a prelude to independence. These bodies had small numbers and dissent of this nature continued throughout the 1970s.[77] In Lithuania, mass demonstrations had occurred in Vilnius in 1956 and Kaunus in 1960, while in 1972 a full-scale riot occurred in Kaunus when a young man, Romas Kalanta, set fire to himself as a protest against the

---

75 Taras Kuzio and Andrew Wilson, *Ukraine: Perestroika to Independence* (London, 1994), pp. 61, 192–202; Subtelny, *Ukraine*, pp. 575–6; David Saunders, 'What Makes a Nation a Nation? Ukrainians Since 1600', *Ethnic Studies* 10 (1993), pp. 103–6.
76 Mart Laar, *War in the Woods: Estonia's Struggle for Survival, 1944–1956* (Washington, DC, 1993); Anatol Lieven, *The Baltic Revolution: Estonia, Latvia, Lithuania and the Path to Independence*, 2nd edn (London, 1994), pp. 87–92.
77 Rein Taagepera, *Estonia: The Road to Independence* (Boulder, CO, 1993), pp. 102–3.

regime.[78] As many as one-third of the dissidents during the 1970s consisted of Roman Catholic priests, while students and academics made up the majority of the rest.[79] During the early 1980s activity in the Baltic states intensified under inspiration from the Solidarity-led protests in Poland so that there followed strikes and marches and further anti-Soviet publications in the Baltics, although the Soviet state reacted with repressive policies which meant that, on this occasion, the protestors would not prove able to change the constitutional position of the Baltic states within the USSR.[80]

They had to wait several more years for such developments, inspired by the liberal atmosphere of Perestroika. Demonstrations began in 1987, sparked off by the Chernobyl disaster, which led to concern about the effects of industrialisation upon the Baltic region. In Estonia protestors in 1987 displayed particular concern about the consequences of phosphate mining within their country. However, within a year demonstrators had become more overtly nationalistic so that mass meetings took place commemorating events connected with the Soviet annexation. At the same time – as the first step towards the formation of political parties – cultural associations also developed, such as the Estonian National Heritage Society. By May 1988 full-blown political parties had come into existence in the form of the Estonian Popular Front, which claimed to have 40,000 members, the Latvian Popular Front and the Lithuanian Restructuring Movement (Sajūdis). By the following spring, when elections to the Congress of People's Deputies occurred, the new movements had already begun to strive for sovereignty, an aim which all three Baltic states had achieved by the autumn of 1991, despite armed intervention by Soviet troops earlier in the year.[81]

Nationalism played the fundamental role in the collapse of Yugoslavia, but in this instance a range of conflicting ideologies led to the head-on collision of the 1990s. In the first place, several Muslim groups in Yugoslavia politicised themselves. A Bosnian religious Islamic movement emerged under the influence of Alia Itzebegović in the late 1960s, when he wrote his *Islamic Declaration*, for which he faced trial in 1983, along with twelve other activists during a state clampdown against Muslims. Itzebegović went to prison for advocating the creation of an ethnically pure Bosnian Muslim state and the introduction of western parliamentary democracy. He was released in 1988 and two years later founded the Party of Democratic Action (PDA), which had branches throughout Yugoslavia and won 86 out of 240 seats in elections to the Bosnian assembly in 1990, with Itzebegović becoming the first President of the Assembly.

78 Romuald J. Misiunas, 'The Baltic Republics: Stagnation and Strivings for Sovereignty', in Lubomyr Hajda and Mark Beissinger (eds), *The Nationalities Factor in Soviet Politics and Society* (Boulder, CO, 1990), pp. 221–2.
79 Thomas A. Oleszczuk, *Political Justice in the USSR: Dissent and Repression in Lithuania, 1969–1987* (Boulder, CO, 1988).
80 V. Stanley Vardys, 'Polish Echoes in the Baltic', *Problems of Communism* (July–August 1983), pp. 21–34.
81 Misiunas, 'Baltic Republics', pp. 207–13; Lieven, *Baltic Revolution*, pp. 214–315; Taagepera, *Estonia*, pp. 121–96.

But the PDA split in October when Adil Zulfikarpašić became leader of the newly established Muslim Bosnian Organisation. During 1991 the groups carried out violent acts against each other. In addition, there followed the Muslim Democratic Party in 1992, which wanted to see a confederation between Bosnia-Herzegovina and Croatia.

At the same time that these Muslim organisations appeared in Bosnia, there also developed groupings representing the interests of Serbs and Croats within the Republic. These consisted of the Bosnian branch of the Serbian Democratic Party, founded in July 1990 by Radovan Karadžić, and the Bosnian branch of the Croatian Democratic Union, founded in October 1990. By the end of 1990 these parties controlled different villages in Bosnia as ethnic politics began to take control here, as elsewhere in Yugoslavia, waiting to explode.[82]

Similar developments occurred in one of the other major Muslim areas of Yugoslavia, Kosovo. In this case, Albanian and Serbian nationalists clashed. The background for the emergence of Albanian nationalism lay in the demographic growth of the area, which, however, did not manifest itself in economic advance or the granting of republican status. Discontent amongst the Kosovo Albanians surfaced during the 1970s, under the leadership of Adem Demaqi, who faced imprisonment along with eighteen other Albanians in February 1976 for creating the National Liberation Movement of Kosovo, which aimed at unifying Kosovo with Albania – the real fear of Serbs. The sentences did not quench nationalist desires so that in 1979 pamphlets began to circulate in Kosovo which attacked the Yugoslav state. In 1981 large-scale demonstrations (involving five major groupings) occurred, leading to the sentencing of nearly 3,000 people. The repressive policy continued throughout the 1980s.[83] In a classic situation of ethnic conflict, the position in Kosovo deteriorated further with the development of Serb nationalism at the end of the 1980s, leading to violence and – countering this – further repressive policies from the Yugoslav state, resulting in a spiral of conflict in which each side reacted to the other. This reached a head in 1998–9 when the Kosovo Liberation Army began to emerge and face repression from Yugoslav forces.[84]

For much of the post-War period the major nationalist cleavage in Yugoslavia involved Croats and Serbs. This conflict surfaced during the late 1960s and early 1970s over the issue of the redistribution of resources within Yugoslavia. The Croatian nationalism of these years was led by members of the intelligentsia in the Republic and had the support of the Communist Party here, as well as the backing of students and workers. By 1971 a movement calling for reform of the Yugoslav constitution had developed, known as Maspok or the Croatian Spring. It involved street demonstrations, riots at football matches,

82 The above account is based on: Noel Malcolm, *Bosnia: A Short History* (London, 1994), pp. 200–1, 208, 222–3; Bugajski, *Ethnic Politics in Eastern Europe*, pp. 25–32; and Misha Glenny, *The Fall of Yugoslavia: The Third Balkan War*, 2nd edn (London, 1993), p. 147.
83 Poulton, *The Balkans*, pp. 60–6.
84 See Noel Malcolm, *Kosovo: A Short History* (London, 1998), pp. 314–57, for the 1980s and 1990s.

anti-Serb articles in the Croatian press and the destruction of signs written in the Cyrillic alphabet (used by Serbs), as well as the development of non-communist organisations such as Matica Hrvatska, ostensibly of a cultural nature but in reality political. General Tito reacted to these developments using a 'carrot-and-stick' policy. On the one hand a new constitution of 1974 addressed some of the grievances of the Croatian nationalists, but before that the Maspok had been crushed, involving hundreds of arrests and the purging of the Croatian League of Communists. Croatian nationalism remained under control until the end of the 1980s, although dissidents such as Franjo Tudjman faced imprisonment at the start of that decade.[85]

Much of the fuel for the fire of Serbian nationalism came from what the movement viewed as concessions made to smaller minorities. Resentment grew in intensity, especially after 1974 when Kosovo, an integral part of Serbia, gained a status which gave it almost as much autonomy as the rest of the republics; this resentment became especially powerful at the end of the 1980s and into the 1990s.[86] Serb nationalism essentially revolved around the concept of a greater Serbia.[87]

Yugoslavia in the late 1980s and early 1990s represents the best example of one form of nationalism giving birth to another as each group decided to defend its interests against the other. Each variety of nationalism which developed usually had more than one enemy. The complexity of historically evolved settlement patterns meant that not only did nationalist movements evolve in the former republics, but every representative of another minority living within the borders of one of these states developed its own irredentist organisation. Nothing could better illustrate the dangers of nationalism than the number of organisations which developed during these years, as well as the murderous policies to which they gave rise. The starting point for the growth of contemporary nationalism amongst the Yugoslav republics may be the death of Marshal Tito (who represented the symbol holding the whole system together) in 1980, but the rise of the intolerant and aggressively patriotic Slobodan Milošević to the head of the Serbian League of Communists in 1986 and to the Presidency of Serbia in 1989 provided the fuse for the explosion which followed. Essentially, his policy – backed by the Serbian press and intellectuals – developed into one supporting a Greater Serbia in which he would ignore the views of the other Yugoslav peoples.

Inevitably, as these events unfolded, similar developments occurred in the other Yugoslav republics. In Slovenia, where nationalism had begun to stir during the 1970s, it had become more of an organised artistic, intellectual and political movement by the end of the 1980s. The self-confidence of Slovenian nationalism led to the development of an opposition party called DEMOS,

---

85 Christopher Bennet, *Yugoslavia's Bloody Collapse* (London, 1995), pp. 70–4; Poulton, *The Balkans*, pp. 31–2; Franjo Tudjman, *Nationalism in Contemporary Europe* (Boulder, CO, 1981), pp. 132–5.
86 Poulton, *The Balkans*, p. 16.
87 Fred Singleton, *Twentieth Century Yugoslavia* (London, 1976), p. 229.

which won a majority in elections in the Republic held in April 1990. By the end of 1990 Slovenia had essentially split away from the increasingly Serb-dominated Yugoslavia, despite threats from the Yugoslav army and Milošević.

By this time Croatian nationalists had also asserted themselves in their own republic, again largely as a reaction against Serbian chauvinism. In this instance, the party that came to the fore consisted of Franjo Tudjman's Croatian Democratic Union, which won the 1990 elections in Croatia and took the same action as Slovenia in declaring independence in June 1991. However, the presence of a substantial Serbian minority in Croatia complicated matters and acted as the pretext for armed intervention by the Serb-controlled Yugoslav army. The rest of the 1990s witnessed the practice of state-inspired brutality from all sides in the former Yugoslavia.[88]

Like Yugoslavia, Cyprus was destroyed by the simultaneous rise of conflicting ideologies. The development of Turkish nationalism, which essentially aimed at partition of the island into Greek and Turkish sectors, coincided closely with the growth of the movement for union with Greece (*Enosis*), making both nationalisms irreconcilable. In fact, the moves of Turkish nationalists, backed by mainland Turkey, really represent a reaction against the concept of *Enosis* of a predominantly Greek island with a substantial Turkish population.

The idea of *Enosis* began to circulate almost immediately after Britain gained control of Cyprus in 1878 and intensified in the first half of the twentieth century.[89] But the turning point in the development of Greek and Turkish Cypriot nationalism – the catalyst for the irreversible downward spiral – came with the foundation of EOKA on 11 January 1955 under the leadership of Colonel George Grivas but with the support of the figurehead in the struggle against British rule, Archbishop Makarios III.[90] EOKA made its existence known three months later on the morning of 1 April when it set off a series of explosions on the island.[91] This action laid the pattern for the next five years in the history of Cyprus, which involved a combination of violent acts by EOKA against its British, but also its Turkish and Greek opponents, attempts at diplomacy by Britain, Greece and Turkey (as well as Archbishop Makarios), and acts of repression by the British regime in Cyprus, involving the suspension of civil liberties. The Turkish Cypriots, supported from mainland Turkey and egged on by the 'divide-and-rule' tactics of the British, reacted to the situation by developing their ideology of partition, *Taksim*, and establishing their own paramilitary organisation, the TMT.

---

88 Three of the best accounts of the end of Yugoslavia during the early 1990s are: Glenny, *Fall of Yugoslavia*; Bennet, *Yugoslavia's Bloody Collapse*; and Laura Silber and Alan Little, *The Death of Yugoslavia* (Harmondsworth, 1992).
89 Stavros Panteli, *A New History of Cyprus: From the Earliest Times to the Present* (London, 1984), pp. 55–264.
90 Ibid., p. 241.
91 Nancy Crawshaw, *The Cyprus Revolt: An Account of the Struggle for Union with Greece* (London, 1978), p. 114.

The period between the establishment of an independent Cyprus in 1960 and the Turkish invasion of 1974 was characterised by party political divisions along purely ethnic lines. The main Greek parties at the time of independence consisted of the Patriotic Front and the Cypriot Communist Party, while the major Turkish groups were the Turkish Cypriot People's Party and the National Front, both of which favoured partition.[92] The early 1970s witnessed the formation of the Republican Turkish Party and the National Unity Party. The latter, under the leadership of Rauf Denktash, wanted the establishment of an independent Turkish state of Cyprus,[93] an aim which he eventually achieved as its President. He received assistance in this process from a surprising quarter in the form of EOKA B, founded again by General Grivas in 1971, with support from the military regime in Greece, once more with the aim of *Enosis*. After opposition from President Makarios to its activities, the Greek military and EOKA B launched a *coup d'état* against Makarios in July 1974.[94] Rather than achieving their aim, both factions had effectively pressed the self-destruct button, as the coup meant the end of the military regime in Greece as well as the death of the Republic of Cyprus as it existed, with the Turkish state invading the northern half of the island – initially to guarantee the safety of the Turkish minority, thus fulfilling its obligation as one of the signatories of the 1960 Zurich agreement for the independence of the island. In reality the Turkish state had achieved a long-term historical aim of expanding into Cyprus.

Ethnic cleavage of a similar nature to Cyprus has played a major role in Belgium but it has not surfaced in violence in this state partly because of its experience as a mature liberal democracy and partly because of the absence of external powers egging on the conflicting parties. Consequently, the division functions within the existing liberal democratic structures. In the first place it delineates voting allegiances, even amongst parties which are not overtly nationalistic. For instance, the three mainstream parties of Christian Democrats, Liberals and Socialists each have their separate subsidiaries in Flanders and Wallonia. However, while the first of these groups has been strongest in Flanders, the Socialists have gained most of their support from the French-speaking part of Belgium. To these groupings we need to add Flemish and Walloon nationalist parties which particularly concerned themselves with language rights in the case of the former and economic conditions in the case of the latter.

During the 1960s and 1970s the *Volksunie* was the most important Flemish grouping, averaging 7 per cent of the vote at general elections and 12 per cent in Flanders. It was the third party in Flanders between 1968 and 1974 after the Socialists and Christian Democrats.[95] More extreme is the *Vlaams Blok*, which increased in importance during the 1980s and 1990s. The first major Walloon

92 Joseph S. Joseph, *Cyprus: Ethnic Conflict and International Concern* (New York, 1985), p. 53.
93 Floya Anthias and Ron Ayres, 'Ethnicity and Class in Cyprus', *Race and Class* 25 (1983), p. 72.
94 Crawshaw, *Cyprus Revolt*, pp. 386–9.
95 R. E. H. Irving, *The Flemings and Walloons of Belgium* (London, 1980), p. 9.

parties after the end of the Second World War consisted of the Bloc Francophone and the Parti Unite Wallon, followed by the Mouvement Populaire Wallon in 1961. In addition, there existed the Front Democratique des Francophones for French speakers in Brussels. The most successful grouping has been the Rassemblement Wallon, founded in 1968. Although these parties for French speakers have gained parliamentary representation, they have tended to have a short life-span.

In the United Kingdom nationalism has played a major role on the Celtic fringe. In Scotland several groupings developed during the nineteenth century but the turning point came in 1934 with the formation of the Scottish National Party. Initially, it simply asked for Scotland to be treated as an equal in the UK and to retain its share in the management of the Empire. It attracted 16 per cent of the votes in the eight seats it contested at the 1935 general election but its 10,000 members in 1934 had fallen to 2,000 by 1939. Its policy has changed in the post-War period when it has demanded a Scottish Parliament. It gained its first MP, Robert McIntyre, at a by-election in April 1945. The SNP reached a high point at the end of the 1960s, winning the Hamilton by-election in November 1967, gaining numerous local councillors, and counting more members than any other political party in Scotland. It reached a new peak at the October 1974 general election when it won eleven seats on 30 per cent of the vote. It fell back somewhat after that time, but now represents a serious force in Scottish politics, securing 22 per cent of the vote and six seats in the 1997 general election in the anti-Tory landslide. It now wants Scottish independence.[96]

The major Welsh nationalist political party, Plaid Cymru, came into existence in 1926, led by bourgeois nationalists mainly concerned with the Welsh language, Welsh identity and Christianity in Wales. The party has contested elections since 1929 and its level of success has mirrored that of the SNP. It won a by-election in Carmarthen on 3 July 1966, but lost the seat at the 1970 election, when it gained 11.5 per cent of votes cast in Wales, but failed to secure parliamentary representation. Although Plaid Cymru's share of the vote fell to 10.8 per cent in the October 1974 general election, it managed to secure three members of parliament. The proportion of votes received fell further to 7.3 per cent in the 1987 national poll but the party still had three MPs at Westminster, and this reached four in 1997. Plaid Cymru also has many local councillors.[97]

96 The above account of Scottish political nationalism is based upon: Christopher Harvie, *Scotland and Nationalism: Society and Politics, 1707–1977* (London, 1977); H. J. Hanham, *Scottish Nationalism* (London, 1969); Douglas Young, 'A Sketch History of Scottish Nationalism', in Neil McCormick (ed.), *The Scottish Debate: Essays in Scottish Nationalism* (London, 1970), pp. 5–20; Mick Hume and Derek Owen, *Is There A Scottish Solution? The Working Class and the Assembly Debate* (London, 1988), p. 26; *Independent*, 3 May 1997.
97 Denis Balsom, 'Wales', in Michael Watson (ed.), *Contemporary Minority Nationalism* (London, 1990), pp. 8–23; Gwynfor Evans, *A National Future for Wales* (Swansea, 1975), pp. 89–90; Dafydd Elis Thomas, 'Asking the National Question Again', in John Osmond (ed.), *The National Question Again: Welsh Political Identity in the 1980s* (Llandysul, 1985), pp. 286–305; *Independent*, 3 May 1997.

Nationalism in Northern Ireland has taken quite a different path to its Scottish and Welsh equivalents in a state in which ethnic difference controls all aspects of life – above all, politics. Apart from the fact that the British political parties have not gained representation in Northern Ireland, meaning that the overwhelming majority of voting simply takes place on sectarian party political lines, the other major characteristic of the province was the role of violence in political life after the end of the 1960s, leading to a situation resembling war for most of the last three decades of the twentieth century.

The post-War political history of Northern Ireland divides into three phases. The first of these phases simply represents a continuation of the status quo reached after the partition of Ireland in 1921 when the Unionists continued to rule the province, a phase which lasted until the end of the 1960s. The governing group consisted of the Ulster Unionist Party. The main Catholic grouping during this period was the Nationalist Party. The divisions between the two groups are obvious: the former wanted the continuance of the union with Britain decided by the Anglo-Irish Treaty of 1921, while the latter wished to see unification with Eire through constitutional means. In contrast, Sinn Fein (formed in 1905) and the Irish Republican Army (inextricably linked to it) were prepared to use any means to achieve their aims, because, as they stressed, Irish independence had been secured by violence. However, unlike the second period in the post-War history of Northern Ireland, this first phase was characterised by relative peace, although some IRA activity had occurred, resulting in eighteen deaths – two-thirds of them IRA members – during a border campaign between 1956 and 1962.[98]

The second phase in the post-War history of Northern Ireland began at the end of the 1960s when Catholics started to voice their discontent at the fact that they remained second-class citizens. A series of organisations came into existence in an attempt to ameliorate this situation, the most famous of which was the Northern Ireland Civil Rights Association, established in 1967. The first march for civil rights occurred in August 1968, and although it passed off peacefully, those which followed resulted in clashes between marchers and Protestant reactionaries and police, one of the characteristics of this second phase.

The most notable feature of this period was the readiness of the paramilitary forces which developed to use violence, a fact which had characterised Nationalists since the nineteenth century and Unionists from the eve of the First World War. In fact, any explanation for the bloodletting which occurred between the late 1960s and the late 1980s would have to appreciate this tradition of violence in the province. Over 3,000 people were killed during this period while over 50,000 were seriously injured. 'More people have died, per capita, of political violence in Great Britain than in India, Nigeria, Israel, Sri Lanka or Argentina.'[99]

98 This statistic is from Sabine Wickert, *Northern Ireland Since 1945* (London, 1989), p. 78.
99 Ignatieff, *Blood and Belonging*, p. 165.

The violence of this second period is connected with the fragmentation that occurred in both the Nationalist and Unionist parties which had existed in the first five decades of the history of Ulster, to reflect the extremes of opinion which had developed. In the Nationalist case two main tendencies emerged, one of which was the Social Democratic Labour Party, formed in 1970 under the leadership of Gerry Fitt and combining traditional constitutional nationalists with the civil rights activists who had appeared at the end of the 1960s. Also developing from the crisis at the end of the 1960s was the Provisional IRA, splitting away from the official Dublin-based Marxist organisation. The new group accepted the use of violence as a means of protecting the Catholic community and achieving a united Ireland. The political face of the IRA consisted of Sinn Fein, which has been electorally less popular than the SDLP. In addition to the IRA, other Catholic paramilitary organisations developed, including the Irish National Liberation Army.

On the other side of the religious divide the major force has been the Ulster Unionist Party, a continuation of the grouping which governed Northern Ireland from 1920. The second major Protestant political faction has been Ian Paisley's Democratic Unionist Party, established in 1971. Nevertheless, the history and violence characteristic of Ulster has also given rise to Loyalist paramilitary organisations, the most significant of which include the Ulster Volunteer Force, re-established in 1966 (after previously existing at the start of the twentieth century), and the Ulster Defence Association, formed in 1972. Such groups have been motivated by their desire to remain tied to the British mainland and the wish to protect their community from the IRA.

The third phase in the post-War history of Northern Ireland begins with the IRA ceasefire of 31 August 1994. Although it resumed its military campaign on the mainland in February 1996, the subsequent ceasefire of July 1997 and, more importantly, the Good Friday Agreement of 1998 have meant a move into an ostensibly peaceful phase in Northern Ireland's post-War history. Nevertheless, opposing forms of nationalism still control political discourse.

Violence has played a large role in nationalism within Turkey, especially Kurdistan. Political Kurdish nationalism took off during the inter-war years, leading to three major rebellions in 1925, 1930–1 and 1937, which were met by savage repression on the part of the Turkish state, using the armed forces at its disposal. Consequently, during the early post-War decades, there were few signs of Kurdish political nationalism. During the late 1950s, as a response to developing Kurdish nationalism elsewhere in the Middle East – more specifically, revolution in Iran in 1958 in which Kurds had participated – Kurdish political nationalism resurfaced again, with some disorder occurring in 1958 and 1959. Following further liberalisation in Turkey, Kurds were able to publicise their position during the 1960s. In 1965 there followed the formation of a Democratic Kurdistan Party, which wanted to see the establishment of a separate state. Four years later the first legal Kurdish nationalist grouping came into existence in the form of the Revolutionary Cultural Society of the East, but this faced a ban following a military coup in 1971. However, other organisations developed from the middle of the 1970s. The most important of these included the refounded Revolutionary Cultural Society of the East, which now called itself the Revolutionary Democratic Cultural Association, and the Socialist Party of Turkish Kurdistan, established in 1974 but facing much repression shortly afterwards.

The largest and most enduring organisation is the PKK, which came into existence in 1978. It has carried out a violent campaign in the Turkish area of Kurdistan in which its victims have included members of the Turkish armed forces and those it views as 'state informers'. In 1993 the PKK killed 200 people including children, teachers, local politicians and the families of village guards employed by the Turkish state, which has reacted to this by behaving in an equally brutal manner. To give one example of mutual brutality, reported by Amnesty International:

> On 15 August 1993 PKK guerillas attacked the town of Yüksekova in Hakkan province, seriously wounding a special team member and a gendarme. After the guerillas had withdrawn gendarmerie troops reportedly moved about the town firing on houses and shops. They killed one townsperson (described in official communiques as a PKK guerilla) and wounded nine others. Further attacks in Yüksekova in the following months left three killed and four wounded.

Between 1984 and 1995 a total of 20,181 people were killed in Kurdistan, consisting of 5,014 civilians, 11,546 members of the PKK and 3,621 security force members. Many civilians would prefer to have nothing to do with either the PKK or the Turkish state but sometimes find themselves involuntarily drawn into the conflict. Like other liberation movements which employ violence, the PKK has financed itself using illegal means such as banditry, extortion and drug trafficking. The ideology of the PKK looks forward to the establishment of an independent Kurdistan along socialist lines, through an alliance of workers, peasants and intellectuals. In 1991 a Kurdish nationalist party linked with the PKK, the Kurdish HEP, obtained 22 seats in the general election of that year. By this time restrictions implemented by the Turkish state during the 1980s, such as banning the use of Kurdish, had been lifted, as Turkey entered another democratic phase, allowing the growth of a Kurdish media, although the violence between the PKK and the Turkish state continued apace.[100]

100 The above account is based upon a variety of sources: C. J. Edmonds, 'Kurdish Nationalism', *Journal of Contemporary History* 6 (1971), pp. 87–107; Kendal, 'Kurdistan in Turkey', in G. Chaliand (ed.), *A People Without A Country: The Kurds and Kurdistan* (London, 1980), pp. 60–8, 72–81; Michael M. Gunter, 'The Kurdish Problem in Turkey', *Middle East Journal* 42 (1988), pp. 391–8; David McDowall, *The Kurds* (London, 1989), pp. 12–14; Ferdinand Hennerblicher, 'Some Aspects of the Restoration of the Kurdish People's Movement After 1975', in *Internationale Tagung der Historiker der Arbeiterbewegung: 22. Linzer Konferenz 1986* (Vienna, 1987), pp. 180–1; Edgar O'Ballance, *The Kurdish Revolt: 1961–1970* (London, 1973), p. 70; Jonathan Rugman and Roger Hutchings, *Atatürk's Children: Turkey and the Kurds* (London, 1996), pp. 27–43; Kemal Kirişci and Gareth M. Winrow, *The Kurdish Question and Turkey: An Example of Trans-State Ethnic Conflict* (London, 1997), pp. 119–56; Amnesty International, International Secretariat London, 'Turkey: A Time for Action', February 1994.

The example of Turkey illustrates the difficulties facing nationalist movements which have developed in post-War Europe, springing from the emergence of a developing cultural consciousness amongst educated members of minorities within individual nation states. Clearly, those underdeveloped groupings which lack numbers, literacy, concentration, economic power and durability have the greatest problems in developing a full-blown nationalist organisation.

But even when the best-prepared groups move from cultural ethnicity to full-blown nationalism, they face further hurdles. Most importantly, these consist of initial hostility from the ruling state, often followed by the granting of limited autonomy, which represents the goal of many post-War organisations. Full independence only arrives if the dominant state experiences some sort of collapse, as happened in eastern Europe at the end of the 1980s. But even in such cases – as the classic case of Yugoslavia illustrates – this does not lead to an ethnic paradise because counter-nationalisms which have evolved simultaneously often have visions of taking control of the same territory, which consequently leads to conflict.

Inevitably, the new states and the new autonomous regions practise intolerance similar to that carried out by former rulers, as this is inherent in the nature of states inspired by nationalism. To repeat the point again, the basis of ethnicity, in the form of appearance, language and religion, has some degree of reality inherent within it. Politically inspired nationalism, aimed simply at state formation or autonomy, concerns itself primarily with power. It standardises and therefore distorts the component parts of ethnicity for the purpose of securing some level of local control over a particular area.

Nation States,
Majorities and Minorities

CHAPTER 6

The Role of the State

The very existence of a nation state suggests that it will exclude outsiders – otherwise there would appear little justification for its survival. While minorities can certainly succeed, particularly if they assimilate, it usually proves easier for people with the right ethnic credentials to reach the top. The development of a culture in which the state plays a central role is fundamental to this process, both through the education system and, more recently, through arts patronage. National culture creates myths about the people living within a particular state who are said to have certain shared characteristics, the vast majority of them of a positive nature. The concentration of the state education system on its own geography, history and literature ensures that these values are passed down to the next generation. Similarly, national arts patronage is less likely to fund a museum exhibition of, in the French case, paintings by *beurs* than art produced by the Impressionists. In many eastern European socialist autocracies a more overt ideology developed which viewed socialism in any particular country as having reached perfection as embodied in the figure of the leader.

However, most nation states make attempts to include their minority populations in the body politic through constitutions and the passage of legislation. In cases such as Belgium, the United Kingdom or Switzerland, the indigenous groupings have a full stake in the constitutions. Similarly, in the Soviet Union the various constitutions bent over backwards to guarantee that the peripheral populations had the same position as Russians within the representative structure. Legislative guarantees attempt to improve the position of minorities. Most post-War states have legally guaranteed the equality of all citizens before the law and have forbidden discrimination. Nevertheless, it is one thing to say this and another thing to implement it. How can it be possible to outlaw prejudice without a fundamental change in the nature of political and economic organisation? No state seems prepared to establish a police force to outlaw discrimination as this would be absurd. Furthermore, the economic and social position of minorities often makes it impossible for them to take up the opportunities presented to them by a particular state.

While nation states guarantee the rights of minorities, they practise other forms of legislative exclusion. Nationality laws, for instance, grant rights to those with citizenship and deny them to those who do not possess it. Immigration controls, which have gone hand in hand with nationality legislation – and have become increasingly draconian in western Europe since the 1960s – deliberately keep out people with the 'wrong' ethnic credentials, notably Blacks and Asians from the developing world.

Throughout Europe the forces of law and order in the form of the legislature, the judiciary and the police have deliberately targeted minorities for negative treatment. The fact that lawyers and judges usually originate from the establishment of a particular state adds to their desire to uphold it. Consequently, they usually hold biases against minorities. Thus stereotypes circulating about Gypsies as criminals in Britain or Hungary would affect the decision of those who tried them. The police, the security services and the army exist to uphold the laws passed by the dominant ethnic and social elites of any particular nation state. The police and soldiers often have a greater degree of prejudice than people outside the forces. The experience of Black people in Britain and France, immigrants in Germany and Gypsies in post-communist eastern Europe would illustrate this state of affairs.

The state almost inevitably discriminates in favour of one group and against another. Ultimately, perhaps the only way in which state exclusion can disappear is if nation states abolish themselves or wither away, but this seems unlikely to happen in the near future. Since 1945 all nation states in Europe have practised legalistic forms of minority exclusion, although most have made some efforts, with varying degrees of success, to alleviate the situation.

CULTURE AND IDEOLOGY

Nation states have a dominant ideology, which they perpetuate in a variety of ways. The education system, for instance, predominantly teaches children about the history and geography of the state in which they live. Meanwhile, symbols such as national anthems create pride in particular nation states. France has an underlying ideology moulded by a revolutionary tradition, which has determined its attitude towards minorities. The communist regimes in eastern Europe overtly preached a national ideology as the examples of Romania and the Soviet Union would indicate.

Several abstract cultural and political factors link all four of the established British nationalities together. These include a national anthem and flag as well as a national history, especially during the twentieth century when both World Wars played a central role in pushing forward a concept of a Britain united against Germany. While some effort has been made to incorporate post-War immigrant minorities into the dominant ideology and culture, some voices have spoken out against this, epitomised by the following statement made in

1986 by the late Professor Sir Geoffrey Elton, one of Britain's leading historians at the time and, ironically, a refugee from Nazism:

> Schools need more English history, more kings and bishops . . . The non-existent history of ethnic minorities and women leads to incoherent syllabuses.[1]

Multiracist education has come under threat by the implementation of a National Curriculum, which, for instance, placed much emphasis on Christian religious education and the concept of education for citizenship.[2] Some local white teachers, headteachers and parents attacked multiracialism, most notably Ray Honeyford, the headteacher of a Bradford school who, in the 1980s, produced numerous articles attacking 'multicultural education'.[3]

During its existence as a nation state, especially from the middle of the nineteenth century, France has assimilated millions of immigrants in accordance with its Jacobin ideology, springing from the 1789 Declaration of the Rights of Man. Regarding 'the state as a moral being and the nation as the personification of the general will', the Jacobin tradition views special recognition of minorities as 'anathema'.[4] This ideology means minorities in France have difficulty in progressing upward without shedding the skin of their ethnic consciousness, which many are simply not prepared to do.

Some states have gone to the extent of denying the existence of particular minorities. For instance, in 1961 the Political Committee of the Hungarian Socialist Workers Party declared that there was no such thing as a Gypsy nationality. Instead, Gypsies constituted a social category, a view which continued into the 1980s, although scholarly and scientific opinion correctly saw Gypsies as a racial/ethnic minority.[5]

Romania in the early post-War years introduced a series of legislative guarantees which theoretically protected the rights of its minorities. However, the situation of the largest grouping, the Hungarians, began to deteriorate after 1956 and the failed uprising in Hungary, as overt Romanian nationalism developed. This new ideology emerged under both Gheorghe Gheorghiu-Dej as General Secretary of the Communist Party during the 1950s and early 1960s and, more especially, under his successor Nicolae Ceaucescu, who took over in March 1965. The revision of Romania's historiography, which began in 1960, provides one of the clearest indications of the growth of a nationalistic spirit within the Romanian Communist Party.[6] During the course of the 1960s

---

1 Quoted in the Preface to Tony Kushner and Kenneth Lunn (eds), *The Politics of Marginality: Race, The Radical Right and Minorities in Twentieth Century Britain* (London, 1990).
2 See National Curriculum Council, *Curriculum Guidance* Vol. 3, *The Whole Curriculum* (York, 1990).
3 See Mark Halstead, *Education, Justice and Cultural Diversity: An Examination of the Honeyford Affair* (Lewes, 1988).
4 These are the phrases of James F. Hollifield, *Immigrants, Markets, and States: The Political Economy of Postwar Europe* (Cambridge, MA, 1992), p. 187.
5 Frances S. Wagner, 'Ethnic Minorities in Hungary Since World War II', *Central European Forum* 2 (1989), pp. 79–80.
6 Stephen Fischer-Galati, *The Socialist Republic of Rumania* (Baltimore, 1969), p. 73.

the new historiography became overtly chauvinistic and glorified the pre-communist past, devoting particular attention to 'Great Figures in the History of Rumanian Genius', as an advertising supplement placed by the Romanian state in *The Times* in 1972 put it.[7] Historians placed stress upon the continuity of Romanian history from Roman times to the present in terms of the make-up of the population, inevitably meaning that minorities within the country did not matter and even faced vilification.

> According to the government's distorted representation of Hungarian History, the Hungarian people arrived on Rumanian soil as conquering barbarian hordes of Mongolian origin which had migrated to Transylvania in the ninth century. They subjugated the indigenous Rumanian population which is claimed to have originated from the intermarriage of Dacians and Romans. The Invaders took over many of the subjected people's institutions and, during the thousand years following the conquest, oppressed Rumanians and attempted to Hungarize them.[8]

The rise of chauvinistic Romanian historiography developed alongside the increasingly tight control and glorification of Ceaucescu, which became a personality cult, describing Ceaucescu as 'the greatest thinker, philosopher, statesman and scientist the world has ever seen'.[9]

In such an atmosphere, the position of many sections of the population deteriorated, including that of ethnic minorities. In May 1966 Ceaucescu could declare that the term 'multi-nation state' no longer applied to Romania, as it was really one 'united national state'. The Romanian leadership rejected any efforts by minorities to have their interests represented by political groupings as nationalist, chauvinist and irredentist.[10] After that time minorities faced repression, as indicated by the curtailment of their language rights and political institutions and their purging from any kind of sham representative institutions which remained in the country by the 1980s. By 1988, the eve of his overthrow, Ceaucescu spoke of a homogenous future people in Romania. While he recognised that citizens of his state had different historical origins, there was no question regarding collective existence, rights and future. Only under such circumstances could he guarantee full equality of rights to all citizens of Romania.[11] By this time the security police, Securitatea, dealt with Hungarian dissenters using methods such as torture, mysterious accidents (sometimes fatal), house searches, house arrests, interrogations and loss of employment.[12]

7 George Schöpflin, 'Rumanian Nationalism', *Survey* 20 (1974), pp. 77–104.
8 Rudolf Joó et al. (eds), *Report on the Situation of the Hungarian Minority in Rumania* (Budapest, 1988), p. 69.
9 Trond Gilberg, *Nationalism and Communism in Romania: The Rise and Fall of Ceausescu's Personal Dictatorship* (Boulder, CO, 1990), pp. 49–57.
10 Brigitte Mihok, 'Minorities and Minority Policies in Romania Since 1945', *Patterns of Prejudice* 27 (1993), p. 87.
11 Pál Bodor, 'A Minority Under Attack: The Hungarians of Transylvania', *New Hungarian Quarterly* 30 (1989), p. 117.
12 Bennet Kovrig, 'The Magyars in Rumania: Problems of a "Coinhabiting" Nationality', *Südosteuropa* 35 (1986), p. 485.

At the fall of the Ceaucescu regime in 1989 'every commoner in Rumania is a second-class citizen. The members of national minorities are third-class.'[13]

The strength of nationalism and xenophobia in Romania from the 1960s – as well as the Second World War history of fascism in the state – meant that the liberal democracy established after 1989 would have strong traces of this aspect of Romania's past, as evidenced in the growth of extreme right-wing parties and outbreaks of racial violence. But the new rulers did make efforts to guarantee the rights of minorities on paper.[14] For instance, the new constitution of 1991 had some provisions for the protection of minorities as 'it recognizes and guarantees the right of conservation, development, and expression of ethnic, cultural, linguistic and religious identity for persons belonging to national minorities', and declared the Romanian state as the 'common and indivisible home for its citizens without any discrimination as to race, ethnic origin, language, or religion'. On the other hand the constitution declared Romania to be a 'national state, sovereign, unitary, and indivisible' and stated that 'the official language is the Rumanian language', although minority language rights were guaranteed.[15]

In Albania under the old order the national myth viewed the country as a unitary entity because of language and an allegedly consecutive history from the classical period. After 1945, in a situation closely resembling Romania, a personality cult developed focusing upon Enver Hoxha, who controlled the state until his death in 1985. Furthermore, also like Romania, Albania took much pride in developing its own form of socialism, and in its consequent self-reliance.[16]

In the Soviet Union the ideology of Soviet inclusion of minorities differed from the reality. For much of its history concepts about the equality of peoples inherent in Leninist ideology gave way to Russian and Soviet nationalism as the dominant state doctrine, because Russians, their language and their culture dominated the USSR at an all-Union level, despite the extensive guarantees granted to different nations and the widespread use and development of native languages and cultures. While Russian cultural and political control may have reached its height during the Stalinist period and especially during the Second World War – when the defence of Mother Russia and the personality cult of the dictator acted as the galvanising forces – the dominance of Russian nationalism and culture remained after the War, even if the personality cult – certainly on the scale revolving around Stalin – had become a thing of the past. By the Brezhnev period, the concept of Soviet internationalism had become the dominant ideological glue of the USSR, even if many of its components had originated in Russian nationalism.

13 Bodor, 'A Minority Under Attack', p. 93.
14 Leo Paul, 'The Stolen Revolution: Minorities in Romania After Ceauşescu', in John O'Loughlin and Hermann van der Wusten (eds), *The New Geography of Eastern Europe* (London, 1993), p. 149.
15 Ivanka Nedeva, 'Democracy Building in Ethnically Diverse Societies: The Cases of Bulgaria and Rumania', in Ian M. Cuthbertson and Jane Liebowitz (eds), *Minorities: The New Europe's Old Issue* (Boulder, CO, 1993), p. 140; Janusz Bugajski, *Ethnic Politics in Eastern Europe: A Guide to Nationality Policies, Organizations and Parties* (Armonk, NY, 1994), pp. 206–9.
16 Derek Hall, *Albania and the Albanians* (London, 1994), pp. 25–42.

Several explanations offer themselves for the importance of Russia within the Soviet Union. The most straightforward of these would focus simply upon the Bolsheviks as the heirs of the Tsarist Empire. Most of the dominant figures in the Soviet state, both before its inception and during its existence, consisted of Russians by either birth or assimilation. As the largest population they were also likely to dominate in the arena of culture and political nationalism, while their position as one of the most highly educated groups also played a role in their dominance.

Nevertheless, in the Soviet case (more than perhaps any other state in post-War Europe), cultures existed at two levels and Soviet citizens were conscious of possessing a type of dual nationality. By the 1950s Soviet patriotism based upon the ideas of Marx and Engels had universal pretensions, with the aim of transforming national cultural traditions in the cause of internationalism. But it combined various levels of loyalty.

We may view Soviet patriotism as a complex of the highest cultures and loyalties of Soviet citizens, with loyalty to the particular culture of one's own nation in the second order of priority and loyalty to international communism on the third level.[17]

The concept of the Soviet citizen gained ground during the Kruschev and Brezhnev eras at the expense of Russian nationalism. Between 1950 and 1964 Kruschev closed about 10,000 Russian Orthodox churches, and overt signs of Russian nationalism were suppressed by both Kruschev and Brezhnev. At the 24th Congress of the Communist Party of the Soviet Union in March 1971 Brezhnev spoke of the emergence in the USSR of 'a new historical community of people – the Soviet People'. According to ideologues this new entity represented the first-ever socialist interethnic community of people. This group had a single common territory and a single ideology. But reaction against the idea of the Soviet people came not only from the minority national groupings, but also from the dominant Russians so that, in its most extreme form, the view expressed by one Russian nationalist stated that Russians had become 'foreigners in their own country'. Such ideas developed into a cultural and political Russian nationalism during the 1960s and 1970s which emerged as a potent political force under Gorbachev and Yeltsin.[18]

INTERNATIONAL GUARANTEES

Virtually all European states are bound by international treaties protecting the civil rights of minorities. Such measures represent paper guarantees, which

17 Frederick C. Barghoorn, *Soviet Russian Nationalism* (New York, 1956), p. 11.
18 Paul Flenley, 'From Soviet to Russian Identity: The Origins of Contemporary Russian Nationalism and National Identity', in Brian Jenkins and Spyros A. Sofos (eds), *Nation and Identity in Contemporary Europe* (London, 1996), pp. 235–44; Ruslan O. Rasiak, '"The Soviet People": Multiethnic Alternative or Ruse?', in E. Allworth (ed.), *Ethnic Russia in the USSR: The Dilemma of Dominance* (New York, 1980), pp. 159–68.

do not solve the underlying problems preventing the entry of members of minorities into positions of economic and political power. In fact, the signing of international agreements guaranteeing the paper rights of minorities may actually perpetuate discrimination because of the fact that these treaties demonstrate the acceptance by the international community of nation states, which, by the very nature of their existence, exclude. Nevertheless, the post-War agreements were signed to prevent a repeat of Nazism and its brutal consequences, an aim which, in the case of Europe, has been largely achieved.

The first explicit recognition of the rights of minorities dates back to the Congress of Vienna of 1815, when Prussia, Russia and Austria committed themselves to respecting the nationality of their Polish subjects.[19] Similarly, the treaties signed after the First World War guaranteed minority rights.[20] However, it was really in the aftermath of the Second World War, and the foundation of the United Nations and the various organs for European co-operation, that concern for the civil rights of minorities on paper grew. The Universal Declaration of Human Rights proclaimed by the United Nations in December 1948 represents one of the most important paper guarantees in the post-War world, supporting a number of fundamental rights for all human beings, including the right to life, liberty and security of the person, as well as the right to protection against slavery, torture, arbitrary arrest and exile, irrespective of race, colour, language, religion or national origin (although, significantly, no mention was made of people without citizenship).[21] Two years later the fifteen members of the European Council signed the European Convention on Human Rights and Basic Freedoms, which became operative in 1953. It closely resembled the UN Universal Declaration and also set up the European Commission to police breaches by signatories of the European Convention. Since then the Conferences on European Security and Co-operation, which have met on a series of occasions after the first gathering in Helsinki in 1957, have further guaranteed minority rights. A total of 33 European states – together with the USA and Canada – signed the original Helsinki Agreement of 1957, although many of the signatories have subsequently broken its provisions.[22] In 1958 the International Labour Organisation issued the Discrimination (Employment and Occupation) Convention, although by 1994 this had still not been signed, in western Europe, by Ireland, Luxembourg and the UK. In 1965 the UN sponsored the International Convention for the Elimination of All Forms of Racial Discrimination (ICERD), which had been accepted by 134 states by 1994, including most European ones.[23]

---

19 I. L. Claude, *National Minorities: An International Problem*, 2nd edn (Cambridge, MA, 1969), p. 7.
20 Ferdinando Albanese, 'Ethnic and Linguistic Minorities in Europe', *Yearbook of European Law* 11 (1991), pp. 318–19.
21 Tomas Hammar, 'The Civil Rights of Aliens', in Zig Layton-Henry (ed.), *The Political Rights of Migrant Workers in Western Europe* (London, 1990), pp. 76–7.
22 Petrè Nakovski, 'The European Mechanism for the Protection of Human Rights and the Rights of Minority Groups', *Macedonian Review* 21, pp. 59–68.
23 Martin MacEwan, *Tackling Racism in Europe: An Examination of Anti-Discrimination Law in Practice* (Oxford, 1995), pp. 47–52, 54–5.

CONSTITUTIONALISM

As well as the international treaties which nation states sign, many also have similar theoretical constitutional guarantees aimed at protecting the rights of minorities. The newly created states within eastern Europe, which emerged from the fascist debris, displayed particular concern about the position of their indigenous minorities, as did those states, such as Cyprus, which had large competing ethnic groups. But in situations such as Cyprus and Yugoslavia paper guarantees ultimately proved futile because they symbolised controls resented by all groupings, whatever their size.

In the United Kingdom, no written guarantees have existed because of the absence of a paper constitution. If only because of its larger population, England remains dominant within the UK. The three peripheral states have had differences in the way that government functions, with Wales remaining closest to England and Northern Ireland demonstrating the greatest divergence. In Wales the main development until the 1990s consisted of the evolution of the Welsh Office and the Secretary of State for Wales. The post gradually amassed executive power over housing, transport, education and agriculture, although with serious limitations to its power because of responsibility being due to the British parliament and budgetary system rather than exclusively to the Welsh people.[24] In the previous absence of a Welsh assembly or a completely independent Wales, the most cynical interpretation of the post would have viewed the Welsh Secretary as a colonial administrator working in the interests of Westminster. The appointment of people such as William Hague and John Redwood – young English politicians on the make – by the long Conservative government of Margaret Thatcher and John Major, did nothing to dispel this idea.

Several factors indicate the greater autonomy which Scotland has enjoyed over Wales. In the first place, a separate Scottish judiciary exists,[25] while, politically, the Scottish Office has a longer history than its Welsh equivalent, having come into existence in 1885, been headed by a Secretary of State for Scotland by 1926 and been divided into five departments in 1973.[26] Nevertheless, while Scotland and the Scottish Office may have had a greater degree of autonomy than Wales, much of what applies to Wales in its relationship with Westminster is also relevant to Scotland. Under the Thatcher and Major governments, when Scottish Conservative MPs gradually dwindled, it was difficult to view the Scottish Secretary (who actually did remain a Scot) as anything more than an unelected representative of Westminster implementing unwanted government policy. As the Labour Party benefited most from the demise of the Scottish Conservative Party and as they also faced something of a threat from the SNP, they had to make a commitment to devolving further powers

24 Vernon Bogdanor, *Devolution* (Oxford, 1979), pp. 131–44; Charlotte Aull Davies, *Welsh Nationalism in the Twentieth Century: The Ethnic Option and the Modern State* (New York, 1989), pp. 87–92.
25 James G. Kellas, *Modern Scotland* (London, 1980), pp. 74–87.
26 Ibid., pp. 93–111; Bogdanor, *Devolution*, pp. 80–5.

to Scotland in their election manifesto of 1997, so that both Scottish and Welsh assemblies came into existence in 1999, meaning a measure of autonomy, but not independence.

In the case of Northern Ireland, just as its political parties have remained separate from British ones, so has the method of its governance from Westminster. A further complicating factor here lies in the interests of a foreign power, the Irish Republic. Northern Ireland has had the greatest level of autonomy amongst all of the peripheral regions of the UK, although the constitutional intricacies have passed through a series of stages, reflecting the developing political history of Northern Ireland, especially since the end of the 1960s.

The Government of Ireland Act of 1920 determined the early post-War history of Northern Ireland. Originating in the desire of Irish Nationalists for Home Rule at the end of the nineteenth century as well as Unionist opposition to such a step, it originally created two parliaments, one in the Irish Republic and one in the north. In the end the former did not operate because Southern Ireland proceeded along its own constitutional path, as recognised in the Anglo-Irish Treaty of 1921 and the creation of the Irish Free State, which meant Irish independence from the following year.

With regard to Northern Ireland, the Act of 1920 also allowed continued representation at Westminster. The Parliament in Belfast had control over education, planning, local government, law and order, civil and criminal law, and minor taxation. The Prime Minister of Northern Ireland invariably remained a Unionist. In essence, the whole process guaranteed the Protestants ascendancy because of greater numbers. Direct rule from Westminster operated in a series of ways including a Governor, who could reserve royal assent to legislation, but also by the dependence of Northern Ireland upon the British Treasury. This remained the situation until the Troubles from the late 1960s onwards. The continually deteriorating security situation eventually led the British government to intervene directly in a political sense in March 1972 when Edward Heath, the British Prime Minister, suspended the Northern Ireland Parliament and transferred all legislative and executive powers to Westminster.

The constitutional history of Northern Ireland since then has had a series of characteristics. In the first place, direct rule continued, assisted by the Northern Ireland Act of 1972, which suspended local autonomy and established the Northern Ireland Office and a Secretary of State for Northern Ireland. But the British government made several attempts to devolve power, most notably as a result of the Sunningdale agreements in 1973 which established a single-tier assembly. This collapsed, however, after operating for just a few months in the following year. More recently, after the paramilitary ceasefires of 1994, Protestants and Catholics, at the instigation of the British and Irish governments, moved closer together in the establishment of a power-sharing assembly in 1996, although this had significant problems – notably its lack of authority and the exclusion of Sinn Fein, as well as the equivocal attitude of the Unionists. Increasingly, the Irish state has become more and more involved in the affairs of its northern neighbour, having been formalised in the Anglo-Irish Agreement of 1985, which established an Intergovernmental Council. The co-operation of the British and Irish governments, despite much opposition from both Unionists and Sinn Fein, played a crucial role in the outbreak of peace from the end of 1994. The real breakthrough came with the Good Friday Agreement of 1998, which represents the most concrete forward move in the history of Northern Ireland. As well as establishing an assembly, it has also meant a Protestant first minister with a Catholic deputy. In the longer term Northern Ireland may become an autonomous region connected with both Eire and Britain, a process which the European Union may facilitate.

In contrast to the UK, Belgium has often been regarded as a good example of a power-sharing democracy in which constitutional guarantees mean that Flemings and Walloons do not dominate each other but have, instead, an equal share in the control of the state. The fairly equal size of the two groupings has meant that it is difficult to say which is the minority population.

Since 1945 the Belgian constitution has altered on several occasions in direct response to rising Flemish and Walloon nationalist movements. In essence, before the first post-War reforms of the late 1960s, the Belgian state remained a unitary system based upon the 1831 constitution, which meant the existence of three levels of government in the form of central, provincial and communal. Changes in the voting system and in the linguistic laws from the late nineteenth century had not effectively altered the structure of the state, a process which only began to happen with the first constitutional revisions of 1970,[27] followed by two further ones in 1980–1 and 1988, as Belgium entered a period in which 'the topic of dividing the state' became 'a perennial subject of political debate, usually to the exclusion of other questions'. The lateness of the constitutional changes, in the context of the rising regionalist movements of the twentieth century, has a series of explanations including the opposition of the mainstream nationalist parties and disagreement about which areas of the state would be affected by change.[28]

The first reorganisation of 1970 actually resulted from negotiations begun as early as the late 1940s and intensified during the 1960s. The most basic alteration consisted of the division of the country into four linguistic regions, covering the French area, the Flemish district, bilingual Brussels, and the German region. Cultural councils for the two major groups came into existence, made up of members of both houses of parliament who spoke the relevant language. These new bodies had responsibility for cultural and educational matters in the two regions. In addition, the changes also divided Belgium into three regions – the Walloon one, the Flemish area, and Brussels – which would have their own regional institutions made up of elected representatives who would have power over issues decided by Parliament.[29] Furthermore, at the

---

27 R. E. H. Irwing, *The Flemings and Walloons of Belgium* (London, 1980), p. 12.
28 Maureen Covell, 'Belgium: The Variability of Ethnic Relations', in John McGarry and Brendan O'Leary (eds), *The Politics of Ethnic Conflict Regulation* (London, 1993), pp. 287–8.
29 Irwing, *Flemings and Walloons*, p. 12.

national level, a new addition to the constitution meant that the cabinet had to include equal numbers of French and Dutch speakers.[30]

The measures proved unsatisfactory for Flemish nationalists, leading to another constitutional reform in 1980, which increased the economic powers of the regions and established institutions envisaged in 1970. Various mechanisms also came into existence for the purpose of settling disputes between the different levels of government, including a Court of Arbitration, which ruled on such disagreements.[31] Changes in 1988 meant a significant devolution of power away from the centre, recognising the three linguistic communities of Flemish, French and German speakers, and three territorial regions covering Flanders, Wallonia and Brussels. The communities gained complete control of education, which covered 75 per cent of their budget. The regions obtained responsibility for transport as well as for many areas of social and economic policy. In addition, Brussels obtained its own dual legislative and executive institutions. In financial matters the regions obtained one-third of the national budget but limited tax-raising abilities.[32] A further measure in 1992 recognised the fact that Belgium had become a federalised state and devolved power even further.[33]

Belgium clearly represents one of the most egalitarian states in Europe in terms of the power of the linguistic and territorial divisions, a situation guaranteed by the strength of the nationalist parties. One might ask, however, if the ultimate destiny of Belgium may be separation in view of the continual loosening of the powers of the central government.

The Swiss constitution of 1848 forms the basis of the consociational system of government which exists in that country. The recognition of three official languages in the state – German, French and Italian, which have absolute equality – forms the basis of much else that springs from this document. The ethnic stability of Switzerland since the middle of the nineteenth century is due to the fact that many Swiss institutions include representatives from all three groups, including the Federal Tribunal, or Supreme Court. In the bicameral Federal Assembly, both the lower National Council and the upper Council of States reflect the linguistic proportion of the population at large in their make-up.[34] The 1848 constitution also contained guarantees which preserved the ethnic rights of the different linguistic and religious groups. Article 49 declared that 'freedom of conscience is inviolable'. Article 60 stated that 'every canton is obliged to accord citizens of other confederate states the same treatment it accords to its own citizens as regards legislation and that concerns judicial discrimination'.[35]

30 Covell, 'Belgium', p. 289.
31 Ibid., p. 290.
32 Liesbet Hooghe, *A Leap in the Dark: Nationalist Conflict and Federal Reform in Belgium* (Ithaca, NY, 1991), pp. 22–6.
33 See John Fitzmaurice, *The Politics of Belgium: A Unique Federalism* (London, 1996), pp. 145–69.
34 Kenneth D. McRae, *Switzerland* (Waterloo, Ontario, 1983), pp. 119–44; Jürg Steiner and Jeffrey Obler, 'Does the Consociational Theory Really Hold for Switzerland?', in Martin J. Esman (ed.), *Ethnic Conflict in the Western World* (London, 1977), pp. 324–32.
35 Jay A. Sigler, *Minority Rights: A Comparative Analysis* (Westport, CN, 1983), pp. 122–3.

While Switzerland may have avoided the disasters which have befallen areas such as Northern Ireland, it is not an ethnic paradise. From the late 1960s it had problems connected with the desire of some of the Jura provinces, on the French border, to become a new canton, which happened at the end of the 1970s after much negotiation and opposition from the German speakers of the area.[36]

Italy has managed to control its major regional ethnic problem in the South Tyrol since the Second World War by the granting of home rule in a series of stages. The 1948 Autonomy Statute allowed the province of Bolzano restricted rights, so that the local German-speaking population had limited control over the economic and political decisions which determined the fate of their area. The unsatisfactory nature of the 1948 measure and the resulting growth of a nationalist movement in the area meant that a new package for self-rule emerged in 1969 and came into operation in 1972. This transferred a significant measure of legislative and administrative power to the province of Bolzano. In addition, the principle of ethnic proportions in employment, agreed in the 1948 Autonomy Statute, extended in their application beyond the offices of the provincial government to apply to all state organisations in the province except the army and the police. At the end of the twentieth century it looks as though one solution to the South Tyrol problem is the establishment of an Autonomous European Region Tyrol, which would unite both the North and South Tyrol within the EU, which now counts both Austria and Italy as members.[37]

In Spain under Franco the peripheral nationalities lost the considerable degree of autonomy which they had obtained during the Second Republic in the 1930s. However, they managed to regain some of these privileges when Spain re-emerged into its second liberal democratic phase during the 1970s. Article 2 of the new Constitution of 1978 declared that while 'the Spanish nation' was 'indissoluble' and formed 'the common and indivisible motherland of all Spaniards', it recognised and guaranteed 'the right to autonomy of all the nationalities and regions which comprise it and the solidarity among them all'. Article 151 of the Constitution meant that those regions which had enjoyed autonomy during the Second Republic – in the form of Galicia, Catalonia and the Basque land – could reclaim it in the new liberal democratic system of government, while Article 143 allowed other areas to apply for the same status.

What did the granting of autonomy mean? Not as much as some nationalists – especially in the Basque land – would have liked. Under Article 149 of the

---

36 McRae, *Switzerland*, pp. 185–213; Jonathan Steinberg, *Why Switzerland?*, 2nd edn (Cambridge, 1996), pp. 89–99.
37 Minority Rights Group, *Co-existence in Some Plural Societies* (London, 1986), pp. 5–7; Flavia Pristinger, 'Ethnic Conflict and Modernization in the South Tyrol', in C. R. Foster (ed.), *Nations Without a State: Ethnic Minorities in Western Europe* (New York, 1980), p. 165; Antony Alcock, 'Trentino and Tyrol: From Austrian Crownland to European Region', in Seamus Dunn and T. G. Fraser (eds), *Europe and Ethnicity: World War I and Contemporary Ethnic Conflict* (London, 1996), pp. 82–5.

1978 Constitution the central government retained exclusive control over 32 fields of administration, including budgetary matters, although another clause allowed the regions to increase their power by appealing to the central government. In the area of taxation the state had the right to regulate the activity of the regions, although, after negotiation with the centre, the Basque area gained considerable jurisdiction in this field.

In keeping with the less forceful nationalism which existed in Catalonia and Galicia, these two regions had little trouble in accepting the limited provisions granted by the 1978 Constitution. In addition, autonomy also created problems for the Castilian immigrants living within the Basque land. It is questionable whether the Spanish regions have achieved a great deal of autonomy, especially when compared with the situation in other areas of northern and western Europe which have evolved a federal system of devolved power.[38]

Further east in the Mediterranean, Greece has paid little attention to the rights of its indigenous minorities, making few provisions for the autonomy of the Turks of Western Thrace. Instead, the Greek state has not only denied the existence of its long-established groupings of Vlachs, as well as Turks and Macedonians, but has also persecuted them. Under the 1923 Treaty of Lausanne, the Greek state agreed to the establishment of committees for the administration of Turkish properties in Western Thrace, of which four existed during the 1950s. By this time they had broadened their jurisdiction to cover responsibility for aspects of the education of the Turkish minority and also heard complaints from members of the community.[39] Nevertheless, by the end of the 1960s these bodies had ceased to exist, following the seizure of power by the Greek junta, and did not function again even after Greece returned to democracy in 1974. In fact, a law of 1990 prevented the election of Turkish officials.[40]

Article 5(2) of the Constitution of 1975 declared:

This provision guarantees for all persons living within the Greek borders absolute protection of their rights and freedoms, regardless of their nationality, race, language or political beliefs.

But the position of the Turks and other minorities has deteriorated significantly since that time. One way in which the Greek state has ignored the provisions of the 1975 Constitution has been by depriving Turks of Greek citizenship under a law of 1955. Article 19 declared that:

38 See Robert P. Clark, 'Territorial Devolution as a Strategy to Resolve Ethnic Conflict: Basque Self-Governance in Spain's Autonomous Community System', in A. Messina et al. (eds), *Ethnic and Racial Minorities in Advanced Industrial Democracies* (London, 1992), pp. 225–46; K. N. Medhurst, *The Basques and the Catalans*, 3rd edn (London, 1987), pp. 7–9; Michael Keating, 'Spain: Peripheral Nationalism and State Response', in McGarry and O'Leary, *Politics of Ethnic Conflict Regulation*, pp. 217–19; John F. Coverdale, *The Political Transformation of Spain After Franco* (London, 1979), pp. 128–30.
39 K. G. Andreades, *The Moslem Minority in Western Thrace* (Thessaloniki, 1956), pp. 12–14.
40 Sadik Ahmet, 'Grievances and Requests of the Turkish–Moslem Minority Living in Western Thrace, Greece', *Turkish Review* 3 (1989), pp. 43–4; Yusuf Sarinay, 'The Rights of the Turks of Western Thrace and the Greek Policy', *Turkish Review* 5 (1991), pp. 32–4.

A person of non-Greek ethnic origin leaving Greece without the intention of returning may be declared as having lost Greek nationality. This also applies to a person of non-Greek ethnic origin born and domiciled abroad. His minor children living abroad may be declared as having lost Greek nationality if both their parents or the surviving parent have lost the same. The Minister of the Interior decides in these matters with the concurring opinion of the National Council.

By February 1991 a total of 544 Western Thrace Turks had been so affected, while 123 people of all ethnic groups suffered in this way in 1993. They included George Misales, who left Greece for Australia in 1970 and found out from his relatives two decades later that his citizenship had been taken away.[41]

Cyprus provides an example of the disaster of forcing an apparently egalitarian constitution upon two conflicting populations which want to impose their will upon each other. The solution of 1960 very much represents a last-minute solution to a problem which had simmered since the end of the nineteenth century, when Greek nationalism emerged on the island, and had faced powerful opposition from pan-Turkish expansionists for at least two decades. The 1960 Constitution is a shotgun marriage, doomed from the start. It is as if next-door neighbours who had no affection for each other, in the form of the Turkish and Greek communities in Cyprus, had pursued their true lovers, Turkey and Greece, for decades, only to be told by the people that they loved that they could not marry them but had to, instead, marry their worst enemy. However, both the Greek and Turkish states continued to carry on affairs with the newly married couple by interfering in the constitutional arrangements. The end result could only be divorce, which duly happened in 1974, although only one set of lovers (the Turks) married. The Greek Cypriots, in view of the traumatic love experience that they had faced as a result of pursuing the true object of their desire, had decided by 1974 that it would be better to live the rest of their lives in solitude, a situation which, while it might not result in the bliss which once seemed possible, at least meant stability, both political and economic.

Certainly the wedding contract of 1960 had everything to recommend it to the reluctant Turkish and Greek communities, representing the most egalitarian of all constitutional arrangements for bi-ethnic societies at that time. But we need to stress again the situation in which it emerged, where ethnic killing continued apace and where Greece, Turkey and the UK, with the support of the UN, forced the agreement upon Archbishop Makarios at Zurich in 1959, who had no choice but to accept it. It represented the only viable solution at the time, a true compromise for reluctant partners.

The 1960 Constitution contained 199 articles and 6 annexes, and its 'strong bi-communal character' is 'revealed throughout its sections'.[42] It 'recognized

---

41 International Affairs Agency, *The Western Thrace Issue in Turkish–Greek Relations* (Istanbul, 1992), p. 20; Helsinki Watch, *Destroying Ethnic Identity: The Macedonians of Greece* (New York, 1994), pp. 26–36.
42 Norma Salem, 'The Constitution of 1960 and its Failure', in Salem (ed.), *Cyprus: A Regional Conflict and Its Solution* (London, 1992), p. 119.

the separate existence of a Greek and a Turkish community, provided for separate communal institutions, separate holidays, separate seats in the legislature, separate ballots and numerous other devices to ensure separate group development while providing political power to both major groups'.[43] The executive consisted of a Greek President and a Turkish Vice-President, together with a Council of Ministers made up of seven Greeks and three Turks, one of whom would hold one of the key ministries of foreign affairs, defence or finance. The legislature consisted of a house of representatives, with 35 Greek and 15 Turkish MPs, and two communal chambers, with responsibility for religious, educational and cultural matters. The constitution also covered public service, providing for a 70:30 division. The army would be made up of 60 per cent Greeks and 40 per cent Turks. The courts also had both Greek and Turkish judges. The five largest towns of Nicosia, Limassol, Famagusta, Larnaca and Paphos would each have both Greek and Turkish municipalities.[44]

Despite the above provisions, which made the 1960 Cyprus Constitution 'one of the most complex attempts to satisfy competing ethnic groups ever written',[45] government in the new state ran into trouble almost as soon as the ink had dried, due to the negative attitude of both sides to the contract, and had virtually collapsed by 1963. Makarios declared in 1960 that he had signed the Zurich agreement under pressure and that *Enosis* remained his ultimate aim.[46] A series of issues caused particular resentment between the two communities, including civil service appointments, the make-up of the army, the levying of income tax and municipal government in the major towns.[47] Consequently, in November 1963, Archbishop Makarios proposed thirteen amendments to the 1960 Constitution to the Turkish Cypriot leader, Dr Fazil Kutchuk, which the latter rejected with backing from Ankara. This in turn led to an outbreak of ethnic violence on the island, which, despite international efforts to control it, surfaced upon several occasions during the following decade,[48] during which the Turks, with less firepower, came off worse. Partly as a result of this – although realising the inevitable – the Turks governed their own population, which was becoming increasingly territorially segregated, using their own communal chamber, Turkish Cypriot army, police force and judicial system.[49] In many ways the events of 1974 simply meant that Turkish military force shored up the *de facto* reality of the years since 1963, although the Turkish community managed to vastly increase its share of the island's territory.

The eastern European regimes which emerged after the Second World War made sure that their constitutional provisions and nationality legislation

43 Sigler, *Minority Rights*, p. 112.
44 See Salem, 'Constitution of 1960', pp. 119–21.
45 Sigler, *Minority Rights*, p. 112.
46 P. N. Vanezis, *Cyprus: The Unfinished Agony* (London, 1977), p. 19.
47 Salem, 'Constitution of 1960', pp. 121–2.
48 Nancy Crawshaw, *The Cyprus Revolt: An Account of the Struggle for Union with Greece* (London, 1978), p. 366.
49 Robin Oakley, 'The Turkish Peoples of Cyprus', in M. Bainbridge (ed.), *The Turkic Peoples of the World* (London, 1993), p. 98.

guaranteed the position of minorities within their borders, even though, like liberal democracies, this did not result in the existence of an ethnic paradise anywhere. Some states had a greater level of success than others in their attempts to create multi-ethnic societies, such as Yugoslavia during the 1950s, despite its subsequent decay into anarchy and bloodshed. But under the old regime no equivalent of Northern Ireland existed in eastern Europe. Only the collapse of communism during the 1980s and 1990s resulted in situations in which particular minority groups could not be accommodated as aggressive nationalism reared its ugly head, having remained relatively dormant in the political and economic certainties of the previous four decades.

Czechoslovakia progressed through a series of constitutional arrangements after the Second World War, which seriously affected the political position of the Slovak population. In the immediate post-War period, the prospects for Slovak autonomy looked good. The Košice programme, issued by the Czechoslovak government which had returned from exile on 5 April 1945, promised to guarantee the status of Slovakia in the new constitution. Consequently, until the communist take-over of 1948, the Slovaks enjoyed some autonomy, although it had begun to decline even before the communist coup of February 1948 as the Czech communists began to flex their muscles with backing from Moscow. The new constitutional arrangements essentially meant that the Czech Communist Party swallowed up its Slovak sister, leaving little voice for Slovak autonomists. The reorganisation of local government in 1949 and the unification of the criminal and civil law in 1950 further served to kill off concepts of Slovak autonomy. The 1960 Constitution continued the centralising process. The Slovak National Council would act as the instrument of state administration in Slovakia, with executive and legislative power.

The situation did not change until the events of 1968 when Czechoslovakia became a federated state, one of the long-term effects of the Prague Spring. The new constitutional arrangements, negotiated in 1968 and coming into operation during the following year, meant a devolution of power away from the centre to the Czech Socialist Republic, with its capital in Prague, and the Slovak Socialist Republic, based on Bratislava. The central government, also located in Prague, had sole responsibility for foreign policy, defence, currency, the protection of the constitution and federal legislation and administration. The two republics controlled education, culture, justice, health, trade and construction.[50]

Although some centralisation eventually took place after the federalisation of 1968, public opinion polls in the 1990s revealed that the Slovak population viewed the period 1968–89 as the most successful and happiest in their country's history.[51] Consequently, the Velvet Revolution of 1989 was not initially

---

50 Jan Rychlík, 'From Autonomy to Federation, 1938–68', in Jiří Musil (ed.), *The End of Czechoslovakia* (Budapest, 1995), pp. 190–7; Minority Rights Group and TWEEC (eds), *Minorities in Central and Eastern Europe* (London, 1993), pp. 14–15; David W. Paul, *Czechoslovakia: Profile of Socialist Republic at the Crossroads of Europe* (Boulder, CO, 1981), pp. 64–5.
51 Petr Pithart, 'Towards a Shared Freedom, 1968–89', in Musil, *End of Czechoslovakia*, p. 201.

about different nationalisms, but the Slovak desire for independence inevitably emerged in a liberal democratic state with a large, educated, territorially compact minority, to become a reality by the end of 1992. Concerns about the constitutional make-up of the post-communist state represented one of the core issues leading to the eventual break-up of Czechoslovakia, especially for the Slovak leadership, which regarded the degree of their autonomy as the key issue in the future development of the state – in contrast to the Czechs, who viewed the economic reforms as being of utmost importance. The parliaments at the elections of 1992 were actually elected in accordance with the 1969 reforms, indicating the failure to move forward in the constitutional sphere. The potential disruption of long drawn-out negotiations in an attempt to reach an agreement led both sides to decide on the solution of divorce, in this case amicable because of the absence of a virulent centralising nationalism.

Both communist Czechoslovakia and its successor states made attempts to guarantee the rights of the smaller minorities. The 1969 Constitution granted cultural and language privileges to the smaller groupings, as well as recognising the right of individuals to identify themselves with whatever minority they wished.[52] The period after 1989 resulted in the characteristic granting of guarantees to minorities, which could not, however, prevent an increase in overt racism. Article 6 in the Czech Constitution, published in December 1992, simply spoke about the protection of minorities by the majority in decision making. The Slovak Constitution of September 1992 allowed minorities to choose their own national affiliation, develop their own culture and use their own language.[53]

After the Second World War Hungary provided wide-ranging paper guarantees for its minority populations. The Constitution of 1949 prohibited discrimination against any citizen on grounds of religion or nationality and protected cultural and language rights. It further declared that all Hungarian citizens would enjoy equal rights. Paragraph 138 of the 1961 criminal code allowed the imposition of a prison sentence of between two and eight years for anyone who 'caused serious physical or mental damage to a member of a national, ethnic or racial group for simply belonging to these groups'. The 1972 Constitution further guaranteed the cultural and educational rights of minorities, and subsequently the state linked its policies with the Final Act of the Conference on Security and Co-operation in Europe of 1975. A branch of the Ministry of Culture called the National Minority Advisory Committee co-ordinated the social, cultural and political activities of the individual groupings within the National Minority Federations.[54]

In view of the difficulties involved in holding the Yugoslav peoples together during the first two and a half decades of the state's existence – a process

52 Minority Rights Group and TWEEC, *Minorities in Central and Eastern Europe*, p. 16.
53 Bugajski, *Ethnic Politics in Eastern Europe*, pp. 304, 331.
54 Lajos Arday and Gyorgy Hlavik, *Ethnic Groups in Contemporary Hungary* (Budapest, 1988), pp. 26–9; David M. Crowe, 'Minorities in Hungary Since 1948', *Nationalities Papers* 16 (1988), pp. 22–5; Wagner, 'Ethnic Minorities in Hungary', pp. 72–4.

which descended into brutal killing following the Nazi invasion in 1941 – it would always prove difficult for the reconstituted Yugoslav state to exist for any length of time, especially in view of the fact that the Serbs had the bitter memory of having been victims of a genocidal policy in 1941, while Croats regarded themselves as having faced a similar experience from the mainly Serbian partisans in 1945. Nevertheless, the post-War Yugoslav state did survive for four and a half decades, despite the rumblings of discontent from the Croats which had begun to surface during the 1960s.

Part of the reason for the survival lay in the policy of the Communist Party of Yugoslavia (CPY), and its leader Marshal Josef Broz Tito (of mixed Croatian and Slovenian descent, but always regarding himself as a Yugoslav), which had emerged victorious in the struggle against fascism during the Second World War. Before the War the CPY had actually accepted a formula imposed by Stalin and the Comintern which recognised the right of individual minorities within the new state to self-determination and consequent separation. A major turning point in the development of the post-War policy of federalism occurred on 29 February 1943 when Tito put forward this idea at a conference at Jajce attended by members of all of the major nationalities. A statement after the meeting declared the principle of equality of the Yugoslav peoples, all of whom would have their rights guaranteed. This formed the basis of the post-War Yugoslav state, in a new situation in which class would play a role ahead of nation so that all workers of whatever ethnic group would have equal standing. Rather than being divided along bourgeois ethnic lines, the peoples of Yugoslavia would pursue their true interest of proletarian internationalism.[55]

The 1946 Constitution put the above principles into operation. Closely based on the 1936 Soviet Constitution, Article 1 declared:

> The Federative People's Republic of Yugoslavia is a federal people's State of Republican form, a community of peoples equal in rights who, basing themselves on a right to self-determination which includes the right to separation, have expressed a will to live together in a federal state.

Several articles provided for full equality among the Yugoslav citizens. Another forbade incitement and dissemination of national, racial and religious hatred, and a new law in July 1946 imposed severe penalties for such actions. The Constitution created six republics (in the form of Serbia, Croatia, Slovenia, Bosnia and Herzegovina, Macedonia and Montenegro), one autonomous province (Vojvodina, with a mixed population), and one autonomous region (Kosmet, inhabited mostly by Albanians). Both of the autonomous areas lay within Serbia. Power divided between central government and the Republic, with the former having responsibility for finance, economic planning, foreign policy, defence, communications and law. The legislature consisted of a Federal

55 George Schöpflin, 'The Rise and Fall of Yugoslavia', in McGarry and O'Leary, *Politics of Ethnic Conflict Regulation*, pp. 179–80; J. Frankel, 'Communism and the National Question in Yugoslavia', *Journal of Central European Affairs* 15 (1955), pp. 50–3.

Council, elected by a complicated procedure, and the Council of Nationalities, representing the different peoples. The executive consisted of the Politburo, made up of members from the different Yugoslav nationalities. Similarly, the army, which also played a unifying role in the new state, consisted of members of all of the nationalities.[56]

Each of the six republics developed its own structure controlling administrative and cultural matters. In addition, each one had its own Communist Party and Central Committee. At this early stage in the post-War history of the nationalities question, relatively few problems arose. Although the CPY recognised the individual peoples within the state, it also propagated the concept of a Yugoslav people.[57] The national question remained dormant into the 1950s, as the CPY tried to lessen the importance of the individual nationalities, which it achieved in various ways. In the first place, it emphasised the idea of the equality of the Yugoslav people which tied in with a greater emphasis upon the idea of socialism within one country, so that the stress upon the unity of the Yugoslav people became greater, along with growth in the idea that national identities would eventually fade away. On the practical political level the changing view of the CPY – which, in 1952, had renamed itself the League of Yugoslav Communists (LYC) – manifested itself in the New Fundamental Law of Yugoslavia of 1953, which made significant alterations to the 1946 Constitution by absorbing the Chamber of Nationalities into the Federal Chamber and replacing it with the Chamber of Producers. The Chamber of Nationalities would meet only when the necessity arose for deliberation upon questions involving nationality. This essentially meant that power moved away from the Chamber of Nationalities both upwards towards the Federal Chamber and downwards to the 'working people' and their institutions such as workers' councils and associations of citizens in areas such as education, culture and the health services. Such developments were stressed in Article 1 of the Fundamental Law, which defined Yugoslavia as a 'socialist democratic federal state' based on full equality of all the peoples of the country, an aim which could only be achieved by democratic economic and social relations and which required the workers to participate directly in economy and government.[58]

The subsequent 15 years of the history of Yugoslavia, and perhaps the next 25, can be seen as the attempt of the centralisers to ensure the equality of all peoples, which eventually but inevitably hit a wall in the form of nationalist resistance among at least one of the republics. The next major step in the former process consisted of the 1963 Constitution, which – in view of what happened subsequently – might be regarded as the starting point of the destruction of Yugoslavia, because of the resentments which one of its clauses

56 Frankel, ibid., pp. 53–4; Wayne S. Vucinich, 'Nationalism and Communism', in Vucinich (ed.), *Contemporary Yugoslavia: Twenty Years of Socialist Experiment* (Berkeley and Los Angeles, 1969), pp. 252–3; Duncan Wilson, *Tito's Yugoslavia* (Cambridge, 1979), pp. 39–40.
57 Dennison Rusinow, *The Yugoslav Experiment, 1948–1974* (London, 1977), p. 17; Spyros A. Sofos, 'Culture, Politics and Identity in Former Yugoslavia', in Jenkins and Sofos, *Nation and Identity in Contemporary Europe*, p. 258.
58 Vucinich, 'Nationalism and Communism', pp. 253–4; Rusinow, ibid., pp. 70–1.

caused, namely the provision for the redistribution of resources from less developed republics to wealthier ones. The new Constitution also continued to allow citizens of Yugoslavia to choose their own nationality and culture and to use their own language. The legislative and executive provisions of the new Constitution were incredibly complex, drastically revising the 1946 and 1953 measures. The major legislative body now consisted of the Federal Assembly, which had five separate chambers, one of which had responsibility for Nationalities. In addition, the new arrangements of 1963 established a Constitutional Court.[59]

In 1964 Tito claimed the Yugoslav state had solved its minority problems but recognised recent manifestations of nationalism. The dispute over the language issue, which surfaced in Croatia in 1967, played an instrumental role in revisions to the 1963 Constitution which occurred in that year. These measures essentially reduced the powers of the central government in the legislative sphere and broadened those of the Council of Nationalities to include participation in the discussion of social and economic developments, budgetary matters, foreign policy and defence and national security.[60]

But the 1967 reforms did nothing to solve the problem of growing nationalism and may even have aggravated it. Because the state gave in to it, the nationalists were spurred on by their victory. Certainly, the Croatian Spring followed in 1971, but this led to a mixed state reaction in the form of a degree of repression, as well as further constitutional changes. The first of these came into operation in 1968, followed by others in 1971 and the final Yugoslav Constitution of 1974. The amendments of 1971 confirmed the trend which the LYC had already accepted of devolving power away from the centre to the individual republics and even the autonomous regions.

These developments received yet further confirmation in the 1974 Constitution. 'With 405 clauses it was the world's longest constitution, and, probably on account of its absurd length, was virtually untranslatable and largely nonsensical.'[61] Apart from devolving control from the centre and giving power to the Yugoslav regions and republics, it also aimed at guaranteeing a smooth transition of rule after the death of Tito, who had reached 82 years of age in 1974, by making sure that no individual could gain too much power for themselves. In addition, the new arrangement of 1974, despite the devolving of power from the centre, also tried to maintain some sort of unitary control.

Like the previous post-War Yugoslav constitutions the one from 1974 recognised the inherent equality of all citizens of the state. It devolved economic control to what were described as Basic Organisations of Associated Labour. More important – from the point of view of the nationalities problem – was the increase in the power of the individual republics and autonomous regions, which almost became sovereign states with even a measure of control over

59 Vucinich, ibid., pp. 257–8; Wilson, *Tito's Yugoslavia*, p. 150.
60 Vucinich, ibid., p. 258; Wilson, ibid., pp. 171–4.
61 Christopher Bennett, *Yugoslavia's Bloody Collapse: Causes, Course and Consequences* (London, 1995), p. 74.

their own foreign policy.[62] The concrete consequences of 1974 included the representation of the six republics and the two regions in all federal-level institutions, from the Presidency and National Bank to cultural and sporting bodies. Offices were to be held on a rotational basis in order to allow every republic and region equal access to power. The new Constitution instituted three levels of central government in the form of the Presidency, the Federal Executive Council, and a bicameral Federal Assembly made up of the Chamber of Republics and Provinces and the Federal Chamber. However, each republic and region had a veto in all matters and all levels of central government. Any semblance of a unified Yugoslavia continued through the control of the Communist Party – even though it too had devolved its power to eight different leagues – and the figure of Tito. His position received added emphasis, threatening potential disaster (which was to become a reality) because of the vacuum that would be created when he eventually died. The other methods of central control consisted of a security police, run by the LCY, and the Yugoslav People's Army, which had an over-representation of Serbs and Montenegrins in its officer corps. In addition, education and state propaganda tried to create a sense of Yugoslav national unity by focusing especially upon the wartime spirit.

The 1974 Constitution resembles the Cyprus equivalent of 1960 in that it attempted to bind together a series of disparate units whose elites did not want this. The collapse of Yugoslavia may not have become inevitable until the early 1990s, but it is extremely tempting to pick out other dates – perhaps as far back, like its equivalent in Cyprus, as its birth. The attempts at holding the state together during the post-War period also indicate the problem of marrying socialism and nationalism. It may be that less stress upon the economic equality of all of the Yugoslav peoples might have allowed the development of a more successful Belgian style of federalism. But, on the other hand, one is also tempted to make comparisons with Northern Ireland, where the historical traditions of hatred, also relevant in the Yugoslav case, would – perhaps inevitably – eventually resurface until the solution of separation became a reality.

Soviet political structures made great efforts to guarantee the representation of the minority groupings through the various constitutions during the history of the USSR. The Stalin Constitution of 1936 operated for much of the post-War period until its replacement in 1977, although it had undergone frequent amendments in the intervening years. In fact, the 1977 Constitution made virtually no alterations to the structure of the Soviet state. The Union republics continued to have the paper guarantee which allowed secession. The all-Union government still had the same powers as before which meant that, apart from controlling foreign affairs, the centre also held wide-ranging responsibility for internal political issues, which included state security and the establishment of the basic principles in areas such as education and health, and

---

62 Vojin Dimitrijević, 'The 1974 Constitution and Constitutional Process as a Factor in the Collapse of Yugoslavia', in Payam Akhavan and Robert Howse (eds), *Yugoslavia: The Former and the Future* (Washington, DC, 1995), pp. 57–8.

internal economic matters. The levels of administration remained the same as previously. The fifteen Union republics continued as they had from the early post-War period. They had power over the social and economic development of their territories and would participate in a series of central decision-making bodies. At the second level there were 20 autonomous republics which had their own constitutions and also dealt with social and economic matters, although they did not have the same degree of representation at the central government level as the republics. Finally there existed autonomous regions and autonomous areas, which guaranteed cultural rights and social assistance to their populations.[63]

Soviet citizens had constitutional and other guarantees protecting their rights throughout the history of the USSR. For instance, Article 34 of the 1977 Constitution declared that:

> Citizens of the USSR are equal before the law, without distinction of origin, social or property status, race or nationality, sex, education, language, attitude to religion, type and nature of occupation, domicile or other status.

Article 36 stated that 'Citizens of the USSR of different races and nationalities have equal rights'. In contrast to liberal democratic states, this article tried to guarantee the reality of such rights by declaring that they would be ensured by 'a policy of all-round development', which, however, also meant inculcating people with Soviet patriotism. In the normal pattern of both eastern and western European socialist or liberal democratic states, Article 36 of the new Constitution also forbade discrimination, in this case direct or indirect 'on grounds of race or nationality' as well as outlawing 'any advocacy of racial or national exclusiveness'.[64]

The reality of equality of Soviet citizens did not of course match the rhetoric and the paper guarantees, making this state little different from others. The demographic, geographic and economic characteristics of the different ethnic groups within the Soviet Union, as well as the historical dominance of Russians, ensured the perpetuation of the differences between one group and another, which, as in the case of liberal democracies, constitutional guarantees could not rectify.

MULTIRACIALISM

The large influxes of immigrants to western Europe after 1945 presented the liberal democracies which recruited them with, in many cases, potentially disenfranchised citizens. Even if they possessed electoral rights, as in the case of immigrants into Britain from the Empire and Commonwealth, the newcomers

---

63 René Tangac, 'The Soviet Response to the Minority Problems', in G. Chaliand (ed.), *Minority Peoples in the Age of Nation States* (London, 1989), pp. 105–6; Martha B. Olcott (ed.), *The Soviet Multinational State: Readings and Documents* (New York, 1990), pp. 8–11; Leonard Schapiro, *The Government and Politics of the Soviet Union*, 6th edn (London, 1979), pp. 83–6, 171.
64 Tangac, 'Soviet Response to the Minority Problem', p. 106.

often faced discrimination. With the evolution of political consciousness amongst immigrants, as well as the focusing of mainstream media attention upon their situation, most of the western European liberal democracies felt that they had to introduce legislation for the purpose of pacifying immigrant and progressive liberal opinion within their boundaries.

Denmark has introduced various measures to tackle racism. For instance, in 1971 a Race Discrimination Act came into operation, forbidding discrimination on grounds of race, colour, national origin or religion, and covering areas including employment and access to retail and social establishments, although only seven prosecutions took place between 1985 and 1989. The various legalistic provisions have not solved the problem of racial prejudice against immigrants in Denmark. Continued discrimination in employment is indicated in this state, as in all others, by a much higher unemployment rate amongst immigrants than Danish people, caused, here as in the rest of Europe, by a combination of prejudice and the mid-1970s economic downturn which left immigrants in a weak position because of a lack of technical, educational and linguistic skills.[65]

Sweden, like Denmark, has both ratified international agreements and introduced its own legislation against discrimination. During the early post-War period the Swedish parliament displayed particular concern about anti-semitism and consequently passed measures to deal with it. In 1970 the Swedish parliament ratified ICERD, amended the criminal code (making discrimination punishable by a fine or a six-month prison sentence), and forbade defamation of minority groups.[66] By the middle of the 1970s the concept of Swedish multiculturalism had developed upon the three principles of 'equality', 'freedom of choice' and 'partnership'. The concrete manifestations of the new policy included a 1976 law which allowed immigrants to vote in local elections and the growth of numerous educational courses aimed at 'engendering a spirit of ethnic tolerance and an anti-racist morality into local administration and the general public'. None of this prevented the rise of racial violence and neo-Nazism in the country. Furthermore, in 1990 Peter Nobel, a former head of the anti-discrimination board, could describe Swedish refugee policy as 'stupid, inhumane and void of any solidarity'. He continued that he would be unwilling to live in a society 'which is a glossy supermarket for some nationalities and a rigid police state for others'.[67]

British policy towards immigrants within its shores since the end of the 1950s has moved to one in which the concept of integration has become central, partly as a compensation for the erection of immigration controls during the 1960s. This policy is summed up in Roy Hattersley's classic statement that:

---

65 MacEwan, *Tackling Racism in Europe*, pp. 96–100; Meredith Wilkie, 'Victims of Neutrality: Race Discrimination in Denmark', *Nordic Journal of International Law* 59 (1990), pp. 7–77.
66 David Glueck, 'Sweden Bars Racial Discrimination', *Patterns of Prejudice* 4 (1970), pp. 7–8.
67 Aleksandra Ålund and Carl-Ulrik Schierup, 'The Thorny Road to Europe: Swedish Immigrant Policy in Transition', in John Wrench and John Solomos (eds), *Racism and Migration in Western Europe* (Oxford, 1993), pp. 99–101, 105.

'Integration without limitation is impossible; limitation without legislation is indefensible.'[68] While, as a result of such views, the establishment of bodies such as the Commission for Racial Equality is positive, legislation does not solve the underlying structural problems which cause racial prejudice.

The first Race Relations Act, which came into operation in 1965, outlawed discrimination in public places and incitement to racial hatred verbally or in writing, but did nothing about the core areas of prejudice in housing and employment. The Act also established the Race Relations Board for the purpose of enforcing the legislation, but the Board could not deal with most of the complaints which it received because they lay beyond its scope. In the same year as the 1965 Act came the White Paper on Immigration, epitomising the Labour Party policy of integration combined with limitation. As well as referring to the fact that 'immigrants . . . do not outrun Britain's capacity to absorb them',[69] the document also established the National Committee on Commonwealth Immigrants for the purposes of co-ordinating integration.

Not surprisingly, the 1965 Act did not prevent racial discrimination, as revealed in two reports during the following couple of years: one from the research institute, Political and Economic Planning, and the other by a group of three lawyers consisting of Professor Harry Street, Geoffrey Howe QC, and Geoffrey Bindman. Apart from pointing to the presence of racial prejudice in Britain, both inquiries recommended the strengthening of the 1965 legislation, which duly happened with the passage of the 1968 Race Relations Act, significantly progressing through Parliament just a few weeks after the 1968 Immigration Act, which aimed at curtailing the influx of Ugandan Asians. The new Race Relations Act extended the provision of the 1965 legislation to cover the obvious areas of housing and employment, and also established the Community Relations Commission for the purpose of creating harmonious community relations and of advising and assisting local voluntary community relations councils with this end in mind.

The next major piece of legislation – which has remained the longest lasting – came in 1976 in the form of another Race Relations Act. Once again a series of reports revealed that racial discrimination continued to exist in Britain, and made further recommendations to deal with it. The establishment of the Commission for Racial Equality represents the major achievement of the 1976 Act, taking over the functions of both the Race Relations Board and the Community Relations Commission. In addition, the new legislation also strengthened the provisions of the previous measures, introducing the concept of indirect discrimination, which was, however, not very clearly defined. Unfortunately – but hardly surprisingly – the CRE has not solved racial prejudice on the grounds of colour in Britain. No major piece of legislation has superseded the 1976 Act.

As well as the measures passed by central government, local councils in Britain have also made attempts to lessen racial prejudice and promote integration.

68 Quoted in John Solomos, *Black Youth, Racism and the State* (Cambridge, 1988), pp. 38–9.
69 Quoted in Shamit Saggar, *Race and Politics in Britain* (London, 1992), p. 82.

For instance, from the early 1960s a limited number of Local Education Authorities made provision to help children of immigrants who could not speak English,[70] although many, because of their lack of linguistic skills, found themselves in specially created classes for misfits, consisting primarily of immigrants' children.[71] In addition, the race relations legislation of the 1960s and 1970s had also provided for the establishment of local Community Relations Councils, which after 1976 became Racial Equality Councils, of which 91 existed in 1991. In that year (1991) they received £4.5 million, from both the CRE and local councils, to employ racial equality officers.[72] During the 1980s certain inner-city local authorities began to introduce measures to deal with racial inequality, especially within London (the Greater London Council, Lambeth, Brent, Hackney and Haringey). The policies pursued included anti-racist education within schools, the granting of local authority contracts to firms which pursued an equal opportunities policy in their hiring of labour, and the use of anti-racist training to make individuals aware of their own potential prejudice as well as to bring attention to the existing legislation against discrimination.[73]

The anti-racist legislation and the measures pursued by local government in Britain since the 1960s have had some success, especially in areas where immigrants have concentrated. Nevertheless, racism is alive and well in contemporary Britain, as the employment and housing situations of immigrants and their children remind us. What the changing political and legislative climate has done is to make overt discrimination more difficult, although not impossible. The CRE cannot eradicate racism because so much else in Britain acts against it. Ultimately, Britain has not become a multiracial society because the state has not changed enough. The liberal British state has, however, managed to create the myth that this is actually the case.

> The multiracial illusion is that dominant and subordinate can somehow swap places and learn how the other half lives, whilst leaving the structures of power intact. As if power relations could be magically suspended through the direct exchange of experience, and ideology dissolve into the thin air of face to face communication.[74]

Despite the apparent contradictions of the Jacobin creed of standardisation – although perhaps in keeping with the revolutionary catchwords of 1789 – the French state has, in common with most western European countries of immigration, made efforts to deal with discrimination. As well as signing up to the various post-War international agreements, most notably ICERD, it has introduced its own domestic measures. The first attempts to deal with

70 Catherine Jones, *Immigration and Social Policy In Britain* (London, 1977), pp. 216–17.
71 This was my own experience as a 5-year-old.
72 MacEwan, *Tackling Racism in Europe*, p. 165.
73 These issues are covered in contributions to John Solomos and Wendy Ball (eds), *Race and Local Politics* (Basingstoke, 1990).
74 Philip Cohen and Harwant S. Bains, *Multi-Racist Britain* (Basingstoke, 1988), p. 13.

discrimination occurred in 1959 and the major piece of legislation reached the statute book in July 1972, outlawing both incitement to racial hatred and discrimination. Subsequently, a law in 1981 also made Holocaust denial a criminal offence. The provisions of the 1972 measure covered all spheres of public life including employment, housing and retailing. Those who disregarded any of the provisions of the Act could face a fine of between 2,000 and 20,000 francs and a prison sentence of between two months and one year. But the effectiveness of the legislation is questionable. For instance, victims of discrimination have to prove that the refusal which they faced resulted from their ethnicity or nationality. In addition, in examples of overt discrimination the person prosecuting has to provide witnesses. 'In cases of job discrimination, in addition, how does one prove that there was discrimination when an employer is free to hire whomever he chooses and is under no obligation to justify his choice?'[75]

The Netherlands has also made attempts to guarantee the rights of its minority populations. Like virtually every other western European state, it has signed the various international agreements since the Second World War. Furthermore, the Dutch constitution guarantees equal treatment and prohibits discrimination. Other legislation has reinforced this as well as outlawing defamation on racial grounds. In 1985 the National Institute Against Racial Discrimination came into existence, funded by the Department of Justice, for the purpose of combating all forms of racial discrimination in the Netherlands. Its activities include research on structural racism and initiating lawsuits against institutions and individuals who have carried out acts of overt racism.[76]

Germany has passed no specific anti-discrimination legislation, although it has ratified most of the relevant international agreements. In addition, the constitution of reunified Germany forbade discrimination on the grounds of sex, birth, race and language, and national or social origin, provisions which applied to foreigners in the new state.[77] It is interesting to speculate whether the legal exclusion of foreigners in the Federal Republic influenced the outbreak of racial violence in Germany during the early 1990s. It is difficult to envisage quite the number of attacks which did take place in such a short space of time occurring in, for instance, Britain, with its programmes of multiracial education, although we need to bear in mind that many of the attacks in Germany occurred in the east which had little experience of immigration.

LEGISLATIVE EXCLUSION

At the same time as liberal democratic states have passed legislation to tackle discrimination, they have also introduced measures which exclude minorities.

75 Jacqueline Costa-Lascoux, 'French Legislation Against Racism and Discrimination', *New Community* 20 (1994), pp. 371–9; Danièle Lochak, 'Discrimination Against Foreigners Under French Law', in Donald L. Horowitz and Gérard Noiriel (eds), *Immigrants in Two Democracies: French and American Experience* (New York, 1992), pp. 391–410.
76 Peter R. Rodrigues, 'Racial Discrimination and the Law in the Netherlands', *New Community* 20 (1994), pp. 381–91.
77 MacEwan, *Tackling Racism in Europe*, pp. 149–55.

The most obvious way in which they have done this lies in the introduction of immigration laws which physically keep people out. In fact this represents the most blatant example of exclusion practised by liberal democratic states, which have constantly tightened such legislation whereby the central aim is to keep out as many dark-skinned poor people from the developing world as possible. This situation has not always existed and really began to develop from the early 1960s in Britain and the middle of the 1970s in continental Europe. Before these watersheds, the European states had desperately sought supplies of labour from wherever they could find them.

Hostility towards post-War immigrants in Britain, from both government and populace, began even before the first West Indians arrived upon the *Empire Windrush* in 1948, leading to the development of an anti-Black and Asian press campaign in the late 1950s. This resulted in the Commonwealth Immigrants Act of 1962, which aimed to keep out citizens of the Commonwealth and Empire.[78] However, this measure did not prevent the entry of Black and Asian people with British citizenship, which resulted in the passage of the Commonwealth Immigrants Act of 1968 and the Immigration Act of 1971. These two pieces of legislation still allowed people from the White Commonwealth with British-born parents or grandparents to enter the country. Since the early 1970s it has proved increasingly difficult for people from the Third World to move to Britain. Refugees could still enter the country, but numerous new measures have turned Britain into one of the most impenetrable fortresses on Earth.[79]

A similar situation has developed in France. Like Britain, this state initially had desperately tried to recruit as many people as possible, preferably with white skins, in the early post-War years. By the early 1970s overt hostility had developed against immigrants, particularly those from Algeria, manifesting itself most obviously in the form of racist murders and growing support for extreme right-wing groupings. This coincided with the oil crisis of 1973, the economic recession consequent upon it and a decline in the demand for unskilled labour. All of these factors combined in the decision to ban the arrival of new foreign workers in 1974, as France also entered an age of restrictions upon immigration, including a short-lived attempt at preventing family migration and the implementation of a scheme between 1977 and 1981 aimed at the repatriation of Africans, who received 10,000 francs if they left. In reality, Spaniards and Portuguese took more advantage of the offer. In 1983 the government of Pierre Mauroy reintroduced the scheme, imposed stricter border controls for people coming from North Africa, brought back limits on admitting dependants and resumed seeking out illegal immigrants. Since then French immigration controls have tightened even further.[80]

78 Kathleen Paul, *Whitewashing Britain: Race and Citizenship in the Postwar Era* (Ithaca, NY, 1997); Ian R. G. Spencer, *British Immigration Policy: The Making of Multi-Racial Britain* (London, 1997).
79 Panikos Panayi, 'The Evolution of British Immigration Policy', in Albrecht Weber (ed.), *Einwanderungsland Bundesrepublik in der Europäischen Union: Gestaltungsauftrag und Regelungsmöglichkeiten* (Osnabrück, 1997), pp. 134–7.
80 See, for instance, Max Silverman, *Deconstructing the Nation: Immigration, Racism and Citizenship in Modern France* (London, 1992), pp. 37–69.

The mid-1970s also represented a major turning point in the migration of foreign workers into Germany. As a result of the recession caused by the oil crisis of 1973, the government immediately banned the recruitment of foreign workers. The recession and a consequent rise in unemployment coincided in the 1970s and 1980s with the entry into the labour market of large numbers of people born during the 'baby boom' of 1955–66, although politicians were also displeased at the fact that so-called 'guest workers' tended not only to remain for long periods, but also to bring over their families to Germany, consequently adding to social costs within the economy. Despite the stop on recruitment in 1973, the number of foreigners in Germany increased dramatically during the following two decades, due mostly to the migration of dependants.[81] In addition, the Federal Republic accepted 369,215 asylum seekers between 1984 and 1988, the most steady stream fleeing repression in Poland.[82]

Numbers to Germany increased further during the late 1980s and early 1990s. Geographical location – bordering eastern Europe – provides one major explanation. Another is Article 16 of the Constitution of the Federal Republic, which offers a right of asylum to refugees – although we should not overestimate its importance because all western European states, having signed the Geneva Convention, should accept refugees. Article 116 of the Federal Constitution, accepting ethnic Germans from eastern Europe, offers a third explanation for the level of immigration into Germany during the early 1990s. The actual intake between 1990 and 1992 totalled 887,366 asylum seekers and 849,606 ethnic Germans, averaging out at over half a million newcomers per year for these three years alone.[83] A rise in racial violence in the new Germany, as well as government and media obsession with the number of foreigners entering the country, led to an amendment to Article 16 of the Constitution, which made deportation easier and did not allow refugees into Germany if they had not come direct from the state from which they fled.[84]

The high rate of immigration into Germany in the early 1990s did not look good to European policy-makers who, by this time, had moved towards the development of a unified strategy for European migration, with the creation of a fortress where those within could move as they wished (with border control virtually disappearing); while those outside, especially to the south and east, had great difficulty entering.[85]

81 Hartmut Berghoff, 'Population Change and its Repercussions on the Social History of the Federal Republic', in Klaus Larres and Panikos Panayi (eds), *The Federal Republic of Germany Since 1949: Politics, Society and Economy Before and After Unification* (London, 1996), pp. 59–67.
82 Barbara Marshall, 'Migration into Germany: Asylum Seekers and Ethnic Germans', *German Politics* 1 (1992), p. 125.
83 Cornelia Schmalz-Jacobsen, Holger Hinte and Georgios Tsapanos, *Einwanderung und Dann: Perspektiven einer Neuen Ausländerpolitik* (Munich, 1993), p. 314.
84 Wolfgang Bosswick, 'Asylum Policy in Germany', in Philip Muus (ed.), *Exclusion and Inclusion of Refugees in Contemporary Europe* (Utrecht, 1997), pp. 59–74.
85 These developments have attracted the attention of many scholars, including Rey Koslowski, 'European Union Migration Regimes, Established and Emergent', in Christian Joppke (ed.), *Challenge to the Nation-State: Immigration to Western Europe and the United States* (Oxford, 1998), pp. 153–88.

Just as important – and perhaps slightly more subtle than immigration legislation in excluding outsiders – have been nationality laws which are fundamentally concerned with the process of inclusion and exclusion. French nationality law, for instance, has become more and more restrictive since the Second World War. It illustrates the assimilationist attitude of the French state, in the sense that the granting of citizenship has depended upon conforming to French values. Immigrants who have moved into the country since 1945 have consisted of both people who already possessed French nationality as well as non-citizens. From the end of the nineteenth century children born in France to foreign parents had been able to acquire French citizenship without too much trouble once they reached adulthood, meaning that the principle of *jus solis* basically operated. By the 1980s this principle had begun to come under attack from the far right, as large immigrant communities became increasingly visible and ostensibly unassimilable. In addition, many members of the second generation had dual citizenship. The right-wing government formed in 1986 set up a Nationality Commission, although a new law abandoning the principle of *jus solis* did not appear until 1993.[86]

German nationality laws appear far more exclusive towards post-War immigrants because they revolve around the principle of *jus sanguinis* rather than *jus solis*. This fact has its root in the absence of a German state at the start of the nineteenth century, which meant that in order to prove German nationality the principle of birth within particular territorial boundaries did not matter. *Jus sanguinis* became formalised as the guiding principle of German citizenship under the Nationality Law of 1913, which has operated in all of the systems of government which Germany has passed through since that time. The main consequence of the 1913 legislation for immigrants has been the potential perpetual exclusion from German nationality of people born in the country through numerous generations, as German citizenship is essentially hereditary. Naturalisation represents the only way around this problem, but this has been a difficult process which only became slightly easier during the early 1990s as a consequence of the presence of millions of people born in Germany without citizenship, increasing at a rate of 55,000 a year by the end of the 1980s.[87] New legislation in 1991 and 1993 aimed at giving such people citizenship, otherwise a situation would exist in which potentially millions of people born within Germany would remain without civil and political rights. But the onus remained upon the individual to make the move, and anyone who did take up the offer would have to indicate their willingness to integrate, most clearly by the absence of a criminal record and, more importantly,

---

86 See Rogers Brubaker, *Citizenship and Nationhood in France and Germany* (Cambridge, MA, 1992), pp. 138–64; André-Clément Decouflé, 'Historic Elements of the Politics of Nationality in France (1889–1989)', in Horowitz and Noiriel, *Immigrants in Two Democracies*, pp. 357–67; Adrian Favell, *Philosophies of Integration: Immigrants and the Idea of Citizenship in France and Britain* (London, 1998), pp. 40–93, 150–99.
87 See: Brubaker, ibid.; and William A. Barbieri, Jr, *Ethics of Citizenship: Immigration and Group Rights in Germany* (Durham, NC, 1998).

by giving up any other nationality which they may have[88] – which could create problems for those who may decide, at some future date, to return to the land of their parents or grandparents.

In Switzerland nationality laws, based solely upon *jus sanguinis*, play a large role in guaranteeing the status of immigrants and their descendants as second-class citizens. Consequently, it 'has not been uncommon to find three and four generations of foreigners born in Switzerland retaining the nationality of their homeland',[89] although it seems difficult to see how another state can represent their 'homeland', if it was their great-grandparents who were actually born there. In order to obtain Swiss citizenship, applicants must have lived in the country for twelve years, or shorter if they resided there between the ages of 10 and 20. Furthermore, they have to renounce their former citizenship and face an investigation into both their own character and that of their family. The fee for naturalisation varies from SF100 in some cantons to SF75,000 in others.[90] Not surprisingly, in view of the above hurdles, 'barely 1 per cent of the immigrant population has attempted to attain Swiss citizenship in any given year since World War II'.[91]

The Russian Federation has had problems with the development of nationality laws partly due to the presence of millions of Russians outside its border, a problem which has also affected the nationality legislation of the states in which large numbers of this group live. The Russian Federation Law on Citizenship came into operation immediately after the dissolution of the Soviet Union at the end of 1991, operating upon a mixture of *jus sanguinis* and *jus solis*, demonstrating concern with the residual Russian populations living in other states of the former USSR, who could acquire citizenship of the Russian Federation.[92]

This was just as well because some of the new states in which the Russian populations found themselves made efforts to exclude them from their new citizenship, especially within the Baltics. Lithuania actually had the most inclusive policy among the new Baltic states. In fact, it became the first Soviet republic to adopt a new citizenship law in November 1989, several months before declaring independence in the following spring. The measure granted citizenship to citizens of inter-war Lithuania and their descendants as well as to people living and residing permanently in Lithuania who did not possess the citizenship of any other state. Other permanent residents had a period of two years in which to acquire Lithuanian citizenship, during which time they

---

88 Bundesminister des Innern, *Das Neue Ausländergesetz* (Bonn, 1991); Mary Fulbrook, 'Germany for the Germans? Citizenship and Nationality in a Divided Nation', in David Cesarani and Mary Fulbrook (eds), *Citizenship, Nationality and Migration in Europe* (London, 1996), p. 102.
89 Patrick Ireland, *The Policy Challenge of Ethnic Diversity: Immigrant Politics in France and Switzerland* (London, 1994), p. 152.
90 Gérard de Rham, 'Naturalisation: The Politics of Citizenship Acquisition', in Layton-Henry, *Political Rights of Migrant Workers*, pp. 168–70.
91 Ireland, *Policy Challenge of Ethnic Diversity*, p. 152.
92 See Galina K. Dmitrieva and Igor Lukashuk, 'The Russian Federation Law on Citizenship', *Review of Central and East European Law* 19 (1993), pp. 267–92.

simply had to apply for it. At the end of the two-year period a total of 370,000 permanent residents had still not acquired nationality. The relatively liberal Lithuanian law is explained by the time of its passage – before the gaining of independence, which meant that there was an obvious reluctance to alienate the Soviet authorities – and by the relative lack of resentment towards the small Russian population. In the early 1990s a series of other measures has displayed less tolerant characteristics. For instance, the Law on the Legal Status of Foreigners in the Republic of Lithuania, passed on 4 September 1991, did not automatically guarantee freedom of expression to foreigners.[93]

This reflected the picture in the other two new Baltic states, Estonia and Latvia, with their considerably larger Russian populations. A parliamentary commission on citizenship reporting in September 1991 proposed that all of those resident in Estonia on 30 March 1990 could obtain citizenship but, after a storm of protest from extremist opinion, this did not become law. Instead, the 1938 Estonian Law on Citizenship came into operation at the start of 1992. This meant that inter-war citizens and their descendants held Estonian citizenship. Everybody else could apply for naturalisation after two years' residence, providing they had the required knowledge of Estonian, but would have to wait for a further year before they could obtain it. Applications for citizenship could begin in 1992 but would not become operative until April 1993. The measure prevented Russians from voting or standing in elections to the Estonian Assembly in September 1992, which meant that all 101 deputies were Estonians. By the start of 1995 nearly 50,000 people had been naturalised, although 60,000 had taken up Russian citizenship. Nevertheless, a new, tighter law followed in January 1995 stipulating 'five years residence plus a one year waiting period to process applications and a test on the basics of the Estonian Constitution and the citizenship law, in addition to the Estonian language test'.[94]

Debates about citizenship in Latvia at the end of the Soviet period mirrored those in Estonia, which has meant the passage of legislation overtly discriminating against the Russian minority. Calls for a citizenship law began in 1988 and at least one appeared in draft by the summer of 1989. After much discussion – and international criticism – the Latvian legislature did not actually pass a law until July 1994. This meant that 400,000 of the 700,000 residents of the state classed as non-Latvians could apply for citizenship, although the process would continue until 2003. This ensured that the Russian community would remain on the margins of Latvian society and economy for some time to come,

93 Rogers Brubaker, 'Citizenship Struggles in the Soviet Successor States', *International Migration Review* 26 (1992), pp. 279–80; Paul Kolstoe, *Russians in the Former Soviet Republics* (London, 1995), pp. 139–41.
94 Brubaker, ibid., pp. 281–2; George Ginsburgs, 'The Citizenship of the Baltic States', *Journal of Baltic Studies* 21 (1990), pp. 12–15; Neil Melvin, *Russians Beyond Russia: The Politics of National Identity* (London, 1995), pp. 44–5; Jeff Chinn and Robert Kaiser, *Russians as the New Minority: Ethnicity and Nationalism in the Soviet Successor States* (Boulder, CO, 1996), pp. 98–102; Alexander Segounin, 'The Russian Dimension', in Hans Mountzen (ed.), *Bordering Russia: Theory and Prospects for Europe's Baltic Rim* (Aldershot, 1998), pp. 39–40.

representing a type of apartheid. A new law of 1995 actually meant the issue of 'non-citizen passports', allowing holders to enter and leave the country.[95]

PERSECUTION

All post-War European nation states have practised exclusion of ethnic out-groups, whether directly, through the introduction of immigration or nationality laws, or indirectly, by essentially ignoring the guarantees for minorities which exist in their constitutions. In addition, most European states have, at one time or another, practised persecution through the forces of law and order. Those countries which have weak constitutional guarantees have represented the worst offenders in this sense.

But western liberal democracies have also used heavy-handed methods, as Northern Ireland best illustrates. After the partition of Ireland at the start of the 1920s, the Royal Ulster Constabulary (RUC) combined with the part-time B Specials, who had their origins in the paramilitary Ulster Volunteer Force, to police the new Northern Ireland. 'The Specials were nakedly sectarian, Protestant to a man.' The RUC was not much better because at the end of the 1960s just 10 per cent of its members consisted of Catholics. In addition, the Civil Authorities (Special Powers) Act of 1922 'was one of the most draconian pieces of legislation ever passed in a liberal democracy', allowing the government of Northern Ireland 'to take all such steps and issue all such orders as may be necessary for preserving the peace and maintaining order'. These steps included interning people without trial, arresting people without warrant and issuing curfews. Such measures were basically aimed at controlling the activities of Roman Catholics. Protestants overwhelmingly dominated the judiciary so that in 1969 there were six Protestant High Court judges and just one Catholic, a proportion reflected at all levels of judicial appointments, which counted 68 Protestants and just 6 Catholics.[96]

Not surprisingly, the forces of law and order acted in a biased manner when the Troubles broke out at the end of the 1960s. Catholic and Protestant demonstrators received different treatment at the hands of the B Specials and the RUC, with Catholics becoming victims of open aggression, although the level of bias led to the disbanding of the B Specials in October 1969. Nevertheless, the Westminster government intervened in other direct ways during the late 1960s and early 1970s. In the first place it sent in troops in August 1969, ostensibly for the purpose of keeping the peace between Catholic and Protestant rioters, although in the long run the British Army developed into the most visible sign of the British presence in Ireland. At the height of the

---

95 Brubaker, ibid., pp. 282–4; Melvin, ibid., pp. 43–4; Chinn and Kaiser, ibid., pp. 112–15; Segounin, ibid, pp. 40–1.
96 Brendan O'Leary and Paul Arthur, 'Northern Ireland as the Site of State- and Nation-Building Failures', in Brendan O'Leary and John McGarry (eds), *The Future of Northern Ireland* (Oxford, 1990), pp. 16–17; John Darby, *Conflict in Northern Ireland: The Development of a Polarised Community* (Dublin, 1976), p. 63.

Troubles in 1972 over 21,000 British troops found themselves stationed in Northern Ireland, assisted by the 9,000 members of the Ulster Defence Regiment,[97] which had replaced the B Specials and resembled it very closely in the almost entirely Protestant composition. The number of British troops in Northern Ireland declined from the early 1970s, falling to 10,500 in 1982, although increasing again to 12,000 in 1992.[98] The outbreak of peace in 1994 led to further dramatic reductions. The RUC remained as a force made up of over 90 per cent Protestants throughout the period of the Northern Ireland Troubles.

All sections of the security forces acted in a biased manner against the Catholic minority. This scenario reached its nadir on 'Bloody Sunday', 30 January 1972, during which British troops shot and killed fourteen civil rights demonstrators taking part in an unauthorised march. The use of plastic bullets against Catholic demonstrators also proved lethal. For instance, the RUC killed four people and injured three others in May and June of 1981 when they fired them into Catholic crowds, who were demonstrating following the deaths of IRA hunger strikers.[99] The RUC continued to use such bullets against Catholics, but not Protestants, as late as the summer of 1996, when members of both groups participated in street disorder over the issue of whether or not to allow an Orange Order march through a Catholic street in Portadown.

As well as the security forces, persecution of the Catholic minority in Ireland has taken place in other ways. When Westminster took direct control in March 1972, it replaced the Special Powers Act with the Northern Ireland (Emergency Provisions) Act in the following year, which basically had the same powers as the 1922 measure. In the first half of the 1970s, IRA suspects had also faced internment, although this policy was eventually phased out and replaced with the Diplock Courts, which operated without a jury on the basis that jurors faced intimidation.

Throughout western Europe, immigrants have also experienced victimisation from the police and judiciary, as a few examples will illustrate. One British report from 1983 stated: 'There can be no doubt that police officers are racist. The police themselves accept this is so, and argue that the police are only a cross-section and therefore reflect the make-up of that society.'[100] This issue reached the forefront of public attention in 1998 because of the Stephen Lawrence Inquiry. For Black people, 'the liberal notion that the courts and the legal system are impartial and a bulwark between the state and the citizen is a myth' because at the end of the legal process they 'are more likely than whites to be sent to prison',[101] due essentially to the fact that the legal profession consists primarily of members of the white establishment who have no dealings with Black people other than as defendants.

---

97 Padraig O'Malley, *The Uncivil Wars: Ireland Today* (Belfast, 1983), p. 216.
98 Kevin Boyle and Tom Hadden, *Northern Ireland: The Choice* (London, 1994), pp. 85, 86.
99 O'Malley, *Uncivil Wars*, pp. 214–16.
100 Paul Gordon, *White Law: Racism in the Police, Courts and Prisons* (London, 1983), p. 72.
101 Ibid., p. 116.

In Denmark during the late 1980s and early 1990s many Blacks in Copenhagen were warned to stay away from public places because of a suspicion – common throughout western Europe – that they were involved in drug smuggling.[102] In Germany, during the 1990s, some policemen participated in acts of violence against minorities already facing attack from the population as a whole. One example of German police brutality occurred in June 1994 and involved 'Emelia Ogubuike Madu, a Nigerian whose asylum application had been rejected' and who 'was taken from Volkstedt Prison in handcuffs and leg chains to the airport in Berlin to be deported'. The pilot refused to allow him into his plane. The victim describes what happened next:

> I was still handcuffed. I was taken into an airport building and pushed into a small cell. The airport police started beating me. There were about ten of them beating me with sticks and with their hands. They were calling me 'Nigger'. I said, 'Yes my name is Nigger' to get them to stop. I was bleeding; my eyes were puffy.[103]

Similarly, in France, policemen have mistreated people whom they have perceived as foreign.

> For example, on August 11, 1995, following a routine identity check, three uniformed policemen in Marseille beat a French citizen of Algerian origin. The victim was driven by police to a deserted quarry where he was beaten and allegedly robbed by police. The police were apprehended when one of them returned to the scene of the crime to recover his club. The officers were suspended and imprisoned for three weeks. During the investigation, one of the officers testified that the police hierarchy was aware of the use of intimidation tactics and did not condemn such practices.[104]

Much worse than this individual incident are the events of 1961 when France experienced one of the most brutal and murderous examples of police racial violence in Europe since the Second World War: in the context of the Algerian War of Independence they murdered at least 200 Algerians in Paris protesting against the implementation of a curfew against them.[105]

While liberal democracies practise persecution and victimisation of minorities, some of the worst of such actions have occurred in eastern Europe, illustrated by Bulgaria, within the old Soviet bloc, and – perhaps the worst offender of all – the essentially arbitrary totalitarian state of Turkey, which has carried out acts of intolerance verging upon genocide.

The position of the Turks in Bulgaria began to deteriorate from the end of the 1940s. On 17 July 1970 the Bulgarian Communist Party decided on

---

102 Bashy Quraishy and Tim O'Connor, 'Denmark: No Racism by Definition', *Race and Class* 32 (1991), pp. 114–16.
103 Helsinki Watch, *'Germany for Germans': Xenophobia and Racist Violence in Germany* (New York, 1995), p. 48.
104 *Human Rights Watch World Report, 1996* (New York, 1996), p. 216.
105 Details of these events can be found in Jean-Luc Einandi, *La Bataille de Paris: 17 Octobre 1961* (Paris, 1991); and Michel Levine, *Les Ratonnades d'Octobre: Un Meurtre Collectif A Paris en 1961* (Paris, 1985).

'converting the race and religion by terrorism', which meant violent attacks upon the Turkish areas of settlement involving both the police and populace and resulting in perhaps thousands of deaths in the years 1968–72.[106] In 1984 the Bulgarian Communist Party tried to deal with the deep economic and political crisis within the state by whipping up a nationalistic atmosphere with its homogenising consequences, which resulted in an attempt at forced assimilation of the ethnic Turks, who served to deflect attention away from the shortcomings of the regime. The new policy manifested itself most clearly not just in measures against the Muslim religion and the use of the Turkish language, but also in a forced name-changing campaign. The state used crude methods to carry out this last policy:

> Villages with predominantly Turkish inhabitants were surrounded by police with dogs and troops with tanks, often in the early hours of the morning. Officials with new identity cards, or in other reported instances with a list of 'official' names to choose from, visited every household and the inhabitants were forced, in some cases allegedly at gun-point, to accept the new cards and to sign 'voluntary' forms requesting their new names.

Those who refused the name changes lost their jobs or faced imprisonment, internal banishment or even murder by the security forces during the operations in the villages.[107] But the Bulgarian state claimed that hundreds of thousands of Bulgarians 'voluntarily' and 'spontaneously' asked for new names. The same government asserted that no Turkish minority existed in Bulgaria, 'only ethnic Bulgarians who have re-established the culture and traditions that have been suppressed during five centuries of Turkish rule'.[108]

Of all post-War European states, Turkey represents the most intolerant of minority rights. This is at least partly explained by the absence of either a liberal democratic or socialist regime ruling the country for any length of time in the post-War period, during which the army has effectively controlled power either directly or indirectly. Despite this, the Turkish state has signed several international agreements which are supposed to guarantee the rights of minorities, including the European Convention on Human Rights[109] and the Helsinki Final Act.[110] But Turkey has displayed little regard for the human rights of either ethnic Turks who have held the wrong – usually left-wing – political views, or members of minorities. The arrogant behaviour of Turkey has received tacit support from the west, because of the country's strategic position during first the Cold War and then the Gulf conflict.

---

106 Ilker Alp, *Bulgarian Atrocities: Documents and Photographs* (London, 1988), pp. 133–7.
107 *Bulgaria: Imprisonment of Ethnic Turks* (London, 1986), pp. 7–15; Ali Eminov, *Turkish and Other Muslim Minorities of Bulgaria* (London, 1997), pp. 85–91.
108 Helsinki Watch, *Destroying Ethnic Identity: The Turks of Bulgaria* (New York, 1986), p. 9.
109 Yvo J. Peters, 'The Rights of Minorities in Present-Day Turkey', *Europa Ethnica* 44 (1987), pp. 132–7.
110 Helsinki Watch, *Denying Human Rights and Ethnic Identity: The Greeks of Turkey* (New York, 1992), pp. 34–5.

Turkey's repression of its Kurdish minority offers an example of its contempt for paper guarantees. The basis of much of the Turkish policy towards the Kurds revolves around the denial of their status as an individual minority grouping, a view which began in the inter-war years as a reaction to Kurdish nationalism, and which has continued into the post-War period. One of the most ruthless periods in the history of Turkish repression of Kurdistan partly coincided with the rule of Turgut Özal, as part of the reaction against the growth of the PKK. In 1987, during Özal's premiership, a state of emergency came into operation in ten provinces in the south-east of Turkey. A governor-general ruled the area with extensive power, including the evacuation of villages and pasturage if he regarded such a step as necessary. In 1990 about 50,000 people had their homes razed. In addition, the security forces have arrested, beaten and tortured anybody they have suspected of having assisted the PKK. One of the torture victims from 1992 was a 20-year-old Kurdish student who was arrested in April for selling an illegal newspaper and taken to police headquarters in Sakariye. He described his ordeal to Lois Whitman, deputy director of Helsinki Watch:

When we got to Sakariye, they stripped me naked and gave me electric shock on my penis and finger. For fifteen days after that I could not use my right hand. They said I must be an Armenian, but I said, 'No, I'm Kurdish'. They used *falaka* on me [beating the soles of the feet] and highly pressurized water. My feet were so swollen I couldn't put my shoes on. For five days they kept that up – the electric shock, *falaka* and pressurized water.

In 1993, at least 24 people died after interrogation involving torture, while in police custody. This number included students, villagers, journalists, human rights activists and lawyers. The US State Department pointed this out to the Turkish government but a Foreign Ministry spokesman simply replied by stating that Turkey had made much progress in the field of human rights violations and continued to move forward in this area. The state of emergency in Turkey has also resulted in milder forms of repression. For instance, in April 1990 the governor-general of Kurdistan received powers to close down any publishing house in the country which 'falsely reflects events in the region or engages in untruthful reporting or commentary'. In addition, the state has also banned any political parties which have gained parliamentary support as representatives of the Kurds, describing them as fronts for the PKK. The groups affected included the HEP in July 1991, some of whose deputies formed the Democratic Labour Party, the offices of which faced closure in the summer of 1994.[111]

111 The facts for the above discussion come from: David McDowall, *A Modern History of the Kurds* (London, 1996), pp. 425–31, 435–40; Philip Robins, 'The Overlord State: Turkish Policy and the Kurdish Issue', *International Affairs* 69 (1993), pp. 657–76; Mark Muller, 'Nationalism and the Rule of Law in Turkey: The Elimination of Kurdish Representation during the 1990s', in Robert Olson (ed.), *The Kurdish Nationalist Movement in the 1990s* (Lexington, 1996), pp. 173–99; Amnesty International, International Secretariat London, 'Turkey: A Time for Action', February 1994; Helsinki Watch, *The Kurds of Turkey: Killings, Disappearance and Torture* (New York, 1993), *passim* and p. 27 for the quote.

While Turkey may represent an extreme example of ethnic intolerance, all nation states practise ethnic exclusion of one form or another. Paper guarantees prove unsatisfactory because they do not solve the social and economic inequalities faced by minorities. Ultimately – to repeat the point again – nation states are in the business of excluding: if they were not, they would not exist.

CHAPTER 7

'Public Opinion'

THE METHODS OF EXCLUSION AND PERSECUTION

Political activity within nation states operates in the context of the existing political and ideological structures. The population living within the borders of a nation state responds to the inherent ethnic exclusionism. The media represent the first way in which 'public opinion' practises ethnic exclusion because the press, radio and television play a central role in determining the thoughts of the population of any given state. Under such a situation everyday discrimination is heightened while racist political groupings and racist violence can develop – the other ways in which public hostility towards minorities manifests itself.

The media tap the nationalism and xenophobia inherent in nation states. This applies to all types of newspapers, just as it applies to all levels of television and radio programmes. *The Times* and the *Sun* in England, the *Frankfurter Allgemeine Zeitung* and *Bild Zeitung* in Germany sell a similar nationalist message, but, because of the relative levels of education of their readers, *The Times* and the *Frankfurter Allgemeine Zeitung* use more sophisticated language. Even apparently more progressive newspapers such as the *Guardian* in the British case and the *Frankfurter Rundschau* in Germany examine everything from an English or German perspective.

The media clearly represent a major method of excluding and persecuting minorities. By exclusion we mean the creation and highlighting of people outside the national community. Persecution refers to victimisation because of this fact. The media exclude and victimise minorities in two main ways. First, they function, on an everyday basis, using ethnic stereotypes. According to such stereotypes, the core national grouping has particular characteristics, which represent the 'correct' ones. In contrast, outgroups do not possess these virtues, which usually include cleanliness, thrift, hard work, honesty and acceptance of the national norms. Instead, outsiders often have the opposite characteristics.

Apart from perpetuating everyday stereotypes, the media also launch campaigns against particular minorities – especially recently arrived immigrants, when it is felt that too many have entered the country, as in the case of Britain in the late 1950s or Germany in the early 1990s. In such instances, the media have played a central role in outbreaks of large-scale and widespread racial violence, as well as persuading governments to introduce legislation to control immigration. In the case of eastern Europe under the old order, the media, controlled by the state, focused especially upon Jews.

Everyday discrimination thrives in a situation in which media stereotypes and campaigns focus upon the differences between the dominant population and minorities. This can take various manifestations including refusal to enter into social discourse, friendship and marriage. Similarly, prejudice in employment, whether in the form of unwillingness to offer work to members of minority groups or discrimination in the work-place, also develops. Opposition towards the settlement of minorities in particular areas also represents a major form of everyday hostility, leading to the emergence of ethnic ghettos.

Within liberal democracies, extremist groups, led by committed nationalists and racists, also develop. Such right-wing political parties play a role in perpetuating negative images of minorities, as well as influencing government and even media attitudes towards them, and causing outbreaks of racial violence, so that they represent a third major way of excluding and persecuting minorities.

Extreme right-wing political parties have existed in every liberal democracy in Europe since the end of the Second World War. They have basically taken two forms, although considerable overlap exists between these categories. At the far end of the scale there exist neo-Nazi groupings which overtly or covertly look back towards the inter-war fascist governments, and often work towards the re-establishment of the inter-war political order in states where fascism gained control of power. In many states neo-Nazis cannot stand for parliament, which limits the level of their success as does the overt and obscene racism they preach. Their views alienate respectable opinion but, precisely because of their outrageous nature, tend to appeal to young alienated working-class males. Their propaganda often leads to outbreaks of racial violence in the areas in which they campaign, and their members often participate in such attacks. However, the influence of such groups remains limited.

In contrast to such parties – which have remained beyond the pale of 're-spectable opinion' and have therefore made little impact upon electoral politics – overtly nationalist groupings, which play down their racist propaganda and do not sell the concept of resurrecting fascist regimes, have had considerable electoral success in several states since 1945. In reality, if such parties ever did seize power, they would pursue overtly racist policies, which would encompass deportation at the very least.

Political groupings which achieve success threaten the established political order and the centrist parties ignore them at their peril. Gaining or losing a tenth of votes cast at any election can determine the outcome. Mainstream political parties react to this threat in two apparently contradictory ways. On

the one hand, they overtly distance themselves from these nationalist groupings and refuse to enter into electoral pacts with them. On the other hand,
because of the level of electoral success of overtly nationalist groupings, the
mainstream parties steal some of their ideas, particularly in the area of nationality laws and immigration control.

Violence represents the most clinical and least respectable method of persecuting minorities. It has occurred throughout the European continent since
the end of the Second World War and has manifested itself in at least three
different ways. In the first place, sporadic attacks have occurred against individuals and their homes and property. Immigrants in western democracies
have been especially affected by this sort of incident, as have Gypsies in post-
communist eastern Europe. While such events may occur on a regular basis in
a wide variety of locations, they intensify at times of growing hostility towards
outgroups fuelled by the media and extremist political parties.

A second and less common form of racial violence has involved rioting,
which has affected a variety of groups as victims, especially immigrants in the
west. In such instances, hundreds or thousands of members of the dominant
grouping have gathered together in order to attack the homes and properties
of a particular outgroup. The media play a large role in such outbreaks of
mass disorder, which only occur in times of heightened attention and hostility
towards particular groupings, such as befell Britain in the late 1950s and east
Germany in the early 1990s. Such incidents take place in states which have not
yet developed concepts of 'multiracialism'. In countries such as post-1960s
Britain, where minorities have evolved their own publicity and power bases,
as well as having access to the mainstream media, mass racial violence would
simply be disreputable and stigmatised as such by 'respectable' politicians,
TV, radio and newspapers.

The most extreme form of racial violence in post-War Europe has consisted
of killing, in which the state plays either an active or passive role.[1] During the
first four decades after the end of the Second World War this occurred on a
limited scale. It has intensified in eastern Europe and the former Soviet Union
since the collapse of communism and has manifested itself in a variety of
ways, although none of these has ultimately involved a return to genocidal
Nazism, even though elements of such policies may have been present. In
former Yugoslavia, the militias and armies of all of the various peoples, with
the knowledge of the state authorities, have participated in what western
media have described as 'ethnic cleansing'. This process involves forcing
people with the 'wrong' ethnic credentials into camps, deporting them to areas
where members of their group are concentrated, or simply killing them.
In several parts of the former Soviet Union, including Nagorno-Karabakh,
Georgia and Chechnya, significant levels of killing have taken place, involving
either soldiers or unarmed people or both.

---

1 See also above, pp. 211–14.

THE ROLE OF THE MEDIA

Press reaction towards immigrants in post-War Britain illustrates the role of the media in excluding minorities. Negative attitudes to newcomers, especially Asians and West Indians, surfaced during the 1950s and early 1960s when press articles constantly complained about the influx of people from former British colonies. Such writing focused upon a series of issues including the health threat posed by the immigrants, as evidenced by a campaign in the *Yorkshire Post* and the *Telegraph and Argus* in 1962, which concentrated upon the fact that a small number of Pakistanis in Bradford had smallpox – a story blown up out of all proportion, in a classic example of press sensationalism.[2] Similarly, after the anti-Black Notting Hill riots of 1958 national newspapers, led by *The Times*, voiced concern about the effects of immigration.[3] On 4 September, for instance, *The Times* declared:

> There are certain crimes in this country, such as living off prostitutes' earnings, in which immigrants from outside Britain play too large a part. It is quite wrong that offenders of this kind should be immune from deportation just because they happen to be born in the Commonwealth and not in a foreign country. For one thing, their presence tends to excite prejudice against the innocent. It is possible, incidentally, that if legislation of this kind were passed it would not be the negro who was most affected.
>
> The time has come to admit that there is a colour problem in our midst. It would be disastrous to appear to give way in the face of violence. But to ignore the existence of the problem altogether is to invite disaster.

Any explanation for the regular occurrence of racial attacks in Britain since 1945, as elsewhere, would have to apportion much blame to the press – especially, but certainly not exclusively, the popular variety, which is involved in a constant campaign against foreign influences on Britain. A few examples can illustrate the point, although a reading of any British newspaper on any day of any year would reveal nationalist and xenophobic content, however subtle. On 2 July 1970, for instance, seven national daily newspapers carried a front-page headline about the discovery of 40 illegal immigrants in a cellar in Bradford, with the *Daily Express* declaring, 'Police Find Forty Indians in "Black Hole"'. In contrast, physical attacks against Pakistanis hardly ever made front-page news.[4] Sixteen years later the *Sun*, *Daily Mail* and *Daily Express*, amongst other newspapers, carried headlines which focused upon the allegedly deceitful nature of Asians moving to Britain, indicating the way in which the British press and state have criminalised immigrants and refugees. This process has also affected organs such as the apparently free-thinking

2 Eric Butterworth, 'The 1962 Smallpox Outbreak and the British Press', *Race* 7 (1966), pp. 347–64.
3 Robert Miles, 'The Riots of 1958: Notes on the Ideological Construction of "Race Relations" as a Political Issue in Britain', *Immigrants and Minorities* 3 (1984), pp. 252–75.
4 Paul Hartmann and Charles Husband, *Racism and the Mass Media* (London, 1974), p. 175.

Independent, which, on 10 October 1991, for example, could declare that 'we simply cannot provide a home for those who only want to live in a richer country. Such people are economic migrants' and, in the context of existing legislation, criminals.[5]

Germany in the early 1990s also offers an example of the media playing a role in the intensification of hostile perceptions of immigrants, again leading to serious racial attacks. Simply the act of reporting an outbreak of racist violence led to similar incidents elsewhere in a copycat fashion, because perpetrators felt that it had become legitimate to attack foreigners. Just as importantly, the focus of the media upon the influx of asylum seekers into Germany and the language used also gave the attackers legitimacy. Even the (apparently) most respectable of publications could carry articles and pictures of Germany being flooded by foreigners.[6] For instance, on 15 August 1991 the left-of-centre *Stern* magazine, accompanied by pictures of an ark overflowing with people, could carry the following apocalyptic headline:

ASSAULT UPON EUROPE

They come from the east, where their states were ruined by communism.

They come from the south, from Africa's hungry countries. The tragedy of the Albanian refugees in Italy demonstrates what lies before all of us: a mass migration as never seen before.

Such language made rioters feel that they could act with impunity against people not regarded as part of the national community. The asylum seekers, who bore the brunt of the attacks of the early 1990s, became scapegoats for the significant downturn in the German economy which had taken place consequent upon unification.

In eastern Europe, much of the state-controlled press hostility under the old order focused upon Jews, as several examples illustrate. In Poland, with a powerful tradition of anti-semitism, Judeophobia reached one of several post-War peaks in 1967 – following the Israeli victory over Soviet-backed Syrian and Egyptian forces during the Six Day War in June of that year – and continued in 1968 consequent upon demonstrations against the regime in Poland. Press organs controlled directly or indirectly by the state played a large role in propagating anti-semitism. The journals of the Party and professional groups within Poland such as lawyers and the army all carried hostile comments towards Jews in 1967–8, as did radio and television broadcasts. Meetings occurred in all editorial offices and Jews had to condemn Israel in public. In offices and factories mass meetings took place against Israeli aggression, while small demonstrations, involving the secret police and Party stalwarts, took place after the break of diplomatic relations with Israel on 12 June. Public institutions received lists

5 Robin Cohen, *Frontiers of Identity: The British and the Others* (London, 1994), pp. 88–92.
6 For instance, for the debate leading up to and during the outbreaks of violence in the autumn of 1991 see, for example: *Spiegel*, 9 and 30 September 1991; *Frankfurter Rundschau*, 23 September and 7 October 1991; *Welt Am Sonntag*, 6 and 13 October 1991; *Rheinischer Merkur*, 2, 9 and 16 August 1991; *Stern*, 14 August 1991.

of names of Jews which they employed, who subsequently lost their jobs and, instead, would have to work in manual occupations. Jews furthermore lost their housing and faced expulsion from the Communist Party and from their universities. They also received 'encouragement' to emigrate in the form of anonymous letters and phone calls. Consequently, only about 5,000 Jews – most of them sick and elderly – remained in Poland after the anti-semitic campaign of 1967–8.[7] But this did not prevent the development of further outbursts of anti-semitism, indicating the inextricable nature of Judeophobia and Polish nationalism, no matter which form of government exists. As a result of an opposition campaign to the state in 1976–7, newspapers drew links between Jewish leaders and those who had led support for Israel in 1967.[8]

Attitudes towards Jews in the Soviet Union were, at best, ambivalent and, often, outwardly negative during the post-War period. One of the peaks of anti-semitism in the USSR occurred at the end of the Second World War as part of the general repression of the various forms of nationalism which had received a new lease of life during the conflict. Perceptions of Jews specifically did not become completely negative until 1948 when it became clear that Israel did not wish to become a client state of the USSR. The rise of anti-semitism is also connected with the onset of the Cold War which, in both the USSR and the USA, created the need for a scapegoat to blame for the failures of each state's diplomacy. While the USA became gripped by McCarthyism with its conspiracy mentality focusing upon American communists, the Stalin equivalent, in classic anti-semitic language, directed attention towards 'rootless cosmopolitans', who supposedly had connections with the West.[9]

Newspapers played a leading role in the spread of anti-semitism during the early post-War years. A wide range of articles hostile to the Jewish population appeared in the press, beginning with one by Ilya Ehrenburg in *Pravda* published on 21 September 1948. This denied the existence of a Jewish people, condemned Jewish nationalism and described Israel as a bourgeois state and a tool of Anglo-American capitalism which could not solve the Jewish problem.[10] Another article in *Der Shtern* from 1948 criticised Jews for constantly referring to the Holocaust.[11] In January 1949 a press campaign began against a group

7 See Josef Banas, *The Scapegoats: The Exodus of the Remnants of Polish Jewry* (London, 1979); *The Anti-Jewish Campaign in Present-Day Poland: Facts, Documents, Press Reports* (London, 1968); Michael Checinski, *Poland: Communism, Nationalism, Antisemitism* (New York, 1982), pp. 106–253; Robert S. Wistrich, *Anti-Semitism: The Longest Hatred* (London, 1991), pp. 160–4; Bernard Wasserstein, *Vanishing Diaspora: The Jews in Europe Since 1945* (London, 1996), pp. 211–14; I. Irwin-Zarecka, *Neutralizing Memory: The Jew in Contemporary Poland* (Oxford, 1989), pp. 56–63.
8 Lucasz Hirszowicz and Tadeusz Szafar, 'The Jewish Scapegoat in Eastern Europe', *Patterns of Prejudice* 11 (1977), pp. 7–9.
9 See Benjamin Pinkus, *The Jews of the Soviet Union: The History of a National Minority* (Cambridge, 1988), pp. 145, 147, 150–1, 154; Wistrich, *Anti-Semitism*, pp. 176–7; Joseph Dunner, 'Anti-Jewish Discrimination Since the End of the Second World War', in W. A. Veenhoven et al. (eds), *Case Studies on Human Rights Violations and Fundamental Freedoms: A World Survey*, Vol. 1 (The Hague, 1975), p. 77.
10 Bernard D. Weinryb, 'Antisemitism in Soviet Russia', in Lionel Kochan (ed.), *The Jews in the Soviet Union Since 1917*, 3rd edn (Oxford, 1978), p. 322.
11 Pinkus, *Jews of the Soviet Union*, pp. 148–9.

of cosmopolitan theatre critics.[12] Anti-semitism then developed into a state-inspired hysteria which spread beyond the press to affect the radio, literature, cinema, theatre, scientific and popular lectures, while posters appeared in the work-place to make the point even plainer.[13]

The anti-semitic campaign of these years resulted in the closure of Jewish institutions and the purge and murder of prominent Jews. Thus the Jewish Anti-Fascist Committee established during the Second World War was banned in 1948 and its chairman, Solomon Mikhoels, was murdered, while the Jewish State Theatre which he directed, along with numerous other Jewish theatres, was also closed down. Jews faced arrest on charges of economic sabotage, theft, speculation, bribes and work evasion. The purges affected journalists, musicians, writers and academics, as well as people involved in industry.[14]

The anti-semitic campaign reached a peak with the so-called 'Doctor's Plot' of 1953, an idea which had evolved over the course of several years. On 13 January all of the leading Soviet newspapers carried a story about the arrest of a group of nine doctors, six of them Jews, who had tried to poison leading Soviet figures using harmful methods of medical treatment under instruction from an American Jewish philanthropic organisation. The following months resulted in an outburst of unbridled anti-semitic propaganda, which affected all of the leading Soviet newspapers. Jewish doctors faced accusations of negligence, sloppiness, nepotism and malpractice, and many were arrested. The sackings of Jews in other professions also continued, while some Jewish people experienced assaults on the street. In addition, plans also developed for the deportation of Jews to Siberia, to be housed in camps and barracks in the process of construction.[15] But a Soviet Holocaust of the Jews did not materialise because of a lessening of anti-semitism following the death of Stalin on 5 March. The trial of those accused in the Doctor's Plot, scheduled for 15 March, did not go ahead. Those Jews dismissed since 1948 gradually got their jobs back, while those who had been exiled were individually rehabilitated.[16]

Anti-semitism certainly did not disappear, however. During the 1950s and early 1960s Jews went on trial for committing economic crimes. Worse still, incidents characteristic of western liberal democracies occurred in the form of fire-bomb attacks upon synagogues in Malakhovska near Moscow in 1959 and Georgia in 1962, while in Uzbekistan in 1961 and 1962 Muslims accused Jews of using blood for ritual purposes.[17] Overt anti-semitic media images in the Soviet Union, which had never actually died down after the Doctor's

---

12 Gennadi Kostrychenko, *Out of the Red Shadows: Anti-Semitism in Stalin's Russia* (Amherst, NY, 1995), pp. 153–78.

13 Pinkus, *Jews of the Soviet Union*, p. 155.

14 Ibid., pp. 174, 177; Weinryb, 'Antisemitism in Soviet Russia', p. 322; Wistrich, *Anti-Semitism*, p. 176; Kostrychenko, *Out of the Red Shadows*, pp. 179–247.

15 Iakov Etinger, 'The Doctor's Plot: Stalin's Solution to the Jewish Question', in Yaacov Ro'i (ed.), *Jews and Jewish Life in the Soviet Union* (London, 1995), pp. 103–24; Wistrich, ibid., p. 178; Kostrychenko, ibid., pp. 248–303.

16 Pinkus, *Jews of the Soviet Union*, p. 209; Weinryb, 'Antisemitism in Soviet Russia', p. 323.

17 Weinryb, ibid., pp. 326–7.

Plot, took off again after the Six Day War in 1967 as hostility towards Israel increased. Between 5 June 1967 and 5 June 1972, 1,107 anti-Jewish caricatures appeared in 44 Russian newspapers dealing simply with the Arab–Israeli conflict.[18] Similarly, numerous anti-Zionist books appeared during this period which spoke in conspiratorial terms reminiscent of classic inter-war fascist hostility towards Jews.[19] Such images continued into the 1970s, with ideas harking back to the anti-semitic language of the Dreyfus affair in France during the 1890s, revolving around Jewish–Masonic plots.[20]

During the 1980s anti-semitism in the USSR received a new lease of life from several sources. In the first place, the Israeli invasion of Lebanon in 1982 and 1983 led to the appearance of more hostility towards Jews in the Soviet press. A Public Anti-Zionist Committee produced publications and held conferences subscribing to theories of a worldwide Jewish conspiracy.[21] Perestroika simply meant the replacement of state with public anti-Jewish hostility, a process which continued under Yeltsin.

In Czechoslovakia anti-semitic stereotypes circulated in the media after the failure of the Prague Spring, while opponents of the regime during the 1970s and 1980s also faced accusations of Zionism. These developments occurred despite the presence of only tiny numbers of Jews in the country.[22] The Velvet Revolution and Divorce led to an increase in negative images of both the Jewish and, more especially, Gypsy minorities in the Czech Republic and Slovakia. The *Protocols of the Elders of Zion*, the anti-semitic forgery which has claimed, since it first surfaced at the end of the nineteenth century, that Jews control the world, began to circulate in Slovakia in the early 1990s, distributed by radical nationalists.[23]

EVERYDAY DISCRIMINATION

Partly as a result of media attitudes, outsiders in any nation state face everyday hostility. The clearest manifestations of this lie in the area of securing employment and housing, where the attitude of majorities has controlled the working and living conditions of minorities, particularly immigrants.[24] Other manifestations of everyday discrimination include hostility in socialising and animosity in the work-place.

18 Pinkus, *Jews of the Soviet Union*, pp. 233–4.
19 Dunner, 'Anti-Jewish Discrimination', pp. 78–80.
20 Howard Spier, '"Zionists and Freemasons" in Soviet Propaganda', *Patterns of Prejudice* 13 (1979), pp. 1–5.
21 Theodore H. Friedgut, 'Passing Eclipse: The Exodus Movement in the 1980s', in Robert O. Freedman (ed.), *Soviet Jewry in the 1980s: The Politics of Anti-Semitism and the Dynamics of Resettlement* (Durham, NC, 1989), pp. 11–12.
22 Eva Schmidt-Hartmann, 'The Enlightenment that Failed: Antisemitism in Czech Political Culture', *Patterns of Prejudice* 27 (1993), p. 123; Wistrich, *Anti-Semitism*, pp. 155–6; Wasserstein, *Vanishing Diaspora*, pp. 224–5; Hirszowicz and Szafar, 'Jewish Scapegoat', pp. 9–11.
23 Yeshayahu A. Jelinek, 'Historical and Minority Problems in Czecho-Slovakia', *Patterns of Prejudice* 27 (1993), pp. 102–5.
24 These issues are examined in detail in Chapters 2 and 3 above.

Britain during the 1950s illustrates such processes. For instance, George Powe faced hostility from pub landlords in Nottingham, one of whom called for the police to remove him and his friends, some of whom were white.[25] Such social prejudice continued into the 1980s, as described by a Black resident of Birmingham:

When you go to a nightclub, no matter how you're dressed, if you're wearing a shirt and tie and all that, they say you're not dressed right, and then a white guy comes up in casual clothes and gets straight in.

All the clubs in town have a system where they only let in a handful of blacks, just to cover themselves. One of them even has a black bouncer to turn away black people, so that you can't say they're prejudiced. Even if you're perfectly dressed they'll find some reason to stop you, like no single men, or no groups, or they don't like your hair. I was even told once there weren't enough buttons on my shirt.[26]

During the 1950s and 1960s British trade unions also displayed hostility towards Black and Asian immigrants, because they feared that bringing foreign workers into the country 'can only lead to a worsening of their own position' due to their potential to undercut the wages of the native membership.[27] In some instances concern about immigrants in the work-place led to industrial disputes. One of the most famous of these occurred in 1955 when workers at West Bromwich Corporation Transport held a series of one-day strikes in protest against the employment of an Indian trainee conductor.[28] As late as 1964, members of the Associated Engineering Union at the English Steel Corporation in Sheffield refused to speak to a Pakistani upgraded from the position of crane driver to take charge of a machine.[29] In reality, everyday relations between native English people and newcomers consisted of 'a jumbled and largely unpredictable mixture of friendliness and veiled hostility'.[30]

In Switzerland hostility towards immigrants revolved around a series of fears, summed up by the concept of *Überfremdung*, literally translated as 'overforeignisation'. Certain sections of the Swiss population believed, in a pattern typical of the whole of post-War Europe, that too many immigrants in Switzerland would harm the economy, society and culture of the country and the interests of natives. Trade unions played a leading role in the campaigns against immigrants during the 1960s, led by the Schweizerischer Gewerkschaftsbund (SGB), the largest labour organisation in the country. In fact, for much of the decade, employers had a more positive attitude to immigrants than trade unions, because of the economic benefits available. In contrast,

25 Edward Pilkington, *Beyond the Mother Country: West Indians and the Notting Hill White Riots* (London, 1988), p. 45.
26 Quoted in *Black Birmingham* (Birmingham, 1987), p. 49.
27 Michael Banton, *White and Coloured: The Behaviour of British People Towards Coloured Immigrants* (London, 1959), p. 167.
28 Ron Ramdin, *The Making of the Black Working Class in Britain* (Aldershot, 1984), p. 200.
29 Clifford S. Hill, *How Colour Prejudiced is Britain?* (London, 1965), p. 125.
30 Banton, *White and Coloured*, p. 162.

unions feared *Überfremdung*, although the underlying causes for concern, (demonstrating the classic ground for trade union opposition to immigrants) lay in anxiety about the effects of immigrants on wages and their reluctance to join established trade unions.[31]

The everyday experience of newcomers in Germany has resembled that of immigrants in Britain and Switzerland. Opinion surveys from 1961–2 revealed that 83 per cent of Germans believed that each group of people had naturally inherited distinctive racial characteristics, while 65 per cent thought that even if people of all nationalities had the same life chances, some races would be more successful than others.[32] Such attitudes meant that, as late as the 1970s, relations between Germans and immigrants 'during leisure time and in human association were few and far between – and almost non-existent among neighbours'. Lack of knowledge of German by the immigrants did not help their position. Derogatory names circulated widely, including 'sheep thieves, camel drivers, Hottentots (North Africans), Mohameds, Caraway Turks, Mussulmen (Turks), Partisans, bear trainers (Yugoslavs), spaghetti eaters, Macaronis, lemon shakers (Italians)'.[33] Such attitudes continued in the following decades, leading one 28-year-old woman from Macedonia, Dana, to declare that: 'I feel that if xenophobia intensified the Germans would grind us to soap powder'. She consequently went to extreme lengths to hide her ethnicity, including looking at the ground as she walked along the street so that Germans would not see her dark eyes. In addition, Dana only spoke German to her children in public.[34]

NATIONALIST AND RACIST POLITICAL GROUPINGS

All parties which participate in the political processes of nation states are nationalist because they all accept that they work within the parameters of the existing boundaries. However, a difference exists – to take the example of Britain – between the Conservative Party of the 1970s and the National Front of the same period, in the explicitness of their racial discourse, the extremity of some NF ideas and the centrality of race (as opposed to nation) in their ideology. Racist organisations, together with the more extreme neo-Nazi groupings, which have not managed to make an electoral breakthrough, have nonetheless existed in liberal democracies all over Europe since 1945.

31 Anne Sue Matasar, 'Labor Transfers in Western Europe: The Problem of Italian Migrant Workers in Switzerland' (Columbia University unpublished PhD thesis, 1968), pp. 114–24; Stephen Castles and Godula Kosack, *Immigrant Workers and Class Structure in Western Europe* (London, 1973), pp. 144–52.
32 Badi Panahi, *Vorurteile: Rassismus, Antisemitismus, Nationalismus in der Bundesrepublik Heute* (Frankfurt, 1980), p. 268.
33 Clemens Amelunxen, 'Foreign Workers in West Germany', in Veenhoven, *Case Studies in Human Rights Violations and Fundamental Freedoms*, Vol. 1, pp. 127–8.
34 Dagmar Burkhart-Chatzfeliader, 'Das Schicksal von vier Jugoslawinnen im deutschen Westen: Die ewige furcht, sich falsch zu verhalten', in R. Italiaander (ed.), *Fremde Raus* (Frankfurt, 1983), p. 202.

Even the most apparently tolerant of western European liberal democracies, within Scandinavia, have witnessed the growth of right-wing groups. Sweden, for instance, has counted a wide range of nationalist and xenophobic parties since 1945, which can trace their origins back to inter-war fascist activity within the country. One of the most significant early post-War groupings, neo-Nazi in nature, was the Nordiska Riksparteit, established in 1956 and continuing to function until the 1990s, although in the meantime it split into several groups which carried out a violent factional war against each other. One of these new groups was the Riksaksjonsgruppe, responsible for a series of acts of violence and threats against anti-racists, left-wingers, immigrants and gays in Gothenburg in the middle of the 1980s. At around the same time a neo-Nazi anti-immigrant grouping, Bevara Sverige Svenskt (Keep Sweden Swedish), became active in the Stockholm area, initially engaging in extra-parliamentary activity, involving skinhead violence. In 1987 the group changed its name to Sverigepartiet (the Swedish Party) and in the following year it became the Sverigedemokratene (the Swedish Democrats). The transformation involved a progression from a violent organisation to one which tried to make itself respectable for the purpose of securing parliamentary representation. This group had some success in elections during 1991, when it gained a single local council seat in Dals-Ed, although it failed to obtain the 20,000 parliamentary votes for which it had aimed. Part of the reason for its relative failure to achieve its target lay in competition from two other groupings, the Sjöbopartiet and the Framtegspartiet, which ran as a coalition and gained 27,637 votes, which translated into 12 local council seats. In the 1994 elections the Swedish Democrats managed to obtain five seats at the local level. The above group-ings represent simply the tip of the iceberg, as numerous other extremist parties have existed in the course of post-War Swedish history. In terms of the characteristics of members, in common with similar groupings all over Europe, many have been young males from working-class backgrounds with-out a university education.[35]

In Norway the major parliamentary right-wing grouping has consisted of the Progress Party, established in 1973. Initially, it devoted relatively little attention to the issue of immigration, because the country counted virtually no foreigners within its borders. It made a significant breakthrough in 1987, when it obtained 12 per cent of the votes in local elections, increasing further to 13 per cent in the general election of 1989, when it became the third-largest party, although it fell back to 6 per cent in the 1993 national poll. At the time of the 1987 elections, hostility towards immigrants made up a major part of the Progress Party's campaign, so that at one rally its leader, Carl I. Hagen, read out a letter which he claimed he had received from a Muslim in Norway,

---

35 Heléne Lööw, 'Racist Violence and Criminal Behaviour in Sweden: Myths and Reality', in Tore Bjørgo (ed.), *Terror from the Extreme Right* (London, 1995), pp. 119–61; Tore Bjørgo, 'Militant neo-Nazism in Sweden', *Terrorism and Political Violence* 5 (1993), pp. 28–57; David Arter, 'Black Faces in the Blond Crowd: Populist Racialism in Scandinavia', *Parliamentary Affairs* 45 (1992), pp. 367–70.

stating that Norway would become a Muslim state and that mosques would become as common in the country as churches. The success of the Progress Party made racism respectable, which led to a tightening of immigration controls in 1988. The Party also helped to give rise to new one-issue movements concerned solely with immigration, in the form of the People's Movement Against Immigration and Stop Immigration.[36]

In 1972 a Progressive Party came into existence in Denmark, which focused upon immigration from the end of the 1970s. By the middle of the 1980s it was campaigning on the slogan of: 'Make Denmark a Muslim Free Zone'.[37] By 1990 a series of specifically anti-immigrant groupings had taken root in Denmark. The most significant of these was the Danish Society, which simply wanted to expel all foreigners from Denmark, with the exception of executives of multinational companies. Its leaders consisted of professional academics and priests, and its membership included pensioners, shopkeepers, artisans and workers. It published its own monthly magazine, *Danskeren*, and devoted particularly hostile attention to Muslims. Other organisations have included the neo-Nazi National Party and the Ku Klux Klan (Danish Chapter).[38]

Anti-immigrant groups began to take off in Britain from the middle of the 1950s, as evidenced by the rise of Union Movement, founded in 1948 and led by the leader of the pre-War British Union of Fascists, Oswald Mosley. The new organisation focused upon areas in London which had experienced significant levels of immigration, including Brixton and Notting Hill. The 1958 riots in the latter area encouraged Mosley to stand as a candidate for North Kensington, which included Notting Hill, in the 1959 general election, where he obtained 8 per cent of the votes cast. His campaign focused on issues which ranged from repatriation to the dietary habits of immigrants.[39] Outside London, the Birmingham Immigration Control Association came into existence in October 1960. Its activities included protest meetings, the distribution of leaflets, the organisation of petitions and the writing of letters to local newspapers.[40]

In 1967 the National Front, the only overtly racist party of any significance in post-War Britain, came into existence. Its leading figures consisted of John Tyndall and Martin Webster and its campaign focused on the 'degeneration'

36 Arter, ibid., pp. 363–4; Herbert Kitschelt, *The Radical Right in Western European Perspective* (Ann Arbor, 1995), pp. 128, 133–4; Khalid Salimi, 'Norway's National Racism', *Race and Class* 32 (1991), pp. 113–14.
37 Arter, ibid., p. 363; Jørgen Goul Andersen, 'Denmark: The Progress Party – Populist Neo-Liberalism and Welfare State Chauvinism', in Paul Hainsworth (ed.), *The Extreme Right in Europe and the USA* (London, 1992), pp. 193–205; Hans-Georg Betz, *Radical Right-Wing Populism in Western Europe* (London, 1994), p. 5.
38 Bashy Quraishy and Tim O'Connor, 'Denmark: No Racism by Definition', *Race and Class* 32 (1991), pp. 116–19.
39 Roger Eatwell, *Fascism: A History* (London, 1996), pp. 261–3; Richard Thurlow, *Fascism in Britain: A History, 1918–1985* (Oxford, 1987), pp. 246–7; Pilkington, *Beyond the Mother Country*, pp. 98–100.
40 Robert Miles and Annie Phizacklea, *White Man's Country: Racism in British Politics* (London, 1984), p. 38.

which had accompanied immigration from the Commonwealth; it called for repatriation, while its leading figures also privately stressed anti-semitism. At the West Bromwich by-election of 1973 it obtained 16 per cent of the vote and it counted a membership of 14,000. But, by the following year, its decline had set in, as it obtained less than 4 per cent of the votes at the general elections of 1974. Subsequently, it split apart, with the British National Party its most notable successor, while Margaret Thatcher attracted many NF voters.[41]

In France the Front National has become part of the mainstream political scene since the early 1980s, although it had various predecessors, as the extreme right in France has long historical traditions. These date back to the late nineteenth century in the form of Action Française and culminate in the collaborationist Vichy Regime of the Second World War, which attracted the extremists who had developed fascist groupings during the inter-war years.

Because of the stigma of collaboration, right-wing groups had difficulties immediately after the end of the Second World War, especially as supporters of Vichy faced execution. Although some minor parties existed by the early 1950s,[42] the first significant development on the right of the political spectrum occurred around the figure of Pierre Poujade, who formed a pressure group called the Union for the Defence of Shopkeepers and Artisans, which in 1955 became a political party with the name of French Union and Fraternity (UFF). Poujadism attracted members of the petty bourgeoisie, such as small shop-keepers and artisans who felt threatened by the expansion of big business, and complained about corrupt politicians. The movement believed Jews lay behind both big business and politics.[43] The UFF had a spectacular success in the 1956 general election when it obtained 11.6 per cent of the vote and 52 seats in the National Assembly (including one held by Jean-Marie Le Pen, future leader of the FN), although the movement disappeared with the rise of De Gaulle during the late 1950s.

The Front National came into existence in October 1972 and 'spent its first ten years crossing the electoral desert, unable to make any significant impact on the political scene'.[44] The first significant result occurred in the 1983 muni-cipal elections when the party gained 2 million votes. In the following year the FN obtained 10.87 per cent of the votes cast at the European elections. By this time it counted 20,000 members, a figure which had risen to 50,000 by 1985. In the next year 9.9 per cent of the electorate supported the FN at the general election, which meant that it obtained 35 seats. In 1988 the party reached a high point when Le Pen gained 4.4 million votes at the Presidential election, or 14.4 per cent of all votes cast. The FN continued its success into the 1990s, securing 12.6 per cent of votes at the parliamentary elections of

41 See Roger Eatwell, 'Why Has the Extreme Right Failed in Britain?', in Hainsworth, *Extreme Right*, pp. 176–80.
42 Eatwell, *Fascism*, pp. 241–2.
43 Ibid., p. 243.
44 Jonathan Marcus, *The National Front and French Politics: The Resistable Rise of Jean-Marie Le Pen* (London, 1995), p. 52.

1993, while, two years later, Le Pen again finished a respectable third in the first round of the Presidential election.

What has been the basis of the success of Le Pen and his party? Part of the reason for the breakthrough of the early 1980s lay in a reaction against the socialist government which had come to power in 1981, although this would not explain the continuing success of the group into the 1990s, as right-wing governments became the norm until 1997. The FN's ideology may also have played a role in its rise to power: while it may revolve around nationalism and racism, this also has other elements, some inherited from previous extreme right-wing groupings in France such as Poujadism, and others which have had much in common with contemporaneous ideologies such as Thatcherism and Reaganism. But the concentration upon the issue of race played a large role in the breakthrough of the 1980s. Rather like Adolf Hitler's attitude towards Jews, Le Pen has blamed every problem which France faces upon foreigners. 'For Jean-Marie Le Pen, politics is nothing less than a Manichean struggle for the survival of the French nation and French identity.'[45] As well as the enemy within, in the form of immigrants, the external foe consisted, during the 1980s, of Soviet communism and Islam. Internally, the 'presence of a small proportion of North African workers in the French economy is identified as the single most significant factor contributing to the decline of the French nation'.[46] The newcomers have caused crime, lowered educational standards, constructed mosques at the rate of one every four days, imposed their culture upon France, caused the building of high-rise blocks to house them, and contributed to the balance of payments deficit of the country by sending 31 billion francs abroad every year. The solution to France's problems lies in putting French people before immigrants in all fields of life including employment, housing and education. Illegal immigrants and foreign criminals should be deported. Mosque building should stop and ethnic ghettos face dismantling. Concern with the declining French birth rate, especially in comparison with that of immigrants, led to attacks on abortion, homosexuality and contraception. Whether or not the FN would describe itself as neo-fascist, many of the above policies link it with the right-wing ideological movements of the 1930s. In any case, if the FN seizes power, it would behave as it wishes.

The FN has appealed to particular sections of the French population. In geographical terms, the party has tended to gain its highest proportion of votes in the areas with the greatest concentration of immigrants, particularly around Paris and Marseilles. In addition, areas with a heavy concentration of 'pieds-noirs' have also voted strongly for Le Pen, especially in view of much of his anti-Arab rhetoric.[47] Furthermore, people who have voted for the party

45 Ibid., p. 101.
46 Jim Wolfreys, 'An Iron hand in a Velvet Glove: The Programme of the French Front National', *Parliamentary Affairs* 46 (1993), pp. 423–4.
47 Philip Ogden, 'Immigration, Cities and the Geography of the National Front in France', in Gunther Glebe and John O'Loughlin (eds), *Foreign Minorities in Continental European Cities* (Wiesbaden, 1987), pp. 176–82; Henry G. Simmons, *The French National Front: The Extremist Challenge to Democracy* (Oxford, 1996), p. 180.

have tended to switch their allegiances from moderate right-wing groups. In addition, the FN has also attracted more men than women and has also appealed to people who had previously abstained from voting.[48]

The amount of support obtained by the FN meant that it played a large role in bringing issues of immigration and nationality to the centre of French politics during the 1980s, especially amongst mainstream right-wing politicians from whom the FN gained much of its support. The blunt and openly racist language of Le Pen and his acolytes has meant that candidates of the main-stream right, including Jacques Chirac, could link aspects of what they saw as the decline of France, such as increased criminality, to the fact that too many foreigners lived within the country.[49] The rhetoric of the mainstream right was accompanied both by the tightening of French controls upon immigra-tion, and by the growing concern with who gained French nationality. Thus while such groups may have refused to enter into ruling alliances with Le Pen at either a local or national level, they stole some of his policies.[50]

In view of the existence of the Nazi dictatorship between 1933 and 1945, it was unlikely that the liberal democratic state which came into existence in Germany after 1945 could ever be completely free from extremist groupings. Even in the immediate aftermath of the Second World War, during the 1940s and 1950s, when Germany was apparently trying to come to terms with the consequences of twelve years of Nazism, parties of the extreme right had a certain level of electoral success. These consisted of the Socialist Reichs Party and the German Reichs Party, the former of which obtained 11 per cent of the vote in elections in Lower Saxony in 1951,[51] but which faced a ban from the Federal Constitutional Court in 1952 through a provision in the 1949 Federal Constitution which allowed for the abolition of anti-democratic parties. These first two parties essentially represent a regrouping of the original forces of Nazism during a period when the Allies eliminated the most obvious supporters of the regime.

The next significant group consisted of the National Democratic Party which came into existence in November 1964. Its programme harked back towards Nazism, calling for the restoration of pre-War borders, a united Germany and priority for German workers in employment over foreigners. The programme of the party opposed all foreign influences upon Germany, especially Jewish, American and immigrant. Foreign workers had, it claimed, led to an increase in crime, and were after German women. In 1969, the NPD gained 1,422,010

---

48 Paul Hainsworth, 'The Extreme Right in Post-War France: The Emergence and Success of the Front National', in Hainsworth, *Extreme Right*, p. 44.
49 Marcus, *National Front*, pp. 93–4.
50 Such issues are considered by: Martin A. Schain, 'Immigration and Changes in the French Party System', *European Journal of Political Research* 16 (1988), pp. 597–621; and Christopher T. Husbands, 'The Mainstream Right and the Politics of Immigration in France: Major Develop-ments in the 1980s', *Ethnic and Racial Studies* 14 (1991), pp. 170–98.
51 David Childs, 'The Nationalist and Neo-Nazi Scene Since 1945', in Klaus Larres and Panikos Panayi (eds), *The Federal Republic of Germany Since 1949: Politics, Society and Economy Before and After Unification* (London, 1996), p. 212.

votes in the federal elections, when it secured 4.3 per cent of the poll.[52] Although this represents the highest proportion of votes ever achieved by an extreme right grouping in federal elections, the NPD did not gain parliamentary representation, because of the necessity under the Federal Constitution to obtain 5 per cent of the vote, a target which no extreme right group has achieved at this particular level of elections. This has meant that no such group has gained representation in the Bundestag, although both the NPD and the Republikaner have surpassed 5 per cent at other elections.

Despite the economic crisis of the 1970s, which caused a rise in unemployment, no upsurge in support for the extreme right occurred. In fact, the 1970s 'were a dismal period for the far Right in Germany',[53] a situation which continued for much of the 1980s. Nevertheless, at the beginning of the 1980s, the German far right 'was organized in 73 groups with a membership of 20,300', of which the largest consisted of Gerhard Frey's Deutsche Volksunion, which had surpassed the NPD as the leading extreme right group in the country. Out of the 73 groups mentioned above neither the NPD nor the DVU fitted into the category of neo-Nazi – and consequently illegal – groupings as classified by the Office for the Protection of the Constitution (Amt für Verfassungsschutz), although 18 (most of which counted just a handful of members) of the 73 groups were classed in this way.[54]

Extreme right groups began to take off towards the end of the 1980s at the same time as did attacks against foreigners. Although a series of short-term factors played a large role in these developments, they also took place against a growing self-confidence and re-definition of German national identity, in which the state began to reinterpret its Nazi past and lose some of its guilt and shame. This revulsion against Nazism – and, in fact, against the whole of nineteenth-century German history – reached its height during the 1960s and 1970s, a period during which positive attitudes towards national identity focused upon post-War liberal values and constitutional patriotism, as well as the concept of never forgetting the German past. During the 1980s a series of leading political figures, above all Chancellor Helmut Kohl, together with right-wing intellectuals, began to speak about reinterpreting German history, a process in which shame about Nazism would disappear as German history stretched beyond the years 1933–45. In addition, the new perspective also stressed the fact that Germans had been victims during the Second World War. The rising tide of German self-confidence received a powerful shot in the arm during the process of German reunification, especially on the night of the collapse of the Berlin Wall, 9 November 1989, when hysterical nationalism became respectable. Reunification also allowed a move away from a focus

---

52 Richard Stöss, *Politics Against Democracy: Right-Wing Extremism in West Germany* (Oxford, 1991), pp. 146–7.
53 David Childs, 'The Far Right in Germany Since 1945', in Luciano Cheles, Ronnie Ferguson and Michalina Vaughan (eds), *The Far Right in Western and Eastern Europe* (London, 1995), p. 297.
54 Childs, 'Nationalist and Neo-Nazi Scene', pp. 221–2.

upon Nazism as the sole evil phase in German history. Concern with the GDR joined it as the *Stasi* united with the Nazis as the bogeymen of German history.

Inevitably, the changing concepts of German national identity resulted in a growth of xenophobia, which took off during the 1980s, to reach a peak at the start of the 1990s. This manifested itself, in the first place, in an increase in racial attacks and a take-off in support for the extreme right. Several new groups came into existence, including the Nationale Alternative and the Nationale Offensive.

More important than any of the neo-Nazi groupings was the Republikaner, which had existed since 1983, under the leadership of Franz Schönhuber, who had served in the Waffen SS. During the 1980s and into the 1990s, the Republikaner had an ideology similar to the DVU and the NPD. All three supported the collective over the individual – the collective consisting of a homogenous nation, people or state – meaning that they were more overtly racist than the democratic parties and called for more extreme measures to deal with the 'threats' posed by foreigners within Germany, including deportation and a tightening of the right of asylum. They blamed immigrants for unemployment and for social problems and feared that German national identity would be destroyed by foreign cultures. All three parties also advocated a move away from the guilt feeling about the Nazi past, asserting that the country should take pride in its history. Furthermore, they were hostile to the EU and wanted to see Germany return to its 1937 borders, rather than those imposed at the end of the Second World War.

The Republikaner had a membership of 25,000 by the early 1990s, while the DVU reached 11,500 and the NPD totalled over 6,100.[55] More spectacular was the electoral support obtained by the DVU and the Republikaner. The latter was catapulted into the limelight in 1989 when it gained 7.1 per cent of the vote in the elections to the European Parliament and 7.5 per cent in the regional election in Berlin. The Republikaner fell back to just 2.1 per cent in the federal elections of 1990, but subsequently obtained its most spectacular success in the early years of the new German state, rocketing to 10.9 per cent of the vote in the state election in Baden-Württemberg in 1992 and gaining around 5 per cent on several other occasions.[56] The electorate of both the DVU and Republikaner consisted more of men than of women. Both parties also had a disproportionate percentage of voters among the younger age groups. Socially, the parties of the right attracted members of the working classes and lower middle classes, as well as the unemployed: all felt that their economic position had come under threat.

Nevertheless, at the federal election of 1994, the extreme right did not make the breakthrough which threatened in 1991 and 1992, but which became

55 Hans-Gerd Jaschke, *Die 'Republikaner': Profile einer Rechtsaußen-Partei* (Bonn, 1993), p. 118; Bundesministerium des Innern, *Verfassungsschutzbericht, 1992* (Bonn, 1993), p. 36.
56 Hans-Joachim Veen, Norbert Lepszy and Peter Minch, *The Republikaner Party in Germany: Right-Wing Menace or Protest Catchall* (Westport, CT, 1993), pp. 11–12.

increasingly unlikely from 1993. The DVU did not field any candidates while the Republikaner gained just 1.9 per cent of the vote, falling below the 2.1 total it achieved in 1990 and way under the 4.3 per cent gained by the NPD in 1969.[57] We might offer two explanations for this poor showing. First, the Republikaner suffered internal divisions which came to a head two weeks before the election when 'the party's executive voted to dump' Schönhuber as its leader.[58] A second explanation is that the election results are simply typical protest votes characteristic of a contemporary liberal democracy in the middle of a parliament, with voters moving back to the mainstream for the 'real thing'. But if they are protest votes, then we need to ask what they were protesting about. Part of the answer lies in the liberal asylum laws of Germany which had been tightened up, meaning that the ruling coalition could attract back some of these votes.

The extreme right has also played a role in post-War Belgium, although activity in this state is complex because of the existence of two major indigenous communities as well as a large immigrant population. Like several other European states, Belgium witnessed an upsurge in overt racism during the 1980s and 1990s, although the events of these decades have roots which go back to the early post-War period.[59]

By the middle of the 1980s, a total of 29 active extreme right-wing groups existed in Belgium: 18 in Flanders, 8 in Wallonia, and 3 with bilingual names.[60] The most successful of all of these groupings consisted of the Vlaams Blok, which came into existence in 1979. During the course of the 1980s the VB gained electoral success and became overtly xenophobic, focusing much attention upon immigrants. In the 1981, 1985 and 1987 general elections the party received no more than 2 per cent of the votes cast, although it did have slightly more success at the local level, especially in Antwerp. The first major breakthrough occurred in municipal elections in 1988, once again particularly within Antwerp where the VB gained 17.7 per cent of the votes cast. In the European elections of the following year the party attracted 240,668 votes, which allowed Karl Dillen to gain a seat in Strasburg. More significant success occurred in the general election of 1991, when the party obtained 10.3 per cent of the Flemish vote, giving it twelve seats in the lower house and six in the senate. Further success followed during the 1990s, so that in the 1994 local elections it had increased its share of the vote in its Antwerp stronghold to 28 per cent.

Nationalism and xenophobia have formed the core of VB ideology. The group believes in the existence of a Flemish 'Volk' community, whose 'cultural, ethical and intellectual interests need to be preserved'. It wants to see an

---

57 *Die Zeit*, 21 October 1994.
58 *Searchlight* (November 1994), p. 21.
59 Guy Delore, 'The Far Right in Belgium: The Double Track', in Cheles, Ferguson and Vaughan, *Far Right*, pp. 248, 250–1.
60 Christopher T. Husbands, 'Belgium: Flemish Legions on the March', in Hainsworth, *Extreme Right*, p. 129.

independent Flanders which would enter into a Dutch federation with the Netherlands, South Flanders in north-western France, and South Africa. During the course of the 1980s the VB began to focus more and more upon the issue of immigration, which played a significant role in the increase of votes which it experienced. The policies it put forward have included the repatriation of all illegal immigrants, the creation of a separate social security system for foreigners, the banning of multicultural education and the creation of a separate school system for foreigners. It has spoken about putting its own people first and has regarded racial mixing in a negative light.[61]

In the French-speaking part of Belgium the most important far right grouping since the 1970s has consisted of the National Front, which took its name from Le Pen's party. Although it sees itself as a Belgian organisation, it has had little success in Flanders. Even within Wallonia, the level of its support has remained far lower than that for the VB. The National Front describes itself as anti-immigrant, anti-communist, anti-socialist and against the 'cowardice of the liberals'.[62]

The views of the extremists have found an echo in mainstream politics. Most remarkably, in 1987 the Minister of the Interior, speaking on the decline of the Belgian birth rate, declared:

> We risk suffering the same fate as the Roman Empire when it was engulfed by the Barbarians. These are the Moroccans, the Turks, the Yugoslavs, the Muslims . . . They have nothing in common with our civilization.[63]

In the Netherlands some racist parties and pressure groups have developed on a small scale at a local level, such as a working group on immigrants established in the 'Old West' district of Rotterdam in September 1971 due to concern about the settlement of Turks in the area. Its activities included 'squatting in houses for the benefit of Dutch families' and campaigning 'against nuisance caused by immigrants'.[64] In the same year as these activities began, a far more significant organisation called the Nederlandse Volksunie came into existence, with the aim of creating a greater Dutch state which would include Belgian Flanders, but exclude aliens. This group had actually been preceded by several other extreme right-wing organisations, with origins dating back to the inter-war years, but, following the pattern in several other continental European liberal democracies, many of these early groups demonstrated limited concern about immigrants. The NVU did not achieve more than 1 per

61 Ibid., pp. 134–43; Cas Mudde, 'One Against All, All Against One!: A Portrait of the Vlaams Blok', *Patterns of Prejudice* 29 (1995), pp. 5–28; Marco Martiniello, 'The National Question and the Political Construction of Immigrant Ethnic Communities in Belgium', in Alec G. Hargreaves and Jeremy Leaman (eds), *Racism and Politics in Contemporary Europe* (Aldershot, 1995), pp. 136–7; Betz, *Radical Right-Wing Populism*, pp. 19–21.
62 Husbands, 'Belgium', pp. 133–4; Delore, 'Far Right in Belgium', pp. 252–3.
63 Freddy Mercx and Liz Fekete, 'Belgium: The Racist Cocktail', *Race and Class* 32 (1991), pp. 73–9; Glyn Ford, *Fascist Europe: The Rise of Racism and Xenophobia* (London, 1992), pp. 51–5.
64 Wiesbe de Jong, 'The Development of Inter-Ethnic Relations in an Old District of Rotterdam Between 1970 and 1985', *Ethnic and Racial Studies* 12 (1989), p. 263.

cent of the vote in national elections by the time of its demise in the early 1980s, due partly to its overtly fascist image. Slightly more successful was the Centre Party which came into existence in 1980. Its main aim consisted of the 'preservation of Dutch culture', which meant opposing immigrants from beyond Europe. Although this group made little impact on a national scale, it did have some success at the local level. The other major recent grouping on the extreme right of the Dutch political spectrum consists of the Centre Democrats, which has an ideology similar to the Centre Party (which had declined in importance by the end of the 1980s), but which has gained slightly more support. The activities of the above three extremist groupings gave legitimacy to acts of racial violence during the 1980s.[65]

In Switzerland a protest movement against foreigners developed during the 1960s which spawned a series of organisations. In December 1964 a meeting took place in Zurich – sparked off by a liberalisation of regulations for Italians who worked in Switzerland – to protest against the 'foreign invasion' of the country. The federal government also received a petition with 38,000 signatures calling for an immediate stop to immigration and a reduction of 30 per cent in the number of aliens in Switzerland. By 1964 an Anti-Italian Party existed, together with a Popular Movement Against Foreignisation. In 1969 the National Action Against the Overforeignisation of People and Homeland demanded a reduction in the number of foreigners in Switzerland to 10 per cent of the total within four years. The organisation put forward similar proposals during the course of the early 1970s.[66]

In 1971 an anti-immigrant group called the Schweizerische Republikanische Bewegung managed to obtain 7 per cent of the vote at the national election. By the end of the 1970s, in keeping with the common European pattern, racism became less respectable, following the development of anti-racist initiatives.[67] This did not mean that it disappeared, however, and during the 1980s and 1990s hostility towards newcomers tended to manifest itself in racial attacks. In addition, numerous anti-immigrant organisations, covering all shades of the extreme right political spectrum, existed in Switzerland during the course of those decades. The more moderate and respectable of these groupings have continued to enjoy electoral success at both the national and local level.[68]

65 Gerrit Voerman and Paul Lucardie, 'The Extreme Right in the Netherlands: The Centrists and their Radical Rivals', *European Journal of Political Research* 22 (1992), pp. 35–54; Christopher T. Husbands, 'The Netherlands: Irritants on the Body Politic', in Hainsworth, *Extreme Right*, pp. 95–125; Jaap van Donselaar, 'The Extreme Right and Racist Violence in the Netherlands', in Tore Björgo and Robb Witte (eds), *Racist Violence in Europe* (London, 1993), pp. 55–9.
66 Matasar, 'Labor Transfers in Western Europe', p. 111; Kurt B. Mayer, 'Migration, Cultural Tensions, and Foreign Relations: Switzerland', *Journal of Conflict Resolution* 11 (1967), p. 142; Barbara Schmitter Heisler, 'From Conflict to Accommodation: The "Foreigners Question" in Switzerland', *European Journal of Political Research* 16 (1988), pp. 691–2.
67 Christopher T. Husbands, 'The Dynamics of Racial Exclusion and Expulsion: Racist Politics in Western Europe', *European Journal of Political Research* 16 (1988), pp. 714–15; Patrick Ireland, *The Policy Challenge of Ethnic Diversity: Immigrant Politics in France and Switzerland* (London, 1994), pp. 173–85.
68 See Urs Altermatt and Hanspeter Kriesi, *Rechtsextremismus in der Schweiz: Organisationen und Radikalisierung in den 1980er und 1990er Jahren* (Zurich, 1995).

Racism has also remained potent in post-War Austria, although much of the hostility has been of an anti-semitic nature, despite the small numbers of Jews in the country, demonstrating the tenacity of this aspect of Austrian political culture. Even in the immediate aftermath of the War hostility towards Jews existed but it reached a new peak in the 1980s due to the Waldheim Affair, the revelation that the former Secretary-General of the United Nations, who stood for the Austrian presidency in 1986, had played a role in the deportation of Jews from the Balkans during the Second World War. This had a series of effects, including a polarisation of Austrian society into those who supported Waldheim and those who opposed him, a division which even encompassed Austrian Jewry.[69] The other major spark for the increase in Austrian racism during the 1980s and 1990s was the rise in the number of asylum seekers moving to the country.

The main beneficiaries of the growth of anti-semitism and hostility towards foreigners were Jürg Haider and the Freiheitliche Partei Österreichs. This organisation had actually come into existence as early as 1955, and until 1986 it remained a nationalist organisation, which attracted former Nazis but which had failed to make a significant electoral breakthrough. For much of the 1970s and early 1980s some of its leadership had tried to steer it towards a liberal ideology to such an extent that it entered into a coalition with the governing socialist party. A turning point in the history of the FPÖ occurred in 1986 when Haider became party chairman and moved the organisation back towards its more right-wing origins. This served it well in the 1986 general election, which occurred against the background of the Waldheim Affair and resulted in the party's best-ever result when it gained 9.7 per cent of the votes cast. Since that time it has surpassed 20 and even 30 per cent of the vote in regional and municipal elections. The party has made much out of the influx of east European refugees into the country, especially after the collapse of communism, and has tried to persuade the government to introduce tighter immigration controls. Like similar organisations throughout western Europe during the 1980s and 1990s, the FPÖ succeeded in this task as well as in creating an atmosphere which allowed a growth of racial violence.[70]

Throughout the post-War period Italy has had a tradition of extreme right parties which have put forward a nationalist or regionalist vision and which have their origins in the fascism of Mussolini. For most of the years since 1945 these groupings remained largely absent of overt xenophobia, a fact connected both with the relative absence of such policies in inter-war fascist Italy (certainly in comparison with Nazism) but also with the lack of immigrants in the

---

69 Bruce F. Pauley, *From Prejudice to Persecution: A History of Austrian Anti-Semitism* (Chapel Hill, NC, 1992), pp. 310–12; Ruth Wodak, 'The Waldheim Affair and Antisemitic Prejudice in Austrian Public Discourse', *Patterns of Prejudice* 24 (1990), pp. 18–33; Richard Mitten, *The Politics of Anti-Semitic Prejudice: The Waldheim Phenomenon in Austria* (Boulder, CO, 1992).
70 Max E. Riedlsperger, 'FPÖ: Liberal or Nazi', in F. Parkinson (ed.), *Conquering the Past: Austrian Anti-Semitism Yesterday and Today* (Detroit, 1989), pp. 257–77; Betz, *Radical Right-Wing Populism*, pp. 11–13; Richard Mitten, 'Jörg Haider, the Anti-Immigration Petition and Immigration Policy in Austria', *Patterns of Prejudice* 28 (1994), pp. 27–47.

country. Throughout the post-War years the most important far right group in Italy has been the Movimento Sociale Italiano which came into being in December 1946 and has existed continually since that time. It made its major breakthrough in 1994, by which time it formed part of a grouping called the National Alliance, which gained 13.5 per cent of the vote and 107 deputies and played a role in Silvio Berlusconi's short-lived Forza Italia government.[71] Racism in Italian politics and society began to take off with the influx of immigrants during the 1980s. The MSI, for instance, opposed the newcomers on the basis that both they and Italians suffered. For the migrants movement to Italy meant separation from family and country of origin as well as a form of economic exploitation comparable with slavery, while for Italy the influx threatened Italian identity.[72]

In eastern Europe, extremist organisations, which could not exist under the old order, surfaced in the new-found freedom of the 1990s, as the example of Poland illustrates. By March 1990, 22 political parties which openly preached anti-semitism existed in Poland. The most active of these has been the Polish National Community–Polish National Party, led by Bolesław Tejkowski, which is openly anti-semitic and anti-German. It has claimed that far fewer Polish Jews actually died in the Second World War than is generally accepted, as most survived, changed their names and now controlled Solidarity and the state. The organisation fielded candidates in both the 1991 and 1993 elections, although it failed to win any seats. It has also had connections with the up-surge of racial attacks which occurred in post-communist Poland – the targets of which included German tourists – as well as with demonstrations against Holocaust memorials.[73]

Similar developments have occurred in Russia. In May 1987 an anti-semitic organisation called Pamyat surfaced, although it had previously existed under another name. This group supported Russian culture and the Orthodox Church and opposed Soviet ideology. In addition, it placed the problems which had beset Soviet society at the door of a 'Zionist–Masonic Conspiracy' which worked against the interests of Russia and the Russian people.[74]

By the early 1990s Pamyat consisted of numerous smaller groups of which the best known included the Russia Party, founded at the end of 1990. In February 1992 this latter group announced that it had established a shadow cabinet and declared that if it came to power it would appoint an official 'to check the

71 For the MSI see, for example: Roberto Chiarini, 'The Italian Far Right: The Search for Legitimacy', in Cheles, Ferguson and Vaughan, *Far Right*, pp. 20–40; Eatwell, *Fascism*, pp. 195–215.
72 Luciano Cheles, 'The Italian Far Right: Nationalist Attitudes and Views on Ethnicity and Immigration', in Hargreaves and Leaman, *Racism, Ethnicity and Politics*, pp. 170–1.
73 *Antisemitism World Report 1994* (London, 1994), pp. 108–13; Alina Cała, 'Antisemitism in Poland Today', *Patterns of Prejudice* 27 (1993), pp. 124–6; Anita J. Prazmowska, 'The New Right in Poland: Nationalism, Anti-Semitism and Parliamentarianism', in Cheles, Ferguson and Vaughan, *Far Right*, pp. 208–12; Jolanta Ambrosewicz-Jacobs and Annamaria Orla-Bukowski, 'After the Fall: Attitudes Towards Jews in Post-1989 Poland', *Nationalities Papers* 26 (1998), p. 272.
74 Howard Spier, 'Soviet Anti-Semitism Unchained: The Rise of the "Historical and Patriotic Association", Pamyat', in Freedman, *Soviet Jewry in the 1980s*, pp. 51–7.

nationality of couples about to marry so as to prevent marriages which breach this "purity of blood" principle'.[75] Other anti-semitic manifestations, typical of liberal democratic states, had also begun to surface by the beginning of the 1990s, including vandalism against cemeteries and synagogues.[76] Not surprisingly, opinion polls have also revealed the existence of anti-semitic attitudes.[77] The rise of Vladimir Zhirinovsky's overtly nationalistic Liberal Democratic Party, in the early 1990s – which, however, had become insignificant by the 1996 Presidential elections – provides another example of the strength of anti-semitism in the USSR and its successors.

RACIST VIOLENCE

In view of the centrality of nationalism in European political development and the spreading of negative views about minorities, especially immigrants, by newspapers and racist political groupings, it should come as no surprise that attacks upon immigrants, Jews, Gypsies and other minorities have been endemic in post-War Europe – events from which no state has been totally free. While some violence occurred under the old order in eastern Europe, attacks upon minorities have become increasingly common in liberal democratic states, where, in western Europe, immigrants have borne the brunt of hostility. Nevertheless, some of the worst racial violence since 1945, in which elimination has been the aim, has taken place in situations either where states are extremely weak (such as Poland in 1946), or where the state is directly or indirectly involved in the violence (such as Yugoslavia in the 1990s). In the latter situation, the background of a war – in which killing is an everyday occurrence – made the maltreatment of minorities easier. The early 1990s also witnessed riots throughout central and eastern Europe, due to a resurgence of overt nationalism and the economic crisis which followed the collapse of the old order.

Isolated attacks, and sometimes riots, have greeted the arrival of immigrants in all western European states in which they have settled. Attacks upon individuals are endemic and far more occur than are actually recorded. Riots, on the other hand, tend to break out when the media focus upon race as an issue, as happened in Britain during the late 1950s and Germany in the early 1990s.

In Britain, countless examples exist of individuals facing attacks during the 1950s, especially in crimes perpetrated by 'Teddy boys'. Victims included both West Indians and Greek Cypriots. As one perpetrator recalled:

> we'd try to fight Blacks. We used to shout at them in the street 'You Black Bastards' to try to provoke them, like. Over Brixton way, we'd try to stop

75 Natalia Yukhneva, 'Political and Popular Antisemitism in Russia in the Period of *Perestroika*', *Patterns of Prejudice* 27 (1993), pp. 65–6.
76 British Refugee Council, London, R21.2, 'CIS, Baltic States and Georgia: Situation of the Jews', July 1992.
77 Robert J. Brym, *The Jews of Moscow, Kiev and Minsk: Identity, Antisemitism and Emigration* (London, 1994), pp. 38–65.

them getting off buses, to frighten them. We'd often go for the Blacks we don't like them round here, we hate them.[78]

The 1940s and 1950s also witnessed larger-scale disturbances against immigrants. The first of these occurred in Liverpool between 31 July and 2 August 1948. During the course of the violence a hostel for Black seamen came under attack, but 60 Black men and just 10 whites faced arrest, indicating a policy of apprehending the victim for having the wrong skin colour. Riots also occurred in May 1948, when 250 whites attacked a house inhabited by Indians in Birmingham, and in Deptford Broadway in south London in July 1949, when about 1,000 whites launched an assault on a hostel housing Black people.

The major anti-immigrant riots in post-War Britain occurred in Nottingham and Notting Hill in 1958, between 23 August and 2 September. The first incident began outside a public house in Nottingham and then spread to other parts of the city, and involved 1,000 whites fighting in the street with a significantly smaller number of Blacks. Police prevented potential disorder in the city on 30 August and 6 September when crowds of hundreds of whites gathered in the streets. In Notting Hill, in London, although isolated incidents had occurred in early August, the first major outbreak of violence took place on 23 August, followed by further large-scale attacks upon both individuals and property on 30 and 31 August and 1 and 2 September, resulting in 177 arrests of mostly whites, although Blacks had retaliated. As in Nottingham, hundreds of people had participated.

After the Notting Hill disturbances, similar incidents occurred on a few more occasions, although not on the same scale. Between 19 and 23 August 1961 the few Asian businesses which existed in Middlesbrough came under attack from several thousand natives. One year later hundreds of whites attacked Black people in Dudley. Since that time, virtually no anti-immigrant riots have occurred in Britain, replaced, instead, by small-scale, but often fatal, attacks.[79]

The major disturbances of the late 1950s and early 1960s occurred against the background of the 'general race conscious climate of the country',[80] whipped up by the press, MPs and extremist organisations, during the campaign for the Commonwealth Immigrants Act of 1962. As early as November 1954 the Labour MP John Hynd proposed that immigration should be regulated and received backing from both sides of the House of Commons, most notably from Cyril Osborne. During the 1950s and into the 1960s, Osborne pursued a personal crusade against the arrival of Commonwealth immigrants who, in his view, would undermine the British way of life.[81]

---

78 Quoted in T. R. Fyvel, *The Insecure Offenders: Rebellious Youth in the Welfare State* (Harmondsworth, 1963), p. 34.
79 For slightly more detail on the above incidents see Panikos Panayi, 'Anti-Immigrant Violence in Nineteenth and Twentieth Century Britain', in Panayi (ed.), *Racial Violence in Britain in the Nineteenth and Twentieth Centuries* (London, 1996), pp. 16–17.
80 *Pakistan Times*, 22 August 1961.
81 Pilkington, *Beyond the Mother Country*, pp. 68–9; Colin Holmes, *John Bull's Island: Immigration and British Society, 1871–1971* (London, 1988), pp. 260–1.

The activities of the National Front, which concentrated in areas of heavy immigrant settlement, encouraged racist attacks, many of which have resulted in the death of the victim. In fact between 1970 and 1985 a total of 63 racist murders took place in Britain.[82] In 1986 one in four Black residents in the London Borough of Newham 'had been victims of some form of racial harassment in the previous twelve months'.[83] Such incidents continued into the 1990s. During the Gulf War in 1991, mosques came under attack up and down the country. In one incident, 'the doors of a mosque in Woking, Surrey, were set on fire' while 'several cars in the area were daubed with anti-Iraqi graffiti'.[84] Such incidents occurred against the background of an anti-Iraqi and anti-Muslim propaganda campaign by the press and in a situation in which the state arrested or deported 176 Iraqis and other Arabs merely upon suspicion of acting against the British national interest in a time of war.[85] Even after the Gulf War attacks upon immigrants and their offspring continued apace in Britain. Between 1989 and 1994 the annual number of such incidents rose from 4,383 to 9,762.[86]

Racist violence has also occurred throughout post-War French history. In 1973, for instance, widespread attacks occurred following the murder of a bus driver by a mentally disturbed Arab. The reaction against this incident, which affected North Africans and included bombings and machine-gun attacks against cafés, hotels and *bidonvilles*, resulted in death or serious injury to 52 people, including the murder of 10 people during the week after the killing of the bus driver. Similar incidents of racist violence continued throughout the middle of the 1970s[87] and beyond. Between 1986 and 1991 about 20 immigrants or their children – virtually all of them North Africans – were murdered.[88]

No other western European state has a legacy of minority persecution comparable with Germany, for during the years 1941–5 a core function of the German state consisted of murdering 'racial inferiors', focusing particularly upon Jews, but also targeting other groups who threatened the existence of the Nazi dictatorship, either internally or externally. Within such a historical context, it is unlikely that the liberal democratic German state, which emerged at the end of the 1940s, could fully escape from the ghosts of its past. Consequently, racist violence has been fairly endemic in post-War Germany, although – like the growth of extremist groupings which accompany it – it has reached a series of peaks.

Significant acts of racial violence did not take place to any great extent in the immediate post-War years, but exploded with a series of anti-semitic

82 Keith Tompson, *Under Siege: Racial Violence in Britain Today* (London, 1988), p. 171.
83 Commission for Racial Equality, *Living in Terror: A Report on Racial Violence and Harassment in Housing* (London, 1987), p. 9.
84 *Guardian*, 23 January 1991.
85 Tony Kushner and David Cesarani, 'Conclusion and Epilogue', in Cesarani and Kushner (eds), *The Internment of Aliens in Twentieth Century Britain* (London, 1993), pp. 214–15.
86 *Human Rights Watch World Report 1996* (New York, 1996), p. 215.
87 Cathie Lloyd, 'Racist Violence and Anti-Racist Reactions: A View of France', in Björgo and Witte, *Racist Violence in Europe*, pp. 212–13.
88 Ford, *Fascist Europe*, p. 63.

incidents in 1959 and 1960. The first of these occurred on Christmas night in 1959 and involved, in a standard neo-Nazi action throughout post-War Europe, the daubing of graffiti on Jewish cemeteries, synagogues and memorials throughout the Federal Republic, most notably in the Jewish synagogue in Cologne, where two members of the German Reichs Party painted swastikas and statements such as 'Jews Out'. By the end of January 1960 the police had recorded 685 incidents of a similar nature all over West Germany, many of them provoked simply by the reporting of the first incidents and the trial of their perpetrators.[89]

These events occurred at a time when only a small number of foreign workers had made their way to Germany. In fact, in the early stages of labour recruitment during the later 1950s and early 1960s, the migrants attracted little hostile political or media attention.[90] While isolated attacks upon immigrants occurred throughout the 1960s, 1970s and 1980s a dramatic increase occurred in 1991 with a rise in the number of right-wing offences – attacks against people or their property – from the previous year's 270 to 1,483, which re-sulted in 3 deaths.[91] Most of the incidents took place between August and October, essentially sparked off by the most serious incident, and its report-ing, which occurred in Hoyerswerda in Saxony, in the old GDR. After a build-up of hostility towards asylum seekers and foreign workers in the town during the summer, a full-scale riot broke out against them between 17 and 22 September involving hundreds of local residents, together with skinheads who had made their way to the town from other locations in east Germany. The violence sparked off by Hoyerswerda reached a crescendo during the first two weeks of October 1991. Morning radio news broadcasts began simply by listing the attacks which had taken place the previous evening. Incidents took place from the North Sea to the Alps and from the French to the Polish borders, with the perpetrators carrying out their activity with virtual impunity.

The high number of racist attacks during 1991 – 1,483 – increased even further during the following year to a new height of 2,584, a rise of 74 per cent. Just as notable was the rise in the number of murders from 3 in 1991 to 17 in the following year. A riot in Rostock, also in the former GDR, and its reporting between 22 and 27 August, acted as the spark for events in 1992. Throughout September 1992 immigrants and refugees were attacked with impunity, with the state apparently powerless to halt the violence. On 23 Nov-ember a fire-bomb attack in the town of Mölln in Schleswig-Holstein resulted in the death of three Turks.

89 Wolfgang Benz, 'Die Opfer und die Täter: Rechtsextremismus in der Bundesrepublik', in Benz (ed.), *Rechtsextremismus in der Bundesrepublik: Voraussetzungen, Zusamenhänge, Wirkungen* (Frankfurt, 1984), pp. 28–31; Peter Dudek and Hans-Gerd Jaschke, *Enstehung und Entwicklung des Rechtsextremismus in der Bundesrepublik*, Vol. 1 (Opladen, 1984), pp. 266–9.
90 See Karen Schönwälder, 'Migration, Refugees and Ethnic Plurality as Issues of Public and Political Debate in (West) Germany', in David Cesarani and Mary Fulbrook (eds), *Citizenship, Nationality and Migration in Europe* (London, 1996), pp. 161–4.
91 Bundesministerium des Innern, *Verfassungsschutzbericht, 1991* (Bonn, 1992), p. 75.

The year 1992 represents the high point in racial violence in post-War Germany. In 1993 a 15 per cent decline in the number of assaults against asylum seekers and foreign workers and their families occurred, although the number of attacks still exceeded the total for 1991. The major incident of 1993 took place on 29 May when a fire-bomb attack on a Turkish house in Solingen resulted in the death of three children and two women.[92] The most significant violence of 1994 occurred in March and May. The first involved an arson attack on a synagogue in Lübeck on 25 March, just before the start of the Passover. A few weeks later, on 12 May, foreigners were attacked in the streets of Magdeburg by 60 neo-Nazi youths.[93] Although violence against foreigners declined after 1994, it certainly did not disappear.[94]

The explosion of racial violence in Germany during 1991 and 1992 has a complexity of causes. In the first place, politicians and the press bear a large amount of responsibility. The focus upon the influx of asylum seekers filtered through to disaffected youth as a message to attack foreigners. The economic downturn following unification also played a part in violence. In east Germany unemployment rose from zero to 17 per cent between 1990 and the beginning of 1994, although in some cities only about half of the working population had proper jobs rather than artificial employment created by the state. Even in the old Federal Republic the unemployment rate had increased from 6.2 to 8.8 per cent in the same period.[95] By focusing upon the scapegoats, attention could move away from the real cause of the economic downturn in the form of the negative economic effects of reunification and the responsibility of Helmut Kohl's government for this state of affairs.

Racial violence has taken place in the Netherlands on a regular basis in the post-War period, despite the country's reputation for tolerance, although it has never reached the scales experienced in Germany in the early 1990s. As early as 1958 attacks occurred upon Indonesian youths in Schildersbuurt, a working-class district of The Hague, sparked off by the ease with which the young men attracted Dutch girls,[96] although during most of the 1960s racist attacks remained small in scale. Violence against foreigners took off during the early 1970s. In 1970 and 1971 fights took place on a regular basis between Dutch and Moluccan youths. Also in 1971 clashes occurred between Dutch and Turkish young men in The Hague and Rotterdam, while in the following year the latter city experienced large-scale riots involving Turks and Dutch people. In common with countries throughout western Europe, large-scale disturbances declined during the course of the 1970s, but were replaced by more ruthless and murderous attacks upon individuals during the 1980s and 1990s, involving

92 For more detail on the above see Panikos Panayi, 'Racial Violence in the New Germany (1990–3)', *Contemporary European History* 3 (1994), pp. 266–74.
93 For events in 1994 see Helsinki Watch, *'Germany for Germans': Xenophobia and Racist Violence in Germany* (New York, 1995).
94 *Human Rights Watch World Report, 1996*, p. 219.
95 Panayi, 'Racial Violence in the New Germany', pp. 282–3.
96 Christopher Bagley, *The Dutch Plural Society: A Comparative Study of Race Relations* (London, 1973), p. 90.

fire-bombs, knives and guns.[97] In 1994, the fatalities caused by racists included the shooting of a 19-year-old Ethiopian by Dutch youths in Dordrecht.[98]

Those southern European states which experienced an influx of immigrants in the 1980s and 1990s also witnessed an accompanying rise of racial attacks. In Italy one of the most publicised incidents involved the murder of a South African, Jerry Masslo, at the end of August 1989, by youngsters in Villa Literno, near Naples. In February of the following year a gang of Italian youths in Florence attacked and injured North African and Slavic migrant workers using baseball bats and iron bars. When they appeared in court, the attackers claimed that they had support from the entire Florentine population. Similar incidents followed all over the country. Such developments have been encouraged by media reporting of immigration, culminating in hostility towards the movement of Albanians to southern Italy during August 1991, which one of the leading newspapers in Italy, *La Republica*, described as 'an Albanian invasion'.[99]

'Spain's first racist murder' took place in November 1992 when four men, including a member of the police force, killed Lucrecia Pérez, an immigrant from the Dominican Republic.[100] Two years later, in 1994, at least three racist murders occurred in Spain, including that of Ben Amar Cheringuene, a North African, 'killed after being beaten and thrown off the "Expresso del Sol" – the night train from Malaga to Madrid'.[101] Spain also has a longer history of violence against Gypsies, which peaked in 1986 when more than 30 families in Andalusia had their homes burnt down and then faced hostility in the places to which they fled, including one town where riots broke out.[102] Some attacks have also occurred against immigrants in Portugal involving skinheads and small neo-Nazi groups, while tourists have also faced hostility.[103]

Elsewhere in western Europe, animosity has focused upon groups other than immigrants. In Greece and Cyprus the bulk of hostility has inevitably concentrated upon the Turkish minority. In Western Thrace riots against the Turks occurred on 29 January 1990 following the trial of two leading figures in Komotini on trumped-up charges. The disturbances resulted in attacks upon 400 businesses belonging to Turks, as well as in injury to 21 people, and the death of one Greek after a fight with a Muslim.[104]

97 Van Donselaar, 'Extreme Right and Racist Violence in the Netherlands', pp. 50–5.

98 *Campaign Against Racism and Fascism* 18 (January/February 1994), p. 5.

99 Jacqueline Andall, 'New Migrants, Old Conflicts: The Recent Immigration to Italy', *Italianist* 10 (1990), pp. 163–5; Giovanna Campani, 'Immigration and Racism in Southern Europe: The Italian Case', *Ethnic and Racial Studies* 16 (1993), p. 517; Ford, *Fascist Europe*, p. 70; Ellie Vasta, 'Rights and Racism in a New Country of Immigration: The Italian Case', in John Wrench and John Solomos (eds), *Racism and Migration in Western Europe* (Oxford, 1993), p. 96.

100 David Corkill, 'Multiple National Identities, Immigration and Racism in Spain and Portugal', in Brian Jenkins and Spyros A. Sofos (eds), *Nation and Identity in Contemporary Europe* (London, 1996), p. 164.

101 *Campaign Against Racism and Fascism* 18 (January/February 1994), p. 5.

102 Ford, *Fascist Europe*, p. 62.

103 Ibid., pp. 75–7; Corkill, 'Multiple National Identities', p. 168; Martin Eaton, 'Foreign Residents and Illegal Immigrants: *Os Negros em Potugal*', *Ethnic and Racial Studies* 16 (1993), pp. 549–50.

104 Helsinki Watch, *Destroying Ethnic Identity: The Turks of Greece* (New York, 1990), p. 20; Hugh Poulton, *The Balkans: Minorities and States in Conflict*, 2nd edn (London, 1993), p. 187.

In the context of the way in which Greeks and Turks have treated each other these disturbances remain mild. In Cyprus the hostility between the two communities led to the 1974 war, although attacks perpetrated by both communities preceded these events on several occasions. During the struggle for independence, violence had broken out between the two communities in 1958 and had resulted in several deaths, including the murder of a Turkish policeman in Paphos and the stabbing to death of two Greeks in Larnaca.[105] The most serious incident occurred near the Turkish village of Geunyelli, when eight Greeks were murdered by Turks.[106] The next major outbreak of communal violence happened in December 1963 at the time when relations between Makarios and the Turkish leader Dr Kutchuk had broken down. The incidents which occurred – with the knowledge of Makarios and his cabinet – involved an attack on the Turkish area of Nicosia which resulted in several killings, as well as the seizure of 700 Turkish hostages. In the first half of 1964 fighting between Greeks and Turks in villages north of Nicosia may have resulted in as many as 400 Turkish and 170 Greek deaths. After the possibility of a Turkish invasion emerged, a partial solution to the problem of ethnic violence was found when British troops, followed by UN forces, began to police parts of the island.[107] This did not prevent further outbreaks of violence which occurred on several occasions before the final collapse of 1974. In the worst instance, on 15 November 1967, fighting at Agios Theodoros and the neighbouring village of Kophinou resulted in the death of 24 Turks and one Greek.[108] In a sense the 1974 war brought the previous years of sporadic disorder to their logical conclusion and resulted in the worst violence in the post-War history of Cyprus, perpetrated by the overwhelming might of a Turkish army supplied by the USA and NATO, with over 500,000 troops facing a Greek Cypriot force of less than 20,000.[109] The atrocities committed by the Turkish forces included rape, ill-treatment of prisoners and the killing of civilians.[110] Even those who were 'only' victims of ethnic cleansing had, like all uprooted individuals in post-War Europe, mental scars, as one former resident of Argaki village described:

> You know how much property I had in the village; I had many orange plantations and I was completely occupied in working them. I was concerned with my kids and interested in party politics not in the slightest. We left the village on Thursday early morning, with nothing, and I sat idle for two or three months . . .

105 Halil Kiamran, *The Rape of Cyprus* (London, 1983), p. 56.
106 Nancy Crawshaw, *The Cyprus Revolt: An Account of the Struggle for Union With Greece* (London, 1978), pp. 288–94.
107 Ibid., pp. 366–70; Keith Kyle, *Cyprus: In Search of Peace* (London, 1997), pp. 11–12.
108 P. N. Vanezis, *Cyprus: The Unfinished Agony* (London, 1977), p. 33.
109 Stavros Panteli, *A New History of Cyprus: From the Earliest Times to the Present* (London, 1984), p. 382.
110 Friends of Cyprus for an Independent, Sovereign and Unitary State, *Report of the Commission of the Council of Europe on Human Rights in Cyprus, 1974*, n.d.

I am in complete uncertainty. That is, no-one knows from morning to night what will happen each day, or what to expect from the barbarous Turkish conqueror. I have neither the courage nor the appetite to find land to cultivate to live.[111]

The 1974 invasion of Cyprus did not represent the only occasion on which Turkish violence affected Greeks. Apart from the earlier incidents on the island, one of the worst examples had occurred against the Greek minority of Istanbul on 6–7 September 1955, once more against the background of the Cyprus dispute, but fuelled by anti-Greek sentiment in the Turkish press. Stories circulated stating that the Greek population of Cyprus was preparing to attack the Turks on the island, which led one major newspaper, *Hürriyet*, to comment that 'if the Greeks dare touch our brethren, then there are plenty of Greeks in Istanbul to retaliate upon'. The spark for the events, indicating yet again the tit-for-tat way in which Greeks and Turks have mutually mistreated their minorities, consisted of a bomb attack on the Turkish consulate in Thessaloniki which also damaged the nearby birthplace of Kemal Atatürk. The ferocity and consequences of the disturbances lead to comparisons with an anti-Jewish pogrom in late Tsarist Russia, although they also fit into the violent nature of post-War Turkish politics and society. The riots resulted in the destruction of 4,000 Greek shops, as well as the burning of 38 churches and the vandalising of 35 others. Furthermore, 52 Greek schools were destroyed and had their furniture, books and equipment stolen, while 2,000 homes faced similar treatment. The death toll reached 15. The cost of the damage may have totalled $300 million. Despite apologies from the Turkish government, the 1955 riots represented the beginning of the end for the Greek community of Istanbul as it fled out of the city, a process speeded up by subsequent state policies, despite the 1923 Treaty of Lausanne.[112]

Attacks against minorities, at least on a large scale, rarely occurred in eastern Europe during the communist period, connected with the level of control exercised over the population, which tried to prevent riots of any sort taking place. The collapse of the old order has led to both individual attacks and riots in states which have maintained fairly solid state structures, and ethnic cleansing in those where war has occurred.

Before 1989, one of the most serious incidents of racial violence in eastern Europe occurred against Jews in Poland immediately after the Second World War. The explanation for the shocking events of 1945–7 – especially in the immediate aftermath of the Holocaust – lies at least partially in the historical strength of Polish anti-semitism which facilitated the implementation of the Final Solution on Polish soil during the Second World War.

111 An interview quoted by Peter Loizos in his article on 'Argaki: The Uprooting of a Cypriot Village', in Michael A. Attalides (ed.), *Cyprus Reviewed* (Nicosia, 1977), p. 13.
112 Alexis Alexandris, *The Greek Minority of Istanbul and Greek–Turkish Relations, 1918–1974* (Athens, 1983), pp. 256–66; Helsinki Watch, *Denying Human Rights and Ethnic Identity: The Greeks of Turkey* (New York, 1992), p. 8; Tozun Bahcheli, *Greek–Turkish Relations Since 1955* (Boulder, CO, 1955), pp. 172–4.

The post-War violence may have led to the death of as many as 1,500 Jews.

Each case, though different and tragic in its own right, followed the same pattern: Jews were killed when they came to ask for the return of their houses, workshops, farms and other property. They were assaulted when they tried to open stores or workshops. Bombs were planted in orphanages and other Jewish public buildings. Jews were shot by unknown snipers and in full view of witnesses. Jews were attacked in their homes and forcibly removed from buses and trains. Jews were terrorized and forced to leave when they began to settle again in a small town or village.[113]

It is as if the Polish population wished to complete the work of the Nazis by making sure that the country became completely free of Jews, a task which it all but achieved because of the exodus of most of the Jews who remained in Poland in 1945.

Apart from the ubiquity of smaller incidents described above, larger-scale riots also occurred in several other locations including Dzialoszyce, Chelm, Rzezow and Cracow. The most serious incident of all occurred in Kielce in July 1946. About 250 of the 25,000 Jews who had lived in the town in 1939 returned after the War and focused on one particular block of flats, which had come under attack from a grenade in the autumn of 1945. The spark for the disturbances of 4 July came in the form of the alleged kidnapping of a 9-year-old boy by the Jews of Kielce. After this story spread, crowds, which included soldiers, shot and lynched about 40 Jews. Even those Jews who escaped the violence found themselves attacked on trains leaving the town, while trains entering it were searched for Jewish passengers.

> After the arrival of the Lublin–Wroclaw train at the Kielce railway station at about 1 p.m., two Jews were removed from it and attacked by a crowd of more than 100 people. Two people tried to protect them. Boy Scouts and civilians searched for other victims in the cars as the train pulled out of the station. At the successive stops Jews were hauled out and murdered.[114]

Both the Czech Republic and Slovakia provide examples of the milder types of violence which have occurred in eastern Europe in the 1990s. Both have experienced racial attacks, carried out by skinheads, which have particularly targeted Gypsies but have also focused upon other groups, such as the small numbers of foreign workers imported by the communist regime. A peak of violence occurred in April and May 1990. In one of the worst incidents on 1 May in Prague, '200 skinheads raised havoc in central Prague, turning on a Canadian tourist group after they had beaten up or dispersed all

113 Lucjan Dobroszycki, 'Restoring Jewish Life in Post-War Poland', *Soviet Jewish Affairs* 3 (1973), p. 67.
114 Bozena Szaynok, 'The Pogrom of the Jews in Kielce, July 4, 1946', *Yad Vashem Studies* 22 (1992), pp. 199–235, gives a complete account of what actually happened. The above quote comes from p. 232. For the background to these events see: Dobrocszycki, ibid., pp. 66–70; and Michael Checinski, 'The Kielce Pogrom: Some Unanswered Questions', *Soviet Jewish Affairs* 5 (1975), pp. 57–72.

the Roma and Vietnamese from the main square'.[115] By 1992 about 1,000 skinheads were active in Prague, as well as 500 in Pilzeň and around 2,000 in northern Bohemia. They carried out acts of violence throughout the 1990s, which resulted in the murder of 30 Gypsies in the Czech Republic between 1989 and 1995.[116] Similar developments occurred in Slovakia. To give just one example: on 21 July 1995, about 40 youths set fire to Mario Goral, a Roma, in Ziar nad Hronom. 'Goral suffered burns over 60 per cent of his body. He died ten days after the attack.'[117]

Hostility towards Gypsies also took off in Hungary during the 1990s. Skinheads actually appeared here, as in several other parts of eastern Europe, during the 1970s and 1980s. By the end of the latter decade they had carried out numerous attacks against journalists and Cuban foreign workers. In the early 1990s the skinheads organised themselves into about six regional group-ings, counting less than a thousand members each.[118] The first major attacks against Gypsies occurred in the eastern cities of Eger and Miskolc in September 1990.

> Trouble had been brewing between locals and Roma in Eger when some eighty to 100 skinheads, clad in the standard outfits of their Europe-wide counterparts, raided houses in the Roma quarter, beating their inhabitants, including pregnant women, children, and elderly people. The police stood by as they ransacked the flats, smashing furniture and windows.[119]

Incidents such as these, involving skinheads as perpetrators, have continued since 1990, reaching another peak in the autumn of 1992. Furthermore, both large- and small-scale attacks have taken place without any involvement from skinheads. In some cases the police have beaten Gypsies, as happened in Szombathely in February 1997.[120]

In view of the overt nationalism and xenophobia which sustained the Ceaucescu regime, it is hardly surprising that such sentiment did not dis-appear after his fall from power and that it surfaced in an explosive way during the early 1990s. 'Violence and injustice towards the Roma are a part of every-day life',[121] although the worst attack of all took place against Hungarians in the city of Tîrgu Mureş. Such incidents have occurred against a background in which mainstream parties have continued, in the traditions of Ceaucescu, to stress Romanian nationalism.

115 Paul Hockenos, *Free to Hate: The Rise of the Right in Post-Communist Eastern Europe* (London, 1993), pp. 215–17.
116 *Human Rights Watch World Report, 1996*, p. 214.
117 Ibid., pp. 235–6.
118 Helsinki Watch, *Struggling for Ethnic Identity: The Gypsies of Hungary* (New York, 1993), p. 38.
119 Hockenos, *Free to Hate*, p. 154.
120 Ibid., p. 154; Helsinki Watch, *Struggling for Ethnic Identity: The Gypsies of Hungary*, pp. 48–56; *Roma Rights* (Spring 1997), p. 8.
121 Brigitte Mihok, 'Minorities and Minority Policies in Romania Since 1945', *Patterns of Preju-dice* 27 (1993), p. 91.

The party which took over from Ceaucescu, the National Salvation Front, comprehensively won the elections of May 1990, securing 66 per cent of the vote for Parliament, while its Presidential candidate, Ion Iliescu, obtained 85 per cent of votes cast. The party's continuation of chauvinistic nationalism has clear indications. For instance, it did not eliminate the Securitatae. In addition, in April 1991, the Romanian Parliament paid tribute to the country's wartime fascist leader, Ion Antonescu, condemned and executed as a war criminal in 1946.[122]

In a situation characteristic of western European liberal democratic states, the ruling party surrendered to pressure from more extremist groups, the most notable of which is Vatra Rumâneasca, which came into existence in January 1990, claiming that it aimed to defend Romanian national interests and the Romanian language. However, with the passage of time, it became overtly nationalistic and chauvinistic,[123] speaking about Romanian soil 'being defiled by the feet of Asiatic Huns, Gypsies and other scum'.[124]

Vatra played a significant role in the outbreak of murderous racial violence against the Hungarian minority in Tîrgu Mureş in March 1990. Tension had begun to develop in the city during the first two months of 1990 when demonstrations by Hungarians demanding separate schools and bilingual signs were met with counter-demonstrations from Romanians opposing such moves, in which Vatra played a leading role. Violence began to surface on 16 and 17 March when Vatra supporters attacked Hungarians in the street after two bilingual signs appeared in the city centre calling for 'Justice for Minorities' and 'Schools in Hungarian'. On 18 and 19 March student rallies opposing the demands of the Hungarians took place at universities all over the country. The major violence in Tîrgu Mureş broke out on 19 March and did not die down until 23 March. Troops did not intervene until 21 March. One of the victims was András Sütő, who recalled:

> From behind our backs the entire delirious mob, armed with all manner of bludgeoning and hacking tools, attacked us in the truck. For several minutes they stabbed, flogged and beat everyone they encountered.

The disturbances resulted in about 8 deaths and 300 injuries, with members of both communities affected. The government, conscious of rising Romanian nationalism and forthcoming elections, did not unequivocally condemn the violence and, a few weeks later, Iliescu met with the leaders of Vatra.[125]

---

122 Leo Paul, 'The Stolen Revolution: Minorities in Romania After Ceauşescu', in John O'Loughlin and Hermann van der Wusten (eds), *The New Geography of Eastern Europe* (London, 1993), pp. 151–2; Hockenos, *Free to Hate*, pp. 151–2.
123 See Tom Gallagher, 'Vatra Rumânească and Resurgent Nationalism in Romania', *Ethnic and Racial Studies* 15 (1992), pp. 570–98.
124 Paul, 'Stolen Revolution', p. 152.
125 Hockenos, *Free To Hate*, pp. 177–9; Gallagher, 'Vatra Rumânească', pp. 574–8; Vladimir Socor, 'Forces of Old Resurface in Rumania: The Ethnic Clashes in Tîrgu Mureş', *Report on Eastern Europe* 13 (April 1990), pp. 36–43; Helsinki Watch, *Struggling for Ethnic Identity: Ethnic Hungarians in Post-Ceacescu Romania* (New York, 1993), pp. 14–18.

Violence against Gypsies in post-communist Romania has involved both members of the state security services and individuals acting alone or collectively. Attacks have taken place in any location which contains a Gypsy settlement, from the largest city to the smallest village, with the aim of forcing out the local Gypsy population. Deaths have occurred regularly. The violence has taken place against the background of a mass-media vilification, which has pictured the Gypsies as a criminal class responsible for the social and economic ills of the country. The attacks are usually sparked off by a criminal act by a Gypsy for which the entire Roma population of a particular locality is held responsible. Violence breaks out with the overt or covert support of the local state in the form of mayor, policeman or priest.[126]

Despite the undoubted severity of the xenophobic attacks which occurred in Romania after Ceauşescu, it remained relatively mild compared with the violence which developed further south in former Yugoslavia and which western observers have described as genocide. This may represent an apt description of events in this part of the world but – whatever has happened and whoever may bear responsibility – events here do not compare with the Nazi extermination of Jews in 1941–5. The most obvious difference consists simply of scale, but there is also one of intent, especially in the case of the Nazis who specifically aimed at eliminating all Jews, although this may have been the aim of some Croatian and Serbian extremists. Events in Bosnia and Croatia would certainly fit into the UN definition of genocide, which encompasses a wide range of activities which aim at destroying, 'in whole or part, a national, ethnical, or religious grouping, including the killing of members of a particular minority, and deliberately inflicting on the group conditions of life calculated to bring about its physical destruction in whole or part.

The main reason for the descent into the type of violence which former Yugoslavia experienced during the early 1990s lies in its political situation: in other words, the former Yugoslav states had entered a state of war. Only in such circumstances can widespread killing proceed, above all because, as killing becomes one of the main functions of the state, only a very short step is involved in moving from the elimination of soldiers to the use of similar treatment against civilians.

The Yugoslav war brought to the boil the simmering conflicts which had begun to surface during the course of the 1980s. The first major theatre of war consisted of Croatia, where fighting began in the second half of 1991, involving clashes between Croatian forces and Serbians already living within the country, as well as with the intervening Serbian-controlled Yugoslav army. In a time of war, both sides inevitably suffer casualties. Initially, during the summer months, Serb extremist organisations and Serb irregulars carried out murders of Croatians in the major areas of Serb concentration but, as Croats

---

126 Helsinki Watch, *Destroying Ethnic Identity: The Persecution of Gypsies in Romania* (New York, 1991), pp. 36–71; Mihok, 'Minorities and Minority Policies in Romania', pp. 91–3; Katrin Reemtsma, 'Between Freedom and Persecution: Roma in Romania', in Björgo and Witte, *Racist Violence in Europe*, pp. 194–206.

united and became more radical, Serbian civilians also became victims of the actions of irregulars. Apart from forcing people to move, the regular and irregular armed units also blew up the houses of people who had the wrong ethnic characteristics in the areas which they controlled, as well as torturing detainees. By the end of 1991 when the Serbian forces held the initiative – which meant that the Croats had come off worse – about 5,000 people had been killed, while thousands had suffered injuries and over a quarter of a million refugees had fled their homes.[127] In the following year Croats 'torched or bombed' 3,200 Serb homes as a reprisal for ethnic cleansing.[128]

The most brutal actions occurred in Bosnia, to which the Yugoslav war spread in 1992. In this case a three-way killing process took place involving Croatians, Serbs and Muslims. Although most journalistic and academic commentators who wrote on the war in Bosnia admitted that all sides committed atrocities, most of the experts tended to focus upon the activities of the Serbs. The reason for this state of affairs may find a simple explanation in the fact that the Serbs have been the worst offenders. Alternatively, vilifying the Serbs may simply have represented an example of attempting to find an easy answer for western consumption to what is clearly an extraordinarily complicated state of affairs. The pursuing of such a line also provided the pretext for western intervention either through the UN or through NATO for either humanitarian or military reasons.

The first stories about Serb atrocities in Bosnia broke in the summer of 1992. The killing of civilians and the destruction of homes occurred here as it had done in Croatia. But the most shocking aspect of the reporting from Bosnia consisted of the focus upon concentrations camps, used by Bosnian Serbs to round up Muslim men of fighting age. It appears that four main camps existed, in Trnopolje, Manjača, Omarska and Keraterm, together with numerous smaller detention centres. It seems clear that beatings, torture and killings took place in some of these camps, as well as starvation, although it is inaccurate to describe them as 'death camps', certainly not of the Second World War Nazi type. Nevertheless, the suffering was real enough, as described by Ed Vulliamy, one of the first western journalists to report on the concentration camps, upon entering Omarska. He spoke of men 'at various stages of decay and affliction; the bones of their wrists and elbows protrude like pieces of jagged stone from the pencil-thin stalks to which their arms have been reduced'.[129]

Other aspects of the Yugoslav war, again especially in Bosnia, also attracted western media attention, especially events in Sarajevo. In this case, although both Serbs and Muslims were affected, the worst atrocities were suffered by the latter, with routine bombing of civilian targets, because of the greater

127 Janusz Bugajski, *Ethnic Politics in Eastern Europe: A Guide to Nationality Policies, Organizations, and Parties* (Armonk, NY, 1995), p. 51.
128 Ibid., p. 58.
129 Ed Vulliamy, *Seasons in Hell: Understanding Bosnia's War* (London, 1994), p. 102.

firepower of the Bosnian Serbs. Stories also circulated about the rape of women, again committed by all sides.[130]

In 1995 Serbs suffered the most inhumane treatment at the hands of Croatians as they fled from western Slavonia and Krajina after Croatian forces captured these areas. Croatian soldiers burnt down houses, while, during their trek into Serbia, the refugees had to endure stoning from Croatian civilians. About 200,000 Serbs left western Slavonia and Krajina as a result of these events, meaning that only 4 per cent of Croatia's remaining population consisted of Serbs.[131] Those who fled included 60-year-old Mira Sudzokovic and her family who 'travelled for six days to Belgrade' while 'planes shelled the convoy. People were killed, entire families. Sometimes we had to get off the road, hide in the forest, or go through the fields to avoid the shelling.'[132]

The events in Yugoslavia during the 1990s represent the most serious all-out war in Europe west of the Soviet Union since 1945. Despite the shock felt by many western journalists and public opinion, the brutality which occurred was, under wartime conditions, inevitable. The events of these years represent the persecution of minorities reaching its most basic level, in a situation in which killing became one of the central functions of the various state authorities, whether civilian or military, which existed in former Yugoslavia. That this region descended into war finds explanation in the extreme nationalism of all sides, which had built up over decades, due to political and economic factors, and which exploded in the summer of 1990.

Some areas of the USSR experienced the sort of developments which occurred in Yugoslavia. This applies especially to Transcaucasia, with settlement patterns as complex as the Balkans. The worst acts of minority persecution in the Russian Federation during the 1990s have actually taken place in Chechnya, which has striven for independence and which Boris Yeltsin resisted by sending in Russian soldiers, resulting in the destruction of the capital Grozny. This represented a test case of the future of the Russian Federation because if the Chechens gained independence, then numerous other peoples within Russia may also have desired to do so. Hence the determination with which Yeltsin tried to hang on to control of the area.[133]

Similar developments occurred in Georgia, where two populations, the Abkhazians and the Ossetians, have also striven for independence. Like the conflict in former Yugoslavia, the situation in Georgia developed out of opposing nationalisms which emerged during the 1980s. Furthermore – also similar to both the situation in Yugoslavia, as well as the one in Chechnya – these struggles have resulted in killing, destruction and ethnic cleansing.

130 Adam Jones, 'Gender and Ethnic Conflict in ex-Yugoslavia', *Ethnic and Racial Studies* 17 (1994), pp. 116–21.
131 Helsinki Watch, *Civil and Political Rights in Croatia* (New York, 1995), p. 18.
132 Quoted in Julie Mertus, Jasmina Tesanovic, Habiba Metekos and Rada Bovi (eds), *The Suitcase: Refugee Voices from Bosnia and Croatia* (Berkeley and Los Angeles, 1997), p. 66.
133 See, for example, Carlotta Gall and Tomas de Waal, *Chechnya: A Small Victorious War* (London, 1997).

Hostilities also broke out from the Gorbachev period in Karabakh, the disputed region between Armenia and Azerbaijan. In 1987 Armenians began to ask Moscow about the possibility of unifying with Armenia the landlocked territory of Karabakh within Azerbaijan and its Armenian majority. The pressure mounted in the following year both on the Soviet centre and within Karabakh and Armenia, where the local Armenian population began to hold mass demonstrations throughout the area. But this simply resulted in a violent reaction by the local Azeri population, which began hunting out and killing Armenians. During the course of the late 1980s and early 1990s thousands of deaths occurred, carried out by civilians, the Soviet army and the forces of Armenia and Azerbaijan.[134]

Karabakh represents an extreme example of persecution involving a war situation. Clearly, killing is the most brutal form of exclusion and persecution but in order to reach such a phase a series of other developments has to occur, including media persecution and the growth of extremist parties. In most cases in the history of post-War Europe, significant levels of killing have not occurred, usually because the process of state formation took place decades or centuries before 1945, or in other instances because non-violent methods of exclusion act just as effectively in dealing with minorities. Nevertheless, the function of all nation states always remains the same: to include those who have the correct ethnic characteristics and to exclude those who do not. It is only the methodology which varies from one case to another.

---

134 See Jonathan Davis, 'Spontaneous Pogroms or State-sponsored Racial Violence? Assessing the Nature of Ethnic Violence in Nagorno-Karabakh' (University of Birmingham unpublished Master of Social Science dissertation, 1997).

Select Bibliography

The following list simply represents the sources which proved most valuable in the writing of the current volume. Much more bibliographical information can be obtained from the footnotes.

Abedin, Syed Z. and Sardar, Ziauddin (eds), *Muslim Minorities in the West* (London, 1995).

Acton, Thomas, *Gypsy Politics and Social Change* (London, 1974).

Adams, Barbara, Okely, Judith, Morgan, David and Smith, David, *Gypsies and Government Policy in England* (London, 1975).

Akhavan, Payam and Howse, Robert (eds), *Yugoslavia: The Former and the Future* (Washington, DC, 1995).

Alderman, Geoffrey, *Modern British Jewry* (Oxford, 1992).

Alexandris, Alexis, *The Greek Minority of Istanbul and Greek–Turkish Relations* (Athens, 1983).

Andreades, K. G., *The Moslem Minority in Western Thrace* (Thessaloniki, 1956).

Anthias, Floya, *Ethnicity, Class, Gender and Migration: Greek Cypriots in Britain* (Aldershot, 1992).

Apostolski, M. and Polenakovich, Haralampie (eds), *The Republic of Macedonia* (Skopje, 1974).

Arter, David, 'Black Faces in the Blond Crowd: Populist Racialism in Scandinavia', *Parliamentary Affairs* 45 (1992).

Ashworth, Georgina (ed.), *World Minorities*, 3 volumes (Sunbury, 1977–9).

Bade, Klaus J. (ed.), *Deutsche im Ausland – Fremde in Deutschland: Migration in Geschicte und Gegenwart* (Munich, 1992).

Baer, Lars-Anders, 'The Sami: An Indigenous People in Their Own Land', in Birgitta Jahreshog (ed.), *The Sami National Minority in Sweden* (Stockholm, 1982).

Bainbridge, M. (ed.), *The Turkic Peoples of the World* (London, 1993).

Bennett, Christopher, *Yugoslavia's Bloody Collapse: Causes, Course and Consequences* (London, 1995).

Berghoff, Hartmut, 'Population Change and its Repercussions on the Social History of the Federal Republic', in Klaus Larres and Panikos Panayi (eds), *The Federal Republic of Germany since 1949: Politics, Society and Economy Before and After Unification* (London, 1996).

Betz, Hans-Georg, *Radical Right-Wing Populism in Western Europe* (London, 1994).

Biffl, G., 'Structural Shifts in the Employment of Foreign Workers in Austria', *International Migration* 23 (1985).

Björgo, Tøre and Witte, Rob (eds), *Racist Violence in Europe* (London, 1993).

Boscardin, Lucio, *Die italienische Einwanderung in die Schweiz mit besonderer Berücksichtigung der Jahre 1946–1959* (Basle, 1962).

Breitenbach, Barbara von, *Italiener und Spanier als Arbeitnehmer in der Bundesrepublik Deutschland* (Munich, 1982).

Brock, Colin (ed.), *The Caribbean in Europe: Aspects of West Indian Experiences in Britain, France and the Netherlands* (London, 1986).

Bugajski, Janusz, *Ethnic Politics in Eastern Europe: A Guide to Nationality Policies, Organizations and Parties* (Armonk, NY, 1995).

Castles, Stephen, *Here for Good: Western Europe's New Ethnic Minorities* (London, 1987).

Castles, Stephen and Kosack, Godula, *Immigrant Workers and Class Structure in Western Europe* (London, 1973).

Castles, Stephen and Miller, Mark J., *The Age of Migration: International Population Movements in the Modern World* (London, 1993).

Cesarani, David and Fulbrook, Mary (eds), *Citizenship, Nationality and Migration in Europe* (London, 1996).

Chaliand, Gerard (ed.), *Minority Peoples in the Age of Nation States* (London, 1989).

Chaliand, Gerard and Rageau, Jean-Pierre, *The Penguin Atlas of Diasporas* (Harmondsworth, 1995).

Cheles, Luciano, Ferguson, Ronnie and Vaughan, Michalina (eds), *The Far Right in Western and Eastern Europe* (London, 1995).

Chinn, Jeff and Kaiser, Robert, *Russians as the New Minority: Ethnicity and Nationalism in the Soviet Successor States* (Boulder, CO, 1996).

Cohen, Robin, *Frontiers of Identity: The British and the Others* (London, 1994).

Commission of the European Community, *Linguistic Minorities in Countries Belonging to the European Community* (Rome, 1986).

Comrie, Bernard, *The Languages of the Soviet Union* (Cambridge, 1981).

Condon, Stephanie A. and Ogden, Philip E., 'Afro-Caribbean Migrants in France: Employment, State Policy and the Migration Process', *Transactions of the Institute of British Geographers* New Series 16 (1991).

Condon, Stephanie A. and Ogden, Philip E., 'The State, Housing Policy and Afro-Caribbean Migration to France', *Ethnic and Racial Studies* 16 (1993).

Crawshaw, Nancy, *The Cyprus Revolt: An Account of the Struggle for Union with Greece* (London, 1978).

Cross, Malcolm and Entzinger, Hans (eds), *Lost Illusions: Caribbean Minorities in Britain and the Netherlands* (London, 1988).

Crowe, David M., 'Minorities in Hungary Since 1948', *Nationalities Papers* 16 (1988).

Crowe, David M., *A History of Gypsies of Eastern Europe* (London, 1995).

Davidóva, Eva, 'The Gypsies in Czechoslovakia: Part II: Post-War Developments', *Journal of the Gypsy Lore Society* 50 (1971).

Denber, Rachel (ed.), *The Soviet Nationality Reader: The Disintegration in Context* (Boulder, CO, 1992).

Dobroszycki, L., 'Restoring Jewish Life in Post-War Poland', *Soviet Jewish Affairs* 3 (1973).

Eaton, Martin, 'Foreign Residents and Illegal Immigrants: *Os Negros em Portugal*', *Ethnic and Racial Studies* 16 (1993).

Eatwell, Roger, *Fascism: A History* (London, 1996).

Elklit, Jørgen, Noack, Johan Peter and Tonsgaard, Ole, 'A National Group as a Social System: The Case of the German Minority of North Schleswig', *Journal of Intercultural Studies* 1 (1980).

Favell, Adrian, *Philosophies of Integration: Immigrants and the Idea of Citizenship in France and Britain* (London, 1998).

Ficowski, Jerzy, *The Gypsies in Poland: History and Customs* (Warsaw, 1989).

Ford, Glyn, *Fascist Europe: The Rise of Racism and Xenophobia* (London, 1992).

Foster, C. R. (ed.), *Nations Without A State: Ethnic Minorities in Western Europe* (New York, 1980).

Freedman, Robert O. (ed.), *Soviet Jewry in the 1980s: The Politics of Anti-Semitism and the Dynamics of Resettlement* (Durham, NC, 1989).

Freidenreich, Harriet Pass, *The Jews of Yugoslavia: A Quest for Community* (Philadelphia, 1979).

Gellner, Ernest, *Nations and Nationalism* (Oxford, 1983).

George, Vic and Millerson, Geoffrey, 'The Cypriot Community in London', *Race* 8 (1967).

Gerholm, T. E. and Litman, Y. E. (eds), *The New Islamic Presence in Western Europe* (London, 1988).

Giesinger, Adam, *The Story of Russia's Germans: From Catherine to Kruschev* (Battleford, Saskatchewan, 1974).

Gilroy, Paul, *'There Ain't No Black in the Union Jack': The Cultural Politics of Race and Nation* (London, 1987).

Glenny, Misha, *The Fall of Yugoslavia: The Third Balkan War* (London, 1993).

Goldhagen, Erich (ed.), *Ethnic Minorities in the Soviet Union* (New York, 1968).

Hainsworth, Paul (ed.), *The Extreme Right in Europe and the USA* (London, 1992).

Hajda, Lubomyr and Beissinger, Mark (eds), *The Nationalities Factor in Soviet Politics and Society* (Boulder, CO, 1990).

Hargreaves, Alec G., *Immigration, 'Race' and Ethnicity in Contemporary France* (London, 1995).

Hargreaves, Alec G. and Leaman, Jeremy (eds), *Racism and Politics in Contemporary Europe* (Aldershot, 1995).

Häufler, Vlatislav, *The Ethnographic Map of the Czech Lands* (Prague, 1973).

Heiberg, Marianne, *The Making of the Basque Nation* (Cambridge, 1989).

Helsinki Watch, *Destroying Ethnic Identity: The Turks of Greece* (New York, 1990).

Helsinki Watch, *Destroying Ethnic Identity: The Persecution of Gypsies in Romania* (New York, 1991).

Helsinki Watch, *Denying Human Rights and Ethnic Identity: The Greeks of Turkey* (New York, 1992).

Helsinki Watch, *Struggling for Ethnic Identity: Czechoslovakia's Endangered Gypsies* (New York, 1992).

Helsinki Watch, *Struggling for Ethnic Identity: The Gypsies of Hungary* (New York, 1993).

Helsinki Watch, *'Germany for Germans': Xenophobia and Racist Violence in Germany* (New York, 1995).

Herbert, Ulrich, *A History of Foreign Labour in Germany, 1880–1980: Seasonal Workers/Forced Laborers/Guest Workers* (Ann Arbor, 1990).

Hill, Clifford S., *How Colour Prejudiced is Britain?* (London, 1965).

Hiro, Dilip, *Black British: White British* (London, 1971).

Hirszowicz, Lukasz, 'Jewish Cultural Life in the USSR: A Survey', *Soviet Jewish Affairs* 7 (1977).

Hobsbawm, Eric, *Nations and Nationalism Since 1780: Programme, Myth, Reality*, 2nd edn (Cambridge, 1992).

Hockenos, Paul, *Free to Hate: The Rise of the Right in Post-Communist Eastern Europe* (London, 1993).

Hollifield, James F., *Immigrants, Markets, and States: The Political Economy of Postwar Europe* (Cambridge, MA, 1992).

Holmes, Colin, *John Bull's Island: Immigration and British Society, 1871–1971* (London, 1988).

Höpken, Wolfgang, 'From Religious Identity to Ethnic Mobilization: The Turks of Bulgaria Before, Under and Since Communism', in Hugh Poulton and Suha Taji-Farouki (eds), *Muslim Identity and the Balkan State* (London, 1997).

Horak, Stephan M. (ed.), *Eastern European National Minorities, 1919–1980: A Handbook* (Littleton, CO, 1985).

Horrocks, David and Kolinsky, Eva (eds), *Turkish Culture in German Society Today* (Oxford, 1996).

Human Rights Watch World Report, 1996 (New York, 1996).

Huttman, E. D., Blauw, W. and Saltman, S. (eds), *Urban Housing: Segregation of Minorities in Western Europe and the United States* (Durham, NC, 1991).

Ignatieff, Michael, *Blood and Belonging: Journeys into the New Nationalism* (London, 1993).

International Affairs Agency, *The Western Thrace Turks Issue in Turkish–Greek Relations* (Istanbul, 1992).

Ireland, Patrick, *The Policy Challenge of Ethnic Diversity: Immigrant Politics in France and Switzerland* (London, 1994).

Irving, R. E. M., *The Flemings and Walloons of Belgium* (London, 1980).

Itkonen, T. I., 'The Lapps of Finland', *Southwestern Journal of Anthropology* 7 (1951).

Jafar, Majeed R., *Under-Underdevelopment: A Regional Case Study of the Kurdish Area of Turkey* (Helsinki, 1976).

Jahreshog, Birgitta (ed.), *The Sami National Minority in Sweden* (Stockholm, 1982).

Jenkins, Brian and Sofos, Spyros A. (eds), *Nation and Identity in Contemporary Europe* (London, 1996).

Jones, Mervyn, *The Sami of Lapland* (London, 1982).

Joó, Rudolf (ed.), *The Hungarian Minority Situation in Rumania* (New York, 1994).

Joó, Rudolf et al. (eds), *Report of the Situation of the Hungarian Minority in Rumania* (Budapest, 1988).

Joppke, Christian (ed.), *Challenge to the Nation-State: Immigration to Western Europe and the United States* (Oxford, 1998).

Kalvoda, Josef, 'National Minorities Under Communism: The Case of Czechoslovakia', *Nationalities Papers* 16 (1988).

Kalvoda, Josef, 'The Gypsies of Czechoslovakia', *Nationalities Papers* 19 (1991).

Katz, Zev, Rogers, Rosemarie and Harned, Frederic (eds), *Handbook of Major Soviet Nationalities* (New York, 1975).

Kellas, James G., *Modern Scotland* (London, 1980).

King, Russell and Black, Richard (eds), *Southern Europe and the New Immigration* (Brighton, 1997).

Kirişci, Kemal and Winrow, Gareth M., *The Kurdish Question and Turkey: An Example of Trans-State Ethnic Conflict* (London, 1997).

Kirkwood, Michael (ed.), *Language Planning in the Soviet Union* (London, 1989).

Kochan, Lionel J. (ed.), *The Jews in Soviet Russia Since 1917* (Oxford, 1978).

Kolstoe, Paul, *Russians in the Former Soviet Republics* (London, 1995).

Koser, Khalid and Lutz, Helma (eds), *The New Migration in Europe: Social Constructions and Social Realities* (London, 1998).

Kozlov, Viktor, *The Peoples of the Soviet Union* (London, 1988).

Kyle, Keith, *Cyprus: In Search of Peace* (London, 1997).

Layton-Henry, Zig, *The Politics of Immigration: Immigration, 'Race' and 'Race' Relations in Post-War Britain* (Oxford, 1992).

Layton-Henry, Zig (ed.), *The Political Rights of Migrant Workers in Western Europe* (London, 1990).

Leggewie, Claus and Şenocak, Zafer (eds), *Deutsche Türken: Das Ende der Geduld* (Hamburg, 1993).

Levin, Nora, *The Jews in the Soviet Union Since 1917*, 2 volumes (New York, 1988).

Lewis, Bernard and Schnapper, Dominique (eds), *Muslims in Europe* (London, 1994).

Lewytzkys, Boris, *Politics and Society in the Soviet Ukraine* (Edmonton, 1984).

Lieven, Anatol, *The Baltic Revolution: Estonia, Latvia, Lithuania, and the Path to Independence*, 2nd edn (London, 1994).

McDonald, J. R., 'Labour Immigration in France, 1946–1965', *Annals of the Association of American Geographers* 59 (1969).

McDonald, M., *'We Are Not French!' Language, Culture and Identity in Brittany* (London, 1989).

McDowall, David, *The Kurds* (London, 1989).

McDowall, David, *A Modern History of the Kurds* (London, 1996).

MacEwan, Martin, *Tackling Racism in Europe: An Examination of Anti-Discrimination Law in Practice* (Oxford, 1995).

McGarry, John and O'Leary, Brendan, *Explaining Northern Ireland* (Oxford, 1995).

McGarry, John and O'Leary, Brendan (eds), *The Politics of Ethnic Conflict Regulation* (London, 1993).

Malcolm, Noel, *Bosnia: A Short History* (London, 1994).

Malcolm, Noel, *Kosovo: A Short History* (London, 1998).

Marcus, Jonathan, *The National Front and French Politics: The Resistable Rise of Jean-Marie Le Pen* (London, 1995).

Matasar, Anne Sue, 'Labor Transfers in Western Europe: The Problem of Italian Migrants in Switzerland' (Columbia University PhD thesis, 1968).

Medrano, Juan Díez, *Divided Nations: Class, Politics, and Nationalism in the Basque Country and Catalonia* (Ithaca, NY, 1995).

Melvin, Neil, *Russians Beyond Russia: The Politics of National Identity* (London, 1995).

Merriman, Nick (ed.), *The Peopling of London: Fifteen Thousand Years of Settlement from Overseas* (London, 1993).

Mihok, Brigitte, 'Minorities and Minority Policies in Romania Since 1945', *Patterns of Prejudice* 27 (1993).

Miller, Mark J., *Foreign Workers in Western Europe: An Emerging Political Force* (New York, 1981).

Minority Rights Group, *Minorities and Autonomy in Western Europe* (London, 1991).

Minority Rights Group and TWEEC, *Minorities in Central and Eastern Europe* (London, 1993).

Musil, Jiří (ed.), *The End of Czechoslovakia* (Budapest, 1995).

Mušynka, Mykola, 'The Postwar Development of the Regional Culture of the Rusyn-Ukrainians of Czechoslovakia', in Robert Magocsi (ed.), *The Persistence of Regional Cultures: Rusyns and Ukrainians in their Carpathian Homeland and Abroad* (New York, 1993).

Nielsen, Jørgen S., *Muslims in Western Europe* (Edinburgh, 1995).

Nuorgam-Poutasuo, Helvi, Pentikäinen, Juha and Saressalo, Lassi, 'The Sami in Finland: A Case Study', in Finnish National Commission for UNESCO, *Cultural Pluralism and the Position of Minorities in Finland* (Helsinki, 1981).

Ogden, Philip E. and White, Paul E. (eds), *Migrants in Modern France* (London, 1989).

Okely, Judith, *The Traveller-Gypsies* (London, 1983).

Panayi, Panikos, 'Racial Violence in the New Germany (1990–3)', *Contemporary European History* 3 (1994).

Panayi, Panikos, *Outsiders: A History of European Minorities* (London, 1999).

Panteli, Stavros, *A New History of Cyprus: From the Earliest Times to the Present* (London, 1984).

Paul, Leo, 'The Stolen Revolution: Minorities in Romania after Ceacescu', in John O'Loughlin and Hermann van der Wusten (eds), *The New Political Geography of Eastern Europe* (London, 1993).

Peach, Ceri, *The Caribbean in Europe: Contrasting Patterns of Migration and Settlement in Britain, France and the Netherlands* (Coventry, 1991).

Pilkington, Edward, *Beyond the Mother Country: West Indians and the Notting Hill White Riots* (London, 1988).

Pinkus, Benjamin, 'The Germans in the Soviet Union Since 1945', in I. Fleischauer, B. Pinkus and E. Frankel (eds), *The Soviet Germans Past and Present* (London, 1986).

Pinkus, Benjamin, *The Jews of the Soviet Union: The History of a National Minority* (Cambridge, 1988).

Poulton, Hugh, *The Balkans: Minorities and States in Conflict*, 2nd edn (London, 1993).

Ramdin, Ron, *The Making of the Black Working Class in Britain* (Aldershot, 1987).

Ramet, S. P., *Nationalism and Federalism in Yugoslavia, 1963–1983* (Bloomington, 1984).

Rapaport, Lynn, 'The Cultural and Material Reconstruction of the Jewish Communities in the Federal Republic of Germany', *Jewish Social Studies* 49 (1987).

Rehfisch, Farnham (ed.), *Gypsies, Tinkers and Other Travellers* (London, 1975).

Renner, H., 'The National Minorities in Czechoslovakia After the End of the Second World War', *Plural Societies* 7 (1976).

Rex, John, Joly, Daniele and Wilpert, Czarina (eds), *Immigrant Associations in Europe* (Aldershot, 1987).

Richarz, Monica, 'Jews in Today's Germanies', *Leo Baeck Institute Yearbook* 30 (1985).

Ro'i, Yaacov (ed.), *Jews and Jewish Life in Russia and the Soviet Union* (London, 1995).

Rose, E. J. B. et al., *Colour and Citizenship: A Report on British Race Relations* (London, 1969).

Rugman, Jonathan and Hutchings, Roger, *Atatürk's Children: Turkey and the Kurds* (London, 1996).

Ruong, Israel, *The Lapps in Sweden* (Stockholm, 1967).

Rusinow, Denison, *The Yugoslav Experiment, 1948–1974* (London, 1977).

Saunders, David, 'What Makes a Nation a Nation? Ukrainians Since 1600', *Ethnic Studies* 10 (1993).

Sawyer, Thomas E., *The Jewish Minority in the Soviet Union* (Boulder, CO, 1979).

Schöpflin, George and Poulton, Hugh, *Rumania's Ethnic Hungarians*, 2nd edn (London, 1990).

Shaikh, Farzana, *Islam and Islamic Groups: A Worldwide Reference Guide* (Harlow, 1992).

Sheehy, Anne, *The Crimean Tatars and Volga Germans: Soviet Treatment of Two National Minorities* (London, 1971).

Shlapentokh, Vladimir, Sendich, Munir and Payin, Emil (eds), *The New Russian Diaspora: Russian Minorities in the Former Soviet Republics* (Armonk, NY, 1994).

Sibelman, Simon P., '*Le Renouvellement Juif*: French Jewry on the Eve of the Centenary of the *Affaire Dreyfus*', *French Cultural Studies* 3 (1992).

Siguań, Manuel, *Linguistic Minorities in the European Economic Community: Spain, Portugal, Greece* (Luxembourg, 1990).

Singleton, Fred, *Twentieth Century Yugoslavia* (London, 1976).

Singleton, Fred and Carter, Bernard, *The Economy of Yugoslavia* (London, 1982).

Smith, Anthony D., *The Ethnic Origins of Nations* (Oxford, 1983).

Smith, David J. and Chambers, Gerald, *Inequality in Northern Ireland* (Oxford, 1991).

Smith, Graham (ed.), *The Nationalities Question in the Post-Soviet States* (London, 1996).

Solomos, John, *Race and Racism in Britain*, 2nd edn (London, 1993).

Steinberg, Jonathan, *Why Switzerland?*, 2nd edn (Cambridge, 1996).

Stephens, Meic, *Linguistic Minorities in Western Europe* (Llandysul, 1976).

Stone, Gerald, *The Smallest Slavonic Nation: The Sorbs of Lusatia* (London, 1972).

Straka, Manfred (ed.), *Handbuch der europäischen Volksgruppen* (Vienna and Stuttgart, 1970).

Subtelny, Orest, *Ukraine: A History*, 2nd edn (Toronto, 1994).

Tägil, Sven (ed.), *Ethnicity and Nation Building in the Nordic World* (London, 1995).

Tillhagen, C. H., 'The Gypsy Problem in Finland', *Journal of the Gypsy Lore Society* 37 (1958).

Trankell, Ingrid and Arne, 'Problems of the Swedish Gypsies', *Scandinavian Journal of Educational Research* 12 (1968).

Tucker, Thomas, 'Political Transition and the "Jewish Question" in Hungary Today', *Ethnic and Racial Studies* 19 (1996).

Ulč, Otto, 'Communist National Minority Policy: The Case of the Gypsies in Czechoslovakia', *Soviet Studies* 20 (1969).

Ulč, Otto, 'Gypsies in Czechoslovakia: A Case of Unfinished Integration', *Eastern European Politics and Societies* 2 (1988).

Vakhtin, Nikolai, *Native Peoples of the Russian Far North* (London, 1992).

Veenhoven, Wilhelm A. et al. (eds), *Case Studies in Human Rights and Fundamental Freedoms: A World Survey*, Vol. 1 (The Hague, 1975).

Vucinich, Wayne S. (ed.), *Contemporary Yugoslavia: Twenty Years of Socialist Experiment* (Berkeley and Los Angeles, 1969).

Wagner, Frances S., 'The Gypsy Problem in Postwar Hungary', *Hungarian Studies Review* 14 (1987).

Wagner, Frances S., 'Ethnic Minorities in Hungary Since World War II', *Central European Forum* 2 (1989).

Waldinger, R., Aldrich, H. and Ward, R. (eds), *Ethnic Entrepreneurs: Immigrant Businesses in Industrial Societies* (London, 1990).

Walker, Christopher J., *Armenia: The Survival of a Nation*, 2nd edn (London, 1990).

Wasserstein, Bernard, *Vanishing Diaspora: The Jews in Europe Since 1945* (London, 1996).

Watson, James L. (ed.), *Between Two Cultures: Migrants and Minorities in Britain* (Oxford, 1977).

Webber, Jonathan (ed.), *Jewish Identities in the New Europe* (London, 1994).

Wichert, Sabine, *Northern Ireland Since 1945* (London, 1991).

Wilpert, Czarina (ed.), *Entering the Working World: Following the Descendants of Europe's Immigrant Labour Force* (Aldershot, 1988).

Wilson, Duncan, *Tito's Yugoslavia* (Cambridge, 1979).

Wistrich, Robert S., *Anti-Semitism: The Longest Hatred* (London, 1992).

Wrench, John and Solomos, John (eds), *Racism and Migration in Western Europe* (Oxford, 1993).

Zaprudnik, Jan, *Belarus: At a Crossroads of History* (Boulder, CO, 1993).

Map 3   Location of Some Concentrated Ethnic Groups in Europe

Finns

FINLAND

Swedes

ESTONIA

VIA

UANIA

BELARUS

RUSSIA

Russians

UKRAINE

MOLDAVIA

Hungarians
Hungarians

Germans

ROMANIA

Russians

Tatars
Russians

BLACK SEA

Abkhazians South Ossetians

GEORGIA

AZERBAIJAN

ARMENIA

Armenians

CASPIAN SEA

BULGARIA

ONIA   Turks

Turks

CE

TURKEY

K u r d s

CYPRUS

| 0 | | 300 mls |
| 0 | | 400 km |

Index